© 2009 by Andrew M. Patterson. No part of this book may be reproduced, published, restored in a retrieval system, or transmitted by electronic, mechanical, photo-copying, or recording without the written consent of the author.

Dedicated to former Congressman Paul Findley

ISBN 9781489572271

ISBN 9781530815272

First edition: July 13, 2010
Second edition: October, 20011
Third edition: February 13, 2012

Author and Publisher: Andrew M. Patterson
Book Cover Design: Manoj. www.covrdesign.com

Deadly Diplomacy

by

Andrew M. Patterson

A documentary produced from short wave news broadcasts, newspapers of the Bosnina War, 1991-1996 from the news media of 16,000 dren murdered, over twenty thousands women raped, hundreds of thousands dead, over a hundred of thousands maimed and wounded by Serbian aggression aided by the United Nations Security Council, the British House of Lords. Prime Minsiter John Majors, US President William Jefferson Clinton, Under Secretary of State StrobeTalbot, French President Edouard Balladur, and Russian President Boris Yeltsin.

Table of Contents

Introduction p. 3

Author's Notes p. 10

Karadzic Lied to Mike Wallace p. 14

Political Moves on Bosnia January 2, 1992 to 1994 the *New York Times* p. 18

News Media: Newspapers, Short-wave Radio & Television, Feb. 28, 1994- Aug1996 p. 23

What is Terrorism? p. 394

Bios & War Crimes Indictments p. 400

Richard J. Goldstone, of the International Criminal Tribunal charges: p. 300

Bibliography p. 336

Introduction

The author felt the trauma and heartache of Marianne Perle the wife, of journalist Danny Perle when he saw the movie, *A Mighty Heart*. Angelina Jolie played the part of Marianne Perle.. Angelina Jolie re-enacts how Marianne Perle is traumatized when her husband, Danny Pearl, a reporter for the *Wall Street Journal,* was abducted by Pakistani extremists to publicize the **mistreatment** of Taliban and Al Qaeda *detainees* at Guantanamo, Cuba and CIA secret prisons elsewhere.

The story showed how two altruistic young people became involved in international journalism. Danny and Marianne married in the Jewish tradition even though Danny did not practice Judaism. Assigned to Pakistan to cover the Afghan War, Marianne is pregnant with their son, who they will name Adam, the name of Man in Turkish. The Afghan War and its violent consequences are not the issue here. At issue is the brutality of what had happened to Danny and the effect on his wife. Pakistan is a country with a nuclear bomb. Its next door neighbor India has a nuclear bomb. There were some tremendous battles between the two countries including the largest tank battle ever fought.

When Danny doesn't come home, Marianne goes to the Pakistani police to report him as missing. She informs the U.S. Consul in Karachi, where she is living and the Consul gave her all the support he could, which is rare for any U.S.

Consul. Most US Consuls will say, "We are not required to help you. We take care for only our own people," and end it with, "We didn't ask you to come here."

The head of Pakistan's intelligence in Karachi uses his full powers to arrest and question suspects. Eventually, the kidnappers send a note accusing Danny of being an agent of the Mossad and CIA. Marianne recalls that the news media reported the CIA forcibly took Danny's computer and copied its hard drive. She stresses that Danny does not work for the CIA and that he doesn't have any connection with the CIA.

Tad Sculz who covered Latin America for the *New York Times* told that he passed on information to the CIA at dinners he attended. But Danny worked for the *Wall Street Journal* which has a reputation for unbiased reporting. Americans can be accused of ignorance about other countries, those in other countries should be reminded that they too are ignorant about America. Not all Americans are CIA or FBI as there are loyal Americans who are persecuted by the CIA and FBI. It slowly comes out that they are Muslims angry over the torture of detainees at Guantanamo and against Pakistan's government which they accuse as being controlled by the United States.

Marianne enjoys the friendship of Muslim Pakistanis and never felt she or Danny were in any danger. Five months pregnant she is fearful, erratic, and traumatized but must remain strong because of the baby she is carrying. .

The author has learned that the British established three extremist Muslin and anti-Hindu schools in the part of India around Peshawar and established four extremist Hindu anti-Muslim schools in what is India to create divisions between Hindus and Muslims. It was the three Islamic extremist schools in Peshawar that refugees from Afghanistan sent their sons to receive an *Islamic education*. But they were not trained in the Koran or Islamic thought but in fighting and became the Taliban (students).

Not to be outdone by the British, the CIA recruited and trained an *Arab Foreign Legion* they called the *Mujahideen* (Freedom Fighter) that chased out the Russians and destroyed the pro-Russian Afghans. When the different tribes failed to create a viable government the CIA brought in the Taliban.

After that turned sour, the CIA discovered Hamid Karzai working in an Afghan restaurant in Washington and installed him as the leader of Afghanistan. His brother was the largest opium producer of opium and controlled Helmand Province.

Richard Reed, a British born Muslim convert was alleged to have been involved with one of the three extremist Muslim schools in Pakistan. On a trans-Atlantic flight from Amsterdam to the US he was subdued after attempting to blow off his legs by igniting plastic explosives in his shoes. This was followed by the underwear bomber who was Nigerian.

The night of January 2, 2002, the Pakistani police arrest the Taliban Ambassador to Pakistan, Mullah Abdul Salam Zaeef. He was stripped naked on the airport tarmac by Pakistani soldiers, then kicked and beaten before he was loaded on a plane that took him to Guantanamo. He was held for nearly four years with no charges and no proof he had any knowledge about 9-11 or any terrorist plots against America. The arrest of an ambassador who is an accredited diplomat is a violation of international law.

There is no anti-Semitism in Pakistan as Imran Khan, the football great of Pakistan, was married Jemima Goldsmith, the daughter of Lord Goldsmith who is a Jew.

Christian Amanpour made live broadcasts from Sarajevo for CNN news while BBC was implanting the idea that

Serbs were taking revenge for centuries of persecution at the hands of Bosnian Muslims. There is not one historical incident where Bosnians killed or committed crimes against Christian Orthodox Serbs. It was the Turkish Armies that told the Serbs that if they attacked the Turkish Army from behind while they were fighting the Russians they would send in the criminally insane *tomarani*. But in 1914, the Serb *Black Hand* killed and terrorized Bosnians as they wanted Bosnia to annex Bosnia to be Serbia's outlet to the sea.

During the Bosnian War, Germany took in over 400,000 Bosnians. Some Serbs claimed to be Muslims were admitted to the camps where they tried manipulating Bosnians to resort to terrorism. But no Bosnians fell for this trap.

The author wrote a movie scripts about a friendship between a Bosnian Serb who was a professor of history and a Bosnian Muslim who was a professor of astronomy at the University of Sarajevo. In the story, the professor of history gives the historical account and the professor of astronomy to show the differences between the Muslims, Croat Catholics, and Orthodox Serbs in their beliefs.

The author traveled to California to interest a producer to make *Coffee and Conversation* into a movie. Hard to reach people in the movie industry as they have blocks to keep people away the author managed to interest Mike Farrell and agreed to meet with the author.

The author's best friend accompanied him to the meeting with Mike but when they met Mike, there was a tall *CIA agent* standing next to him. While talking with the producer about the story of a friendship between a Serb and a Muslim, this agent told the author's friend that he should tell me to go back to teaching and stop writing. The author wonders why the CIA has nothing better to do then to send one of their agents to stop this story from being made into a movie. Then the CIA Redneck asked the author's friend to work for the CIA but his friend said he wasn't interested.

The author flew to London four times and to the Continent to see film producers. A Hungarian film producer seemed interested but after the author went to Budapest he seemed disinterested to discuss the movie script. The author did get a phone call from a Babelsberg producer after returning to America who wrote the author some letters but then these stopped coming. .

As the author and his son have the same name, he asked his son if he could use his P.O. Box and his son replied that he was welcome to use it. One day, his son came home to say that when he opened his P.O. Box and saw a tab sticking out in the back. He asked the postmistress what the tab was for. She candidly replied that ***it was to see that certain kinds of mail did not get into the box.***

As the author was doing nothing illegal or immoral, he fired off a letter to the Senators from Texas detailing what his son had told him. The Senators responded that they were told no such thing occurred.

On the author's trips to London he stayed at a cheap hotel. The manager was a Serb with a nasty disposition. He might have been a War Criminal as many Serb. One evening, the author saw him throw a drunk on the floor of the hotel lobby and threaten to kill him if he moved and he would have..

Shortly before the author made his third trip to London, he fell from the roof of his house and landed on his right arm. It was swollen and painful. A Bulgarian woman doctor who worked at the hotel was kind enough to tell the author to buy some ointment that would relieve the pain. On the next trip to London, the author learned Daniel fired her because she was kind enough to give the author some medical advice.

After returning from a third trip to London, the author received a call from friend in London who had read his book, **The Hypocrites**. He enjoyed the book and had stopped by the hotel to take the author to his home for dinner. Now he called to say Daniel made a false report to the London Police that he a *dangerous man* because was frightened as MI5 had gone to his place of work and tried to get him fired.

It was learned that Daniel had some workers at the hotel tell lies to the London Police and as jobs are hard to come by in London, they did as he told them. The author could never find what accusations Daniel had made to the London police and British Intelligence. Daniel's like that of a sociopath. Daniel had some political pull somewhere to get his cousin from Mostar into England. His cousin was a Yugoslav Army paratrooper who trained in Russia and fought on the side of the Bosnian Serbs. He laughed as he told how they fooled the UN monitors. Daniel and the hotel owner were helped by the local constable who was pure evil.

The author is truly sorry for Mr. Shabbir, but this kind of thing is typical of British police and MI5 who threaten the livelihood of Muslims in Britain which is against the Magna Charta. Prime Minister John Majors stated that if he lifted the arms embargo on Bosnia the House of Lords would cause his government to fall. (See Nov 4, 1994 news, Swiss Radio International).

British Intelligence *persuaded* five Muslim men of Pakistani ethnicity to participate in a *practice drill* of a terrorist bombing. The men agreed as they wanted to show they were loyal British citizens. The result was that they were killed in the simultaneous bombings of four London buses in July 7, 1996. The same kind of trick was perpetrated in Boston

The British did make an Inquiry into the Iraq War which is more than the Obama Administration has done to pursue the Truth. Former British Prime Minister Tony Blair and Gordon Brown showed how badly they handled that war.

The author is truly sorry about anyone who has suffered persecution because of their kindness to him. It is the nature of the CIA, Pentagon, and British Intelligence to make false accusations in hopes of provoking their targeted victim into doing something rash.

The British tried provoking Gandhi and Indians in South Africa to get them to strike back. Gandhi knew that and succeeded with his peaceful resistance and the British came to hate him. It wouldn't surprise the author if they were behind the assassination of Gandhi.

The author collected the news from unbiased new media before he began to write, **Coffee and Conversation**. In 2002, he went to Sarajevo to check on how accurate he was. Bosnians who read his story there insisted that he must have been in Bosnia during the conflict.

The author met with two professors at the University of Sarajevo to discuss starting a summer school at the University of Sarajevo for foreign students. He found both of them friendly but a few days later on returning to visit one of the friendly professors he entered the secretary's office and saw the professor in his office as the door was wide open. On seeing the author, this professor walked over and slammed the door to his office. That and other behaviors that followed showed the author that he was being followed. Frankly, the author considers the professor was a coward for not being forthright.

An *Austrian* lady pushed herself into his table at an outdoor café when he was talking with his translator. The woman said she was working with an aid organization which checked out she was lying.

Ignoring this woman, the translator told him about the time during she was running across the large open space in front of the Basharshia Mosque when she slipped and fell. A bullet ricocheted off the stone pavement a few feet in front of her. She felt a guardian angel kept her from being killed.

She translated the author's collection of children's stories from around the world which he was going to publish and give the proceeds to children orphaned by the war. After the author left Bosnia to teach in China, where he received an email from his translator that read, *"Look what those dirty Nazis sent my daughter"*.

Curious, the author attempted to open the attachment but got a warning "there is a very dangerous virus inside." He sent an email asking why she sent him an email with a virus. She answered that she didn't. She was unable to open her computer for three weeks and was going mad as her computer was vital to her business and she had to work to survive.

After pushing all Bosnian Muslims into UN Safe Havens, the UN Peacekeepers did nothing to protect them as they said they had no mandate to protect them. Yashushi Akashi was Boutros Boutros Ghali's favored envoy and Japan's senior diplomat. But he was bigoted in his statements about Muslims and blatantly pro-Serb.

The author would often stop to talk with a man at the information desk in downtown bank of Sarajevo. Suddenly he was transferred but someone gave the author his new phone number. When he phoned the man was hysterical and asked who gave you my telephone number?

There was a watch repair man who told the author about this tall American Embassy employee with the name

Andrew who was going around talking against the author. But again the author never learned just what this *Andrew,* was saying.

Then the author's friend, Hazim, lost his job and the school where he was teaching lost its rental agreement and forced to move to another location. Then there was the Egyptian Consul who was friendly but the next time the author came to visit him the Consul refused to see him.

Every three months, the author left Bosnia for a day and then would come back to get another visa for three months. When he came back from Zagreb the third time the Bosnian Croat official at the border stamped everyone's passport but the author's. The rules were suddenly changed from allowing someone to stay in Bosnia for a year to allow only those persons who had a job. Volunteering was not allowed.

A Bosnian man who had joined the 1,400 Mujahedeen and summoned to appear in a Bosnia Court accused of being involved in terrorism. There was no evidence and the judge released him. As he left the court room, IFOR forces arrested him and the CIA sent him to Guantanamo.

The author details some murders in his other books. One murder in *The Hypocrites* is about two French girls who were offered 10,000 dollars to model in Yemen. They were flown to Sana'a, Yemen's capital, in a four engine jet plane and were the only passengers. In Sana'a they were murdered along with the President of Yemen and his brother. Newspapers around the world reported their murder was done by *Muslim extremists* angry they were *cavorting with foreign perfumed women.* **Problem with that was that everyone in Yemen knew the president did not like girls, he liked men.**

The Author's Notes:

In July of 2005, the author went to the internet to check on some dates on events in the Bosnian Conflict and found an article from a Voice of America broadcast made on July 21, 1995, that stated, "Richard Holbrooke, the U.S. Envoy sent by President Clinton and State Department officials, signed a *secret agreement* with Serbian President Slobodan Milosevic and Croat leader Franjo Tudjman, dividing Bosnia between Croatia (51%) and Serbia (49%)."

This was done in advance of the *Dayton Peace Accords* and clearly demonstrated that Serbia was behind the aggression in Bosnia. So when the World Court absolved Serbia of the atrocities and aggression it was one of the greatest travesties of justice.

During the negotiations at Wright Patterson Air Force Base in Dayton, Ohio, Izetbegovic refused to sign. All had sent orders to refuel their planes and all were going home the next day. At three in the morning, the Bosnian Delegation was awakened and told that Croatia and Serbia had signed, so Bosnians signed onto this federation. For his success in tricking the Bosnians, Richard Holbrooke was appointed lifetime US Ambassador to the UN by Bill Clinton.

From 1994 to 1996, the reader can read how see the UN Security Council, Boutros Boutros Ghali, and the U.S. President, Bill Clinton, destroyed Bosnia, a member of the United Nations.

The Muslims of Bosnia had been reform Christians called Bogomils and were besieged by Hungarian Catholics. As the Turkish Army had gone up the Danube River and conquered the Serbs, the Bogomils asked the Turks for help. After the Turks chased the Hungarians out of Bosnia, the Bogomils decided that as Turks did not drink alcohol or chase after women, the Muslim Turks were closer to their *reform Christian ideals* and converted.

In 1911, Dragutin Dimitriyevic of Serbia's Military Intelligence created the Bosnian Serb Black Hand which was to terrorize Bosnian Muslims and Croats into submission and annex Bosnia as Serbia's outlet to the sea. In 1913, he organized the Balkan Alliance that pushed the Turks off the Balkans and separated Bosnia from Turkey. Turkey then gave Bosnia to Austria to protect Muslims from the extremism of the Serbs.

In 1914, the Serb leadership was called to London to sign the Secret Treaty of London. If Serbs would murder Archduke Ferdinand and his wife in Sarajevo which was to give the excuse to start *the War to End All Wars,* Britain, France, and Russia would reward them with Greater Serbia and twenty year old Gavrilo Princip, fatally infected and dying from tuberculosis, killed Archduke Ferdinand and his wife to start the war in June 1914.

After Princip shot Archduke Ferdinand and his wife in Sarajevo Bosnia, he wound up in a Serb prison and died six months after Britain, France, and Russiawife declared war on Germany and Austria because as they said Princip could not get a fair trial. But there were 7 assassins waiting to kill the Archduke which was a conspiracy hatched in London.

Josef Bros (Tito) formed the Yugoslav Federation of six Republics and gave all the Republics the right to secede to curb Serb Nationalism. Slobodan Milosevic began stripping power from the Republics and Croatia and Slovenia seceded voted for independence in 1991. Bosnians voted in 1992 for independence and **Dr. Radovan Karadzic said in the Bosnian parliament on March 4, 1992, "If you Bosnians vote for independence you will take the same highway of hell Slovenia and Croatia took. Muslims will be** *annihilated. Muslims can't defend themselves if there is a war here."* But the Serbs had already planned it.

In September 1991, the UN placed a weapons ban on Bosnia that helped Serbs in their killing. Bosnia had only a few thousand rifles and was defenseless, *which the UN Security Council* (Britain, France, and United States) knew. The Russians sent all their weapons from East Germany to Serbia when they withdrew from the DDR and Milosevic sent Bosnian Serbs from the Yugoslav Army into Bosnia fully equipped to form the *Bosnian Serb Army*.

An internet dis*information* web site accused the late Bosnian president, Alija Izetbegovic of wanting to create an Islamic Republic in Europe. This web site portrayed Slobodan Milosevic, Radovan Karadzic, and Ratko Mladic as *brave men* trying to hold Yugoslavia together.

How could the World Court ignore the documents that showed Bosnian Serb civilians were given sniper rifles and paid 500 Deutschemarks for every man, woman, and child they killed?

Arkan and his Serbian Tigers were paid with money from Belgrade. All his men were psychopaths that enjoyed killing innocent children, raping women, torturing, and massacring. Slobodan Milosevic and Mladic always lied.

Radovan Karadzic Lied to Mike Wallace when he said: "My police and my army never commit War Crimes."

Mike Wallace then show a video of starving men behind the barbed wire of a Serb detention camps. Karadzic demurely says, "These will have to be investigated." But

Karadzic threatened in the Bosnian Parliament to annihilate Bosnian Muslims if they voted for independence.

Serb leaders Slobodan Milosevic and Radovan Karadzic also threatened to bomb London and New York if America and Britain got involved in the Bosnian Conflict.

On January 8, 1993, Radio Free Europe reported that Bosnian Serb leader, Karadzic boasted, "It is not difficult to procure nuclear weapons on the open market."

On January 8, 1993, the UN requested an official from the Bosnian Government be sent to mediate a truce with the Bosnian Serbs. The UN sent a UN armored personnel vehicle to take Deputy Prime Minister Turajlic to the meeting. One version says he was sitting in the UN vehicle when two French UN Peacekeepers opened the door and stepped back while a Serb soldier walked up to open door of the vehicle and fired his machine gun point blank at Deputy Prime Minister Turajlic reducing his body to a bloody pulp.

But there is another version of the story that says he was dragged from a UN Personnel Carrier and shot and killed. The UN apologized but no Serb was punished for this murder. Nothing was done because the family of Secretary General Boutos Boutros Ghali served the British in Egypt after Britain moved into Egypt declaring it a British Protectorate.

After NATO took over from the UN Peacekeepers in Bosnia, Secretary Boutros Boutros Ghali was given the authority to halt any punishing air strikes of the Serbs for breaking the truces or for any atrocities they committed in doing so. **This authority should never have been given to Boutros Boutros Ghali as he had already demonstrated he was inadequate for the position of Secretary General of the United Nations.** He permitted only a few NATO punishing air strikes **and should have stood trial in The Hague while** *other United Nations officials in Bosnia should be charged with corruption and a sex trade with women of Eastern Europe, and War Crimes.*

Regarding the murder of Deputy Prime Minister Turaljic, Bosnian Interior Minister, Jusef Pusinic, the Bosnian Government said it would charge UNPROFOR with negligence in his murder. General Sir Michael Rose who was given command of UN forces in Bosnia became very pro-Serb after he was knighted and given a title of "Sir Michael."

The Bosnian Conflict was an invasion of Bosnia by Serbia as shown in the August 31, 1995 *Wall Street Journal,* a news article that Milosevic *released* 100,000 Bosnian Serbs from the Yugoslav Army along with 512 tanks, 506 armored personnel carriers, 18 transport helicopters, ten high performance military jets, more than 250 mortars, howitzers, and other artillery, and 8,700 tons of fuel. The list does not include the thousands of artillery and mortar shells or the thousands of the mines used to ring Sarajevo and all so-called **UN Safe Havens**. *This was known in* Germany, Hungary, and Eastern Europe so how could the UN Security Council call it a Civil War? The UN Security Council was replaced by the **International Contact Group** replaced the UN Security Council to let the Russians in. Russia broke UN embargoes on Serbia that was supplying Serbs fighting against a member nation of the United Nations and all this was covered up as well as knowledge that Milosevic bought over one hundred German businesses to ship goods into Serbia to supply Serbs, Russian, Greek, and Macedonian volunteers in Bosnia.

On the worst days, Sarajevo would be bombarded with 4,000 artillery and mortar shells into Sarajevo. Milosevic also sent in the elite Yugoslav paratroopers who fought alongside the Bosnian Serbs against Bosnians. **The UN**

Monitors and NATO permitted 4,000 helicopter flights from Serbia into Serb occupied Bosnia, lifted UN sanctions against Serbia as and Bill Clinton and Strobe Talbot kept this news about Boris Yeltsin's crimes and this info out of the news media.

The 4,000 helicopter flights supplied the 4,000 artillery shells used to bombard Sarajevo in defiance of the UN *no fly zone*. There was no change after NATO took over from the UN Peacekeeping Force. Milosevic restricted UN *monitors* to a few main crossings. The UN Security Council had to have known all this and so all who served on the UN Security Council should be investigated by the War Crimes Tribunal.

It was the news about the secret agreement to divide Bosnia between Serbia and Croatia that was the blockbuster. It came two days after Bosnian Serbs redirected three American diplomats to take a back road, which the Serbs said *offered more security.* **There definitely was a cover-up to their murder. To ensure their safety, the diplomats were locked inside an armored personnel carrier. The fourth US envoy to Bosnia, Mr. Richard Holbrooke, was put in another vehicle in the same convoy and separated from these three.** Wouldn't the families of these men like to know why?

The first newspaper report was accompanied by a photo of a round hole about 1 1/2 meters in diameter and very deep that showed was blown off the road. *But U.S. State Department issued a contradictory bulletin, stating that a vehicle that carried the three American diplomats "slipped off the road into a ravine."* **State Department denied the vehicle had been blown up by a land mine.**

The author got the information about Richard Holbrooke dividing Bosnia between Croatia and Serbia from the VOA broadcast of August 1965. Bosnia was not invited and six months later at the Dayton Peace Accords Izet Begovic refused to sign on the accords presented at Dayton. Orders were given to all participates to fuel their planes for the flight back to Bosnia and everyone retired to their rooms to sleep. But at three in the morning, the Bosnian delegation was rousted out of bed and told that Croatia and Serbia, had signed the Dayton Peace Accords and Bosnians the psychological trick by Holbrooke worked and they signed.

For Richard Holbrooke's role in helping Clinton show Congress that he know how to conduct foreign policy even though Richard Holbrooke sold out the Bosnians, had President William Jefferson Clinton appoint him as a *permanent* U.S. Ambassador to the UN French TV news people angrily accused President Clinton of selling out Bosnia to Croatia and Serbia just to enhance his image as a man who knew how to conduct foreign affairs. It was, as they said, to improve his chances for re-election in 1996. It appears the French were not only courageous but also right.

France's Prime Minister, Eduard Balladur, gave strong support to the Serbs at the beginning of the outbreak of hostilities. After he failed in his election for the presidency of France the truth about atrocities committed by Bosnian Serbs and Serbs against French UN Peacekeeping forces was revealed. The abuse of two French pilots who were shot down and captured by Bosnian Serbs was kept from the French People. After the French people learned of the torture of the French pilots and the mistreatment of one hundred French Peacekeepers, the French turned against Balladur. Jacques Chirac defeated Balladur who was called by the French *a man you can hate.* French television criticized President Bill Clinton for selling out Bosnia to the Serbs just to show his ability to conduct foreign affairs.

The Christian Science Monitor radio on August 21,

1995, reported, "Very little of President Clinton's peace plan is known as things are being kept secret. Trying to understand President Clinton's peace plan is like trying to find a black cat in the dark."

The man who was the most important in bringing peace to Croatia and Bosnia was Iran's Foreign Minister, Ali Akhbar Velayati. Iran has been savagely attacked as a nation supporting terrorism but Russia's Boris Yeltsin lied, broke UN sanctions on Serbia, sent in Russian paratroopers as Russia's *contribution* to the UN Peacekeeping Force and they trained, supplied, and fought alongside Bosnian Serbs against Bosnia, a member of the United Nations. President Yeltsin of Russia ordered Russian generals to commit atrocities in Chechnya some brave **Russian generals refused his order to commit war crimes. Russia's Minister of Defense, General Pavel Grachev threatened to have them executed. And President Boris Yeltsin of Russia continually broke UN sanctions placed on Serbia and gave orders to his Russian Army officers to commit atrocities against Chechen civilians. He also threatened to declare war on Bosnia.**

Those Russian Generals should have gotten the Nobel Peace Prize and President Boris Yeltsin and his Minister of Defense, General Grachev should have been tried for War Crimes.

"To the military mind, freedom is a privilege but humans living in democracies think freedom is a right." - Andrew Patterson

Political Moves on Bosnia from January 2, 1992 to 1994 from the *New York Times*

January 2, 1992 - UN mediator Cyrus Vance (U.S.) negotiates cease-fire for Croatia; UN peacekeepers will patrol it, with headquarters in Sarajevo, in attempt to stave off conflict in Bosnia.

February 21, 1992 - The UN Security Council sends 14,000 peacekeeping troops to Croatia.

February 29, 1992 - Bosnia-Herzegovina declares independence. Bosnian Serbs proclaim a separate state. Fighting spreads.

April, 1992 – Serb General Mladic sows mine fields above and around Sarajevo and other UN created "safe havens". Bosnian Serb artillery begins shelling civilian.

April 4, 1992, Bosnian President Izetbegovic announces full mobilization to quell the violence mounting around the country. Karadzic opposes the move. Bosnian-Serb militias attack the Sarajevo police academy, located above the city, on 5 April.

On 4-5 April, 1992: Thousands of Sarajevans of all ethnic backgrounds take to the streets to march for peace. When they descend on the SDP offices in the capital, Bosnian-Serb snipers open fire on the crowd, killing six people. Karadzic proclaims his Serbian Republic of Bosnia-Herzegovina, on 6 April 1992.

Sarajevo's sixty thousand Christian Serbs were never persecuted or attacked by Muslims. Bosnian Muslims fled into the surrounding hills to escape the bombardment of Serb artillery positioned behind mine fields on the hills overlooking Sarajevo. There are no military targets in

Sarajevo as Mladic begins to bombard its streets and markets.

In May 1992, Radovan Karadzic is proclaimed president of Serpska Republic. His capital is Pale, 10 km southeast of Sarajevo. Colonel Ratko Mladic is promoted to general and commander of the 100,000 Yugoslav Army troops (ethnic Bosnian Serbs) stationed in the Bosnian Republic which becomes the Bosnian-Serb Army.

April 6, 1992 European Community recognizes Bosnia. Washington follows on April 7. Fighting intensifies in Bosnia.

May 3, 1992 Bosnia's Muslim president, Alija Izetbegovic, is taken hostage by Yugoslav troops (at the airport) on his return from peace talks in Lisbon. He was freed following day.

May 5, 1992 - Yugoslav army relinquishes command of its estimated 100,000 troops in Bosnia handing them over to Ratko Mladic.

May 27, 1992: A mortar attack on a bread line in Sarajevo kills 16. More die later from wounds suffered in the attack.

May 30, 1992 - United Nations imposes sanctions on the new "Rump" Yugoslavia (made up of Serbia and Montenegro) for fomenting war in Bosnia and Croatia.

June 29, 1992 - Peacekeepers hoist UN flag at Sarajevo airport after Serbs leave.

July 3, 1992 - International airlift to Sarajevo begins.

August 1992 - Major international conference on Yugoslavia was held in London. Agreements on aid and cease-fire are never implemented.

September 19, 1992 - UN Security Council drops Yugoslavia from General Assembly (the war is five months old by now).

November 16, 1992 - UN Security Council authorizes a naval blockade of Serbia and Montenegro.

January 2, 1993, International mediators Cyrus Vance and Lord Owen unveil plan to divide Bosnia into 10 provinces, along ethnic lines.

January 8, 1993, Bosnian Deputy Prime Minister Hakija Turajlic killed by a Serb soldier as he sat in a UN armored vehicle near Sarajevo airport (previously reported in the *Introduction*).

February 22, 1993, UN Security Council sets up a War Crimes Tribunal for former Yugoslavia.

March 25, 1993, Bosnian President Izetbegovic signs Vance-Owen peace plan in New York.

March 1993, Bosnian Croats and Muslims begin fighting over the 30 percent of Bosnia not seized by Bosnian Serbs.

April 12, 1993, NATO jets begin to enforce UN no-fly zone over Bosnia (but no shots are fired until February 28, 1994).

April 26, 1993, The UN tightens trade sanctions against Yugoslavia.

April and May, 1993, Following Serb assault on Srebrenica and dramatic crisis of refugees arriving in Tuzla, UN Security Council creates six "safe havens" for Bosnian Muslims: Sarajevo, Tuzla, Bihac, Srebrenica, Zepa and Gorazde.

May 2, 1993, Bosnian Serb leader Radovan Karadzic signs Vance-Owen plan in Greece but his assembly rejects it.

May 15-16, 1993, In a referendum, Bosnian Serbs overwhelmingly reject Vance-Owen plan in favor of an independent Bosnian Serb state.

May 31, 1993, Yugoslav federal Parliament ousts Dobrica Cosic as he is seen as too peaceable by Milosevic, the Yugoslav federal president. Thousands demonstrate and clash with police in Belgrade.

June 16, 1993, Mediators meet with Milosevic, Izetbegovic, Croatian President Franjo Tudjman and Bosnian leaders in Geneva. Plan emerges to split Bosnia three ways. Bosnian leader Izetbegovic walks out.

June 23, 1993, First U.S. Ambassador to Bosnia, Victor Jackovic, goes to Sarajevo and presents his credentials, then leaves Sarajevo for his base in Vienna (hundreds of kilometers away from Sarajevo).

July 30, 1993, Warring sides reach preliminary agreement in Geneva on Union of Republics of Bosnia and Herzegovina with three states. Izetbegovic walks out of talks August 2 after Serbs violate ceasefire.

August 26, 1993, *Albany Times,* Albany, New York, USA: A 9-year old Muslim girl raped by Serb militiamen was left lying in a pool of blood while her parents were kept behind a fence from going to her. They watched as she died two days later.

September 1, 1993, Geneva peace talks collapse.

November 9, 1993 – In Mostar, south of Sarajevo, a Croat tank shells and destroys famous moon bridge. Later it is discovered that there is a powerful but unknown worldwide Croatian Mafia in Mostar.

December 19, 1993 – Slobodan Milosevic calls for early parliamentary elections in Serbia and his Socialists obtain largest majority.

February 5, 1994 - More than 60 people killed and some 200 wounded as a mortar shell slams into downtown marketplace in Sarajevo. Serb snipers target people going to the market for food and people going to the river for water as well as school children at play or going to school.

February 9, 1994, NATO gives Bosnian Serbs 10 days to withdraw heavy guns from Sarajevo region or face air strikes.

February 17, 1994, Karadzic agrees to remove guns from around Sarajevo if soldiers from Russia, a historical Serb ally, join peacekeeping mission.

February 20, 1994, Russian peacekeepers arrive and the NATO deadline expires. UN says it is satisfied heavy guns are being removed but they were not withdrawn. Another lie by the UN.

February 28, 1994, U.S. F-16 fighters, flying for NATO, down four Bosnian Serb warplanes violating the *no fly* zone. These were the first shots fired by NATO in the Bosnian conflict.

March 18, 1994, The Bosnian Muslim-led government and Bosnian Croats sign a U.S.-brokered accord, ending a yearlong war.

April 22, 1994, after two air strikes against Serbs advancing on Gorazde, NATO delivers fresh ultimatum to Serbs to stop firing and pull back or face more air strikes.

April 27, 1994, UN says the Serbs have *mostly* complied with NATO ultimatum.

May 13, 1994. The five-nation Contact Group announced a new peace plan, including a four-month cease-fire and eventual partition of Bosnia.

July 20, 1994, Serbs refuse the Contact Group plan.

August 4, 1994, Milosevic cuts ties with Bosnian Serbs for rejecting plan.

December 20, 1994, Former U.S. President Jimmy Carter ends mediating mission with announcement of Bosnian cease-fire.

This ends the political coverage for 1992 an 1994.

A video clip of Mr. Colin Powell, the American Secretary of State saying *detainees* in Guantanamo are treated *humanely.*

"I have found mercy bears richer fruit then justice. Am I not destroying my enemies when I make a friend of them?"- A. Lincoln

"Be courteous to all and intimate with few. And let those few be well tried before you give them your trust." - **Abarham Lincoln**

News from Short-wave Radio, Television, & Newspapers February 28, 1994 – August 18, 1996

February 28, 1994, *New York Times;*
Fighters flying for NATO shot down four Bosnian Serb warplanes violating the 'no fly' zone. These were first shots fired by NATO after assuming the role of the UN Peacekeepers in Bosnia.

June 23, 1994, *New York Times,* Katharine Seelye
: "Clinton tries to head off Senate debate on Bosnia (arms) embargo." Emotions rise over bitter debate on whether to allow Bosnia to buy arms for its defense. Senator Sam Nunn rounds up European 'military officials' to testify that lifting the arms embargo on Bosnia "would throw NATO into chaos and disrupt the fragile ceasefire." Many Senators on the Senate Foreign Relations Committee favored lifting the arms embargo so the outgunned Bosnians could be able to defend themselves. Senator Nunn said if the United States reneged on the embargo, it would have no authority in other

cases such as North Korea (where the US never had a position of authority).

The Senate is preparing to vote next week on a bipartisan amendment calling for the United States to defy the embargo.

Bosnian Vice President, Ejup Ganic, "We are not asking for your troops to fight for us on the ground. That is our job and our task. But please do not combine any more big words with small deeds."

President Clinton said he **will *veto* any bill** that calls for defiance of the embargo. "It's too bad we can't get the views of the people (in Bosnia who are) getting killed," said a seething Senator John McCain (R. Arizona)

June 27, 1994, *The New York Times:* Roger Cohen:
"*New strife in Bosnia?*" Paris: Diplomats from the United States, Russia, and the European Union are putting together a peace plan that will give 49 percent to Bosnian Serbs and 51 percent to a Bosnian Croat Federation.

The Bosnian and Croat Armies are planning an attack in a few days on the Bosnian Serbs who control 75% of Bosnia. "The issues of Bosnia and Croatia are coming together fast," said one Western diplomat. The 1991 Croatian War ended in an uneasy ceasefire.

Thus cities like Visegrad, Pogelica, Zvorka, Brcko, and Dobor, would be divided and come under United Nations administration. But this would be little solace to the Muslims of Banja Luka and Prijador, who have lost their homes.

Bosnian Serb leader (and War Criminal) Dr. Radovan Karadzic said, "If our territory in Bosnia is not united we will not accept the international peace plan."

June 27, 1994, Special to the *New York Times:* Elaine Sciolino:

"The White House turns again to an old G.O.P. image maker (spin doctor) David Gergen. In an interview last November, David R. Gergen made it clear that he wanted to be regarded as a man of substance and not a spin doctor. 'I would not pretend to know as much about foreign affairs as Tony (Anthony Lake) or Warren (Christopher). But I didn't take the job to do P.R. (Public Relations)."

When a White House official was asked about Mr. Lake's initial reaction, he replied, "I can't imagine he (Mr. Lake) was pleased."

What is not clear is exactly what Mr. Gergen will do. He will neither prepare daily guidelines nor brief report. Mr. Strobe Talbot is encouraging Mr. Gergen to travel with Secretary of State, Warren Christopher.

Mr. Gergen was asked, "Does that mean Mr. Christopher is subcontracting America's foreign policy to a damage control expert?"

"Oh God, please don't think that," Mr. Gergen replied.

June 29, 1994, *Washington Post:* John F. Harris:
"Europeans urge The Hill (Congress) to keep the arms embargo against Bosnia"

July 18, 1994, All newspapers and television in the US:
The Jewish Center and Synagogue in Buenos Aires is bombed. Israel and the American Government blame five Iranians. The United States and Israel pressure Argentina to try the men for the bombing but the Argentine courts found the evidence was insufficient to make an indictment and freed the men. The Clinton Administration brands Iran a

terrorist nation and tries to get world wide sanctions against Iran.

August 13, 1994, Die Deutsche Welle: (shortwave)
   Bosnian Serbs have been returning heavy weapons into the exclusion zone (the 20 kilometers or 12.5 miles zone) around Sarajevo.

August 13, 1994, Radio Netherlands:
   Bosnian Serbs attacked three UN depots in Sarajevo. This time, they were not successful in stealing back weapons they had turned over.

August 14, 1994, Radio Netherlands:
   Serbs and Bosnians signed an agreement by Thorvald Stoltenberg to stop sniping around Sarajevo Airport. It is expected to be reopened as all flights have been cancelled for three weeks after sniping from around the airport hit three planes.
   In the demilitarized zone between Kuwait and Iraq two UN officials are shot and one UN official from Bangladesh is killed.
   The Iraqi Government denies it seeks a peace treaty with Israel.

August 15, 1994, Die Deutsche Welle:
   Former mayor of Bremen, Germany, Hans Koschnick, who is in charge of EU plans to rebuild Mostar, has had seven attempts on his life (by Mostar Croats). The German Government has sent a detachment of security police to Mostar to protect him.

August 15, 1994, Radio Netherlands:
   Five ethnic Greeks are on trial in Albania for spying in Albania along its border with Greece.

Nelson Mandela, whose South African Government recently broke relations with Israel over the Mossad murders committed in South Africa was given the Ann Frank award by the Dutch Government (the September/October 1994 issue of the *Washington Report on the Middle East* names the two men). The **Truth and Reconciliation** in South Africa has helped smooth out problems resulting from the historical injustices of Apartheid.

August 16, 1994: Die Deutsche Welle:
The Bosnian Army is planning a greater offensive. Yashushi Akashi (UN Secretary General Boutros Boutros Ghali's favored envoy) asked the Bosnian Government to hold back (the intended attack).

Thorvald Stolenberg returned to the UN in New York and asked the UN (Security Council) to lift the arms embargo against Bosnians because the Serbs have consistently refused the peace plan.

Sudan arrested "Carlos the Terrorist" (Jackal) and handed him over to the French authorities. In return, France gave arms to the Sudan Government and satellite photos of rebels in southern Sudan.

August 16, 1994: Radio Netherlands:
Airlifts (of supplied) into Sarajevo have been renewed despite the renewed sniping at civilians in Sarajevo (by Serbs).

In Central Bosnia, near Gorme Viluf, a British soldier was killed in an operation to remove (land) mines.

Nigeria: The trial of opposition leader, Mashad Abiola, is expected to cause riots and violence. The sale of gasoline is prohibited (as a measure) to keep Molotov cocktails from being made.

August 17, 1994, Die Deutsche Welle:

The Nigerian Military Government has dissolved two labor unions and jailed Chief Mashad Abiola. Oil exports have dwindled since the strike started six weeks ago.

German police say that Russian radioactive material seized in Germany this past week was destined for Pakistan.

Israel will release 250 Palestinians as part of the PLO-Israeli Peace Plan. (August 19, 1994, Moscow Radio said 5,000 Palestinians were held by Israel which Israel increased to 10,000 by 2007).

August 17, 1994, Radio Netherlands:

Two Germans, a Pole, and a Pakistani are being held in Berlin on charges of smuggling Russian radioactive material to Pakistan.

Bosnian Serbs have said they will only allow UN convoys into Sarajevo it they if they pay for passage with fuel. The UN calls this blackmail.

Israeli forces shot and killed a Palestinian in the demilitarized zone between Egypt and the Gaza Strip.

August 18, 1994: *The Wall Street Journal,*

Despite continuing hostilities (and threats against his life by Serbs) Pope John Paul II still plans to visit Sarajevo next month.

August 18, 1994: Die Deutsche Welle:

Bosnian Serbs have called for the formation of a *Greater Serbia* composed of conquered parts of Bosnia, Croatia, along with Serbia and Montenegro.

A mortar shell landed (exploded) near Sarajevo Airport and the UN has suspended flights into the airport.

Previous reports that weapons grade nuclear material was smuggled into Germany from Russia and destined for

Pakistan were in error. It is now learned from within security circles that the material was destined for North Korea.

August 18, 1994, *Wall Street Journal:*
Despite continuing hostilities (and threats against his life by Serbs) Pope John Paul II still plans to visit Sarajevo next month.

August 18, 1994: Radio Netherlands: **Carole Van Den Ring**
Despite the fact that there is no evidence connecting Iran to the bombing (of a Jewish synagogue) in Buenos Aires, the U.S. and Israel are pressuring Argentina to put the blame on Iran.

Bosnian Serbs are refusing to allow critically ill Muslims in Gorazde to leave the besieged city unless Bosnia releases Serb prisoners of war.

Bosnian Serbs have dropped many mortar shells around Sarajevo Airport to intimidate the UN forces and have succeeded in making the UN close the airport. (Die Deutsche Welle reported only one mortar shell had exploded near the airport, which must have been an error).

The town of Duroi under Serb control has had an exchange of artillery fire with Bosnian Government Forces.

August 18, 1994: Swiss Radio International:
A powerful earthquake (5.6) struck northwest Algeria. An estimated 12 thousand are homeless and 125 reported dead.

A mortar attack on Sarajevo Airport prevents the UN Envoy, Yashushi Akashi from landing at the airport to meet with Bosnian Serbs. Akashi was going to discuss raising the embargo against Serbians (the Serbs were constantly supplied by Serbia and the Russians so this was not needed).

Tension mounts in Nigeria between General Suni Abacha's military government and the pro-democracy movement. The heads of the striking (oil worker's) union are being replaced with military men.

August 19, 1994: Die Deutsche Welle:

The BND (German intelligence) head, Paul Lassiter has ruled out the Mafia's involvement in the smuggling of Russian nuclear materials.

Yashushi Akashi spent three hours in Pale talking with Serbs to widen the (supply) corridors to Sarajevo.

A French soldier was shot and the UN Command says that it looked as though the soldier was deliberately singled out and shot.

August 19, 1994: Moscow Radio:

Israel freed 247 Palestinians but still holds 5,000 Palestinians as prisoners (without charges so they can be detained for years)..

The US Senate is resolute to lift the arms embargo on Bosnia, but the position of the US (against lifting the arms embargo) is reaffirmed by Secretary of State Warren Christopher, who says that Clinton seeks a multi-lateral lifting of the arms embargo (Clinton's roommate at Oxford was Strobe Talbot who he appointed as Under Secretary of State and strongly supported Boris Yeltsin of Russia who was behind the War in Bosnia) Moscow Radio says this is the correct decision to take.

Bosnian Muslim troops (there were no *Bosnian Muslim troops* but this is Radio Moscow) charged against Bosnian Serb positions in three areas. The 'Muslim' commander of Muslim forces, General Rasim Delic, is getting ready for an all-out offensive. Moscow Radio says this plays into the hands of Bosnian Serbs who seek a military solution (Moscow Radio calls the Croatian/Bosnian cooperation as a *Muslim-Croat Federation* long before the Dayton Peace Accords).

August 19, 1994: Radio Netherlands:
Israeli Cabinet Minister, Simon Peres, paid a visit to Yasar Arafat. (The control of educational affairs) Education in the West Bank (Palestine) will be handed over to the PLO next week.
Tadzhikistan resistance with support from Afghan rebels continues its attacks against the neo-communist government of Tadzhikistan. Russian troops have been caught in the middle receiving fire from both sides. The attacks have been launched from Afghan territory.
The Bosnian Army has gained territory from the renegade Bosnian leader, Abdic, and is within three kilometers of (the encircled) Bihac. Rebel troops (from Abdic) have been coming over to the Bosnian Army side as Bosnians win more territory Abdic denies there are any defections and is seeking a meeting with UN officials.
Deaths from the Algerian earthquake are now officially 159, with an estimated 10,000 homeless.

August 19, 1994: Swiss Radio International:
The Nigerian Government has arrested two (oil worker's) union leaders in a hotel in Lagos. The government has called up retired oil workers in an effort to break the strike by the oil worker's unions.
Boutros Boutros Ghali is asking to reconsider the UN positions in Somalia and reduce UN forces there. The US says the operation is costing too much.

Bosnian Forces are within two kilometers of Velika Kadusa (close to the Croatian border south of Zagreb) which is the headquarters of Abdic, the breakaway Bosnian commander. Abdic is trying to involve the UN in talks between his group and the Bosnian Government.

August 20, 1994: Die Deutsche Welle:
The Bosnian Army is rapidly taking over the Bosnian breakaway enclave of Bosnian millionaire Abdic: Abdic's followers are fleeing the area around Bihac (Bee hatch) which had the highest standard of living in Bosnia (before the conflict) due to its accommodation with the Serbs. Abdic is said to have killed many Muslims. The Bosnian Army is asking for unconditional surrender as they surround Abdic's headquarters near Velika Kadusa.

Five children in Bihac were killed when a shell landed on a school. The Bosnian Army is slowing its advance as many refugees have crowded into the area and they do not want to risk the lives of the refugees.

Croatian Serbs have turned down Radovan Karadzic's plea to join a Greater Serbia.

Four hundred Kurdish protesters demonstrated in Frankfurt. Turkish troops clashed with Kurds in eastern Anatolia.

August 20, 1994: Radio Netherlands:
The death toll in Algeria's earthquake is now put at 171 with an estimated 15,000 homeless.

August 20, 1994: Radio Swiss International:
In Banja Luka, Radovan Karadzic tried to show Bosnian Serb's approval of his leadership with speeches and demonstrations.

August 21, 1994: Asian News TV program, Channel 33, Houston, Texas:

Pakistan celebrated Independence Day August 14. Prime Minister Benazir Bhutto said Pakistan should rely less on conventional weapons and should hold talks with India to resolve the Kashmir-Jammu dispute.

Pakistan demands that the $615 million dollars paid to the US for F-16 fighters should be returned (to Pakistan as the fighters were never delivered. There are other alternatives open to Pakistan to supply its defense needs.

After Indian forces removed their bunkers from around the Islamic shrine in Srinagar, Kashmir, there was much celebration.

August 21, 1994: Die Deutsche Welle:

Twenty to twenty-five thousand refugees fleeing the Bosnian Army that overran Bihac are streaming over the border into Croatian Serb territory.

A Deutsche Welle editorial says that Milosevic is unhappy with Radovan Karadzic's call for a Greater Serbia at this time while the war is still going on in Bosnia. This puts Milosevic on the spot as he is disappointing the most fanatical of the Serbian nationalists and is in danger of losing their support.

August 21, 1994: Radio Netherlands:

Israel will turn over the education and taxation matters to the West Bank (Palestine) by Wednesday. Al Fatah is expected to repudiate its demand that Israel be destroyed.

An airliner flying from Agadir to Marrakech (Morocco) crashed. Of the 40 passengers on board, 14 were said to be foreigners.

August 21, 1994: Swiss Radio International:

Thousands of refugees have fled into Serbian Croatia including Abdic himself. Abdic, a businessman turned politician, joined with the Serbs in an eleven-month revolt. His breakaway from Bosnia was completely crushed by the Bosnian Army but he has vowed to continue fighting against Bosnia. Croatian Serbs (across the border from Velika Kadusa) have accepted (Abdic's followers as) refugees.

August 22, 1994: BBC:

Albania's president accused Greece of *cold-war* tactics by dropping leaflets from Greek planes over Albanian territory. There are 300,000 Albanians working illegally in Greece and the Greek Government threatens to expel them to Albania which would cause Albania more economic hardship.

The UN condemns the attack on UN Forces in Somalia in which seven Indian troops were killed in an area controlled by warlord Mohammed Fareh Adib. The attack was premeditated, well coordinated, and completely unprovoked. Fighting outside of Mogadishu is spreading throughout Somalia.

The PLO and Israel are confident that the deadline of Wednesday (agreed upon in meetings in Alexandria, Egypt) concerning the turnover of education, tourism, and taxation, can be affected.

Marzdieh, Iran's favorite singer has defected to Paris and backs the Mujahideen (Khalk) as the only real opposition to the Iranian Government. She says that ordinary Iranians are disaffected with the present Iranian Government.

As Russian troops withdraw from the Republic of Moldavia, the Russian commander is being transferred to Tadzhikistan (capital, Dushanabe) to support the neo-communist government there against Islamic revolutionaries (Tadshik Mujahidden).

August 23, 1994: Radio Netherlands:

Serbia's Slobodan Milosevic has told the United Nation's envoy, Yashushi Akashi, he is opposed to stationing UN observers along the Serbian border with Bosnia (to enforce the arms embargo against Bosnian Serbs). The UN wants to verify that Serbia really has stopped supplying Bosnian Serbs with weapons, fuel, munitions, etc.

The Bosnian Government has asked refugees fleeing from the Bihac area to return to their homes and offered amnesty to Abdic's soldiers if they lay down their arms. Renegade leader Abdic has vowed he will continue to fight for autonomy in Bihac.

August 23, 1994: *Wall Street Journal:*

On Monday, the university teachers in Nigeria joined the crippling strike by the oil workers. Colleges will stay closed until the military government surrenders power to civilians. General Abacha has ordered banks to reopen but banks have remained closed despite threats to have their licenses revoked. The only traffic on Lagos highways was lines of cars waiting to obtain gasoline at the few filling stations with gas.

August23, 1994: *Wall Street Journal:*

Egypt hanged five Islamic extremists for attempting to assassinate Egypt's security chief and killing nine people. All were accused of belonging to the Jihad Movement, which assassinated Anwar Sadat in 1981. This brings the number of executed people to 42 during its past two and a half year campaign to topple the (Egyptian) government.

Nigerian security agents arrested at least 25 prominent Nigerians since last Friday as General Abacha tries force an end to the unrest that began with the annulment of the 1993 elections, which were to have ended military rule.

August 23, 1994: Die Deutsche Welle:

Germany is asking the EU for closer ties to Israel as the peace plan between Israel and the PLO can only succeed if the well-being of the people living there (Palestine) is guaranteed.

Foreign Minister Klaus Kinkel of Germany and Alain Juppe of France called on Serbia to place checkpoints along the Bosnian–Serbian border o monitor if Serbia is complying with the stated boycott of Bosnian Serbs.

Two hundred and fifty French (UN) troops have been held up by Croatian Serbs of the Krajina region (the Serbs are) wanting to utilize the situation (in Bihac) to voice their concerns. They seek Austria's help to take in the (Serb) refugees from Bihac.

Meanwhile, the Bosnian Army is pouring into the region around Velika Kladusa.

Slobodan Milosevic says he doesn't want UN Observers verifying that Serbia is boycotting (enforcing the UN arms embargo) the Bosnian Serbs. He also says that Serbia doe not want the lull in fighting to be used by both sides to build up supplies and weapons.

UN's Yashushi Akashi (specially appointed by Boutros Boutros Ghali) failed to obtain Milosevic's permission to put in UN observers. Milosevic told Thovald Stoltenberg that he does not want UN monitors, as he would lose support of the Serbian Orthodox Church.

The Bosnian Serbs are receiving petrol supplies from Albania crossing through Montenegro and dozens of roads in southern Bosnia.

August 23, 1994: Radio Netherlands:

The Attorney General of Argentina, Aguero Iturbe, said there was insufficient evidence against four Iranians alleged to be involved in anti-Jewish bombings in Buenos Aires which killed 96. He sent the case back to investigating Judge Juan Jose Galeano who named the Iranians in his report on the July 18 bombing.

Ex-premier, Nawaz Sharif, has said that Pakistan does have an atomic bomb and other nuclear weapons capabilities. Prime Minister Benazir Bhutto says that Pakistan has the capability to make an atomic bomb but that it has not made an atomic bomb.

Despite the loss of seven Indian soldiers in Somalia, India has no plans to withdraw from Somalia.

Alain Juppe (French Foreign Minister) and Klaus Kinkel (Germany's Foreign Minister) have called for a monitoring of the Serbian boycott of the Bosnian Serbs. Milosevic refuses, and claims that this is a case of Serbian sovereignty.

In Zagreb (Croatia), the Croatian Government refuses to let in refugees that fled the Krajina region of Bihac. Roads are clogged with thousands of (Abdic's followers) vehicles fleeing Bosnia.

Nigerian general, Abacha, is a tough and very capable leader who has installed and equipped a very efficient security system. He will be difficult to overthrow and can count on a solid support from northern Nigeria, the region from which he comes.

August 23, 1994: Swiss Radio International:

The PLO and Israel will sign an agreement in Cairo, extending Palestinian autonomy over its social welfare, taxation, education, tourism, etc.

Argentina's (Aguero) Iturbe says the case against the four Iranians is insufficient.

Syria's election today has seven thousand candidates running for office. Regardless of how the election goes, it is not expected to change Syria's foreign policy.

Water is in short supply for the refugee followers of Abdic who have fled into the Krajina district of Croatian Serbia.

August 24, 1994: *Wall Street Journal:*

Bosnian Serb's leader (Radovan Karadzic) predicted that the International Peace Plan would be overwhelmingly rejected in a public referendum this weekend. Meanwhile, Bosnian Army troops flushed out soldiers loyal to ousted Muslim separatist, Abdic, in the northwest and the Bosnian Government assured thousands of refugees that is was safe to return home.

A Nigerian judge temporarily reinstated the oil union leaders dismissed by military rule, Abacha in his bid to end a seven-week-old pro-democracy strike. The government threatened to deal ruthlessly with saboteurs who closed down a key oil terminal.

August 24, 1994: Die Deutsche Welle:

Thirty thousand Muslims (Abdic followers from Bihac) who fled to Krajina (Croatian) Serbian territory are without food and water.

Germany's Foreign Minister, Klaus Kinkel, at the Institute for Foreign Affairs in Bonn, said Belgrade should show its commitment to the International Peace Plan by permitting UN observers to monitor the Bosnian/Serbian border.

August 24, 1994: Radio Netherlands:

India has called for the International Atomic Energy Agency to intervene in Pakistan's development of an atomic bomb.

Tehran wants Washington to apologize for accusing Iran in the bombing of a Jewish synagogue in Buenos Aires, Argentina,

The Air Morocco plane that crashed into the Atlas Mountains was taking evasive action o avoid a collision with another plane.

Former (Pakistan) Premier, Nawaz Sharif, statements that Pakistan has the atomic bomb, was made in Kashmir. In his speech, he warned that India should not act without fear of retaliation from Pakistan.

Indonesian President Suharto is being taken to court by environmentalist for diverting funds to invest in the national aircraft industry.

August 25, 1994: *Wall Street Journal:*

Israel signed over the Ramallah school district to Palestinian authorities, giving them the first foothold outside Jericho in the West Bank.

Refugees from the Bihac enclave claim the Muslim led government troops raped and killed civilians and looted and burned houses.

Russian's Foreign Minister will go to Belgrade this weekend to persuade Yugoslav leaders to accept international monitoring of their border with Bosnia.

Speaking to the Jewish service organization, B'nai B'rith, President Clinton condemned Iran as "the world's leading sponsor of terrorism." He said its *rogue behavior* would not be tolerated.

August 25, 1994: BBC:

The UN Security Council is cutting 1,500 troops from the 19,000 deployed in Somalia at the insistence of the United States.

Croatia has posted troops with rifles and water cannon along the Croat Serb border to turn back 14,000 refugees from the Bihac area. They have invaded the area assigned to French troops under the UN.

Studies of torture and killing by Indian forces in Kashmir show these are systematically planned and deliberately carried out on order high up in the Indian Government.

August 25, 1994: Die Deutsche Welle:

Karl Pashka is the German diplomat appointed as the watchdog in the UN to investigate corruption and malfeasance in the UN and various agencies.

Over16,000 children have died in Bosnia and the Pope was to visit Bosnia to commemorate a Mass for the loss of their lives and to denounce the killings there. Serbian forces are threatening the life of the Pope if he comes.

There is a belief that Karadzic and Milosevic are trying to pull the wool over the eyes of the world and that the Serbian boycott of the Bosnia Serbs is non-existent. Milosevic is losing popularity in Serbia with an Orthodox Serb priest putting a curse on him and members of the Serbian Parliament are continually denouncing him.

August 25, 1994: Radio Netherlands:

UN Security Council considering withdrawing from Somalia if the warring factions do not stop fighting.

The UN proposes lighter sanctions against Serbia if Milosevic allows international observers to see if Serbia is complying with the boycott against Bosnian Serbs. But Milosevic refuses.

Recent attacks on Turkish organizations in SW Germany are said to be the work of right wing (German) extremists, not Kurds.

Greece is initiating talks with Albania over deteriorating conditions between the two countries.

Bosnian Serbs will vote on a referendum this Sunday on whether to accept the international peace plan. Despite Milosevic's insistence they accept the plan, the view is that it will be rejected by the Bosnian Serbs.

TADA, the (Indian) Terrorist and Disruptive Acts law enacted by the Indian Parliament may be scrapped because it has resulted in international criticism of India from human rights groups, especially Amnesty (International). The *rights issue* is becoming an issue in India because thousands of innocent people have been jailed and international (rights) groups are pressuring India.

August 25, 1994: Swiss Radio International:

Britain says the international sanctions against Serbia could be relaxed if Serbia allows monitors to be stationed along the Serbian-Bosnian boarder.

Nigerian oil workers is in the eighth week of the strike. Unions have taken out ads in the newspapers calling for the release of chief Abiola.

Thousands of refugees from Bihac are refusing to return home unless Abdic (political renegade) is allowed to return with them. Thirteen thousand of them are in the UN controlled area. Their mental state has been described as 'manipulate'. The refugees are claiming so many civilians have been killed by Bosnian troops but independent observers only a very few were killed and these exaggerations show the refugees are being manipulated by Abdic and other leaders.

August 26, 1994: *Wall Street Journal:*

Israel rejected a demand that a tomb complex at the site of the February 25th Hebron mosque massacre (where one Israeli settler entered a mosque and killed 36 Muslim men and boys with a submachine gun) be reopened. Chief Rabbis asked that it be reopened for Jewish New Year starting September 5th. But officials at the Tomb of the Patriarchs said it would be closed until security is improved.

Argentina's Supreme Court dropped charges against four Iranian officials who were named as suspects linked to the bombing of a Jewish center in Buenos Aires.

The U.S. and its allies will ease sanctions against Serbia if President Milosevic permits monitoring the Bosnian-Serbian border. UN's British Ambassador is proposing 300 to 400 monitors, but Milosevic has refused such proposals.

Pakistan says it will expel about one million illegal immigrants from Karachi's ten million populations. Most immigrants are from India, Afghanistan, Bangladesh, Burma, and Iran and said to have contributed to the violence, drug trafficking, and crime in general. Karachi has been rocked by ethnic and political violence in recent years.

August 26, 1994: Die Deutsche Welle:

Serbia's ruling Socialist Party pushed through a declaration accepting the Peace Plan and urged Bosnian Serbs to accept it. It also endorsed breaking off with Bosnian Serbs and sealing off the border.

Yashushi Akashi seeks the return of 25,000 displaced Bihac persons and a solution for the 10,000 in a 'no man's land' between Croatia and Croatian Serbs. Izetbegovic (President of Bosnia) has offered amnesty and guaranteed safety for Bihac persons willing to return.

It is certain that Bosnian Serbs will reject the Peace Plan. The rejection is expected to push Washington to lift the arms embargo and the withdrawal of UN troops. It is in conjectured that Washington will offer an Afghan type of operation to train and supply Bosnians.

August 26, 1994: Radio Netherlands:
The US is to withdraw all diplomatic personnel from Somalia by mid September.
Bosnian Serbs are expected to reject the Peace Plan.

U.S. President Clinton threatens to lift the arms embargo if Bosnian Serbs do not accept the Peace Plan by October 15.

Greece has started sending Albanian workers back to Albania. This is in response to the trial of five Greek citizens in Tirana (Albanian capital) on charges of espionage.

In Algeria, the GIA has formed its own alternative government in opposition to Algeria's Government. GIA is the strongest and most militant in opposition t the government.

Four Dutch Jews who died in the Air Morocco crash will be buried in a Muslim cemetery in Agadir despite relative's wishes. Identification of the bodies was said to be impossible.

Six members of the Menon family are arrested in New Delhi after they arrived from Dubai. The Menon family is accused of involvement in the Bombay bombings, which was a reprisal for the Hindu destruction of the Ioda Mosque by Hindu fanatics.

August 26, 1994: Swiss Radio International:
The Bosnian Serb referendum will take two days.

Differences between Albania and Greece are blocking an 18 million dollar aid package to Albania by the EU.

Swiss Radio International describes the Bosnian Serbs as scared as they do no know what the future will be. They are intimidated by Bosnian Serb television and radio to reject the Peace Plan. Lifting the arms embargo on Bosnia is expected to undermine President Milosevic in Serbia and Karadzic in Bosnian Serb territory.

August 27, 1994: Asian TV (channel 33 in Houston, Texas):

Muslim militants are said to have ambushed Hindu pilgrims in Kashmir but none were killed and no group is taking responsibility. They were on their way to Abernaut, a Hindu shrine in the Himalayas at 13,000 feet, which is accessible only a few days every year.

The mosques in Sringar that house a single hair from the head of the Prophet Mohammed was re-opened after and Indian Army bunkers were removed.

Rajiv Gandhi's assassination trial of Tamil Nadu is held up, as the defense lawyers argue for an increase in pay commensurate with the prosecutors in the case. 41 Tamils are being prosecuted for his murder.

India celebrated its independence day, August 28. India's Prime Minister Rao said that Kashmir is an integral part of India. India plans to conduct elections in selected communities in Kashmir.

Rao also said that 20 million children are in child labor and India is threatened with international trade sanctions unless it does something to combat this situation.

Yacub Menon is accused of the serial bombings that killed 280 people and wounded over 1,000 in the Bombay blasts. India claims Pakistanis involved because of Pakistani documentation found on Menon. Yacub was arrested at the New Delhi Railway Station. Anti-Pakistan demonstrations were organized and police with water cannon were brought in to quell the "riots". (Rioters on TV were smiling and laughing as they burned a very crude dummy of Pakistan's Bhutto).

India last year was facing bankruptcy with foreign exchange reserves at only one billion dollars. India is now booming with the economy growing at 8% annually. Sami Rao's government is credited with the turn around.

August 27, 1994: Beijing Radio:

The Bosnian Government said it would welcome troops from any country but didn't answer Iran's offer of Iranian troops. Islamic nations may contribute only when the Peace Plan is put into effect.

Hamas claims two killing in Ramallah.

Egyptian police killed five terrorists in a shootout in Egypt.

Al Fatah met in Palestinian territory with the PLO and voiced its support of Palestinian Council.

Rockets launched by Burkeddin guerillas in Kabul killed 24 people.

Prime Minister Benazir Bhutto (Pakistan) says that Nawaz Sharif's remarks were unfortunate and not correct. Pakistan has the ability to make nuclear weapons from its nuclear energy program, but will not.

China launched an Australian communications satellite into space.

Drought has hit several provinces of China very hard this year.

August 27, 1994: BBC:

Yitzak Rabin (PM of Israel (latter murdered by an Israeli fanatic) ordered a strict adherence to (control) Arab migrant workers after the deaths of two Israelis in Ramallah.

Algerian and Moroccan authorities are making border crossings into each other's territory difficult. The difficulties stem from the robbery in Morocco by five Algerians.

Separatist (Kashmiri) guerrillas kill two Indian soldiers in Kashmir.

August 27, 1994: Radio Netherlands:

Holland has contributed US$58 million in aid to Somalia through the UN. Somalia, Rwanda, and Bosnia all need aid and Holland has to make the choice of priority in placing the aid.

August 27, 1994: Swiss Radio International:

High voter turnout in the Bosnian Serb territory.

France and Algeria have denounced Morocco for demanding visa requirements on Algerians after some Algerians were involved in a hotel robbery in Marrakech.

Ethnic Bosnian Serbs want to show the world they can go it alone. Many Serbs are afraid about the future and that if a peace force does come, how will they be affected? Liberals are organizing in Banja Luka but they are too weak. A lifting of the arms embargo will undermine Milosevic, who after three years of saying one thing and doing another has no creditability in the international arena.

August 28, 1994: BBC:

Russia's (Foreign Minister) Andrei Kozyrev talks with Milosevic about Bosnian Serbs. Kozyrev and Milosevic took a joint position. Milosevic says that his cutting aid to the Bosnian Serbs should be enough to lift sanctions against Serbia.

The *empowerment plan* for Palestinians taking control of education, taxation, social welfare, and tourism in the Gaza Strip is lacking funds for implementation.

Iran's government is critical of the Cairo (world) population conference saying that it promotes promiscuity.

Mr. Jawan, visiting Moscow, says that New Delhi is concerned about money laundering and arms supplies to the Sikh separatists and rebels

August 28, 1994: Die Deutsche Welle:

Overwhelming rejection of the Peace Plan by Bosnian Serbs. They underline their objection to the partition and will continue the war in isolation. Kozyrev denied that his trip to Belgrade was to persuade Serbia to accept international monitors.

Greece expelled 24,000 illegal Albanian workers to Albania and Greek boats are patrolling the waters of Corfu Island and Albania.

King Hussein of Jordan is visiting Germany to obtain financial help.

August 28, 1994: Radio Netherlands:

Asia Watch says China is removing organs from criminals (some before they are dead) and selling them abroad. It asks for a boycott of Chinese organs.

Turkey and Jordan are asking for a lifting of sanctions against Iraq as their countries are suffering economically because of it.

President Milosevic asks that sanctions against Montenegro and Serbia be lifted as a reward Serbia's effort to bring peace to Bosnia.

August 29, 1994: Radio Netherlands:

Controversial trial of five Greeks accused of espionage continues.

A coalmine explosion in Mindanao (southern-most Philippines, which is mainly Muslim) has killed 47 miners and 27 others are missing. They are pumping fresh air into the mine and poison gas coming out of the mine is endangering areas around the mine.

Results show that 85% of the Bosnian Serbs rejected the partitioning of Bosnia as proposed by the international community (what *international community?*) A group of very high U.S. officials met with Radovan Karadzic who they say is ready to defect.

Supplies are low in Sarajevo as winter approaches (Serb blockade of roads into Sarajevo and closing Sarajevo's airport by Serb sniping).

Israel says the identity of two Hamas killers is known. They have fled into the Gaza Strip, but Palestinian authorities have refused requests to arrest and deport them.

Algiers: the dispute between the two strongest Islamic groups: the FIS and Islamic Salvation Front have reduced pressure on President Amin Zerual. They are still demanding the release of two militants, Ali Del Haj and _____ (second name was not clear). The dispute centers on the Armed Islamic Group wanting to name a Caliphate but the other Islamic groups say all Islamic groups must do this and that this would be illegal if only by the Armed Islamic Group named the Caliphate.

Sept/October 1994 ***The Washington Report on the Middle East,*** p. 6.

The Bosnian Government has 200,000 fighters that have received training, discipline, and coordination which was lacking in the first two years of the war. The army is beginning two offensives to secure the area around the newly built airfield at Visoko 120 miles northwest of Sarajevo, which is to receive military supplies expected to flow once the arms embargo is lifted. The other offensive is to shut off the supply corridor to Bosnian Serbs through Brko (175 miles NNE of Sarajevo) with the help of Croatian allies.

August 30, 1994: Die Deutsche Welle:
17 German border guards are dispatched to work with Mostar (Herzegovina) police. These are Germany's crack police, trained to handle all kinds of situations and who can best protect the life of Hans Koschnick (former mayor of Bremen who is Catholic as are the Croats of Mostar), who is in charge of Mostar's reconstruction by the EU. His life has been threatened (by Croats) for his role in rebuilding Mostar.

Milosevic says sanctions against Serbia and Montenegro should be lifted but international groups say it may be possible only if 300 to 400 monitors are placed along the Montenegro and Serbian borders with Bosnia to verify that Serbia is truly boycotting the Bosnian Serbs.

August 30, 1994: Radio Netherlands:
The U.S. Government has approached the Surinam Government to take Haitian refugees to be guarded by 700 US Marines (Surinam is approximately 20% Muslim on the northern coast of South America).

Andrei Kozyrev (Russian Foreign Minister) says the Western Contact Group is too rigid in its actions against Belgrade.

Algeria has sealed off its border with Morocco over Morocco's demand that Algerians must have visas to enter Morocco.

The president of Sudan (Omar Bashem) has been accused by Algerian President, Amin Zeraul, of aiding Algerian rebels.

August 30, 1994: Swiss Radio International:
Lord Owen has said that a united front is needed to approach Bosnian Serbs and that the West should listen more to Russian leaders.

Shimon Peres (Israel) says that (Pakistan's) Prime Minister Benazir Bhutto should be taught a lesson as she has completely ignored Israel in planning her visit to Palestinian territory, which is still under Israeli control of Israel and has its international representation.

August 31, 994: *The Wall Street Journal:*
Andrei Kozyrev chided the West for its international sanctions against Serbia because Serbia has supported the Bosnian Serbs.

Bosnia's Prime Minister says he has little hope that the West will punish the Bosnian Serbs for rejecting the Peace Plan.

A Cairo court has rejected a suit by three Islamic leaders to move the controversial UN conference on population out of Egypt. The conference is being boycotted by Sudan, Saudi Arabia, and more have said they will follow suit.

August 31, 1994: Radio Netherlands:
Japan and Germany will not be admitted to an enlarged UN Security Council this year or in 1995.

Mr. Musa of Egypt wants to have talks with Israel about establishing a *nuclear free Middle East.* Israel has never admitted to the West that is has nuclear weapons.

Two Finnish tourists kidnapped by the Kurdish PKK in southeast Turkey have been released.

A Radio Netherlands Editorial: Colonel Qadaffi says that Allah revealed to him that he should overthrow the (former) government of King Idris twenty-five years ago. He established his "third way, neither capitalist exploitation nor atheist communism", which was published in a Green Book for his government to use as a guide. Libya's three million people have prospered under his regime while at the same time receiving opposition from the West, mainly the U.S. Colonel Qadaffi has been called a madman by former President Reagan and President Anwar Sadat of Egypt.

September/October 1994. *Washington Report on the Middle East:*

The South African government (Nelson Mandela) blames the Mossad for the murders of Alan Kidger, who (whose body) was found dismembered in the trunk of his car, .in November 1991, and chemical engineer Wynand van Wyk, who was beaten to death in a Cape Town hotel, April 1993. Both had received threatening phone calls before their deaths. The two (other) "apparent suicides" were not named. Israel's ambassador, Alan Lial, said, ***"It happens all over the world. Mysterious murder cases with international connotations are attributed to the Mossad. Unfortunately, we are getting used to it."*** (Why does he use the word, 'unfortunately?)

August 31, 1994: *Iranian News* on Los Angeles television:

The chief of Iran's intelligence says the bombing of a Jewish center in Buenos Aires, Argentine, and the bombing of the plane of Jewish businessman over Panama was the work of the Likud Party that is trying to sabotage the peace plan of P.M. Yitzak Rabin (Rabin is later assassinated by a Jewish extremist).

August 31, 1994: Swiss Radio International:
Unidentified guerrillas (in Somalia) killed three Indian doctors in an attack on a hospital in Bidoa, Somalia. Several others were wounded.

September 1, 1994: *The Wall Street Journal:*
Belgrade (Serbia) newspapers report that Milosevic has agreed to allow international observers monitor his blockade of arms and fuel to Bosnian Serbs. Report added that he wants observers along the Croatian Border with Bosnia to monitor the flow of arms to his foes (Bosnians).
 The UN defends itself against charges that the Cairo Population Conference endorses abortion, homosexuality, and promiscuity. Lebanon will boycott the meeting and Palestine may do the same.

September 1, 1994: *VOA (Voice of America):*
U.S. Ambassador to the UN, Madeleine Albright, warned against *ethnic cleansing* in Albania.
 She says an aid package is being put together for (the Republic of Georgia and) Russian troops are in the area to stabilize the situation.

September 1, 1994: Die Deutsche Welle: The trial of five ethnic Greeks in Tirana (Albania) over charges of spying for Greece has continued to cause relations between Albania and Greece to deteriorate. Greece deported 28,000 illegal Albanian immigrants from an estimated 300,000 Albanians living in Greece
.
September 1, 1994: Radio Netherlands:
Radovan Karadzic has threatened to cut off water, fuel, and electricity to all Croat and Bosnian enclaves unless Serbia ends its economic blockade of Bosnian Serbs (They

act as though Milosevic has stopped supplying weapons and fuel to the Bosnian Serbs which never stopped).

Salah Berishe, Albania's president has called on outside help to resolve the situation between Albania and Greece. Greece has managed to stop the economic aid package from EU to Albania.

President Hosni Mubarak of Egypt has called upon all Islamic nations to attend the UN Population Conference in Cairo. Sudan, Libya, and Saudi Arabia have said they will attend. Lebanon and Pakistan have indicated they will not attend.

French police arrested 27 persons over the killing of two Spanish tourists in a hotel robbery in Marrakech (Morocco) committed by five Algerians. Three of the arrested are French citizens of Algerian origin.

Israel and Morocco have agreed to low-level diplomatic relations between the two nations. Morocco is the second Arab nation after Egypt to have diplomatic relations with Israel. Moroccan-Jewish relations go back to a time when Morocco and Spain were one and Jews were protected (by Muslims).

The Yoruba population of Nigeria has asked to withdraw from Nigeria because Chief Abiola (elected president of Nigeria last year) was usurped from the presidency by General Abacha who has continued his detention of Abiola.

September 2, 1994: *Wall Street Journal:*

(Front page article from Tadzhikistan, a country with a population of five million and long border with Afghanistan). The article describes how Russians (Soviets) first supplied heavy weapons to the communists and procommunist government that resulted in the 1992 bloody civil war. Fifteen thousand Russian troops wear the blue berets as symbols of *peacekeeping operations* in the country.

"Western diplomats and aid officials give convincing details of the (Russian) military conducting far-flung intervention without (Russia's) foreign ministry oversight.

September 2, 1994: Beijing Radio:
The PLO and Jordan have signed separate accords that Israel must return the Golan Heights to Syria before they will consider reaching and accord with Israel. (There are huge springs at the bottom of Golan Heights that Israel has dammed up to send that water into Israel. A member of the Rothschild's family was buying land on and around Golan Heights long before Israel was a nation.

Firemen in western South Africa have not been paid for three weeks and King Butalezzi fired his prime minister (Israel was working to destabilize the South African government of Nelson Mandela since he broke with Israel over five murders committed by the Mossad).

Colonel Qadaffi (Libyan leader) called upon the U.K. and the U.S. to negotiate over the two men accused of blowing up the Pan Am plane over Lockerbee, Scotland. Libya has given sanctuary to the two men (causing the U.S. to accuse Qadaffi of complicity in the bombing)

September 2, 1994: Radio Netherlands:
The UN Security Council is meeting about the recent *ethnic cleansing* in Serb-conquered territory in Bosnia. The Council *deplored* efforts of the Serbs in hindering freedom of movement among all people of Bosnia (rather a weak comment to murder).

Several hundred Muslim *Fundamentalists* have been arrested in Cairo to guarantee the safety of the 15,000 delegates to the UN Population Conference to be held in Cairo next week.

Albania's newspapers report that Greek minorities in Albania will have instruction in the Greek language where they predominate.

Karadzic has threatened to cut off all Bosnia enclaves (so-called *UN Safe Havens*) from water, gas, electricity, and food. Serbs are anxious to get economic sanctions lifted. Karadzic said he will seal off the enclaves so completely that not even a bird can get in. Tuzla is surrounded but still has flight into its airport. The people of Goradze and Srebrenitsa know what *siege* means and the hoarding of food, fuel, and water has started.

September 3, 1994: *Eye on Asia* (Houston, Texas TV program produced in India and shown on weekends on Houston's TV)

Nawaz Sharif, who was Pakistan's Prime Minister for 13 months, declared that Pakistan has an atomic bomb. Afwan Shaybani, calls Sharif's 'childish' for making such allegations.

The repercussions of Narwhal's allegations have stirred up demonstrations in India against Pakistan and they are burning Prime Minister Bhutto in effigy accompanied with speeches about Pakistan directing terrorist activities in India.

The arrest in Berlin of a Pakistani over the smuggling of Russian plutonium is now used as evidence that Pakistan has constructed an atomic bomb. Prime Minister Bhutto has refused to comment one way or the other, as there will be repercussions for her if she answers either way (she previously had denied the reportad0.

The BJP Hindu Party raised its flag over a Muslim shrine. This brought criticism against the party for trying to provoke Muslims

The Indian Rupee is now convertible in current accounts. Non-resident Indians can repatriate profits over a three year period. Previously, the Indian Government allowed only $500 a year to be repatriated.

India Air Lines is losing business to private competition.

Dowad Abraham, talking from an undisclosed foreign country, says he had nothing to do with the Bombay bombings

S. Ventralaswamy, (India's Textile Minister) testifies that the U.S. Safety Commission is another ploy to disrupt Indian textile exports. The skirts (in question) have been on sale in the United States for fifteen years and that they have been very popular in the U.S.

Prime Minister Rao (India) says that India does not have an atomic bomb but could quickly assemble one.

Protests in Nepal continue to destabilize Nepal's political situation (already bad from an insurgency of many years). Officials say that the United Marxist Party is behind it all.

September 3, 1994: Swiss Radio International:

The transfer of power from Israel to the Palestinians continues despite Hamas. Opposition seems to be diminishing. The problems of peace with Lebanon, Syria, and Israel are plagued with questions concerning restitution (payment for damage done and the Golan Heights seized by Israel for its springs that once supplied water to Damascus, but were dammed up and turned around to flow into Israel.).

September 3, 1994: Radio Netherlands:

Russia says it may withdraw its peacekeeping forces from Bosnia if the arms embargo is lifted. (Russian peacekeeper trained Bosnian Serbs and even joined them in fighting against Bosnia even though Russia was on the UN Security Council).

Five hundred Muslims arrive in Banja Luka after being driven from their homes by Bosnian Serbs.

Bosnian Serbs have threatened the life of Pope John Paul II because they felt he favored the Croatians when Croatian Serbs were fighting to gain territory in Croatia.

The Ulema, high Islamic council in Saudi Arabia, has expressed its condemnation of the Cairo Conference on Population.

Sniping at Bosnia's Muslims continues are cars are fired on. A girl near the airport was shot and more people in the city were shot.

The South Yemen city of Aden has had fundamentalists attempting to take over the city. Gunmen are on the rooftops firing down on the streets. Thirty-one are dead. Yemen security forces are responding and entering the city.

Trials for war criminals in the former Yugoslavia will start next year. Prosecution for the trials is Judge Goldstone of South Africa. First indictments will be handed down this November with the tribunal to be held in The Hague. The most serious accusations will be considered first, based on evidence. The judge refused to speculate if Radovan Karadzic or Slobodan Milosevic will be brought to trial, but said the court will not be swayed by the positions held by accused war criminals.

September 4, 1994: Shortwave radio "Voice of America in Ecuador":

Seventeen people are killed in fighting between clans in Somalia. UN forces are ready to leave if the clans cannot bring a peaceful solution to Somalia. (In Somalia, the UN forces were more heavily armed and ready to take action on any outbreak of hostilities, but in Bosnia, all things had to be directed from New York.)

September 4, 1994: Radio Netherlands:

Bosnian Serbs are fortifying positions around Sarajevo and are fighting in the *exclusion zone.* They have taken much territory.

Hosni Mubarak (President of Egypt) and Boutros Boutros Ghali will open the Population Conference (in Cairo) on Monday.

September 4, 1994: Swiss Radio International:
Unknown gunmen have shot an Israeli soldier and wounded two others in the Gaza Strip.

Lord David Owen and Stoltenberg met with Milosevic (Serbian president). Milosevic stressed that lifting the sanctions against Serbia would be the best signal for peace in Bosnia.

Arabs going to prayers in East Jerusalem were fired upon, but no one was injured.

Twenty thousand delegates will attend the Population Conference in Cairo.

Nelson Rabela of the Nigerian Oil Workers Union says the strike is not off. They seek the release of Chief Abiola and his installment as president (of Nigeria).

September 5, 1994: Radio Netherlands:
Prime Minister, Benazir Bhutto (Pakistan), spoke out against abortion as a population control measure.

The International Contact Group on Bosnia will meet in Berlin on Sanctions. The U.S. supports the lifting of the arms embargo. Russia is against the lifting of the arms embargo and wants sanctions on Serbia lifted. President Alija Izetbegovic denies the UN accusation that it was the Bosnian Army that mortar bombed the Sarajevo Airport last month.

Oil workers on strike in Nigeria are returning to work. The detention of Mashud Abiola was the main reason for the strike. Fuel supplies are beginning to meet the demand for fuel. At the beginning of the strike, oil prices went up in anticipation of a shortage, but the shortage never materialized. However, prices have not dropped.

September 5, 1994: Swiss Radio International:
The International Contact Group will meet in Berlin. The lifting of sanctions on Serbia will depend on their allowing international monitors on the border between Serbia and Bosnia.

Yashushi Akashi said war criminals in the Bosnian Conflict will face war crimes trials (A German language broadcast from Swiss Radio International said that their seemed to be a disagreement between Ilya Karadzic and her husband, Serb instigator, Radovan Karadzic).

September 6, 1994: The Wall Street Journal:
Two articles, "At the Balkans Crossroads, No Turn is Safe," and "Seeds of Revolt Muslims from Bosnia Find Refuge While Adrift in Europe," attempts to show that there will never be peace between Bosnians and Serbs. The first article deals with the Bosnian Serb mentality of martyrdom and never giving into outside intervention.

September 6, 1996: Die Deutsche Welle:
Tourism flights to Turkey are full because of attraction to ancient ruins, Turkish hand-made carpets, and beautiful beaches. But in the southeast of Turkey, the Kurdish situation is given as the reason for restricting tourism there.

September 7, 1994: *The Wall Street Journal:*
A technical school in Algerian has been set on fire over the weekend by Islamic militants opposed to talks between the leaders of the opposition and the military-backed

government of Algeria. The attack in Bilda, a south Algerian Muslim stronghold, comes after the government said the talks had been 'very positive'

The Indonesian Government (Indonesia has the largest Muslim population in the world) shut down the news weekly, *Tempo* and two other weeklies (*Editor* and *De Tik)* in June. Journalists from *Tempo* are applying for a publishing license for new magazine called, *Opinion.*

September 7, 1994: BBC:

Alain Juppe (French Foreign Minister) says Serbia will allow non-military observers on the Serbian border to *monitor* supplies sent to Bosnian Serbs. The *monitors* **would not be able** to make direct checks and look inside the trucks but to *observe.* If this proposal is accepted, the first easing of sanctions against Belgrade would the opening of Belgrade Airport to international flights.

The Red Cross condemned the Serbs for driving out 2,000 Muslims from their homes in Bhaj (sp?)

On order of Saddam Hussein, there has been a deliberate draining and burning of the vegetation of the marshlands (of eastern Iraq). It has become an ecological disaster affecting the livelihood of the Shia Muslims of the area. The CIA has made available its report to the UN based on satellite photos and UN flights over the area. This was done to prevent Saddam Hussein from making aerial attacks against the Shias. The UN condemns Saddam Hussein, which has in the past been without any effect.

September 7, 1994: Die Deutsche Welle:

The Pope will go ahead with his trip to Zagreb this Saturday.

German Foreign Minister, Klaus Kinkel, is optimistic that the Bosnian Serbs will eventually accept the peace plan.

It was Yashushi Akashi who said the UN could not guarantee the safety of the Pope and the 5,000 people who would attend the mass in the Olympic stadium (of Sarajevo)

September 7, 1994: Radio Netherlands:
Relations between Greece and Albania are at a low point.

Lord David Owen and Thorvald Stoltenberg are in Belgrade working out an agreement on international monitors (the monitors turned out to be worthless in doing any monitoring as they were hindered at every point. But sanctions were eased on Serbia and the UN Security Council said it would not re-impose them on Serbia).

Serbs are driving Muslims from their homes in the northern city of Dzalin (sp?)

The issue of international immigration and those in need is the first issue to be settled in the Cairo Conference (on Population).

Prime Minister Benazir Bhutto (Pakistan) at the Conference of Islamic Nations in Islamabad has said that Muslims are the victims of aggression everywhere but the West is still depicting Muslims as the aggressors. Haris Siladjic is in attendance at the conference and is representing Bosnia.

The Algerian Government and the five opposition groups are getting close to an agreement to end hostilities. Each realizes that none can win over the other. The Islamic Salvation Front is seeking to enter as a political party and is the most radical. The Islamic Armed Group (which has been killing foreigners) has just joined the talks.

September 8, 1994: Houston *Post:*
In Gaza, Palestinian police detained 24 people Wednesday, bringing to 45 the total the number arrested.

All were members of the Islamic Jihad, which is pledged to derail the accord on Palestinian Authority.

September 8, 1994: *The Wall Street Journal:*

(Bosnian) President Alija Izetbegovic lashed out at the UN for failure to retaliate against Serb attacks (continued bombardments). He criticized the UN Envoy, Yashushi Akashi (personally appointed by Boutros Boutros Ghali) wrote the Vatican about security risks to the proposed visit by the Pope to Sarajevo. A. UN spokesman said the letter didn't advise the Pope to cancel his visit. (Yashushi Akashi had made disparaging remarks about Muslims and his words show that there was no real intent by the U.N to defend Bosnian civilians from Serb atrocities. Boutros Boutros Ghali's letter to the Pope John Paul shows that the UN would not protect the Pope from any attempt on his life if he visited Bosnia.)

September 8, 1994: BBC:

A limited Israeli withdrawal from the Golan Heights has been proposed by Israel (but the springs below Golan Heights, that supplied Damascus for hundreds of years, would not be returned but left to supply water to Israel.)

Greece has retaliated further against Albania by slowing down the process of border crossings of Albanians going into Greece. More of the illegal Albanian immigrants have been expelled from Greece.

September 8, 1994: Die Deutsche Welle:

Energy deficient Armenia is about to start up its controversial nuclear electrical generating plant because oil and gas supplies from Azerbaijan have been cut off over its dispute with Azerbaijan over the Nagarah-Karabakh region (which is predominantly Armenian).

September 8, 1994: Swiss Radio International:

Thai and Philippine fundamentalists Muslim guerrillas are fighting for autonomy in their countries and are receiving support form Middle Eastern countries, not Malaysia or Indonesia. The two groups seem to be coordinated.

September 8, 1994: Radio Netherlands:

About 1,000 Croatian Serbs following Bosnian Serb tanks entered into the Bihac area (of northern Bosnia). In addition to attacking the Bosnian Army, heavy artillery rounds were fired at UN troops. NATO planes appeared overhead but flew away without responding to the attack on the UN troops (five hundred lightly armed troops from Bangladesh). The UN is *concerned* about the use of Croatian Serbs in Bosnia.

Syrian Farouk Al Shara spoke in The Hague yesterday and said the offer of Israel over the Golan Heights was no real development. Al Shara asked for a lifting of the arms embargo against Bosnia.

One of the ethnic Greek Albanians has American citizenship. The trial of the five ethnic Greek Albanians has been criticized as a political show and as a move to intimidate the rest of the Greek Albanian minority in Albania.

September 9, 1994: Houston *Post:*

Pope John Paul addressed the people of Sarajevo by radio and television. It was the same message he would have given in his planned visit. Shelling and sniper attacks have intensified in the weeks preceding the Pope's planned visit, which was called off as the Pope feared for the safety of all those who would turn out to see him.

September 9, 1994: BBC:

Greek Prime Minister, Andreas Papandreou, said there would be no talking with Albania so long as the five ethnic Greek Albanians are in jail (in Albania).

The Serbian Government is ready to accept 125 international monitors who will see that no fuel or arms will reach Bosnian Serbs.

September 9, 1994: Die Deutsche Welle:

German police arrest two Turkish citizens who were accused of attacking Turks in Germany.

September 9, 1994: *Eye on Asia,* a television program produced in India for viewing over Channel 31, Houston, Texas)

There was an attempt on the life of Hindu leader, Shabu Shoka, in Uttar Pradesh, by Hindu militants opposed to him.

Ghand Nief and his bodyguard were killed. Nief exposed corruption the Mehrasha State Government. He was also to defend Dowad Abraham against charges he was involved in the Bombay bombings.

Gangs of youths took to the streets throwing stones at trains and buses in their grief over the assassinations. On August 25, the commodity market and Bombay's stock markets were closed.

The former Foreign Minister of India, J.N. Dixt, says that Pakistan is not acting properly in its relationship with India. Pakistan is still continuing to smuggle arms into Kashmir Monaj Joshi says India should 'fight fire with fire."

Senator Larry Pressler (South Dakota) has become interested in the Indian-Pakistan problem over Kashmir.

Three Indian doctors were killed in Baldea, Somalia by an explosion as they were returning to their tent.

Foreign investment has topped two billion US$, surpassing the previous year's investment of US$550 million.

Sony of Japan will invest in television, hi-tech electronics and computers in India.

Prime Minister (of Israel) Yitzak Rabin said Prime Minister Benazir Bhutto (of Pakistan) should be taught some manners. Bhutto telephoned Rabin and patched things up.

In Sringar, Kashmir, 80,000 Muslims gathered to celebrate Prophet Mohammed's birthday. At Hashal Bal Mosque, a lock of the Prophet's hair was shown to the people assembled in the courtyard of the mosque.

All over India, Hindus celebrate Rashan Bahadour and symbols of love and devotion are exchanged between wives, husbands, fathers and mothers to children and between brothers and sisters.

Indian institutions are beginning to clamor for some censorship in the Indian film industry, as there are complaints there is too much sex and violence in films.

September 10, 1994: Die Deutsche Welle:

European Union member attending talks have approved the International Contact Group's easing of sanction on Serbia.

The shelling of Bihac by Croatian Serbs has stopped after NATO threatened to bomb their artillery and tanks

Pope John Paul II has called upon Croats, Muslims, and Serbs to cooperate in a multi-ethnic federation. The Pope has criticized the Serbs for causing the war.

Belgrade claims the Bosnian Army is receiving arms and fuel through the Krajina region near Bihac.

September 10, 1994: Radio Netherlands:

Great Britain sent a warning to Washington that a unilateral lifting of the arms embargo against Bosnia would cause difficulties between the two countries. Great Britain wouldn't object to a lifting of the arms embargo by the UN,

September 10, 1994: Swiss Radio International:
The Pope called upon Croats, Serbs, and Muslims to reconcile and forgive each other. The act of forgiveness is necessary for peace and he regretted that he did not go to Sarajevo as he had planned.

September 11, 1994: Houston *Post:*
Two West Bank Jewish settlers from Keryat Arba just outside Hebron have been detained on suspicion they shot in the head and seriously wounded a Palestinian.
Bangladesh riot police fired rubber bullets and swung their truncheons on a crowd of anti-government protesters demanding Prime Minister Khaled Zia resign and order general elections now instead of waiting for elections in two years time.
Croatia, which is seventy percent Roman Catholic, wants the Pope's visit to focus on the Serb conquest of 1/3 of its territory in the 1991 Civil War.

September 11, 1994: Die Deutsche Welle:
The Pope's visit to Belgrade was called off because there was no interest by the Serbs. Croatian President Tudjman said the Pope's visit to Zagreb gave hope for the future. The opposition to Tudjman did not like the Pope's visit, which they viewed as an endorsement of Tudjman because they do not like the Pope's support of a Bosnian-Croatian Federation.
Hans Koschnick had a rocket destroy his hotel room, but he was in the lobby at the time. Mr. Koschnick, (a Catholic)

former mayor of Bremen, is in Mostar to rebuild the old Muslim sector of the city destroyed by Croat shelling. Croat authorities apologized for the attack and said they will take remedial steps.

Turkish underground leader, Dusos Karatas (sp?) was captured at French-Italian border trying to enter France. He has been out of Turkey since 1990 and is on the list of the 'most wanted" in Turkey.

September 12, 1994: *Wall Street Journal:*

The European Union gave its strongest warning yet on lifting the arms embargo on Bosnian Muslim-led government.

A front-page article on the *Wall Street Journal* discusses the Refah Party (Welfare Party of Turkey) and the surge toward Islamic reform, especially in the more *decadent* areas of Turkish cities (there is a question about the appropriateness of using the word *decadent* as it should be the *poorer areas* of Turkish. Such use of image forming words is not only pejorative but also subjective).

In Kuala Lumpur, Malaysia, the police raided an Islamic Al Arqan settlement which has self-contained communication, businesses, and schools across Malaysia as the sect is banned in Malaysia because it conflicts with the mainstream view of Islam in Malaysia.

September 12, 1994: Die Deutsche Welle:

Hans Koschnick, the E.U. planner for rebuilding Mostar, has made his first appearance since his hotel room and offices were blown up by rockets fired by Croats.

Charles Redmon, former U.S. diplomat to Belgrade is being transferred to Germany as U.S. Ambassador there.

The new Palestinian national anthem will be played for the first time in Oslo at the combined meeting of the PLO and Israel.

Editorial from Die Deutsche Welle: The publishing industry in Serbia has suffered because of the economic sanctions (placed on Serbia) which affects the publication of books and newspapers. This has muted the opposition to the Serbian Government's programs of creating war in Croatia and Bosnia.

September 12, 1994: Radio Netherlands:

Several Muslims groups have complained to the French Ministry of Education's ban on the wearing of headscarves worn by girls in Islamic schools in France is discriminatory.

Dutch Minister of Defense, Vorhoover, says the Bosnian population would suffer if the arms embargo were lifted. He said the arms embargo would not be lifted soon. (Just how this would endanger Muslims more than the massacres of unarmed men and the bombardment of defenseless cities, does not seem very rational, which can be seen when massacres occurred in Srebrenica after the people gave up all their weapons and a Dutch soldier joined in the rape of a sixteen year old girl, who later committed suicide. Both warring parties rejected the UN proposal to have Dutch Troops reinforce the UN's Bangladeshi contingent. (See: November 10, 1994, Die Deutsche Welle broadcast).

September 12, 1994: Swiss Radio International:

The International Contact Group is sending an international force to ease sanctions against Serbia (in return) for their break with Bosnian Serbs (this was proven to be lip service as supplies still flowed and monitors were useless in checking the flights of helicopters into Bosnian Serb territory.)

September 13, 1994: BBC:

The internal fighting in Algeria has cost over 10,000 lives and peace with the five opposition groups and the military of Algeria has reached the stage of negotiations.

Germany will give Turkey 1.5 billion Deutsch Marks in military assistance including tanks and heavy weapons.

Bulgarian police have arrested six people and seized 20 containers of plutonium, strontium, and cesium in the cellar of an apartment house in Sofia. Origin of the nuclear material is unknown.

The five nation International Contact Group meeting in Germany has agreed to send 135 observers to be stationed along the Serbian/Bosnian Serb border.

September 13, 1994: Spanish Radio:

About 100 vehicles a day will pass through Brko carrying humanitarian aid to Bosnian Serbs.

September 13, 1994: Swiss Radio International:

Muslim forces are under heavy shelling in Konjezt (sp?). A village in the Bihac area is evacuated as Croatian Serb artillery is bombarding Bosnian Army troops there.

September 14, 1994: BBC:

The first contingent of inspectors has arrived in Belgrade to be deployed along the Serbian/Bosnian Serb border. They are to make sure that only humanitarian supplies are being sent to Bosnian Serbs. .

September 14, 1994: Die Deutsche Welle:

Heavy fighting along the eastern fringes of Mostar continues.

September 14, 1994: Radio Netherlands:

Heavy shelling of Bosnian troops in Bihac. Serb guns within the twenty-kilometer *exclusion zone* continue to shell Sarajevo (despite promises two weeks earlier to withdraw their heavy weapons).

September 14, 1994: Swiss Radio International:

Croatian and Bosnian authorities have promised to cooperate and repatriate refugees quickly.

The first contingent of twenty international observers has arrived in Belgrade.

The Secretary of the Arab League, Ismat Naguib, praised the Israeli acceptance of Palestinian autonomy for East Jerusalem.

The International Contact Group has decided that Serbia is serious. Lord David Owen negotiating for the International Contact Group said that most of the international observers will be in place this weekend.

Secretary of State Warren Christopher is skeptical of Serbia's split with the Bosnian Serbs, and wants the sanctions to be lifted, not cancelled. There is widespread belief outside the International Contact Group that Milosevic's split with Bosnian Serbs is merely an illusion.

A retired Swedish general is put in charge of the 135 international inspectors, all of whom will be coming from Scandinavian countries.

Cairo supports Palestinian autonomy of East Jerusalem.

September 15, 1994: BBC:

A radical Islamic group called "Battalions of Faith", has threatened the lives of the royal family of Saudi Arabia and foreigners in Saudi Arabia unless Sheik Salman Al Ruda (sp?) is released from detention. The group has ties with students and Islamic groups in Saudi Arabia but the Saudi

Government and family have taken western advice and will not deal with terrorists or threats.

Head of the international inspector's team in Serbia is retired Swedish General Uhl Palmas. They will monitor the flow of humanitarian aid to Bosnian Serbs by inspecting the trucks as they are loaded. He didn't say how they would inspect a truck that appears at the border if it were loaded without having an inspection.

September 15, 1994: Radio Netherlands:

Algerian FIS will not take part with talks between the Algerian Government and other guerrilla groups because the release from house of arrest of its leaders, Abasi Adani and Ali Bel Haq, is not enough.

U.S. diplomatic mission to Somalia is pulling out and the UN will probably leave soon as the operation costs three million dollars a day and there is no end to the conflict between the clans.

Hans van den Bruck of the UN troop deployment said that if the arms embargo against Bosnia were lifted the fighting would escalate.

General Sir Michael Rose and Dutch General de le Presle have been discussing what would result if the arms embargo were lifted.

UN sanctions against Iraq will be continued for another two months in spite of objections by Russia and Turkey. Turkey is complaining that no one is compensating Turkey for the loss of its trade with Iraq. Turkey opened a major road to Baghdad and will send humanitarian aid and receive diesel fuel at rock bottom prices. Turkey says the economic sanctions have not brought Iraq to its knees and it favors an autonomous Iraq with control of Iraq's Kurdistan.

September 15, 1994: Swiss Radio International: First members of the international inspectors will be deployed in Serbia today and if Serbia is truly cutting its military aid toe Bosnian Serbs, sanctions will be lifted.

September 16, 1994: Houston *Post:*
A newspaper article blames Muslim militants opposed to a political solution with the military-backed government of Algeria over the beheading of 16 Algerians in three different regions of Algeria.

September 17, 1994: *Eye on Asia (*produced in India for viewing in Houston, Texas, TV Channel 33).
Home Minister Chevan has instituted TADA (Terrorism and Detention Act) whereby a person can be detained up to 180 days without any evidence or charges. TADA was promulgated in 1985 against Sikh extremists in the Punjab (Indira Gandhi was killed by Sikh extremists and her son, Rajiv, was killed by Tamil extremists). TADA is now being used in the arrests of Abdul and Yusef Memon who are accused of complicity in the Bombay bombings and in the prolonged guerrilla warfare in Kashmir. Andar Pradesh has called for a renewal of TADA, which is subject to renewal every two years. Justice Ragamuth Mishra of NHRC (India's Human Rights Commission) has protested the use of TADA, which he says has injured the rights of innocents.

India's car industry is producing *Esteem* in conjunction with Japan's Suzuki. It will cost $15,000 and is the first Indian car to use safety glass and will be India's first car for export.

India's telephone company hopes to attract foreign capital for planned expansion to all of India's 600,000 villages by 1997.

The six-mile bridge from Bombay to Shurastra will reduce travel between the two cities by 125 miles.

The bodies of ten Indian soldiers killed in Somalia this last week was returned to India for military honors and cremation. Their deaths have renewed calls for the removal of the last of India's UN Contingent in Somalia.

Ladakh is being promoted as a tourist paradise with the government sponsoring a festival this last week. Over 100,000 tourists attended the festival.

Tens of thousands protested in the streets of Dhaka, Bangladesh, for a law that prohibits the slander or blasphemy of the Koran. It was prompted by a book written by Neshrin Taslima.

Nawaz Sharif insists he was right in divulging that Pakistan has the atomic bomb and says that Prime Minister Bhutto was wrong in hindering the development of nuclear weapons. He continues to ruffle feathers when he charges the armed forces intelligence was involved in selling heroin in 1991 to finance covert operations.

September 17, 1994: Die Deutsche Welle:

Focus magazine writes that Abu Nidal's "Arab" terrorist group plans to assassinate Jimna Bubbas, Jewish leader in Germany, according to an internal federal (German) report. There is concrete evidence that they planned to blow up a Jewish synagogue in Berlin's Orangeburgerstrasse. Federal prosecutor's office would make no comment. Baruch Niebar said the (German) government-tightened security around Jewish institutions. 701 anti-Semitic criminal acts were recorded last year, representing a hundred percent increase in crimes of this sort.

** Note: Abu Nidal is known for his *black flag* operations such as the one with the East German Stasi in blowing up a Berlin cabaret where several American soldiers were killed. Israel pointed its finger at Libya and the CIA blamed Libyan President Qadaffi and American President Reagan then responded by bombing Libya.

September 17, 1994: Radio Netherlands:
Seven hundred Muslims have been expelled from Banja Luka (between Bihac and Tuzla). In the past two weeks, 6,000 Muslims, mostly elderly, women, and children, have been expelled from the Bigelgina (sp?) region. Bosnian Serbs plan to expel another 5,000. The UN accused the Serbs of sabotaging water, gas, and electricity supplies to Sarajevo (Karadzic guaranteed on September 3 that these would turned back on).

A ceasefire arranged by the UN in Tadzhikistan has been signed in Tehran by the neo-Communist government and the Islamic opposition. The ceasefire will be placed in effect in one week's time after the arrival of international observers is in place before the November 5th elections are held.

September 17, 1994: Swiss Radio International:
Classical economic models were used in planning the development for the Central Asian Republics that depend mainly on livestock and livestock production. It shows their produce must have some kind of processing before it can be marketed. The report suggests that by using wind power to bring technology in widely scattered areas rather than central distribution or portable generators using diesel fuels which would adversely affect the cultural lifestyles of the people.

(Algerian) President Amin Zerual's release of FIS leaders from house detention has been welcomed, but the

FIS needs further concessions such as access to the leaders before it goes into talks with the government. In 1992, the FIS appeared to have taken power in Algeria when the military cancelled the elections. Both the FIS and the government want to advance carefully to avoid extremists in both groups. Hardliners in the security forces may try to crack down on the FIS or carry out terrorism against them. Meanwhile, the FIS appears to have moved away from demands for a purist Islamic state and still not be upstaged by the Armed Islamic Group, which ahs refused all demands for talks or ceasefire. The French Government has changed its position and is willing to acknowledge that the FIS might take part in sharing the power with the military government.

September 18, 1994: *Eye on Asia* (produced in India for American TV)

UN Secretary General, Boutros Boutros Ghali, was in New Delhi this past week discussing problems of Kashmir, Nepal, Bhutan, Somalia, and Pakistan. Boutros Ghali commended India for its cooperation the UN operation in Somalia.

Outside in the streets of New Delhi, demonstrators chanted for a free Tibet and a Sikh separatist's state.

In Islamabad, Prime Minister Bhutto of Pakistan decried the violence and killing of Muslims merely because they are Muslims. Prime Minister Haris Siladjic of Bosnia told the Conference of Islamic Nations that Bosnia's unarmed people have withstood the attack of one of the world's most powerful armies. Despite the arms embargo against Bosnia, which does not prevent the Serbs from receiving fuel, weapons, munitions, and supplies from Serbia, Bosnia still fights on. He called for an end to the arms embargo and a withdrawal of the UN forces. (Despite the vote by the 106 member nations of the UN to remove the arms embargo against Bosnia, the UN Security Council persists in denying Bosnia the right to defend itself. While The Security Council eases sanctions against Serbia and Bosnian Serbs it does nothing to stop the bombardment of defenseless Bosnian cities. American Muslims for the first time have entered into the political arena to demand Congress and the president to do something but Clinton continues to follow the leadership of John Majors, while Mitterrand vacillates, France's Iranian-born, Eduard Balladur's anti-Bosnian; will prevail as France's foreign policy.)

September 18, 1994: Die Deutsche Welle:
Two people were killed and eighteen wounded in the worst fighting around Sarajevo in months. Sir Michael Rose threatened both Bosnian Serbs and "Warring Muslims" with NATO air strikes. The UN called directly for the removal of heavy weapons within the exclusion zones.

September 18, 1994: Radio Netherlands:
The Bosnian Serb military promised they would pull out heavy weapons remaining in the exclusion zone around Sarajevo. Fighting flared up after Bosnian Forces fired on Serb troops.

September 18, 1994: Swiss Radio International:
The Moroccan Government claims that Algeria is trying to destabilize Morocco with the killing of two Spanish tourists by two Algerian gunmen holding up a hotel in Marrakech. Relations between the two countries are not good and can be traced back some twenty years to the Western Sahara. In 1976, Spain left this colonial country and Morocco invaded. Algeria gave support to the Polisario Liberation Front to liberate the Western Sahara (from Moroccan occupation.) This was scaled down in 1988,

when Algeria decided to let Morocco have the Western Sahara. This (action) allowed a big improvement between the two countries and resulted in border agreements and easier movement of citizens of both countries to travel back and forth.

The security service of Algeria denied it trained the gunmen in the Marrakech killings. The Moroccan Government views the possible influx of Islamic fundamentalist into the Government of Algeria with apprehension. Morocco does not want to see diplomatic relations deteriorate as this happened over Western Sahara with the result that Morocco was forced out of the Organization of African Unity.

Terrorism and provocation are being used against the majority of Albanian population in Serbia's Kosovo Province by the Serbian Government. Many human rights abuses are being reported.

September 18, 1994: Houston *Post:*

Egyptian police killed three suspected Muslim extremists in a raid on Qift in Qena Province, about 300 miles south of Cairo. The suspects were alleged to have taken part in an attack on a Coptic Church. This brought a total of 14 killed this last week in clashes between militants and the military.

One hundred people have been killed and hundreds more wounded in fighting in the Afghanistan capital of Kabul. The latest fighting involved two small groups representing Afghanistan's minority Shiite Muslims. No one knows what started the fighting.

A Nigerian plane with 38 on board, including the Nigerian soccer team, crashed in the desert of southern Algeria, killing four and injuring 24. The plane was en route from Tunis to Lagos and crashed upon landing at Tamanasset Airport.

September 19, 1994: *Wall Street Journal:*

The Tadzhikistan Government forces said they had surrounded rebel troops and taken a strategic region just hours after signing a UN mediated ceasefire in Tehran.

All twelve members of the European Union are discussing plans for a flood of refugees from Algeria if that country comes under Muslim extremist rule.

Afghan Government jets struck targets in southern Kabul where rival Shiite Muslims have been battling the past five days. At least 80 people were killed and five hundred 500.

Azerbaijan's national oil company and Western oil companies are preparing to sign a production sharing 30-year contract tomorrow in Baku. Russian control of the pipelines and a share of the Caspian Sea deposits remain to be worked out.

Muchtar Pakpahan, leader of Indonesia's Workers Union, goes on trial today. He is charged with inciting riots. The government recognizes only one official union and fails to recognize Pakpahan's union. If convicted, Pakpahan could be imprisoned for six years.

Israel and Arab nations ease tensions with multi-lateral talks on economic development, water, arms control, and refugees. Israeli officials appeared for the first time in Tunisia last October. Telephone lines now connect Qatar with Jerusalem, and for the first time an Israeli delegation set foot in Bahrain. Israel and Arab nations have decided to establish a communications network to provide information on military exercises to avoid misunderstandings that could possibly trigger a military response in other countries. .

September 19, 1994: Die Deutsche Welle:

Bosnian Serbs have renewed their siege of Sarajevo and the Muslim sectors and have cut the supply route to UN troops. The Serbs have already cut water, gas, and electricity to the Muslim sector of Sarajevo and (also) cut the supply route to UN troops. Karadzic said he would put more pressure on the Muslims in the city. The Bosnian Forces, which are mainly Muslim, for their part have agreed to stop bombarding Serb units holding Sarajevo under siege. General Sir Michael Rose accused Bosnians of ***provoking*** the heaviest fighting in several months with the intention of pressuring the UN and NATO into attacking the Serbs. (Huh?)

September 20, 1994: Radio Netherlands:
  The Bosnian Serbs were warned to remove their big guns from the 20 kilometer exclusion zone around Sarajevo by midnight. They have brought their weapons into the exclusion zone over the past two weeks into what has been a demilitarized zone since February of this year. Sources say they have been pulling out their guns. Meanwhile the International Contact Group has been holding talks with leaders of Croatia and Serbia.
  More Muslim refugees have been forced to sign over property and forcibly removed from northeast Bosnia. .

September 20, 1994: Swiss Radio International:
  Bosnian Serbs are expelling the remaining Muslims in their area. People are rounded up in trucks, forced to sign over property, cars, etc., and then are driven to Tuzla where they are robbed and some are beaten before crossing into Bosnian territory.

September 20, 1994: Houston *Post:*
  About 1,700 Muslims were forced out of their homes in the Bieljina region of Bosnia Sunday. This latest group, like previous groups forced out of their homes since mid-July,

they were forced to pay the Serbs for a transportation fee and then searched and robbed of their last money and any valuables they had left.

An initial check by the 135 international monitors along the Serbian/Bosnian Serb border indicated that military shipments had not crossed the border (however, helicopter flights from Serbia into Bosnian Serb territory were not monitored nor were roads from Montenegro into southern Bosnia monitored). This was according to Brigadier General de Palmas

A Danish UN Observer was killed in Croatia when his vehicle hit a land mine. About 15,000 UN forces have been stationed in Croatia since the Serb-Croat War ended with a ceasefire in January 1991.

September 20, 1994: *The Wall Street Journal:*

According to diplomats in Riyadh, Saudi Security Forces have arrested hundreds of people in a crackdown on militant Muslims agitating for stricter enforcement of Islamic laws in Saudi Arabia. Previous action has been limited to banning their clerics from preaching in public.

September 20, 1994: Die Deutsche Welle:

Boutros Boutros Ghali has asked for plans to remove UN troops if the arms embargo against Bosnia is lifted. It would take two months and might involve the need to call in the armed forces of another country to help in the withdrawal. The UN would no longer be able to protect civilians in cities of Srebrenica, Gorazde, and Jepre (sp?) nor would the UN be able to monitor the exclusion zone around Sarajevo (there was no protection of Muslims and no real 'exclusion zone'). His remarks preface what may become an extremely bitter fight in the UN. The news journalists speculated that this antagonism will gather momentum as the October 15 deadline nears. At that time, (U.S.) President Clinton said he would lift the arms embargo (he didn't and wouldn't lift the arms embargo on Bosnia).

September 20, 1994: Radio Netherlands:
 The Bosnian Serbs were warned to remove their big guns from within the 20 kilometer exclusion zone around Sarajevo by midnight. They have brought their weapons into the exclusion zone over the past two weeks into what has been a demilitarized area since February of this year. Other sources say that they have been pulling out their guns.
 Meanwhile, the International Contact Group is holding talks with Croat and Serb leaders (they exclude the Bosnian leaders which shows they know Bosnians are wanting peace. Croats have been pulled in two directions since the start of the war).
 More Muslim refugees have been forced to sign over their property and forcibly removed from northeastern Bosnia. .

September 20, 1994: Swiss Radio International:
 The envoys from the International Contact Group are in Belgrade to check the monitoring of aid into Bosnian Serb territory. The only way to force the Bosnian Serbs into accepting the peace plan is to isolate them further. The next step is to have Mr. Milosevic recognize Bosnia.
 Ethnic cleansing in Bieljina has drawn attention. As many as 2,800 Muslims were expelled this last weekend. The Serbs began expelling the remaining Muslims in mid-July People were rounded up in trucks and forced to sign over their property, cars, and trucks and then taken near Tuzla where some were beaten and robbed before being allowed to cross over into Bosnian territory. About 150 young Muslim men of draft age were separated from their

families and held back. The Serbs said they were doing this until Bosnians released Serbs held by Bosnians in the Tuzla area. The Serb government in Pale says there is no policy to expel Muslims. The Serbs claim that this is the work of extremists. There has been a campaign of terror unleashed against Muslims in Bieljina starting last year when mosques were blown up.

September 21, 1994: Die Deutsche Welle:
    Lt. General Sir Michael Rose denied he gave an ultimatum to the Serbs, but says they agreed to remove their heavy weapons from within the *exclusion zone* (see September 14, Radio Netherlands) by midnight Wednesday. UN troops will be monitoring this withdrawal over the next 24 hours to be sure the agreement has been adhered to. The Bosnian Serbs have constantly flaunted the exclusion zone since February when NATO forces them to pull their big guns out of range of Sarajevo.
    The International Contact Group emerged from four hours of negotiations with Milosevic in Belgrade and said the talks had been useful and encouraging. The International Contact Group stressed that Milosevic's aid is necessary if Bosnian Serbs are to be brought to their knees to accept the peace plan. Croatian (Serbs) are said to be supplying Bosnian Serbs.
    Bosnian Serbs pulled back 15 big guns from the exclusion zone around Sarajevo.
    The French Education Ministry has forbidden Muslim girls to wear the veil in French schools. The National Muslim Federation has said the directive was an attack on the freedom of religious expression. There are 160,000 Muslim school children in France. The expulsion of three Muslim schoolgirls in Paris started it all.

September 21, 1994: Radio Netherlands:

(UN Secretary General, B.B. Ghali is an Egyptian Coptic Christian who ancestors were reported to have served the British well in Egypt. His wife is a Hungarian Jewess) Boutros Boutros Ghali has told the UN Security Council that plans to implement the withdrawal of UN troops should take place under the protection of special combat units of NATO.

The International Contact Group has spoken with Milosevic about receiving the peace plan.

September 22, 1994: Swiss Radio International:

(UN Secretary General) Boutros Boutros Ghali recommended that all UN troops remain in Bosnia even if the arms embargo is lifted and NATO air strikes intensify (he contradicts himself continuously). UN troops should be pulled out only if the air strikes or lifting the arms embargo interferes with the U.N Humanitarian Aid efforts. Reducing the 38,000 UN troops in the area would cause the situation to deteriorate on all levels.

September 22, 1994: ECO (Spanish language Channel 33, Houston)
: Dr. Radovan Karadzic submitted more changes in the peace plan to the International Contact Group before the peace plan is *acceptable*

September 22, 1994: PBS-TV *The MacNeil-Lehrer Report:*

Bosnian Serbs fired (rifle) grenades at UN troops near Sarajevo. NATO planes responded by bombing a Serb tank and a heavy gun within the exclusion zone around Sarajevo (which means the Serbs had not removed their tanks and heavy guns from the exclusion zone by Wednesday as Sir Michael Rose said they would).

September 22, 1994: Die Deutsche Welle:

The UN will no longer tolerate attacks on peacekeeping forces (by Bosnian Serbs) in Bosnia and will react with appropriate measure (in the future). NATO planes bombed a Bosnian Serb tank in response to a rocket attack on a UN vehicle injuring five French soldiers. Bosnian Serbs denounced the raid (the tank was empty) and threatened to retaliate against the UN and NATO.

Kuwait and Iraq have agreed to join with the Red Cross in an effort to find 800 missing Kuwaitis after the Gulf War (1991). The repatriation of prisoners of war was by Iraq when it signed the Baghdad Accords at the end of the Gulf War.

September 22, 1994: Radio Netherlands:

UN Observers report hundreds of helicopter flights from Serbia into Bosnian Serb territory. (The) supposition is that these flights are re-supplying Bosnian Serbs. The International Contact Group says Serb sanctions against Bosnian Serbs are working. However, the border between Montenegro and Bosnian Serbs would need monitors linked arm in arm along the border for hundreds of miles to prevent the passing of fuel, munitions, and weapons to the Bosnian Serbs.

UN observers have reported hundred of helicopter flights going back and forth between Serbia and Bosnian Serb territory. This is all happening in the ***no fly zone*** but NATO has ruled that this applies only fixed wing aircraft as helicopter flights are to be used for humanitarian needs as well as flying UN personnel.

Supposition is that these flights are supplying Bosnian Serb forces in Bosnia. This would make nonsense of Milosevic's claim he is boycotting the Bosnian Serbs and negate any lifting of sanctions against Serbia. NATO has

AWACS (radar surveillance planes to track aircraft in the sky day and night. It claims it has not seen these flights in the quantities the UN monitors have. This is embarrassing to those who are working to lift the sanctions against Serbia.

The reason behind this urgency to lift the sanctions is that the Russians want to visibly reward Milosevic to defuse the critics in Russia who say that Yeltsin is betraying the Bosnian Serbs. The UN is expected to raise more sanctions such as banning all traffic on the border rivers which are used for smuggling and freezing the foreign assets of Serb leaders and raising the ban against Serb leaders from traveling abroad. These sanctions are the result of the Bosnian Serbs cutting off Sarajevo's water, gas, and electricity for a week.

The reason for lifting the sanctions on Serbia is also to help keep the Russian on board the peace process. With international conditions differing in every European nation this fall and with elections near nobody seems to care what happens to Bosnia.

September 22, 1994: Swiss Radio International:

Islamic nations and Bosnia want the UN Security Council to delay the vote on lifting the sanctions against Serbia for one week so the issue can be debated by the Foreign Ministers next week. The UN resolution would reward Milosevic for cutting ties to Bosnian Serbs and allowing international observers to monitor Serbia's borders with Bosnia.

Secretary of State, Warren Christopher, has warned Bosnian Serbs that if they continue to violate the exclusion zones and attack UN Peacekeepers that appropriate measure will be taken.

September 23, 1994: Die Deutsche Welle:

(U.S.'s) UN Ambassador, Madeleine, Albright, said the sanctions will be re-imposed if the prohibition for Serbs to stop supplying Bosnian Serbs is not adhered to.

The nations of the Middle East are working with Israel to establish a region free of nuclear weapons (Israel denies it has a nuclear weapons industry near Beersheba in the Negev).

The UN Security Council has reportedly voted on ending the sanctions against Serbia if the ban on war materials is truly in effect. The Council also approved tightening the sanctions against the Bosnian Serbs. The first easing of sanctions will be 100 days of lifting the ban on commuter flights to Belgrade as well as participation in cultural and sporting events. This is considered to be a reward to Milosevic.

September 23, 1994: Radio Netherlands:

Retaliation attacks on UN personnel by Bosnian Serbs have increased since the NATO attack on (an empty) Bosnian Serb tank. NATO Headquarters in Brussels called the air strikes against Bosnian Serb positions around Sarajevo too little and too late. Ganic said good but not good enough. The NATO attacks did not deter Serb attacks on UN personnel.

(Russian) Foreign Minister Kozyrev criticized the Bosnian Serbs for over-reacting and said that Bosnian Serbs cannot count on unconditional Russian support. Kozyrev will meet with the International Contact in the UN in New York, next week. And seek an explanation from Secretary of State, Warren Christopher, as to why the United States will unilaterally lift the arms embargo against Bosnia.

September 23, 1994: Swiss Radio International:

The UN has been demanding access to areas where ethnic cleansing has been taking place in Bosnian Serb territory. The easing of sanctions against Serbia will go into effect the day the international monitors confirm that Serbia is not longer supplying the Bosnian Serbs.

Croatia has demanded the UN in the next few months oversee the return of Croatian territory occupied by ethnic Serbs or withdraw their peacekeeping forces from Croatian territory by the 10th of January. Serbs occupy about a third of Croatia. The Croatian parliament has voted for an end to the UN troops in Croatia.

Fighting has broken out in Sarajevo in the northern part of the city in an attempt to break the siege. This caused Bosnian Serbs to respond by using artillery, which is within the 20 kilometer UN exclusion zone. Sir Michael Rose says the Bosnians **are provoking** the Bosnian Serbs (See Sir Michael's comment November 20 by Die Deutsche Welle.

The Swiss newscaster editorialized that the U.S. is keen on lifting the arms embargo, which is effective only against Bosnia and interested mainly in easing the sanctions on Serbia. Bosnian Serbs are getting more nervous as opposition mounts against them. The Croatians and Muslims are getting ready for an upsurge in the fighting. Newscaster said it was impossible to bring all the warring parties to the peace table.

September 24, 1994: *Eye on Asia (*India for American television*:*

For the first time since their war in 1962, China's Defense Minister visited India to ease the tension between the two countries. Under discussion would be the drawing of a border between the two countries and troop reductions on both sides of the border.

(Pakistan's) Prime Minister Bhutto at the conference of Islamic Nations in Islamabad called upon the international community to bring peace to Bosnia, which is being destroyed every day.

AIDS is spreading in India with an estimated one million carrying the virus (this is an estimate by the Indian Government, but Radio Netherlands reported two million were estimated to carry the virus.)

September 24, 1994: Die Deutsche Welle:
UN Troops have been put on battle alert as a result of threats of retaliation by Bosnian Serb

German security authorities (BND) have evidence that Russian weaponry withdrawn from eastern Europe (when the Russians withdrew from East Germany and Eastern Europe) are in Serbia*
*NOTE: The information given out by Die Deutsche Welle and Radio Netherlands was correct. However, the German Government sought to hide this information. When the information was carried by *Der Spiegel* magazine, the German Government demanded a retraction of this news. However, journalists in Slovakia and Hungary witnessed the Russian convoys shipping the weapons through Slovakia and Hungary to Serbia. This is the same Russia that shipped its anti-aircraft missiles to Serbia and Bosnian Serb territory in 1996 that shot down a NATO plane, piloted by Captain Scott O'Grady.

September 24, 1994: Radio Netherlands:
(Serbian) General Ratko Mladic threatened to take revenge against UN personnel in Bosnia if the UN does not apologize for recent NATO air strikes against his position two days ago. The UN has not responded to the Bosnian

Serbs but said that the strikes were fitting response to Bosnian Serb actions.

On Saturday, Bosnian Serbs paralyzed UN operations around Sarajevo and as a result, the airport had to be shut down.

September 24, 1994: Swiss Radio International (Friday):

UN Peacekeepers are on the alert since (NATO) air strikes on Bosnian Serb positions and threat by Serbs to retaliate. Serbs have been hindering UN monitoring of the exclusion zone for heavy weapons.

On Friday, the UN Security Council voted on easing the sanctions against Serbia as a reward for Milosevic's cooperation in isolating the Bosnian Serbs. But nationalists in Serbia called this a betrayal of the Bosnian Serbs. Countries opposing the easing of sanctions on Serbia do not believe the Serbs have given up on supplying the Bosnian Serbs. It is very difficult to ascertain if there is a complete halt to the military supplies to Bosnian Serbs from Serbia because of the long border with forests and the insufficient number of monitors. There have been reports of numerous helicopter flights from Serbia into Bosnian Serb territory and those flights have not been monitored.

The easing of sanctions represents the ability of Milosevic to sell himself as the peacemaker after sharing a good deal of the responsibility for the crisis and the surge of nationalism in Serbia. It is amazing how Milosevic is able to keep this appearance and win these concessions after his involvement in creating this crisis.

Croatia has demanded that the U.N return the third of Croatia that is occupied by Croatian Serbs.

September 25, 1994: (Sunday) NBC-TV, *Meet the Press*:

(U.S.) Secretary of Defense, William Perry, said if the Bosnian Serbs do not accept the peace plan by October 15, President Clinton will go the UN and ask for a multi-lateral lifting of the arms embargo. If he fails to get a (UN) multilateral lifting of the arms embargo, he will ask Congress for a unilateral lifting of the arms embargo.

September 27, 1994: *The Wall Street Journal:*

Bosnian Serbs entered a UN weapons compound and staged a 'training exercise'.

Serbs denied permission for U.N helicopter flights and relief convoys to pass into Bosnian cities. Serbs also threatened to shoot UN planes landing at Sarajevo Airport.

President Izetbegovic of Bosnia asked the UN Security Council to lift the arms embargo at a fixed future date rather than immediately.

October 5, 1994: *The Wall Street Journal:*

The UN is set to ease sanctions against Rump Yugoslavia following a report from a UN general who says that arms to Bosnian Serbs has ceased. Aeroflot (Russian airlines) will begin flights to Belgrade today (as a result of an easing of the sanctions). Sarajevo Airport by contrast, remains closed under threats of attacks by Bosnian Serbs.

October 7, 1994: Radio Netherlands:

Twenty Bosnian Serb soldiers were killed in an attack on a Serb post (artillery spotting outpost) on Mt. Igman, including a female nurse. **Another six were wounded but survived.** The UN warned Bosnian forces that they would have to clear the demilitarized zone. French UN troops fired four warning shots and more than 200 Bosnian soldiers fled the bunkers.

French destroyed the bunkers where more than 550 Bosnian troops were living. The UN went on to say that more than 1,000 Bosnian troops remained in the demilitarized zone but the UN would give the Bosnian Government time to live up to its word and evacuate the demilitarized zone. The angry Bosnian Serbs demanded an immediate and impartial action by the UN or they would turn Sarajevo into a 'total war zone'.

Karadzic demanded the international community punish the Bosnians for the attack on the Serb outpost. Unless sanctions are made against Bosnia, the Bosnian Serbs said they will make reprisals. (Bosnian President) Izetbegovic has protested the expulsion of the Bosnians and has denied his troops were responsible for the raid.

October 8, 1994: Houston *Post (*Associated Press):

UN officials said that (Bosnian) government troops killed 18 Bosnian Serbs and four were nurses The UN officials went on to say that some of the victims were mutilated, others burned, and some had their throats slit. All twenty had been shot in the head (*Note that Radio Netherlands reported that six Serb soldiers were wounded and left alive. The UN officials didn't mention there were six Serb survivors who were not killed but supposedly watched Muslims mutilate the bodies of Serbs that were killed*). The Bosnian Muslim Government admitted some Serb soldiers died in the attack but denied any Bosnian soldiers mutilated the bodies of Serbs.

Bosnian Serb leader, Radovan Karadzic, threatened to kick UN Peacekeepers out of the 70 percent of Bosnia controlled by Serbs.

A UN plane landed Thursday afternoon at Sarajevo's Airport ending a two-week shutdown imposed by the Serbs who threatened to shoot all planes in retaliation for a NATO assault on one of their tanks.

A Bosnian source said on Thursday that the Bosnian Government Forces launched a further offensive south of Sarajevo toward the Serbian held town of Trnovo.

Note: All television stations in Houston failed to mention that six wounded Bosnian Serb soldiers were left alive and the Bosnian Serb bunker was in the 'demilitarized zone'. The U.N took the side of the Bosnian Serbs and condemned Bosnians for 'mutilating the bodies of the dead'. The UN described the Serb bunker as a 'post' but which was really an observation post for directing artillery fire on Sarajevo.

October 8, 1994: Radio Netherlands:

Since the Bosnian Army killed 18 soldiers and four nurses (first reports said 20 soldiers and one nurse) in an attack on a Serb post, in which the bodies were mutilated. Yashushi Akashi fears that this will set back the re-opening of Sarajevo's Airport.

October 9, 1994: Die Deutsche Welle:

The Bosnian Government has asked that UN soldiers escort city trams in Sarajevo after Saturday's slaying of one passenger and the wounding of eleven passengers by suspected Bosnian Serb snipers. Seven of the wounded were children. Barec Kupercovic said this raises the number of passengers killed to fifteen since service was resume March. There is widespread belief that this attack was in retaliation for the Thursday attack on the Serbian outpost last Thursday.

October 9, 1994: Swiss Radio International:

Gunfire interrupted the opening of Sarajevo Airport as it was fired upon again last Friday. Sarajevo's Airport had been closed for two weeks following threats by Bosnian

Serbs. The airport is now the only way that the city can supply its 389,000 residents.

October 10, 1994: Die Deutsche Welle:

The UN, Bosnians, and Bosnian Serbs are to form a special commission to carry out joint inspection of the demilitarized zone to avoid future attacks such as occurred last Thursday. The French soldiers of the UN forces used artillery guns to destroy the bunkers built by the Bosnians Government troops. Jacques Chirac said there were 1,000 battle-ready Muslim soldiers in these bunkers.

Bosnian Serbs held up 2/3's of the winter supplies destined for Bosnia's civilians despite an earlier agreement to allow the food for Sarajevo and Goradze and fuel for the UN troops to pass. On Sunday, 250 tons were delivered through Sarajevo's Airport.

Bosnian Serbs are threatening to expel UN Peacekeeping forces from their territory in retaliation for Thursday's attack by Bosnians on a Serb command post on Mt. Igman.

Transit services have resumed through "Sniper Alley' after a sniper attack on three trams killed one person and wounded eleven others. Two French soldiers now board every tram for the one kilometer segment of the route (sniper alley) and an armored personnel carrier positions itself between streets and the Bosnian Serb snipers.

Streetcars are the only mode of transportation as Bosnian Serbs are holding up supplies of diesel and gasoline. People in Sarajevo say that it was either risk the sniper fire or walk and they preferred to ride.

The UN doubled its flights into Sarajevo to deliver food and some food trucks were allowed to pass. But 30 tons of winterized plastic materials to cover windows that were shot and homes hit by artillery and rocket fire (along with) candles, shoes, and winter clothing were held back. Mt.

Igman and the mountains around Sarajevo are snow-capped and freezing temperatures emphasize the need for these materials. But Bosnian Serbs continue to block convoys.

West Germany's Foreign Minister, Klaus Kinkel, turned over 50 trucks worth 6 ½ million dollars to UN Envoy Yashushi Akashi in the East German town of Gorta. These trucks are to be used to supply the cities of Sarajevo and Tuzla.

A human rights group, called *The Society for Threatened People,* has passed on information they have collected on 150 War Criminals from the former Yugoslavia who are hiding in Germany.

Earlier this year, the police in Munich arrested Bosnian Serb Duskov Pavic, suspected of atrocities at camps in Bosnia (run by Bosnian Serbs and Serbs from Serbia). The human rights group had collected the information but didn't pass the information on as they had the impression that nothing would be done). As the German Foreign Ministry is pushing human as human rights Bosnians are beginning to have confidence that the PKA (German Federal Police) and (local) police are doing something. Helmut Zuck (giving out the news on radio) speculated that since Pavic's arrest as a War Criminal others may have changed addresses, their names, or gone back to Bosnia or Serbia.

October 11, 1994: Radio Netherlands:

Radovan Karadzic threatened to expel UN forces from his territory. Such a move would halt relief supplies to the besieged Muslim communities and spell disaster (it was already a disaster0,

Bosnian Serbs are accusing the UN of preferential treatment of Bosnia's Muslims. (On one occasion, Serbs stripped a UN soldier of his clothing and tied him naked to a tree in freezing weather. It took several hours for the soldier to die).

Judge Goldstone of the International War Crimes Tribunal of The Hague says **national courts will have to try their war criminals because the UN has not allotted enough money for the War Crimes Tribunal to do its work.** The judge just returned from a trip to Bosnia, Croatia, and Serbia to find out to what extent these countries are willing to cooperate. Croatia and Bosnia are willing to cooperate, but Serbia's president Milosevic says Serbia will not cooperate as they consider the tribunal *ad hoc* (a special) commission because it doesn't consider war crimes the world over. By focusing only on the former Yugoslavia, Belgrade argues that the tribunal is guilty of discrimination. Belgrade will not even allow the tribunal to open an office in Serbia.

Judge Goldstone says there is a great deal of information collected by fifteen investigators but needs fifty investigators which is why he will ask the UN to make more money available.

October 12, 1994: Die Deutsche Welle:

A spokesman for NATO says the UN Secretary General, Boutros Boutros Ghali, has been critical of NATO's request for air strikes on Serb Positions without prior warning and he has asked for clarification. (He was given the power to veto NATO air strikes against the Serbs). It was reported that the United Nations has opposed giving such sweeping powers to the NATO commanders.

Hans Koschnick, in charge of the reconstruction of Mostar by the E.U., has criticized the European Unity for failing to keep its promises. Of the 200 security people to be sent by the E.U., less than 100 have arrived to back up reconstruction and return law and order to Mostar.

October 12, 1994: Radio Netherlands:

Flights into Sarajevo were suspended again after two mortar shells hit Sarajevo Airport. According to UN sources, these shells were fired by *Muslim Forces*.

October 12, 1994: Die Deutsche Welle:

A UN spokesman said that Muslims Forces *marched* into the *demilitarized Zone* and from there they launched an attack on Bosnian Serb Forces.

UN Officials have continued talks with Bosnian Serbs to guarantee the safe passage of food coming for the civilian population.

Muslims in their part of Mostar declared that war has broken out after attacks by Bosnian Serbs, a claim supported by UN spokesmen.

October 12, 1994: Radio Netherlands:

Russia is dismayed by the UN Security Council refusing to condemn an attack by Bosnian Forces which left 20 Serbs dead last week. Russia alleges that the Security Council finds it much easier to issue condemnation when it comes to similar attacks by Bosnian Serbs.

Bosnian Serb Forces are said to have gained considerable ground after heavy fighting around Sarajevo. Bosnian Serbs are said to be consolidating their hold on the major access roads to the capital.

Broadcasts from the 14th to the 28th of October were taped but apparently went missing. This time period was most important as the Clinton Administration was offering to unilaterally lift the arms embargo against Bosnia by October 15th.

October 29, 1994, *The New York Times:*

A week after the Bosnian Government troops had their biggest victory of the war in the Bihac area, Bosnian Serbs, Croatian Serbs, and Serbian Army units in Bosnia mounted a fierce counter-attack.

October 31, 1994: Radio Netherlands:

Bosnian Serbs launched a counter attack against (Bosnian) government forces near the northwestern city of Bosansky Petrovak. This follows threats by Serb leader, Radovan Karadzic, that he would inflict enormous losses on Muslim forces to recapture recent losses.

The (Bosnian) government army has made huge territorial gains in the past few days, not only in the northwestern area of Bihac but also south of the capital of Sarajevo where they took several Serb positions near the city of Trnovo.

On Sunday, Mr. Karadzic declared a state of war in large parts of Bosnia. In response to the recent upsurge of fighting in Bosnia, the United States Government has declared that the offensive by the (Bosnian) government is legitimate. A State Department spokesman in Washington said that the Muslims are the victims of Serb aggression and have understandably taken the right to defend themselves.

November 1, 1994: Houston *Post*:

(Article headline was, "Serbs Suffer Casualties"). Bosnian Army forces have given the Bosnian Serbs their worst defeat in two and a half years of war. They pushed ahead Monday with attacks on the supply route of Sarajevo and Serb held towns in the northwest Bosnia. Serbs claim to have blunted the offensive and promised hard fighting to regain lost territory. Serbs said the attack near Trnovo was backed by an estimated 8,000 troops traveling to the front from besieged Sarajevo through a tunnel under the airport.

November 2, 1994: Radio Netherlands:
The Bosnian Army offensive against the Bosnian Serbs is drawing fire from the Russians. Speaking from New York, Ambassador Sergei Lanoff warned of grave consequences if the (UN Security) Council continues to do nothing (to stop the Bosnian offensive). He was referring to the thousands of new refugees and the precarious position of UN Troops in Bosnia. Russia's criticism was aimed at the (UN) Security Council because the current Bosnian Muslim offensive was launched from a security zone under UN protection. March 17 the Croats and Muslims signed a ceasefire agreement and formed a new federation. But until now, the Croats had not joined in fighting the Bosnian Serbs. The Muslim led Bosnian Army made significant gains against the Serbs over the past two weeks, but the offensive is slowing down in face of the Serb's superiority in heavy weapons.

November 2, 1992: Radio France (Spanish language):
Russia is in Poland to sign an agreement for a new gas pipeline to Western Europe from Siberia that would avoid crossing Ukrainian territory. This avoids crossing the Ukraine which now has a monopoly over all such line from Russia to the rest of Europe. The Moscow's newspaper, *Syvodnya,* expressed surprise at this agreement with Poland considering Moscow's displeasure at Poland's attempt to join NATO, differences over Bosnia, and Poland's inability to control its (Poland's) Mafia and corruption in its military.

November 3, 1994: Houston's *Post:*

Bosnian Serb lines near Kupres are in disarray and thousands of Serb civilians have fled. Fleeing Serb soldiers have left behind their dead and significant supplies of munitions, weapons, and other equipment. The Associated Press reports that Croatians have imposed a news blackout over the Kupres fighting. A Croatian soldier was quoted as saying at a checkpoint near Tomasilovgrad that the "Croats are advancing from the south and Muslims from the west. Hell could break loose when they meet in Kupres."

November 3, 1994: Houston, Texas's Spanish TV channel 33:
Croatians are crossing over the border to join the fight against the Bosnian 5th Army. In the International Contact Group, Russia and the U.K. have lined up against Germany and the U.S. while France is remaining neutral.

November 4, 1994: *The Wall Street Journal:*
Bosnian Croats seized control of the central town of Kupres after a combined Croat-Muslim assault forced the Serbs to retreat. Bosnian Serb leader Karadzic said he would meet today to declare a state of war.

November 9, 1994: *The Wall Street Journal:*
E.U. turned down a request by former East European communist states because of their inability to control their Mafias. This is a political issue in these former Communist states where sophisticated weapons have fallen into the hands of criminal elements led by corrupt military officers working with these criminal elements. The article discusses the murder of Russian journalist, Dimitri Kholodov, who was exposing the corruption in the Russian military that was training Russian Mafia hit men (assassins).

November 9, 1994: Radio Netherlands:

Croatian Serb jet fighters struck at the city of Bihac (a UN protected safe haven). Ten civilians were killed and an industrial installation was badly damaged. The air strikes were carried out from the Krajina region where Croatian Serbs have declared an autonomous republic. Bihac also came under Serb artillery fire.

The self-styled Serb parliament in Pale has not yet taken a position of introducing martial law. It speaks of handing over all authority in the Bosnian Serb territory to the military (Mladic) and Radovan Karadzic. The debate is to continue Thursday.

November 9, 1994: Die Deutsche Welle (in German):

South and southeast of Bihac, Bosnian Serbs have taken back two small towns from Bosnian Government Troops. In Pale, Bosnian Serbs are fed up with *Volkersgruppe and* Karadzic's demand for a proclamation of martial law. A decision for that is soon to come.

The Russian, British, and French on the UN Security Council are against lifting the arm embargo on defensive weapons as this would result in an escalation of the war (their support of Serbia goes back to the *1914 Secret Treaty of London)*

November 9, 1994: Swiss Radio International:

UN officials confirmed the attack on Bihac but had no information on casualties. There has been some territory recovered by Bosnian Serbs in northwest Bosnia.

Note: Former British Prime Minister, Margaret Thatcher decried the hypocrisy of the UN and its lack of abiding by the charter of the United Nations, while British Prime Minister John Majors said that if he allowed the arms embargo to be lifted on Bosnia, it would mean that his government would fall.

When British Prime Minister Majors flew to Moscow to meet with Russian President, Boris Yeltsin, BBC announced that the most hated man in Britain (John Majors) was meeting with the most hated man in Russia (Boris Yeltsin).

Russian President Boris Yeltsin strongly supported the Serb aggression in Bosnia and Croatia to avoid being criticized for betraying Russian *brother Slavs, the Serbs*. Serbs mounted a huge propaganda campaign to say that Bosnian Muslims were planning on creating an Islamic Republic in Europe.

November 10. 1994: Die Deutsche Welle:

Croatia has threatened to intervene in Bihac if the Croatian Serbs do not disengage immediately their attacks on Bihac. UN spokesmen gauge these developments as the most dangerous in recent months to Bosnia-Herzegovina. Special UN Envoy, Yashushi Akaski has condemned the attack on the UN protected zone and the Serbs have been told to end their blockade of relief convoys to Bihac.

Note: There was a designated spot on the Serbian front line where Serbs would allow people of Bihac to buy food at four times the usual price. A loaf of Italian bread was cut into four pieces and then into seven pieces which was to be the rations for four for a week.

November 10, 1994: Radio Netherlands:

UN Officials have warned that the renewed violence has made it impossible for the UN Troops to do their work. Increasingly, the UN has been delayed or prevented from doing their work by the warring parties' counter-measures. UN says the actions over the past few days represent the worst actions for peace in many months.

In northwestern Bosnia, the massive offensive by the Bosnian Serbs against the Muslim enclave is continuing. For the second day running, the support from the Croatian Serbs operating in the breakaway province of the Krajina have continued shelling Muslim positions in the Muslim enclave. The Government of Croatia has warned the Croatian Serbs they will intervene if the Serbs continue their actions in Bosnia.

The warring parties in Bosnia have announced they will not allow UN Dutch Troops in the Muslim enclave of Bihac. The Blue Helmets were to act as scouts preparing the way for the Dutch contingent, which was to reinforce a Bangladeshi UN unit later this month.

Note: The UN Bangladeshi troops were armed only with rifles and stood shoulder to shoulder, without weapon. They told the Serbs that they would have to kill all of them before they could pass further. The Serbs were within blocks of a hospital where they intended to enter and commit atrocities. They turned around and went back.

When asked why the Bangladeshis were not better armed, the UN spokesperson said each country contributing troops to the U.N peacekeeping were responsible for arming to its contingent in Bosnia.

November 10, 1994: Voice of America:

The Serb shelling attacks on Bihac intensified Thursday afternoon. The radio reports of continued Serb infantry assaults and that helicopter flights from neighboring Krajina were supporting Bosnian Serbs. The UN has not confirmed this report but has confirmed that two rockets were fired from a Croatian Serb plane into Bihac and that Croatian Serbs have stepped up their cross-border artillery attacks on Muslim positions in Northwestern Bosnia. If this activity continues, Croatian Defense Minister, Goyco Dusak, warned the Croatian Serbs that the Croatian Army may strike at Serbs in his country.

November 12, 1994: Radio Netherlands:

The UN Security Council will convene Sunday in an emergency session on the Bosnian enclave of Bihac. The meeting was called by Bosnia and Croatia who want a halt to the continuing Serb assaults on the Bihac enclave. Bosnian Serbs with the support of Croatian Serbs in the breakaway province of Krajina are attempting to regain some of the territory they recently had to cede to the Bosnian Government.

The German weekly, *Der Spiegel,* reports that the Serbs are being supplied with **Russian** arms **in direct breach of the arms embargo.**

France, meanwhile has hinted a complete withdrawal of its 7,000 troops from Bosnia, Foreign Minister Alain Juppe has said that the situation could become too dangerous for them on account of the American decision to unilaterally stop enforcing the arms embargo against the Muslims.

November 12, 1994:

The UN Security Council has responded to an appeal by Bosnia and Croatia and will hold an emergency later today to consider the renewed fighting in Northern Bosnia. The meeting will focus on the implications of the counter-offensive by Bosnian Serbs. President, Alija Izetbegovic, said the Bihac enclave is under bombardment by Bosnian Serbs and rebel Serbs in the nearby Krajina, which is part of Croatia. Croatia has turned down a request by Bosnia for military help.

Croats said it was up to the UN Forces to act. Bosnian Serbs say they have retaken three-quarters of the territory lost to Bosnian Government Troops last month. The French Foreign Minister (Alain Juppe) was critical of the withdrawal of American support for the arms embargo and said that if there were any further weakening of the arms embargo, the security of the 5,000 French troops would be compromised. (It was the arms that Iran sent to both Croatia and Bosnia that eventually led to an end to the war in Bosnia)

Three American ships and a number of planes will shortly be withdrawn from the NATO enforcement operation. (A Houston Texas TV station said that of thousands of ships stopped in the Atlantic Ocean only two had arms bound for Bosnia while most of Bosnian Serb supplies were flown in from East European nations in Russian made Tupolovs. The TV then showed videos of planes landing).

November 13, 1994: BBC: As the fighting intensifies in Bosnia, the UN Security Council has called upon UN Secretary General Boutros Boutros Ghali to put forth measures to stabilize the situation.

The BBC correspondent says there are fears of widening the conflict with the Croatian Government Forces renewing hostilities against Croatian Serbs. European Foreign Ministers and Defense Ministers met later today in the Netherlands to consider how to react to the United States withdrawing from cooperation to enforce the arms embargo against the Muslim led Bosnian Government.

November 13, 1994: Radio Netherlands:

There is a demand on the Serbs in Croatia to remain neutral in the conflict in and around the Muslim enclave of Bihac in neighboring Bosnia. The UN Security Council was meeting at the urgent request of Bosnia and Croatia.

In the town of Bihac itself, a designated (UN) *safe area,* the (UN) Security Council has condemned the increased hostilities around Bihac and asked the UN Secretary General Boutros Boutros Ghali, to put forth a proposal to stabilize the situation.

November 14, 1994: CNN (Christine Amanpour, reporting):

Bosnians say that the Croatian Serb units are fighting in the Bihac area raises concern that the Bosnian Serbs are widening the war (See September 18, 1994, where Radio Netherlands reported 1,000 Croatian Serb Troops crossed into Bosnia, behind Bosnian Serb tanks and on November 3rd, ECO, Spanish TV in Spanish, reported activity by Croatian Serb troops in the Bihac activity as well as launching air strikes on Bosnian territory.

The Russians delivered 80 howitzers to Bosnian Serbs as late as this past September. The Russians deny this allegation.

CNN showed pictures of Bosnian Government troops in high spirits with captured Serb weapons, trucks, and supplies. One Bosnian Government Army unit captured five Serb tanks that were rebuilt and put back into the war to fight the Serbs.

Captured Bosnian Serb documents show that morale is low among the Bosnian Serb soldiers and there are many defections.

November 17, 1994: *The Wall Street Journal:*

Bosnian Serbs received help from Abdic's renegade rebel Muslims in northern Bosnia around the enclave of Bihac. The Croatian Government has reached an accord with Croatian Serbs on economic cooperation. International mediators called it a step in achieving an eventual settlement for Croatia.

November 20, 1994: Die Deutsche Welle:

The UN is attempting to protect the Bosnian enclave of Bihac from further attacks. Mr. Claes (NATO commander) said he asked for patience in the slow response of NATO to the Croatian Serb artillery and air raids on Bihac. He spoke after UN Envoy, Yashushi Akashi and UN Commander, Bertrand de la Presle, condemned the Croatian Serbs for intervening in the fighting against Bosnian Government Troops. They demanded Croatian Serbs let supplies into some 1,200 UN Bangladeshi troops deployed in the Bihac enclave.

The Serbs say they have won back all the territory they had lost to Bosnians. Tanjug News Agency says that the Bosnian Serb commander, General Ratko Mladic congratulates his troops.

November 20, 1994: Swiss Radio International:

(NATO commander) Mr. Claes, said that NATO is ready to launch air strikes against rebel Croatian Serbs as soon as the UN makes a request. (This was never forthcoming as the Secretary General of the UN, Boutros Boutros Ghali, was given the power to call these air strikes and he did not like to call punitive strikes against the Serbs). Speaking on American television, Mr. Claes said that NATO is ready to send a strong message to the Serbs that attacks from Serbian held territory in Croatia must stop.

The UN says it is greatly concerned about the deteriorating situation in the Muslim held area of the enclave of Bihac, and strongly condemned attacks from Croatia (by Croatian Serbs). Tensions throughout Bosnia followed a United Nations resolution allowing NATO air strikes against Serbian targets in Croatia in retaliation for two Serbian air raids on Bihac. Muslims in Bihac have been threatening the

UN Peacekeepers because of the UN's inability to protect them from the (Serb) air raids.

Meanwhile, heavy fighting continues around the town of Velika Kadusa north of Bihac as well as in the western front line.

November 21, 1994, *The New York Times:* NATO sends 50 jets and support planes to attack a Serb airfield, but Croatian Serb jets continue to attack Bihac.

Nov. 25, 1994, *The New York Times:* Serbs are holding 55 Canadian peacekeepers hostage to stop further air strikes. (Eventually Serbs took 400 peacekeepers hostage and threatened to kill them if NATO makes air strikes on Serbs near Bihac. NATO calls off the mission after the UN fails to pinpoint targets.

November 29, 1994, Die Deutsche Welle:
In Bonn, the Franco-German summit began with a disagreement over lifting the arms embargo. France is firmly opposed to lifting the arms embargo. A French spokesman briefing journalists after the first round of talks at the summit said Helmut Kohl sought to reassure France's Foreign Minister that Bosnia's stance remained unchanged. France's President Mitterrand and Chancellor Kohl, are reported to have postponed discussions until breakfast on Wednesday morning.

Washington sources say there are two changes in the International Peace Plan being offered Bosnian Serbs are links to Serbia and new talks on partitioning Bosnian territory. The Five Power Contact Group on Bosnia has so far flatly ruled out any changes to carve up the plan. The U.S. Envoy, Charles Thomas, reiterated the standpoint on Tuesday U.S. Secretary of State, Warren Christopher, is to brief America's NATO allies on the change of stance in Brussels on Thursday

While diplomatic speculations about possible changes in the Bosnian Peace Plan goes on, observers of the military situation in the Bihac enclave say they now expect an imminent all-out offensive by the Bosnian Serbs to take Bihac. An artillery barrage on the encircled Bihac continues unremittingly according to a statement from the mayor of the town to a German journalist during telephone calls. UN Monitoring officials reported that a sixteen story building in the town was badly damaged in the shelling. Three rockets also came down in the Bosnian capital, Sarajevo, injuring a woman.

November 29, 1994, Radio Netherlands:

The Bosnian Serbs have kept their promise and released two convoys of Dutch UN Peacekeepers. The ninety Dutch soldiers had been held hostage since Saturday. French, British, and Canadian convoys were also immobilized by the Serbs.

Boutros Boutros Ghali is due in Sarajevo Wednesday where he will discuss continuation of the UN Peacekeeping Mission.

U.S. Secretary of State, Warren Christopher, will attend a meeting with NATO members in Brussels, Thursday and Friday in a bid to settle differences between the U.S. and its European Allies.

Meanwhile, after talks with the Bosnian Government, the International Contact Group on Bosnia stressed that their peace plan will not be altered. It had been rumored that the Serb held areas of Bosnia will be given the option of joining a federation with Serbia in an attempt to get the Serbs to join the peace plan. The idea of a confederation with Serbia had already been rejected by the influential Robert Dole who leads the Republican majority in the U.S. Senate. In his visit to Brussels, Senator Dole called on NATO to take a more autonomous role in Bosnia independent of the United Nations.

November 29, 1994, Swiss Radio International:

UN officials are holding talks in Sarajevo aimed at breaking the deadlock in peace talks. Envoys from Britain, France, Russia, and the U.S. have met with Muslim leaders in a bid to end the siege of the Muslim enclave of Bihac. A U.S. envoy said after the meeting there would be no change to the previous peace plan for 49% of Bosnian territory to go to the Serbs. However, Serbs refuse to give up any of the 70% they currently hold. The (International) Contact Group offered Serbia and Bosnian Serbs a number of concessions if they would stop the fighting.

On Wednesday, Boutros Boutros Ghali is due in Bosnia to offer what a senior UN official called a "rock bottom" condition for the continuation of a UN Peacekeeping mission.

December 3, 1994, Radio Netherlands:

The leader of the Bosnian Serbs, Radovan Karadzic, called upon Croatia to stop its military intervention in Bosnia. He said if Croatia didn't pull its troops out of Bosnia, it would meet with what he called a 'fitting response'. Dr. Karadzic was speaking during a meeting with UN officials at his headquarters in Pale near Sarajevo. The United Nations has voiced concern over the escalation of fighting between Croatian troops and Serb forces from the Krajina, the Serb dominated part of Croatia that has declared its independence from Croatia.

Some 400 UN troops are being held hostage in Bosnia including a convoy with 80 Dutch and four Dutch observers.

(On November 29, Radio Netherlands reported that the Dutch soldiers had been released). The Bosnian Serbs are reported to have agreed to release the 400 Peacekeepers. However, it is not known when exactly this will happen. British Foreign Secretary, Douglas Hurd, has warned that UN Peacekeeping troops could be pulled out if the warring factions fail to win a peace agreement. He further hinted that the arms embargo against Bosnia could be lifted. He travels with his French counterpart, Alain Juppe, to Belgrade on Sunday to discuss the peace plan with (Serb) president Milosevic (accused War Criminal)

December 5, 1994, Radio Netherlands:

In a report to the UN Security Council, UN Secretary General Boutros Boutros Ghali opposed the use of force to defend the designated *Safe Havens* by UN troops.

On May 1, last year, the Security Council designated six towns as *safe areas*. **All are under siege** by Bosnian Serbs except Tuzla.

In Bihac, food supplies have practically run out, and in the capital, Sarajevo, food supplies will last another ten days. One person has been killed in a scramble for food in Srebrenica.

December 5, 1994, Die Deutsche Welle:

Islamic nations meeting at the conference of Islamic ministers in Geneva have threatened to pull out of the international arms embargo against Bosnian Muslims. The Islamic conference said this step would be taken if Muslims were denied the chance to get weapons needed for their defense. Iran's Foreign Minister, Ali Akhbar Velayati, called for the creation of an Islamic Peace Force to be deployed without delay in Bosnia. He said that the troops could quickly replace the UN force being withdrawn from the war theater. The Geneva conference was attended by Bosnia's Muslim President, Alija Izetbegovic and Bosnia's Vice President, Ejup Ganic. Izetbegovic was later quoted as criticizing the Islamic nations for not giving the Bosnian Muslims enough help.

December 6, 1994, Radio Netherlands:
President Izetbegovic has announced in Geneva that the Islamic nations attending the conference in Geneva are prepared to provide more troops for peacekeeping if the western countries withdraw their blue helmets. The Islamic nations have also promised more financial help for the government in Sarajevo. The Islamic Bosnia Group wants talks in the near future with the five countries International Contact Group about the situation in Bosnia.

December 6, 1994, Swiss Radio:
The OECD meeting in Budapest ended in disarray over the war in Bosnia/Herzegovina. The final document at the end of the two-day conference contained no mention of Bosnia after Russia vetoed a statement that would have been included in it. Russia, a traditional supporter of Serbs, refused to accept clauses condemning Serbs for their offensive upon the Muslims in Bihac. Instead, the host country, Hungary, issued a statement calling for a ceasefire in Bosnia. The Bosnian Government categorized the statement calling for a ceasefire a capitulation to the international community.

December 7, 1994, *Wall Street Journal;*
Serb forces allowed one UN food and fuel convoy into government held territory in western Bosnia but said that further cooperation depended on whether NATO ended its threat of aid strikes.

December 12, 1994, *Wall Street Journal:*

Russian tanks and troops moved into the separatist region of Chechnya as many Moscow politicians lamented Yeltsin's use of force there. Russian planes buzzed Chechnya's capital causing civilians to flee. The region's president said that Chechens are ready to fight.

December 13, 1994, *Wall Street Journal:*

Chechen forces fought Russian troops with tanks and rockets in the first major clash since Moscow sent in soldiers to crush the southern region's bid for independence. The Russians attacked with assault helicopters and fighter-bombers in a battle that lasted over four hours.

Russia and the IMF are struggling over the biggest loan in the IMF's history ($6.25 billion to fund Moscow's planned budget deficit). A GOP Senator was on the Senate panel to oversee Russia's assistance and attached stiffer political conditions to the aid. (The war in Chechnya was costing the Russians more than the IMF aid package).

December 26, 1994, Die Deutsche Welle:

The Bosnian Government has refused to enter into talks with the United Nations about a long term ceasefire for the country until attacks on the Bihac enclave have stopped. Despite the ceasefire that went into effect last Saturday, **Bihac is still under attack.**

Bosnian Government and observers on the Bihac scene say that the attacks on the enclave are from renegade Muslims (Abdic) and Serbs firing from across the border from the Krajina region of Croatia who say they do not consider themselves covered by the ceasefire which was brokered by the former U.S. President, Jimmy Carter.

United Nations General, Michael Rose, said he will be traveling to Bihac on Wednesday in an effort to bring about a ceasefire there.

The court in Belgrade the capital of Serbia and Rump Yugoslavia, declared as the attempt by the Belgrade Government to takeover an opposition newspaper, *Borba,* as illegal. The court ruled that the government of the country which consists of Serbia and Montenegro had infringed upon the authority of the parliament. Moreover the government had no license to publish the paper. Earlier, Belgrade had announced a new publisher and a new chief editor. Many of the staff of *Borba* occupied the offices and brought out their own edition of the newspaper. Then in the name of the European Union, the German Foreign Office criticized the (Serbian) government takeover and said that a free press was indispensable in every country.

A report in the German newspaper, *Die Welt,* claims the embargo against Serbia and Montenegro has been broken some 600 times since it went into force. The paper quotes customs officials as saying that in 60 of the cases, the embargo against weapons was violated. In most instances, the companies belonged to Serbs or Croats who had set up legitimate businesses in Germany.

December 26, 1994, Radio Netherlands:

Reports from Bosnia indicate the ceasefire is holding up reasonably well (in other words, there are violations). Reports from the Unites Nations Peacekeeping forces say that it is quiet in Bihac where heavy fighting continued after the ceasefire went into effect Saturday. Sporadic shooting is still heard in the region, heavy fighting is reported only in the town of Valika Kladusa. The U.N commander in Bosnia, General Sir Michael Rose, will be visiting the enclave tomorrow. The United Nations hopes the seven-day truce will pave the way for a four-month ceasefire and eventually an end to the bloodshed.

December 27, 1994, Die Deutsche Welle:
(Bosnian) Vice President, Ejup Ganic stated that his government's position was not to enter into negotiations about extending the truce until Croatian Serbs and Abdic's Muslim renegades stop their attacks on Bihac. On Tuesday, another 90 tons of food and medical supplies reached the enclave.

December 27, 1994, Radio Netherlands: After being held back for five days, trucks carrying 90 tons of food entered Bihac. Some of this food will be for the 180,000 refugees in the enclave. This is the third shipment in the past three weeks.

December 29, 1994, Die Deutsche Welle:
Fighting goes on in the Muslim enclave of Bihac with fierce battles between Government Troops and Serb troops. On Thursday, the self-proclaimed Bosnian Serb parliament in Pale approved the agreement between Carter and their leader, Radovan Karadzic. In addition to the ceasefire, the agreement foresees further peace talks based on the peace plan of the International Contact Group.

December 30, 1994, Die Deutsche Well:
The opposition Social Democrats have called for a condemnation of Moscow's action in Chechnya. The Foreign Affairs spokesman for the CDU-CSU, Karl Lammert, has urged Chancellor Helmut Kohl, the outgoing president of the EU, to act.
But government spokesman, Dieter Fogel, had said that the chancellor does not intend to contact the Russian

President, Boris Yeltsin. Chancellor Kohl said he fully backed the message by Foreign Minister, Claus Kinkel, to his Russian counterpart, Andrei Kozyrev, in a phone call, Where Kinkel voiced concern about the escalating conflict in Chechnya and demanded a political solution'

The EU administration of Mostar, capital of Herzegovina, warned against the deployment of German fighter planes in the former Yugoslavia. While endorsing participation in peacekeeping mission, Hans Koschnick urged that certain areas be avoided for historical reasons. He also opposed lifting the arms embargo on Bosnia.

NATO commander in chief for America in Europe, General George Julian, has described the withdrawal of UN Peacekeeping troops from Bosnia as an extremely difficult operation. There are troops from 35 nations on Bosnian territory with different codes of command and conduct. This alone would make a pullout under pressure very complicated. Assessing the UN Mission, the NATO chief termed the actual situation in the former Yugoslavia as a theater of war, not peace. Troops in peacekeeping missions should be able to defend themselves.

January 2, 1995, Die Deutsche Welle:

The Bosnian Government is retiring its troops from the strategic Mt. Igman, and in return the Bosnian Serbs are to open certain access route for civilian traffic to Sarajevo. These steps are part of the ceasefire that came into effect New Year's Day. According to the U.N, the ceasefire is largely holding. The UN is making an effort to persuade Croatian Serbs in the Krajina to end their fighting. The Krajina Serbs are supporting Muslim *separatists* in the west Bosnian enclave of Bihac.

January 2, 1995, Radio Netherlands:

Bosnian troops will withdraw from the strategically located Mt. Igman and UN troops will monitor the withdrawal. The agreement came into effect on New Year's Day is a four-month ceasefire. The truce so far has been holding reasonably well with the exceptions of a missile attack on the International Hotel in Sarajevo, which caused substantial material damage. The rocket was fired from an area held by the Bosnian Serbs.

Meanwhile, Croatian Serbs and dissident Muslims have also endorsed the ceasefire.

In the former Russian Republic of Tadzhikistan, four Russian soldiers have been killed in an attack by Tadzhik rebels. The Russian's armored vehicle came under fire from across Tadzhikistan's border with neighboring Afghanistan. Several other soldiers were injured.

On New Year's Day eight other Russian soldiers died in Tadzhikistan after drinking champagne spiked with cyanide. The wife of a Russian diplomat and three Tadzhiks and also nineteen people were hospitalized with symptoms of poisoning. It is believed that the poisonings were a premeditated terrorist action.

A 16-year old British computer hack managed to break into the Pentagon's computer files and to Washington's horror put information on Internet that has some 20 million subscribers. Last summer, the Pentagon admitted its computer bank had been penetrated.

January 3, 1995, Houston *Post:*

Yemeni speaker of the House, Sheikh Abdullah al Ahmad in remarks published denied claims by Yemeni Government officials that Saudi forces had penetrated Yemen's borders. An official statement issued in Sanaa Sunday night said an attack was mounted deep inside

Yemeni territory in Saada, a northwestern province on the Red Sea.

In the Russian assault on the Chechen capital of Grozny dozens of Russian vehicles were destroyed and the Russian Army was pushed back from the center of the city. The city was described as in ruins with hundreds of Chechen fighters and civilians dead or wounded. There were reports that the Russians massacred some civilians. Captured Russian soldiers feared that if they are returned to Russia in the future that they will have problems with Russian Intelligence (secret police). The Russian Government claimed that it was mercenaries and not rank and file Chechens who were leading in the defense of Grozny. The Russian Government said they were using artillery, Grad rockets, grenade launchers, and flame-throwers against Russian troops.

January 9, 1995, Radio Netherlands:

The Bosnian Serbs are keeping 80 Muslims civilians in a prison west of the capital, Sarajevo. Among the detainees who have been held since last October, are children and old people. Two have died in the prison. The United Nations has accused the Serbs of violating all human decency and urged the release of the detainees in a letter to Bosnian Serb leader, Radovan Karadzic. The *detainees* originally came from a village in eastern Bosnia. A UN official said they were using them as a bargaining tool to improve their negotiating position.

January 9, 1995, Radio Netherlands (in Spanish):

The original agreement by Croatia with the stationing of UN troops in Croatia was to have the Serbs leave Croatia, that the Croatian Serb militia be disarmed, and that Croatian refugees returned to their homes. None of these conditions have been complied with. The presence of United Nations troops has complicated any solution for the area. The

Croatian Serbs continue to be armed and have not allowed the Croatian Serbs to return to their homes.

In September, the Croatian Parliament noted the failure of the UN to implement those solutions and gave the UN 100 days to comply or they would not renew the mandate previously given by the Croatian Government. This mandate expires officially tomorrow, Tuesday, January 10. The forces inside the Croatian Government that are defending the hard line are disposed to cut relations with UNIFIL even though not all are in agreement. More moderate forces have indicated they have taken a step to resolve the problems. There is the economic pact signed between Serbia and Croatia this past November. The road between Zagreb and Belgrade has been reopened and there has been restoration of water and electricity in some areas. The look to keep 15,000 U.N troops and renegotiate, including the reestablishment of 1/3 of the recognized territory to Croatian authority.

These conditions may determine whether the war will be renewed in Croatia although the Croatian Army has boasted it is ready to take on the Croatian Serbs in the Krajina region (Croatia was receiving weapons from Hungary and from Iran in sufficient quantities to finish the Serb aggression). During this past year, the Croats have improved the army and are ready to recover their territory by force. Thus another chapter in the war in ex-Yugoslavia may be in the making.

January 10, 1995, Die Deutsche Welle:

The Russian parliamentary deputies are holding talks to see how to end the conflict in Chechnya peacefully. Numerous politicians say Boris Yeltsin's handling of the events is a breech of the Russian Federation's Constitution.

After a short lull on Tuesday, fighting resumed around the presidential palace in the Chechen capital, Grozny. The

Russians have estimated 1.2 million Chechens fled from the conflict in the region.

An aid convoy left Zagreb for the mainly Muslim Bihac enclave in northwest Bosnia. The trucks are carrying food and medicines for 180,000 people in Bihac according to a spokesman for UNHCR. The Bosnian Serbs indicate they intend to open roads to Sarajevo this coming weekend. The Serbs had originally said that the re-opening of these routs depended on the Bosnian troop withdrawal from the de-militarized zone around Mt. Igman.

Krajina Serb leaders have rejected talks for peace with the UN.

About 26,000 Muslim fundamentalist live in Germany and the German Government has picked up some Algerians connected to Algerian extremists that threaten to bomb foreign embassies in Algeria.

January 10, Radio Netherlands:

Russian Prime Minister, Viktor Chernomyrdin, wants to establish a ceasefire zones and start a dialogue with Chechen leaders.

The five country International Contact Group is to send a number of top ranking envoys to the former Yugoslavia before the end of this week. They hope to get the Bosnian Serbs to accept the (peace) plan.

(Pakistan) Prime Minister Bhutto has been concerned about the tightening of ties between the U.S. and India...Pakistan and India have been accusing each other of secretly developing nuclear weapons. Secretary of Defense, William Perry, is to fly to India Wednesday.

January 11, 1995, Die Deutsche Welle:

The (Russian) newspaper, *Syvodnya,* has suggested that the war with Chechnya will cost Russia 15 billion rubles or roughly four billion dollars. Of this amount, 1/3 is the cost of the military operations and two thirds is the cost of restoring order and rebuilding the damage caused by the war.

The International Contact Group will meet first in Sarajevo with Russian officials and later in Pale with (Bosnian) Serb leaders.

January 11, 1995, Radio Netherlands:

The influential chairman of the Senate's Foreign Relations Committee, Senator Jesse Helms, says Moscow risks losing American aid if it continues to do what he calls, *Russia's brutality in Chechnya.*

A spokesman for (U.S.) State Department accused Russia of violating several European security treaties of which it has signed.

Meanwhile, in Moscow, President Boris Yeltsin is taking over control of the Armed Forces from Defense Minister (General) Pavel Grachev. Mr. Grachev has come under some fierce criticism for the way in which had handled the campaign in Chechnya

January 13, 1995, Radio Netherlands:

Senator Jesse Helms says Russia risks losing American aid if it continues its brutality in Chechnya. A spokesman for State Department accused Russia of violating several European treaties of which it is signatory.

The Kremlin meanwhile denied earlier reports that President Boris Yeltsin had taken control of Russian Defense Forces from Defense Minister Pavel Grachev.

The International Contact Group has extended the easing of sanctions against Serbia and Montenegro for another 100 days. Sanctions were imposed in 1992 for Serbia's part in the Bosnian *Civil* War and East Slavonia last September. The UN Security Council has imposed new sanctions as well as prohibiting oil convoys from passing from Serbia to the self-proclaimed Krajina republic inside Croatia. According to the Bosnian Government, the Croatian Serbs are suing this fuel in their attacks on the Muslim enclave of Bihac.

The Croatian Government wants the 15,000 UN troops in the Krajina to leave at the end of March when the UN mandate ends. .

January 14, 1995, Die Deutsche Welle:
Western intelligence sources say the assault on Grozny (Chechnya) cannot take place before Sunday. Thirty five military air transports are landing at a north Caucasus airport. Tass says the troops are poised to take the Presidential Palace (in Grozny) today.

Meanwhile, several Russian high officers have expressed fear that the Chechen Conflict could unleash terrorist attacks in Russia.

In Bonn, Government spokesmen confirmed Chancellor Helmut Kohl has been in contact with Boris Yeltsin about the Chechen crisis.

The Croatian Government will not go back on its decision to end the mandate of the UN to monitor the ceasefire between Croatia and rebel Serbs. The mandate ends at the end of March. Croat Minister, Matta Granic, says they want to solve this problem as an internal affair. Butros Boutros Ghali says he is disappointed.

E.U. Administration for the rebuilding of Mostar, Hans Koschnick, said that if the Croatians do not change their minds, there was not only a threat of fighting again in the Krajina region but in all Bosnia itself.

January 14, 1995, Radio Netherlands:
Nearly all of the center of Grozny is under Russian control. The lower house of the Russian parliament passed a

resolution urging President Yeltsin to stop the military campaign and seek a peaceful resolution. President Bill Clinton urged the warring parties to settle the conflict peacefully. He also fully backed the territorial integrity of the Russian Federation.

The roads to Sarajevo will be opened Saturday for civilian and humanitarian traffic. The UN has expressed concern about a new wave of fighting in the Muslim enclave of Srebrenica in eastern Bosnia. Serb Forces have penetrated the area and are fighting mainly Muslim troops.

January 15, 1995, Die Deutsche Welle:

The UN has finally begun food shipments to Chechnya after two weeks of wrangling with Russian authorities. A load of 42 tons arrived in neighboring Osetia after a flight from Amsterdam. The private group, Tepanamore, plans to send more food, medicines and a team of doctors later today.

Fighting in Grozny remains heavy. Rebels still hold the presidential palace despite continued mortar attacks Russian news agencies report the son of Chechen President, Djokar Dudayev, has been killed in battle. U.S. Secretary of State, Warren Christopher, is expected to urge Moscow to end the bloodshed as soon as possible and will meet with Russian Foreign Minister, Andrei Kozyrev, in Geneva today.

Regional Russian leaders as well as the Ukraine and Georgia have called upon Moscow's government to show greater willingness to negotiate. At the end of a three day meeting in The Hague, Netherlands, Shunaiyev, president of Tartarstan said talks between Moscow and Chechen leaders should never have been broken off. Several thousand people demonstrated in Moscow against the war. Sergei Rushikov, head of the Russian Parliament's defense committee, accused President Boris Yelstin as being personally responsible for the bloodshed.

Access roads into Sarajevo remain closed despite the pledge by the Serbs to open them as part of the broad ceasefire signed two weeks ago.

Mortar explosions killed two women in the Bihac enclave of northwest Bosnia. One mortar hit a school and another hit a house. It is not clear who is responsible (more UN euphemism). Also in Bihac a convoy of food has reached the 1,200 Bangladeshi Peacekeepers.

January 15, 1995, Houston *Post:*

Saudi military forces are poised in two areas on the Yemen border 150 miles northwest of Sanaa.

January 19, 1995, Die Deutsche Welle:

The Chechen rebels are ready to continue their fight against the Russian troops despite their fall of the presidential palace in the capital Grozny. According to the head of Chechen forces, Arslan Moskadov, his people only left the heavily damaged palace because it could not longer serve as a headquarters. But he added that it doesn't mean the resistance is over. Russian President Boris Yeltsin has said that with the capture of the presidential palace the military phase has been completed.

Meanwhile, President Yeltsin has sacked three generals from their posts as Deputy Defense Ministers. The three generals, Boris Gromov, Sergei Kongratov, and Viktor Miranov, have all been extremely critical of the Russian invasion of Chechnya in recent weeks. One of them accused the army of using barbaric methods. President Yeltsin accepted the resignation of another general, Eduard Brobidov. He handed his resignation in last month after refusing to accept the leadership of the operation in Chechnya.

In the Algerian capital of Algiers, a member of the Transitional Council has been shot dead in the street. He is the second member of the council to be killed in five days. Shortly before this, a car bomb exploded in the Algerian town of Bolgaria, killing two people and wounding twenty others. According to Algerian television, this was the first car bomb attack on a market place. Earlier in the day, two security officers were killed when a bomb attached to a corpse exploded. The killings come one day after the Algerian Government rejected a proposal by the joint Muslim opposition to seek a solution to the political crisis in the country.

January 20, 1995, *wall Street Journal:*
Chechnya's presidential palace fell today to the Russians troops and Yeltsin declared the military crackdown on Chechnya was practically over. But Chechen fighters who control over half of Grozny vowed to continue fighting.

January 20, 1995, Radio Netherlands:
Russian troops have fought tough battles with the Chechen guerrillas holding their own in Grozny suburbs The Rebel's last supply line, a road running south of the capital, came under fire. A close advisor to the Russian President, Boris Yeltsin, said the conflict in the breakaway republic will continue for some time. He pointed out that after the withdrawal of Russian intervention forces; the rebels are likely to launch a guerrilla war from the mountains in the south of the republic. Russia's news agency, Interfax, reports that the commander of the Chechen forces, Arslan Moskadov, has threatened to start armed attacks outside Chechen territory. The Russian lower house has made a law that allows it to seek the death penalty for Chechen fighters.

The war in Chechnya has deepened Russia's economic troubles. On Friday, the ruble fell to al all time low against the U.S. dollar on fears the military campaign in Chechnya would fan inflation. Estimates put the cost of the war at about one billion dollars with money having to come from the existing budget. The lower house of the Russian parliament, the Duma, has just rejected the proposed 1995 budget. It has also put in jeopardy the six billion dollar loan the International Monetary Fund. The IMF had made approval of the budget a precondition for guaranteeing the credits.

NATO has drafted a contingency plan for the possible evacuation of the UN Peacekeeping Forces from Bosnia. The plan has been submitted to the Defense Ministers of the NATO member states. Crucial to the plan is that NATO will be allowed facilities in Bosnia. But that has become uncertain now that Croatia's President Tudjman doesn't want the mandate of the UN troops in his country to be extended. The current mandate expires at the end of March, which means the UN troops will need to leave Croatia by June.

Meanwhile, heavy fighting is continuing in the enclave of Bihac in Bosnia. Further fighting is reported near the Srebrenica enclave.

In the Bosnian capital, Sarajevo, negotiations about continuing the ceasefire have produced no result because the Bosnian Serbs persist in their refusal to open several approach roads to the city. An exchange of Muslim and Serb prisoners did (however) go ahead.

January 21, 1995, Die Deutsche Welle:
    Small guerrilla units are operating throughout Chechnya.
    Croatia has threatened to use force to recover its territory controlled by ethnic Serbs in the Krajina. *Der Spiegel*

magazine quotes Croatian President, Franjo Tudjman, that his forces are ready to drive the Serb rebels out of the enclave of Krajina and that he would not hesitate to go to war to recover Croatian territory. More than three years there was fierce fighting between Croatia and Serbs. The UN mandate ends soon and peacekeeping force will be required to leave.

Fighting has greatly subsided in most places in Bosnia except about the enclave of Bihac.

The United States has said it would begin direct talks between the Bosnian Serbs and the United States. Direct talks would violate a UN resolution but U.S. Secretary of State Mr. Christopher said that the current ceasefire offered a chance for peace that should not be missed.

Six nations, Tunisia, Algeria, Spain, Portugal, Italy, and France issued sharp condemnation of Islamic terrorists. They warned that fundamentalism and are a threat to the nations of Europe.

January 22, 1995, Die Deutsche Welle:

Germany's Foreign Minister, Klaus Kinkel, issued an appeal to end the bloodshed in Chechnya. Herr Kinkel spoke with Russian Foreign Minister, Andrei Kozyrev, and urged Russia to respect human rights and its obligations under the Helsinki agreements and he said that sanctions against Russia could not be ruled out.

The Economics Minister, Gunther Rechstalt, now in St. Petersburg (Russia) for two days of talks for economic cooperation, made clear that Russia's invasion of Chechnya is an impediment to closer economic ties and to (more) German investment.

Meanwhile, German Defense Minister, Volker Ruhe, has suggested in a newspaper interview that the Russian Minister of Defense, Pavel Grachev, be asked to stay away from an international conference of defense experts to be held in Munich at the beginning of February. Grachev described two liberal politicians, Sergei Kolgarov, and Sergei Yushnikov, as traitors and enemies of Russia because of their open criticism of Russia's military intervention in Chechnya.

Several hundred Russian led by the former reform chief, Yegor Gaidar, and human rights commissioner, Pogayev braved temperature of minus 15 degrees outside the old headquarters of the Soviet Security Police to demand that the fighting (in Chechnya) be stopped.

America's special envoy to Bosnia, Charles Thomas, said that he was hopeful his talks with Radovan Karadzic will clear the way to fresh negotiations to bring an end to the war. Karadzic speaking from in his Pale stronghold this past Sunday, the discussion left him with some hope of resumption of talks with the Muslim led Bosnian Government.

But Bosnia's Vice President, Haris Siladjic, said the negotiations were unlikely unless the Serbs accept a peace plan brought up by the International Contact Group, which would require the Serbs to give up large chunks of (Serb) occupied territory. He doubted the Serbs would give up any territory unless confronted with a formidable military force.

Charles Thomas hopes to join by other members of the International Contact Group and he said he wants to continue contact with the Serbs.

January 22, 1995, Radio Netherlands:

U.S. Negotiator, Charles Thomas, will meet with Serbian leader, Radovan Karadzic with the aim of *jump starting* the peace talks.

Mr. Yegor Gaidar, former reform chief of Russia is in the Netherlands for a two-day visit. Mr. Gaidar says that

Russia faces great financial problems as a result of the high cost of the war in Chechnya. Gaidar predicted that the Russian inflation will cause living standards of the poor to deteriorate even further. Mr. Gaidar, who is Russia's choice in one of the largest parties in the lower house of Russia's parliament, was welcomed by Dutch Foreign Minister, Hans von Mirlo. On Monday, Gaidar is to visit the Dutch trade Promotion Center.

January 23, 1995, Houston *Post:*

A top American negotiator, Charles Thomas, met with Bosnian Serb leader, Radovan Karadzic, in Pale last Sunday. Thomas said he hoped to get Karadzic to deliver on (Serb) promises to open land routes out of Sarajevo. There were indications that Thomas succeeded.

January 23, 1995, Radio Netherlands:

European Foreign Ministers meeting in Brussels have announced the EU will not take any measures at this time to protest the Russian intervention in Chechnya. The EU will give Russia until March to change its policies in Chechnya or face possible sanctions.

The European Union has signed a cooperative agreement with the former Soviet Republic of Kazakhstan. The agreement was signed in Brussels by Kazakhstan's President, Nursultan Nazerbayev, during a meeting with EU Foreign Ministers. The accord provides for improved economic ties and the strengthening of trade contacts between the EU and the Central Asian nation.

Kazakhstan has also strengthened ties with Russia by signing a series of agreements including ones on economic cooperation, citizenship, and financial and economic affairs. The countries will establish a free trade zone in which their central banks will coordinate monetary policy. Kazakhstan's

Prime Minister, Akim Kazaligegan, also expressed his confidence in Russian President, Boris Yeltsin.

After one year as commander of UN Peacekeeping Forces in Bosnia, British General, Michael Rose has handed over responsibilities to a fellow countryman, Lt. General Rupert Smith. On his final day of duty, the outgoing spoke optimistically about the chance of peace in Bosnia. He also announced an agreement has been reached on the opening of routes to the capital of Sarajevo. The Bosnian Serbs have promised to lift the blockade on the first of February

January 24, 1995, Die Deutsche Welle: The Russian parliament will discuss the role of the actions by Russian Defense Minister, Pavel Grachev. The vote of *no confidence* in him is seen as a possibility.

The International Contact Group on Bosnia has held talks in a bid to persuade the warring parties to return to peace negotiations. There is no sign the Serbs, led by Radovan Karadzic, would accept the peace plan, which would give them less than 50% of Bosnian territory.

In Zagreb, the Bosnian President, Alija Izetbegovic, and Croatian President Franjo Tudjman, have agreed to set up a commission to resolve the Croat-Muslim Federation in Bosnia.

January 24, 1995, Radio Netherlands:
Russian forces have cut the southern road that supplies the (Chechen) rebels in Grozny. Evacuation of the estimated 10,000 refugees trapped in Grozny has started (these were mostly ethnic Russians as Chechens had left to live in the countryside with relatives, which the ethnic Russians living in Grozny had no family to turn to for help.

A Scottish newspaper published an American Air Force Intelligence report that said Iran was behind the Pan Am Bombing over Lockerbee, Scotland.

Note: The Air Force Intelligence report was correct but it was rebutted by U.S. officials who said the report contained old and unfounded data. British Intelligence also took the position that Libya is behind the Pan Am bombing. In reality, Saddam Hussein learned America supplied Iran with 400 million dollars worth of weapons. As he had gone to war against Iran in 1979 with the message of American help he was furious with what he saw as Americans reneging on their promises to keep weapons out of Iran. On May 17, 1987, Saddam had a French made Iraqi fighter fire two Exocet missile at the USS Stark killing 37 of the crew and wounding 21.

The immediate response from the United States was that *it was an honest mistake as Saddam Hussein is a friend of America.* The Pentagon said that if an attack were coming it would come from Iran as Iranians were capable of such a premeditated attack.

On July 3, 1988, an Iran Air jumbo jet heading for Bahrain in the Persian Gulf was shot down by a rocket from the USS Vincennes, killing 187 men, women, and children. The US government issued a statement of regret for the loss of life but no apology. The wife of the ship's captain was living in San Diego, California, where her station wagon was blown up by an assassination squad from Iran.

An American journalist in the Gulf War (1991) learned about the multi-billion dollar drug deal by Israel and the American Government with Iran for 400 million dollars in drugs confiscated from drug dealers and drug producers in Iran. In the Gulf War, he began to talk on TV about the secret behind this arms deal. Subsequently he was never seen again on television again.

January 25, 1995, Houston *Post:*

Russian Defense Minister, Pavel Grachev says that Russian generals who refused to serve in Chechnya are unworthy of serving in the armed forces and may face court proceedings. He singled out Colonel General, Eduard Vorobykov, and indicated three dissident deputies who have been critical of the army's performance in Chechnya. Boris Gromov, a hero of the Afghan War might be transferred to an unimportant post as punishment.

Chechen President, Djokhar Dudayev, said that Grozny remains a *no-man's land* with sniper fire continuing non-stop throughout Grozny.

January 25, 1995, *Wall Street Journal:*

On Monday, Mr. Mozartbayev signed an agreement with the European Union on partnership and cooperation, and on Tuesday, he signed with NATO Secretary General, Willy Claes, with NATO's partnership and peace program.

Kazakhstan's President, Nursultan Mozartbayev, agreed to partially unify Kazakhstan's army with Russia's Army.

(Kazakhstan has a population of seventeen million spread over a landmass four times the size of Texas. Its most important exports are oil through Russia. It is also sending gas to Shanghai in China.

Note: Although its 35% minority is called Russian, it has two million ethnic Germans brought in by Catherine the Great to settle in the Volga region of Russia two hundred years ago.

January 28, 1995, Die Deutsche Welle:

At the two NATO conferences in Munich for NATO Defense Ministers, Germany's Defense Minister, Volker Ruhe, said NATO should only take part in UN operations if the alliance if NATO is given freedom of action. He said the division authority of NATO's air power seriously tarnished the alliance's ability and the scope of the alliance should be widened to take not only military but also economic and strategic matters into account.

January 28, 1995, Radio Netherlands:
   Dutch UN troops in eastern Bosnia spotted 20 helicopters flying from Serbia into Bosnia, violating the no-fly zone. The UN suspects the Serbs are using the aircraft for transport purposes. Since the UN Security Council imposed the no-fly zone over Bosnia in 1992 Serbia violated it over 4,000 times and nothing was ever done.
   Chechen rebels shot down a Russian fighter plane over Grozny. The Russian Army has lost several helicopters over Chechnya but this is the first time a fighter plane has been shot down.

January 29, 1995, Die Deutsche Welle:
   Russian Prime Minister, Yushenko, said that western countries must realize their responsibilities for the war in Chechnya, which has already claimed 20,000 lives and was a crime against humanity. Yushenko warned about bringing East European countries into the Western Defense alliance of NATO. He argued that this would create a feeling of isolation within Russia and strengthen anti-western tendencies. Yushenko recommends strengthening the Organization for Security and Cooperation in Europe instead of expanding NATO eastward,
   NATO representatives at the conference have agreed that the war in Bosnia and the Russian campaign in Chechnya will likely speed up interest in the former Eastern Block nations to join NATO (*as they fear Russia will attempt*

move back into Eastern Europe and remake the Soviet Union with a military leading the union).

In Munich, Republican Senator, William Cohen, has called for air attacks on Bosnian Serbs to protect United Nations Troops. The British Defense Minister, Malcolm Rifkind, and French Foreign Minister, Alain Juppe, oppose such action. The German Defense Minister, Volker Ruhe, demanded a free hand for NATO in future actions with the United Nations. He said that conclusions drawn in Bosnia are that NATO cannot be the executive organ.

In Belgrade, the former workers on the newspaper ***Borba*** have formed a new newspaper, ***Nasa Borba.*** Workers on the newspaper claim Serb authorities are harassing them by using Serbian Security Forces to present the staff form entering the offices.

February 4, 1995, Radio Netherlands:
Dutch Foreign Minister, Yores Vorhoever, called for NATO to take over some of the functions carried out by the UN Peacekeepers in Bosnia. He said that NATO should be given the mandate to protect civilians and that troops from moderate Muslim nations should also play a role in this.

February 5, 1995, Die Deutsche Welle:
EU Foreign Ministers agreed to make available about 152 million Marks for reconstruction projects in the city of Mostar.

In the Bosnian capital of Sarajevo, a road is now open for civilian traffic.

February 5, 1995, Radio Netherlands:
UN observers say at least 15 helicopters flew into Bosnian air space last Friday apparently came from Serbia

and may have been carrying supplies to Bosnian Serbs. The authorities in Belgrade deny they were involved

February 6, 1995, Die Deutsche Welle:
Greece has dropped its opposition to a customs union between the EU and Turkey if the EU will negotiate a new membership for Cyrus.

February 8, 1995, Die Deutsche Welle:
Contrary to Russian reports, heavy fighting continues in Grozny.
Willi Wimmer, EU Vice President for Security and Cooperation, said that fears were growing among CIS republics such as Kazakhstan and Kirghizistan that what is happening in Chechnya could happen to them in the future. Russia intends to resume shipments of natural gas to Serbia and Montenegro. Russia's Prime Minister, Oleg Davidoff, signed an agreement in Belgrade today and warned that Russia would resign from the UN Sanctions Committee if that body should object to the delivery of natural gas. Sanctions were imposed on Rump Yugoslavia in 1992 and partially lifted last year after Serbia promised to stop supplying military hardware to Bosnian Serbs. The UN sanctions still apply to natural gas.

February 8, 1995, Radio Netherlands:
President Alija Izetbegovic has stated that he is prepared to negotiate with Bosnian Serb leaders to spare civilians from further suffering. Until now, the Muslim-led Bosnian Government has refused to negotiate with the Serbs unless they accept the International Contact Group's peace plan.
Interviewed on Bosnian TV, Mr. Izetbegovic said that Bosnia would eventually defeat Serb forces. But he

questioned if the struggle would be worth the price paid by civilians.

In Paris, the IMF representing Michael Camdessus said that negotiations for credits of 6.5 billion U.S. dollars have ended without agreement. He said Moscow has not curbed its war in Chechnya this has sent inflation in Russia rising.

February 10, 1995, *Wall Street Journal:*

Serb forces launched a mortar barrage on Sarajevo ending a six-week-old ceasefire.

February 10, 1995, Radio Netherlands:

In a meeting of CIS member states in Alma Ata, Kazakhstan, Russian President, Boris Yeltsin, said measures had been taken to stop the fighting in Chechnya. A Russian proposal for a joint defense of CIS borders (with other CIS member states) was rejected by members of the conference of CIS Ministers.

Bosnian Serbs blocked convoys bound for Sarajevo after the Bosnian Government detained a Serb woman working for the refugee office. The Bosnian authorities have charged her with passing on classified information to Serb forces besieging Sarajevo.

February 12, 1995, Die Deutsche Welle:

Still no supplies are reaching Sarajevo as Bosnian Serbs cut off the road from the airport to the city. Fighting in Bihac has escalated. Heavy artillery fire is reported as Serbs mount an assault.

February 13, 1995, Die Deutsche Welle:

In Ingustia, the Russian Commander in Chief, Aslan Rushidov, discussed a ceasefire. The Russian commander has instructed Artillery to hold fire.

German Foreign Minister, Klaus Kinkel, has said that fighting has become intolerable around Bihac and has contacted Alain Juppe to create a European plan for aid delivery to relieve the people in the town who are starving under a food blockade. The Serbs are trying to force them to surrender by letting barely 50% of the food get through for six months. (The fifty percent figure is exaggerated as it was closer to 20% and considered inedible in western countries. Such was the extent of corruption in the UN program to provide food to Bosnia).

UN Secretary General Boutros Boutros Ghali is quoted as saying that if Croatians do not renew the UN mandate or if the ban against one of the warring sides is lifted, all UN troops will be withdrawn.

In The Hague, the War Crimes Tribunal has indicted 21 Serbs for war crimes in the former Yugoslavia. An arrest warrant has been issued for the arrest of the former commandant of the Omerska *detention camp*, Sergei Mlakesh. Only one of the 21, Tadan Dusek, is in custody in a German prison. Trials are scheduled to begin January 1996.

Bosnian Serb leader, Radovan Karadzic, says he is not prepared to extradite any of the accused. He says he does not *recognize* any on the list of suspects drawn up by the tribunal.

February 13, 1995, Radio Netherlands:
A UN spokesman said the population of Bihac is starving after having been cut off from food supplies by the Bosnian Serbs and (renegade) Abdic's Muslims for six months.

Meanwhile, fierce fighting is report around Bihac. Bosnian Serbs have sent reinforcements into the area. The fighting is a threat to the truce signed in January.

Witnesses and victims of the detention camps of Omerska say the Muslims and Croat civilians held at the camp were subjected to brutal treatment ranging from rape to violent beatings.

The parliament of the self-declared Serb republic in Bosnia has again rejected the latest peace plan put forward by the International Contact Group after an eleven-hour session in the Bosnian city of Sumas. Radovan Karadzic had dismissed the plan as unacceptable. It calls for a division of Bosnia in almost equal parts.

February 14, 1995, BBC:

The International Contact Group's forth proposal is to lift sanctions against Serbia if it recognizes Croatia and Bosnia/Herzegovina of the former Yugoslavia. Officials in Washington said a lifting of the bans would include shipments of fuel to Serbia. In *return, President Milosevic would have to tighten its ban on embargoing the Bosnian Serbs* who refuse to endorse the peace plan put forth by the International Contact Group. An American official said the latest proposal had been approved by the Contact Group and would be presented to President Milosevic soon.

A BBC correspondent in Belgrade said the proposal appears to be overly optimistic as President Milosevic is unlikely to recognize the other former Yugoslav republics unless he is sure of a reward.

The UN says it believes the Bosnian Government troops now control most of the safe areas of Bihac in northwestern Bosnia. The UN spokesman said it had unconfirmed reports Bosnian forces had beaten back Serb forces and captured three areas east of Bihac town. UN officials said that Croatian Serbs of the Krajina have promised to let a UN convoy pass through later today with food and medicines for the civilians of Bihac.

Negotiations are to resume today over the breakaway republic of Chechnya. The talks in Ingustia are between the Chechen military commander, Arslan Rushidov, and Anatoly Kurikov, head of the Russian Interior Ministry of troops. The agreement signed Monday was to halt the use of heavy weapons, but the truce bogged down within hours after the signing.

The BBC correspondent witnessed heavy guns directing continuous fire into a Chechen village.

February 14, 1995, Radio Netherlands:

The International Contact Group is prepared to lift sanctions against Serbia temporarily if the Belgrade Government takes number of steps to bring the conflict in Bosnia and Croatia to an end. The group has called on Serbia to recognize Bosnia and Croatia and to help to tighten its embargo against the Bosnian Serbs. In addition, it wants Serbia to promise to remain neutral if the conflict between Croatia and Croatian Serbs flares up again. Bosnian Serb leader, Radovan Karadzic, has warned he will not sign any ceasefire accords unless the international community comes up with an acceptable peace plan before May the First. The four-month ceasefire currently in effect in Bosnia expires at the end of April.

In Russia, the Committee of Mothers of Military Conscripts intends to take President Yeltsin and the Minister of Defense and the Minister of Foreign Affairs to the International Court of Justice in The Hague. They accuse the Russian leaders of human rights violations in Chechnya. In reference to recent dismissal of generals, the mothers say they have no use for such measures but would prefer to see them brought to trial.

Meanwhile, Russian spokesmen have expressed pessimism about the prospect for a definitive truce. A limited ceasefire announced Monday has been repeatedly violated.

February 15, 1995, Die Deutsche Welle:

A Social Democrat politician interviewed in Cologne said the teaching of Islam as a world religion in German schools would be an important way of counteracting extremism. She said that lessons in Islam should be held in the German language so that all Muslim students attending schools in Germany could participate regardless of their mother tongue.

Alija Izetbegovic will address the German parliament in Bonn next month. The German Foreign Ministry will give a report to the German parliament on the state of the Bosnian nation beginning on March 17. The invitation to Mr. Izetbegovic was extended last week in Sarajevo by Minister of Foreign Affairs, Claus Kinkel.

The European Parliament has protested to Russia over its refusal to allow a delegation from the assembly to travel to Russia and Chechnya. The official protest was announced in Strasbourg by the parliament's president, Klaus Mench. He told reporters that the president of the Russian parliament, Ivan Grukin, had branded the planned visit as interference in Russia's internal affairs. Part of the purpose of the visit would be to examine how the EU could aid in the reconstruction in the parts of Chechnya destroyed by the Russian military invasion.

February 15, 1995, Radio Netherlands:

The 51 member organization of the Islamic Conference has called upon the warring parties in Afghanistan to cooperate with UN peace efforts. The Muslim organization has issued a statement saying the Afghan people have had enough of the fighting various factions have tried to seize the power in Afghanistan over the past three years. The Organization of the Conference says the relatively easy advance made by the fundamentalist Taliban Movement (which wants to restore order in Afghanistan) is evident of the people's desire for peace. The United Nations is hoping to meet with the warring parties this week to discuss replacing the current Afghan Government with a transitional council, which should function as a new interim government.

Three million Afghan refugees in Pakistan sent their children to Islamic schools not knowing the British created these schools for the purpose of inciting hatred against Hindus. In these schools, the children of the refugees were given two years of military training and little true Islamic teachings. They are trained to accept deprivation and hard living conditions as part of the Taliban training and so their fighting spirit is tough. Having little income with which to support a government by the Taliban, they have resorted to drug trafficking. Osama bin laden obtains gifts of money from the Persian Gulf States where he is known as a hero as the CIA made him important because he speaks English well and was educated in the U.S. and Britain. He is esteemed by the Mujahideen for his support. However, due to the inaction of the Clinton Administration to protect the Muslims in Bosnia the Mujahidden became the Al Qaida which became involved in Chechnya when the Russian military began a wave of terrorism on defenseless Chechen civilians.

February 16, 1995, Dei Deutsche Welle:
Russian commander, Yevgeny Penkosin, said further negotiations in Chechnya would only delay the capitulation of Chechen forces.

(Russian) President, Boris Yeltsin, commissioned his first Deputy Prime Minister, Oleg Sokovitz, to deal with the Chechen situation.

UN aid workers have begun distributing food supplies to the starved populace of Bihac enclave in northwest Bosnia. Ninety-six tons of food arrived Wednesday with some destined for UN Peacekeeping troops.

February 16, 1995, Radio Netherlands:

The Republican dominated House (U.S. Congress) has drafted a bill slashing the American contribution the UN Peacekeeping operation. The House wants President Clinton to ask Congress for permission to participate in any future UN Peacekeeping mission.

Next year's presidential and parliamentary elections in Russia are scheduled to go ahead. A summit meeting between President Clinton and President Yeltsin is uncertain.

The evacuation of ten children from the Bihac enclave finally united them with their families. A food convoy arrived in Bihac, the first in some time, and another is scheduled to leave this weekend from Zagreb.

February 17, 1995, BBC:

Mohmoud Masteri is expected to hold talks with President Rabbini in Kabul later today in an attempt to overcome hiatus in the transfer of power to an interim council. This move has been complicated by the growing strength and opposition from the student Taliban Movement.

Chechens and Russians exchanged partial lists of prisoners but the exchange halted with a breakdown in the truce.

Andrei Kozyrev said he did not come to Belgrade to persuade Mr. Milosevic to recognize Bosnia and Croatia but to hear his views on the latest peace proposals by the International Contact Group.

February 17, 1995, Swiss Radio:

The round of violence in Bahrain over the scheduled deportation in December of the Shia religious leader, Sheik Ali Salmon, has brought Saudi Security Forces to the island nation. Bahrain opposition leaders tried to present a petition signed by a reported 20,000 people. This petition calls for the restoration of the constitution, which was suspended in 1975, when the country's parliament was dissolved. Since then, the Emir has ruled by decree.

February 18, 1995, Die Deutsche Welle:

The forces of rebel Muslim leader, Frikret Abdic, have launched an offensive on the Bihac enclave in Bosnia. UN officials say Abdic is holding back a relief convoy destined for the civilian population in the Bosnian Government controlled enclave.

The UN Sanctions Office has given Russia permission to supply natural gas to Serbia if it is used for humanitarian purposes.

The Russians have received permission from Poland to lay a 650-kilometer pipeline through Poland to supply Western Europe. No mention was made about Poland's entry into NATO.

February 18, 1995, Radio Netherlands:

NATO head, Mr. Willy Claes, former Belgian Minister for Economic Affairs, and Mr. Von Mirlo, head of Belgians Socialist Party, are being investigated for taking bribes in 1988 to influence the Belgian Government's decision to purchase 48 Italian Augusta helicopters. Four people were arrested last week in connection with the scandal.

Two mortars landed in a Sarajevo suburb and at least one house was damaged, but no report of casualties was reported. Serbs said this action was taken in response to the deaths of two Serb in Vojhabic, a Serb held village just outside Sarajevo. The Serbs are threatening to block further transportation aid to Sarajevo as reprisal for the incidence.

February 19, 1995, Die Deutsche Welle:
Russian negotiator, Andrei Kurikov, says Russia is still seeking a political solution to the crisis in the Caucasus. He also said that further ceasefire talks are pointless after Chechen rebels attacked Russian soldiers in Grozny last Saturday. Chechen forces in turn have accused the Russians of violating the ceasefire.

In the Serb capital of Belgrade, talks are to take place on the latest peace proposals put forth by the International Contact Group. Representatives of the group are to meet with President Slobodan Milosevic. Prospects of a successful outcome are nil as the Serbs refuse to recognize Croatia and Bosnia/Herzegovina, the conditions for lifting the sanctions on Rump Yugoslavia.

A German magazine alleges that Serbs have threatened to detonate a bomb filled with nuclear waste in a German city if Germany sends troops to Bosnia or otherwise intervenes in the Bosnian crisis.

February 19, 1995, Radio Netherlands:
The Chechen capital of Grozny has come under heavy Russian artillery fire just hours after a weeklong ceasefire expired. Earlier, fighting was report in Ogun east of the capital. But the Russians and the Chechens say there is little hope of extending the ceasefire.

The commander of Russian forces, Anatoly Kurikov, said all chances of a peaceful solution have evaporated.

Serbian President, Slobodan Milosevic, has told Russian Foreign Minister, Andrei Kozyrev, that he won't recognize Croatia or Bosnia/Herzegovina until all sanctions against Serbia have been lifted. Under the plan, Bosnia is to be divided between the Bosnian Serbs and Muslims and Croats who have formed a federation. After his talks with the Serbian president, Mr. Kozyrev said that Moscow wants Serbia to accept the plan without any prior conditions.

February 20, 1995, Radio Montreal:
President Milosevic has rejected the acceptance of the International Contact Groups latest peace proposal which offers to lift economic sanctions against Rump Yugoslavia in return for recognizing Croatia and Bosnia. A point calls for Serbia and the Bosnian Serbs to renounce the idea of uniting Croatian and Bosnian Serbs into Greater Serbia, which Mr. Karadzic calls unacceptable.

February 20, 1995, Radio Netherlands:
Serbia and Montenegro are reported to have bought and installed over their territory an advanced Russian anti-aircraft system. The Sam 11 missile, code-named *Gadfly* by NATO, has a range of more than 30 kilometers. NATO command in Naples has confirmed to Radio Netherlands that the alliance radar recently picked up the distinctive shape of Sam 11's radar signal off the coast of Montenegro. But planes monitoring the skies over Bosnia have not come across any trace of the missile. According to the Russian manufacturer, what makes Sam 11 so effective is its ability to jam signals. Rumors that Serbia and Montenegro purchased the Sam 11's to protect their strategic targets have been circulating for some time.
The United States wants better relations between NATO and Russia.

In Belgium, Secretary General of NATO, Willy Claes and Karel von Meirel of the Flemish Socialist Party were under investigation for allegedly taking bribes in 1988 to influence the Belgian Government's decision to purchase 48 Italian made Augusta helicopters. The party's treasurer, Etienne Manger, has admitted he accepted about one and a half million dollars in bribes. But he said the money was channeled into party funds. Belgium's Department of Justice suspects that Mr. Manger denies that he is covering up for his superiors who include NATO Secretary General, Willy Claes and European Commissioner, Karel von Meirel. The scandal may affect the outcome of Belgium's early elections which have been called for the 21st of May, seven months ahead of schedule.

In Afghanistan, the militia known as the Taliban, has rejected the peace plan in its present form. They said endorsement of the future plan will depend on three conditions: the chief one being the deployment of a neutral force in the capital, Kabul.

The UN's proposal calls for the establishment of an interim council to take over from President Mohammed Rabbini whose term of office ended last year. In their swift onslaught of the past week, The Taliban have managed to seize control of large parts of Afghanistan and on Monday continued fighting was reported.

February 21, 1995, Die Deutsche Welle:

UN Envoy to Yugoslavia, Ashushi Akashi says that for the first time, the Croatian Serbs of the breakaway province of the Krajina have indicated a willingness to negotiate with the Croatian Government. The Croatian Government refusal to renew the UN Mandate has given rise to the idea that the Croatian Government Army will retake rebel Serb territory in the future.

A UN convoy of food has been held up by Frikret Abdic's renegade Muslims in Veluska Kladusa before reaching the civilians of Bihac town where some civilians are close to starvation.

The (newspaper) *Allgemeine Zeitung* in Germany revealed today that secret talks between Iran and Israel have been going on in Bonn in recent months. No disclosure of what the talks were about.

February 21, 1995, Radio Netherlands:

There is a move to strip diplomatic immunity from NATO Secretary General, Willy Claus, over allegations of Mr. Claes' involvement in a one and a half million dollar bribe to influence the Belgian Government's decision to buy 46 Italian made Augusta helicopters in 1988. Mr. Claes was Belgium's Economic Commissioner at the time. It is not clear who received the money. Most of the money was paid to a close friend of the former Socialist Party chairman and present European Commissioner, Karel von Meirel. The associate reportedly channeled the money to the financially troubled daily (newspaper) *Die Mogen*, but Mr. Claes and Mr. Meiret have denied any involvement.

According to a Russian Human Rights Organization, more than 24,000 civilians were killed in the fighting in the Chechen capital of Grozny after the end of January along with 3,700 children below the age of 14. The number of Chechen fighters killed was about 650 but no figures were disclosed on Russian military casualties.

Fighting flared up again today as Russian troops carried out fresh assaults on Grozny and its surroundings. The medical relief organization, *Medicins San Frontiers*, evacuated 11 orphans from the capital and doctors are concerned about the elderly in Grozny.

Yashushi Akashi has announced that the Croatian Serbs are prepared to engage in a new dialogue with the government of Croatia. Two weeks ago, the Serbs in the Krajina region broke all ties with the Zagreb Government when the Croatian Government announced it would not renew the UN Peacekeeping Mandate. One of the points under discussion today was free passage for UN convoys of relief goods for the enclave of Bihac. An agreement has been reached but no details have been made known.

Bosnia/Herzegovina and Russia are to establish diplomatic relations. In a first step, they exchanged official documents in Moscow today. The decision of the two countries to recognize each other was taken when Prime Minister Haris Silajic visited Moscow earlier this month. Russia's recognition of Bosnia increases pressure on Bosnian Serbs to sign the International Contact Group's peace plan for the republic. The Bosnian Government regards Russia as the Serb's most important ally.

February 22, 1995, Die Deutsche Welle:

A food convoy from Zagreb to the starving civilian population in Bihac has been held up for two days at Velika Kladusa by (Friket Abdic's) rebel Muslims and their Croatian Serb allies.

Meanwhile, Germany and Britain are sending envoys to Belgrade on Thursday to convince (Serbian) President, Slobodan Milosevic with a new peace plan for the former Yugoslavia. Last week, Mr. Milosevic told Russian Foreign Minister, Andrei Kozyrev, that he would only consider a plan if the UN lifted sanctions against Serbia.

Russian forces have taken the last road into the Chechen capital of Grozny, and are shelling villages to the south, east, and west of the city. Russian Defense Minister, Pavel Grachev, does not expect a speedy end of the war in the

Caucasus republic. He said that all discussions with Chechen President, Djokar Dudayev were pointless.

February 22, 1955, Radio Netherlands:

An interim council will take over the Afghan Government in March 21 in a proposal put forth by UN mediators in Afghanistan to Mahmoud Mestiri. The setting up of a transitional administration is an essential element in the peace plan for Afghanistan which Mr. Mestiri proposed to the warring parties last week. The UN mediator has indicated the newly emerged Islamic student militia, the Taliban has agreed to the plan. President Rabbini was to have handed over the government to the interim governing council earlier this week, but this became impossible in face of objections from the Taliban and the president's forces.

February 22, 1995, BBC:

Aircraft believed to be Lockheed Hercules military transport were seen to be landing or flying very low over the airfield of Tuzla which is controlled by the Bosnian Government and suspected of supplying weapons or military equipment to the mainly Muslim Bosnian Army.

There have been three sightings of the planes at Tuzla. As Paul Adams reports from Belgrade the mystery of their origin has been compounded by disagreements between the United Nations and NATO.

(Paul Adams speaking): "Three times this month, UN military personnel have reported the presence of large cargo planes at an airstrip near the main Tuzla airport. The sightings were all made after dark with the aid of night vision equipment. UN officials believe that the planes were supplying weapons or equipment to the Bosnian Army using low altitude delivery techniques practiced only by American, British, or French forces. In the first instance, large numbers of (Bosnian) government forces were observed in the area. UN observers were prevented from investigating the area and shots were fired in the air to keep them away from the scene. The UN's report has been the subject of controversy with NATO eager to deny the flights ever occurred. NATO even called on the UN to issue a statement contradicting the first two sighting and has even questioned the competency of those responsible for the report. These include a British officer in charge of information in northwestern Bosnia and a number of forward air controllers. The UN is standing by its observations and waiting for NATO to issue its report. The key question is who is behind the four mysterious flights. In the words of one British diplomatic source, "It would be impossible to do this kind of thing without the awareness of a major western power." He was referring first and foremost to the United States.

February 23, 1995, Die Deutsche Welle:

The prison deaths in the Algerian prison riot came to 98 and 4 guards. Without mentioning the prison deaths, President Yemin Zerual said that improving the economy was the key to ending Algeria's crisis. He said that *savage terrorism is tied to economic conditions.*

February 23, 1995, Radio Netherlands:

Intimidation of UN Peacekeepers in many places by Bosnian Government forces is obstructing the UN from its work. The UN hopes to extend the ceasefire in effect in Bosnia since the beginning of the year. The Sarajevo is refusing to take part in the talks because of continuing clashes in the Muslim enclave of Bihac. The fighting has caused widespread fear in the international community because of the danger it could spread into neighboring Croatia and the rest of Bosnia.

The International Contact Group has again held talks with Serbian president, Slobodan Milosevic in an effort to reach a peaceful settlement to the conflict in Bosnia. According to a French diplomat, the need for a breakthrough is more urgent now than ever.

Speaking to the Human Rights Commission in Geneva, Switzerland, Dutch Foreign Minister, Hans von Mirlo, said that a tribunal for suspected war criminals and a swift prosecution of war criminals after the a war would be guaranteed. The tribunal is currently convened in The Hague for war criminals in Bosnia and another one is being constructed in Tanzania for war criminals in Rwanda.

U.S. Ambassador to the UN, Madelaine Albright, is to tour a number of countries on the Security Council to convince these countries that lifting the oil embargo against Iraq would be an unwise move at this stage. Russia is submitting a resolution calling for an end to the sanctions (on Iraq) but the U.S. says that Baghdad has not met all the conditions: one of which Iraq dismantle its weapons of mass destruction. Ambassador Albright will begin her tour in Britain, then to the Czech Republic, Italy, Argentina, and Honduras.

According to authorities, the mutineers in the Algerian prison riot killed four guards. Eighty-one of the inmates killed were Muslim fundamentalists. The prison is in the center of Algiers and holds a number of fundamentalists waiting execution. It was stormed by Algerian Security Forces Wednesday ending the revolt in one of the bloodiest since political violence broke out three years ago.

UN personnel near Tuzla report that on three occasions, large cargo plane accompanied by fighters made low flights over or landed at Tuzla Airport. The UN personnel were prevented from closely examining what happened. At one point Muslim soldiers fired in the air to prevent the

Peacekeepers away. The UN told Radio Netherlands it has no reason to question the observations of its staff but that NATO should issue the final report on the case.

This report comes from **Hans Debray** of our newsroom.

"Was it a cover American operation as some claim? Did NATO turn a blind eye to an arms delivery to Bosnian Government Forces, which are officially banned under the UN arms embargo or was NATO itself involved? The unexplained event at Tuzla Airport is mysterious for several reasons. It is strange that on three occasions, radar planes flying over Hungarian air space and flying over the Adriatic Sea failed to see any planes flying in the area of Tuzla. There seems to be an information gap between the UN and NATO or as Janos Bokaisky of the Washington Based Center for Strategic and International Studies puts it, 'One can assume that NATO isn't necessarily telling the UN everything. The UN in addition isn't in a position to monitor all the flights over Bosnia and isn't getting all the information.

"Secondly, since the downing of Serb planes over Bosnia and in Croatia and the lack of effect and the lack of impact or follow-up by NATO, I think there has been hesitation to enforce the *no-fly* ban."

Note: The Russians were always included in all groups that made the *peace proposals* but Russian never abided by the arms and fuel embargo on the Serbs despite all UN embargos and sanctions against Serbia and the Bosnian Serbs).

Hans Debray continues, "The question remains whether the Tuzla incident represents an American covert operation. I asked Janos Bokaisky if the Americans would conduct such an operation without informing its allies."

Janos Bokaisky, "It is conceivable although I personally doubt it at this point unless it was a covert operation that went wrong. In terms of the fact that people on the ground monitored it, I would say some of the NATO countries, particularly the United States, are deliberately not enforcing the no-fly ban and not enforcing the delivery to the Bosnian side. A number of flights have been coming into Bosnia over the years originating from various parts of Croatia or outside the immediate conflict zone. One suspects these are weapons deliveries are on behalf of the third world countries, let's say Muslim countries, to the Bosnian Government and in some cases maybe this was another incident that NATO monitored the flight and hasn't interfered."

(While former President, Jimmy Carter, and the International Contact Group are trying to achieve peace in Bosnia, Bokaisky argues illegal flights over Bosnia are just one of the many signs hinting of anything but peace in the area).

Janos Bokaisky, "I think the Bosnian Government has calculated the UN and NATO aren't going to defend them and protect the (territorial) integrity of Bosnia as they are not going to force the Serbs to give up 20% or 30% of the territory they now hold just to comply with the International Contact Group's peace plan. Bosnians are retraining their army and much more professional with weapons and money coming from third world countries and are preparing for an offensive.

"The Serbs on their part aren't gearing up for an offensive. They do continue to get weapons from Serbia. Most of the over-flights over Bosnia originate from Serbia to their brethren in Bosnia. The Croats themselves have been arming themselves for the past two years in collaboration with Bosnian forces. All indications are that we are going to have a major offensive in the next two months."

February 24, 1995, Die Deutsche Welle:

Mostar is a city where Muslims and Croats converge and cultures collide. Once it was one of the architectural jewels of Ottoman Empire, Mostar has seen most of its historical sites destroyed and others in ruins. For Muslims living in the crossfire, it has been harder than ever to mend relations with neighbors. **Guido Banhauer** reports that only by Muslims renewing their faith (Islam) has it been possible for them to move forward. 50,000 Muslims live in the eastern half of the city. The Neratva River was the front line. It appears to be the borderline between east and west. The Starmas Bridge was considered a symbol of a multi-cultural city has already been destroyed and in its place is a hand bridge. Since the war, old Muslims became religious. There is little interest to cross over to the Catholic Croat side which is little damaged. All Muslims have been forced to the eastern side, which is heavily damaged as the Croats trained their big guns on that part of the city. Religious diversity was once a symbol of the city and all civilians were buried in common cemeteries without regard to religion. Now there are Catholic and Muslim cemeteries.

February 24, 1995, Radio Netherlands:

NATO Secretary General, Willy Claes, said NATO discussions on North Africa and the Middle East about the destabilizing effect with the increase of armaments in the region. Mr. Claes repeated that NATO is not looking for a confrontation with Islam. The question of Islamic fundamentalism was not on the agenda.

February 25, 1995, Die Deutsche Welle:

Civilians of Muslim ethnicity are being expelled and their homes ransacked by Bosnian Serbs in the towns around Banja Luka and Glisha. About a half a million Muslims and

Croats lived in the region before the war began in 1992. The count is now down to about 80,000 (When 180,000 Croatian Serb refugees crossed into Bosnia Serb controlled territory, pressure was put on Bosnia to halt its attempt to free its territory while Croatians were not pressured to stop fighting.)

In Central Bosnia, Muslim led Bosnian Government troops are blocking UN buses to protest the presence of two Bosnian Serb liaison officers sent to Begonon and Gradiska under terms of Bosnia's two-month ceasefire.

February 26, 1995, Radio Netherlands:

The Serbs have unleashed a new wave of terror among Muslim civilians in northern Bosnia. A spokesman for the High Commissioner of Refugees said Bosnian Serbs have resumed their policy of *ethnic cleansing*. Muslims in villages around Gradisha and Banja Luka are being systematically assaulted, robbed and shot at. The situation is so serious that entire villages have asked to be evacuated and Bosnian Serbs have blocked three access roads to Sarajevo. The UN says this may be the result of the UN's refusal to give Serbs the fuel they say is necessary to carry out patrols along the route.

Twenty-four elite Russian troops were killed in an explosion in a village near the Chechen capital of Grozny.

Emissaries of Saudi Arabia and Yemen met in Mecca to establish a commission to demarcate the border between the two countries and monitor troop movements and form committees to promote trade and cultural ties between the two countries. The two sides promised not to permit any political, military, or (news) media against the other.

Israel, Mauritania, Egypt, Morocco, Tunisia, and Algeria have met to discuss ways to combat terrorism (Algeria has applied for admission to NATO).

February 26, 1995, Die Deutsche Welle:
President Demirel of Turkey arrived at the Croatian Adriatic port of Split. He will go to Sarajevo for talks with Bosnian President Izetbegovic and then visit UN Turkish forces in Central Bosnia.

February 26, 1995, Radio Netherlands:
Previously, there were only Bosnian Serbs who blocked the UN troops, but the Bosnian Government troops have blocked UN British troops in central Bosnia for three days.

Elsewhere, (UN) Canadian forces are unable to move because Muslim forces are obstructing the road. The UN says these latest actions reflect the Bosnian Government's confidence in its own army and the wish to exert more authority over its own territory.

Russia signed an agreement with Serbia and Montenegro for closer military cooperation. Defense Minister, Pavel Grachev, says the treaty will not take effect until economic sanctions against Rump Yugoslavia have been lifted.

February 27, 1995, Radio Netherlands:
NATO Secretary General, Willy Claes, admitted he was aware of Augusta Military Helicopter Company's offer to bribe Belgium's Socialist Party when he was Economic Minister of Belgium. Yesterday, (U.S.) Vice President Al Gore expressed his country's confidence in Willy Claes.

February 28, 1995, *Wall Street Journal:*
Russian forces have completely surrounded the Chechen capital of Grozny. For the first time since the separatist war began the Russians unveiled plans for rebuilding Chechnya.

Sarajevo suffered its worst day of sniping and shelling since a ceasefire took effect January 1st. One civilian was killed and four others were wounded.

UN officials said Turkish President Demirel's visit had *provoked* the attack by the Serbs and his trip was called off.

February 28, 1995, Die Deutsche Welle:

Russia has signed an accord with Rump Yugoslavia on military cooperation once all UN sanctions have been lifted. Today's signing in Moscow was carried out by Russian Defense Minister, Pavel Grachev, and his Yugoslav counterpart, Pavra Bulotovic. Both said they placed value on the framework document.

In separate talks with Bulotovic, Russian Foreign Minister, Andrei Kozyrev, urged the world community to lift the sanctions against Serbia.

The 15,000 UN Peacekeepers spread across Yugoslavia known as UNPROFOR have a new commander, Lt. General Bernard Janvier, who is taking command in Zagreb from compatriot, General de la Presle in Zagreb. He is the fifth commander of UNPROFOR since UN troops were assigned to the Balkans.

Germany's President Herzog, speaking in Tirana, Albania, called on Serbs to stop human rights abuses in Kosovo. Addressing the Parliament in Tirana, Herzog said the repression could not be justified. He also said Bonn supported a solution that respected present borders by re-establishing Kosovo's autonomy. Serbian President Milosevic stripped Kosovo of its autonomous status in 1989. Ninety percent of its population is ethnic Albanian. In reference to neighboring Macedonia and Greece, President Herzog also urged Albania to show more readiness to compromise in disputes.

In Brussels, Yohan Delain, a former close associate of NATO Secretary General, Willy Claes, has been arrested. Delain was a senior member in the Ministry of Economics which was headed by the then Cabinet Minister Mr. Claes in the 1980's. According to investigators, at this time the Socialist Party of Belgium was paid bribes worth 2.5 million Marks for their part in putting through a deal involving the Belgian Government's purchase of 46 military helicopters made by an Italian armaments firm. In the past, Claes denied all knowledge but observers now say that he vaguely remembers some of the details.

(German) Foreign Minister, Klaus Kinkel, speaking in Bonn, said that Russia could not claim a right to a veto (in NATO). The events in Chechnya demonstrated that a defense structure in Europe could not be achieved without Russia. Kinkel said that NATO and its partners were hoping the Russia would soon sign up for Partnership and Peace NATO Program. In December (1994), Russia refused to sign the document because of NATO plans to expand eastward.

In Washington, Count Otto Landsdorf, honorary chairman of the Liberal Democrats (FDP) said that the time was right to admit Poland, Hungary, and the Czech Republic to NATO. This was logical in view of the fact that these three countries share the same ideals as the countries of the western alliance. At the same time, Count Landsdorf called for a treaty of strategic cooperation between Russian and NATO.

Meeting with the leading members of the Russian military, Defense Minister Grachev defended his tough military offensive in Chechnya and said that there could be no ignoring the Chechen rebels who have used the current ceasefire to recoup losses and regroup. He said the hard core of resistance in the capital, Grozny, had finally been broken.

February 28, 1995, Radio Netherlands:
Fighting has broken out all over Bosnia with the mainly Muslim Army of Bosnia launching a surprise offensive against Bosnian Serbs near Trovnic in central Bosnia. At least 35 Serbs are said to have been killed there.

In the capital of Sarajevo, 600 incidents from sniper fire to heavy fighting between Muslims and Serbs have been reported.

In the south of Bosnia, Serb forces have clashed with Croat forces and heavy fighting has erupted again between Bosnian Serbs and (Bosnian) Government forces in the Muslim enclave of Bihac. The enclave is not covered by the ceasefire.

The Iranian Government recently moved heavy artillery into forward positions in islands in the Straits of Hormuz (the entrance to the Persian Gulf). (U.S. President) Mr. Clinton said the situation would be closely monitored but he added that the deployment was no cause for concern.

March 3, 1995, Radio Netherlands:
Dutch General, Jan Willem Brinkman, will command Dutch troops in the projected evacuation of Peacekeeping troops from Bosnia and Croatia. General Brinkman is to take command of the NATO air division, which is comprised of about 20,000 troops.

March 4, 1995, Die Deutsche Welle: The Islamic Alliance in Mannheim (Germany) inaugurated the largest mosque in Europe. The mosque can hold 2,500 worshippers. Mannheim's mayor, Gerhard Widder, called the mosque a sign of tolerance and cooperation. The chairman of the Islamic Alliance in Mannheim, Altaman Utizeen, said the mosque would help integrate Turks into (German) society.

March 4, 1995, Radio Netherlands:

Bosnian Serbs have allowed ten trucks to proceed into the enclave of Srebrenica. The convoy will supply food to the Dutch Peacekeepers in Srebrenica, which is short of food supplies.

The supporters of Muslim (renegade) Frifret Abdic have been holding a group of medical aid workers for the past five days in the northwest enclave of Bihac who had just delivered medical supplies to a hospital in Bihac and then were taken hostage.

French Peacekeeping forces in Sarajevo fired on snipers targeting civilians in Sarajevo. They fired precision rifles from their armored vehicles. As far as anyone knows, no one was hurt. In a separate incident, a civilian was shot last Saturday while working in his garden. He later died of the wound.

March 6, 1995, Radio Netherlands:

The Afghan Military launched an offensive against a Shiite enclave in Kabul. Some people were killed and at least 140 were injured from rocket and artillery fire. The district in the southwest of the capital is held by the pro-Iranian Hezbeh Wordat. Last month, the Shiite fighters became isolated when the Islamic Taliban Militia defeated their major ally, troops of the opposition leader, Slobidin Hekmatyar. Sixteen aid workers are trapped in a suburb of Kabul.

The Bosnian and Croat Governments have formed a military alliance against Serb separatists who occupy large parts of both countries. The new alliance raises the specter of a wider Balkan War.

In Paris, the three European partners of the International Contact Group are to meet to discuss the specter of a wider Balkan War.

The GIA (Group Islamic Algerian) is considered a threat in Belgium with the Belgian Government moving to protect foreign embassies in Brussels and Air Algeria airline offices.

March 11, 1995, *Wall Street Journal:*

Heavy fighting broke out in the strategic Tuzla region. The Muslim led Bosnian Army launched a major offensive, rocking the already shaky ceasefire. That sparked a stiff Serb response with nineteen people were reported killed in Tuzla from Serb shelling.

March 13, 1995, Houston *Post:*

UN officials said Saturday said they were considering retaliation against guns targeting planes at Sarajevo Airport after two UN planes were hit Saturday.

March 20, 1995, Houston *Post:*

Afghan President Burredin's force has now taken the suburb held by Shia forces. He now controls all of Kabul for the first time in years.

March 22, 1995, *Wall Street Journal:*

Fighting flared for the second day near Tuzla in northeastern Bosnia. Attacks were less fierce than on Monday as the Bosnian Government forces showed signs of waning. UN officials said that both sides were blocking the movement of UN troops.

March 24, 1995, *Wall Street Journal,* Russian Foreign Minister Kozyrev told U.S. Secretary of State Warren Christopher in Geneva, that the U.S.-Russian honeymoon has come to an end with the U.S. objection to the war in Chechnya and U.S. opposition to Russia's sale of a nuclear reactor to Iran.

April 7, 1995, Radio Netherlands:
An attack on the Bosnian Government held suburb in Sarajevo signals the greatest breech of the ceasefire signed last January, and undermines the efforts to extend the truce.

April 8, 1995, BBC:
Last November, the stalemate in Bosnia was broken and the front lines started to move. Bosnian forces and their former enemies (Bosnian Croats) won back territory around Kupres and Herzegovina north of Zenice where the Serbs fled from a string of hill villages without putting up much of a fight. The ceasefire brokered by former (U.S.) President, Jimmy Carter, four days before Christmas, was heralded by the UN as an opportunity for peace.

In fact this was a chance to rearm, reequip, retrain, a half time if you like to call it, coming into the field. There now begins, said a friend of mine, 'the first phase to liberate all of Bosnia.'

This has been seen to come a month in advance of the end of the Carter brokered ceasefire, Bosnian Government forces attacked and made major gains in the Maja Vitza hills east of Tuzla and on Vlasic Mountain above Trovnic in central Bosnia. The winter weather didn't impede Bosnian forces, it helped them. They took Vlasic because of deep snows that covered the mine fields. That enabled Bosnian soldiers to walk over the minefield without detonating the mines. None of this were we able to see for ourselves as (Bosnian) Government forces cut off our access to observe its forces. Not only are we not able to get to the Bosnian Army's 7th Corps at Trovnic, we are not able to get into

Trovnic at all. As I work mostly in TV, the pictures I use mainly are *soldier vision.* These come from high aid cameras resting on the shoulder of a uniformed **Bosnian Serb** soldier.

The United Nations is similarly handicapped and denied freedom of movement. There are two reasons for this: The Bosnian Army is quite naturally spy conscious and believes the Bosnian Community monitors are running a military intelligence gathering operation, to put it pure and simple. Also the Bosnian Government does not want this offensive action to be seen as breaking the ceasefire signed last December. (British *war* correspondents were accused of spying for Serb forces).

So how do we know what is going on at all? Partly from the United Nations which has observation posts and troops on the ground and the reports they put out called "Warring Parties Activity". Except those are not *parties* and they are not engaged in *activities* but *war.* (**Martin Bell,** BBC's correspondent in Belgrade).

April 9, 1995, Die Deutsche Welle:

The Russian Army is preventing Red Cross workers and Western reporters from entering Smashky to verify the massacre of 700 Chechen civilians by Russian troops.

Uzbek opposition leader, Saleh, accused President Izlamkatemov of human rights violations. In an interview with Deutsche Welle: Saleh said the situation in Uzbekistan is worse now than under former Soviet rule. Saleh cited censorship of the media and repression of political opponents by the Uzbek Secret Police and called on German President, Roman Herzog, who is in Uzbekistan, to raise the question of Human Rights. Saleh, an author, currently lives in exile in Germany.

April 10, 1995, Die Deutsche Welle:

NATO ordered flights over Sarajevo to prevent Serb gunners from firing mortar rounds into the city. NATO planes flew over the city Sunday but attacked no Bosnian Serb positions. At least four people have been killed in (mortar) attacks on the Bosnian capital.

Bosnian chief Haris Siladjic, called for more pressure on the Serbs by the international community and the government in Belgrade.

The 62-year old Gradovsky has been charged by the German Government as having acquired arms for East Germany in the seventies from weapons makers through cover firms in Germany and Austria. His lawyer contends the trial is unconstitutional.

Kazakhstan rejected an accord to allow 500,000 ethnic Germans in Kazakhstan to immigrate to Germany. The government in Alma Ata gave the reason for the rejection that other ethnic minorities might make a similar demand. However, an agreement was reached with Germany on the fight against organized crime. German President, Roman Herzog, is currently on a trip in Kazakhstan

April 10, 1995, Radio Netherlands:

The UN Peacekeepers protecting Sarajevo Airport are on maximum alert as Serbs refuse to guarantee the safety of planes involved in the international airlift linking Sarajevo with the rest of the world. An article in Britain's *Daily Telegraph* says that *the International Contact Group is engaged in a mission of helplessness.* As all sides have returned to war, there is little to justify the group's existence anymore.

April 11, 1995, Die Deutsche Welle:

Uzbek President, Karamazov, said he was pleased by the amount of interest shown by German businesses to invest in Uzbekistan.

In Gottingen, an emissary of the Chechen Government, Mr. Yusef, said that Chechen leader, Djokar Dudayev, favors a political solution in Chechnya and that reconciliation with Russia was still possible.

April 12, 1995, Die Deutsche Welle:
UN officials said it was impossible to obtain guarantees from Serb liaison officers at the airport and Serb military barracks nearby to stop attacks on the planes. Di Marco says that hours of fruitless negotiations between the UN and the Serbs, the International Contact Group decided to fly on the Zagreb for talks with President Franjo Tudjman.

April 13, 1995, *Wall Street Journal:*
Fighting flared in Tadjikhistan for the sixth day as Islamic guerrillas attacked a Russian border post along the Tadjikhistan border with Afghanistan. At least 31 border guards and 160 Tadzhik rebels have been killed.

April 13, 1995, Die Deutsche Welle:
Using terror against civilians to break rebel resistance in Chechnya, Russian soldiers who were drunk or under the influence of drugs murdered women and children in the farming town of Samasky, Wednesday.

The Red Cross puts the total of dead at 250, mostly civilians. Russian Human Rights Commissioner, Sergei Kabilov, claims the Russians want to end their campaign in Chechnya by May 9 as that is when world leaders, including President Clinton visit Moscow for the ceremonies marking the defeat of Germany in 1945. News agency, ITATASS says Russian troops have begun an all out assault on the last Chechen stronghold, Barmut in west Chechnya.

Turkey has recalled its ambassador to the Netherlands after that country recognized a Kurdish parliament in exile in The Hague. The Netherlands Government says Turkey violated Human Rights and had no right to put pressure on the Netherlands to bar the Kurdish assembly, which was formed legally under Dutch Law. The sixty-five-member parliament in exile says its membership is drawn from all exiled Kurdish groups including Turkey's outlawed Kurdish Pro-Democracy Group Party and the Marxist Kurdish Worker's Party, the PKK.

The Ministry of Interior in Bonn said that various agreements had been reached by the visit of Germany's President, Roman Herzog, especially in Uzbekistan for cooperation in fighting organized crime and drug smuggling.

Foreign Minister, Klaus Kinkel, told the Algerian Government to respect Human Rights in its fight with Islamic fundamentalists. The Foreign Office in Bonn said Mr. Kinkel told Algerian Foreign Minister, Mohammed Saleh Djambrey, that the Algerian Government should adhere to accepted legal means hold down Islamic violence.

April 14, 1995, Die Deutsche Welle:

Chechen rebels repelled a strong Russian attack on Barmut, the last Chechen rebel stronghold on the lowlands of western Chechnya.

French Prime Minister, Eduard Balladur, expressed his indignation at the cowardly murder of two men (French UNFROFOR solders) and will send French Defense Minister, Francois Lambert, for talks in Sarajevo. Both soldiers were shot by snipers.

Russian President Boris Yeltsin said he would probably sign the _____ treaty with the Ukraine after is has settled its dispute with the autonomous region of the Crimea, dominated by ethnic Russians (the Muslims of the Crimea were ruthlessly killed by Stalin or deported to Siberia in WW II). Ethnic Russians now form the majority of the population in the Republic of Crimea which is a part of the Ukraine. He also told the government in Kiev to observe the Human Rights of the ethnic Russians in the Crimea. Ukrainian authorities began a crackdown at the beginning of this month on pro-Russian separatists.

April 15, 1995, Die Deutsche Welle:
Russian Defense Minster, Pavel Grachev, has called for a review of the CFE (Conventional Forces in Europe) treaty, which limits the number of troops and armor Russia can deploy in the southern Caucasus region which includes Chechnya. Mr. Grachev says the political situation in the area has changed considerably since the treaty was signed. The military limitations agreed to five years ago are now unsatisfactory. Russia has been pressing for some time now to have the treaty altered since the Soviet Union's collapse and subsequent war have made it redundant (*obsolete*). The CFE Treaty was agreed to in 1990 by NATO and the former Warsaw Pact nations.

The Moscow news agency, ITATASS, says Russian forces have paused in their offensive on the town of Barmut giving the reason that the Russians want to avoid losses on both sides. TASS reports that Barmut is liable to fall in the next few days removing the last stronghold of the Chechens.

France has called for a senior cabinet meeting, Tuesday, to evaluate the French military position in Bosnia and consider the withdrawal of their forces from Bosnia. The move follows the deaths of two French Peacekeepers by sniper fire. French Defense Minister, Francois Leotard, visited Sarajevo after the shootings said the shootings had provoked indignation and rage in France and raised the possibility that France could withdraw its forces. Paris wants fresh discussions with European partners and NATO on Bosnia.

In another development, the Bosnian Serb news agency, Serna, has withdrawn a report claiming that leader, Radovan Karadzic had demanded of the Bosnian Serb parliament that he be made supreme commander of the Serb Army.

April 16, 1995, Die Deutsche Welle:

Russia has put forth a proposal to the Commonwealth Independent States to jointly secure and defend their southern border. The head of Azerbaijan's Border Force will not agree to this when it is presented this Saturday at a meeting of Foreign and Defense Ministers of the CIS.

Turkish authorities expelled 11 Germans arrested in the southeast of Turkey on the accusations of taking part in an unauthorized Kurdish pro-Kurdish demonstration.

In Tadzhikstan, the situation along the Afghan border has calmed down following an upsurge of fighting. According to Russian news agency, ITSTASS, the UN mediated talks have been postponed until Wednesday. The ceasefire will officially end next week.

April 17, 1995, Dei Deutsche Welle:

The airport in Sarajevo has been reopened for UN aircraft after being closed for eight days due to sniper fire.

Russian Defense Minister, Pavel Grachev, has asked for more leeway in the CFE Treaty limiting more troops and armor into Chechnya. The possibilities of Russian default on the CFE Treaty has cast an even larger shadow on the planned celebrations in Moscow, May 7, marking fifty year end of WW II. Western governments have harshly criticized Russian conduct in the war in Chechnya especially about the alleged atrocities. Human rights activists said Russian soldiers killed some 250 civilians in the village of Samasky and then tried to cover up the massacre. Observers say the

Russian military has ordered a renewed offensive in Chechnya to clear up the last pockets of rebel resistance before President Yeltsin welcomes western leaders to Moscow this May. But human rights abuses and Russia's willingness to scrap the CFE Treat are causing some fears among western leaders, which do not want to be seen as endorsing military aggression. There is fear that scraping the CFE Treat is only the tip of the iceberg. The speaker of Russia's upper parliament, Vladimir Shomoko, warns that... (The author's tape ran out and the end of the sentence was lost)

April 18, 1995, *Wall Street Journal:*
French presidential candidates argue over withdrawing French UN Peacekeeping troops from Bosnia following the killing of two French soldiers by sniper fire in Sarajevo. Front-runner, Jacques Chirac, has suggested that Peacekeepers in Bosnia should have the right to return fire and counterattack if they are fired upon.

April 18, 1995, Die Deutsche Welle:
Prime Minister Eduard Balladur, says he has proof that the two French UN Peacekeepers shot in Sarajevo was the work of *Muslim Snipers.* (Balladur covered up the abuse and torture French Peacekeepers by Serbs and his declaration was later proven a lie).
French Foreign Minister, Alain Juppe, has called for a meeting to discuss the pullout of French Peacekeeping force in Bosnia. Germany has asked France not to withdraw because of the humanitarian needs.
International mediators, Lord Owen (Lord Owen was later fired by the E.U. and is a rabid anti-Muslim) and Thorwald Stolenberg (later censured by the UN along with Yashushi Akashi for their actions in Bosnia) have met with

Serbian President Milosevic to discuss *possible* violations of Serbian arms and fuel blockade against the Bosnian Serbs.

Croatian Government troops have taken important high ground, which puts them in artillery range of the Croatian towns of Knin, a stronghold of the Krajina (Croatian) Serbs.

April 19, 1995, News in Houston, Texas, from all Houston TV stations:

The Murrah building in Oklahoma City is blown up. Dr. Ron Hatchett and Steve Emerson appear on major national television with the title of *terrorism experts* and say this is the work of Muslim terrorists. President William Jefferson Clinton said on national television network that **this is obviously the work of Muslim terrorists.**

A Jordanian American is arrested in London on his way to Jordan was flown to the USA because there was wiring in luggage that can be used in making a bomb. Oklahoma State Police arrested a man driving a car and identified him as Timothy McVeigh, awarded the Bronze Medal for valor in the Gulf War and he stands trial and convicted of the bombing. (McVeigh was an employee of the CIA which was hidden)/.

April 19, 1995, *Wall Street Journal: P. 11:*

Russian Foreign Minister, Andrei Kozyrev, said Russia might use military force to protect Russians living abroad. He said the status of ethnic Russians was *unsatisfactory* in many former Soviet Republics

April 19, 1995, Die Deutsche Welle:

Prime Minister Tansu Ciller said Turkey's troops would be withdrawn from Iraq soon but she would not give a precise date. The Prime Minister said that Turkish troops would march into the region again if the PKK reformed its forces.

France put forth a resolution demanding an extension to the ceasefire (scheduled to end May 11) and that all warring adversaries resume peace negotiations.

Conflicting reports from Barmut say Russian troops were forced out of Barmut while Moscow says Russian troops held on to the town. Russian commander, General Kulikov, said his troops had moved in on the north of Barmut on Tuesday and forced the last Chechen rebels out of western Chechnya after a battle of several weeks.

UN mediators will meet with Tadzhik opposition Muslim forces and Tadzhik Government representatives in Moscow to discuss a possible ceasefire. Russia told a meeting of CIA Defense Ministers in Moscow that it would take a force of 16,000 troops to seal the Tadzhik-Afghan border from incursions by Tadzhik rebels in Afghanistan.

April 19, 1995, *Wall Street Journal:*

Iraqi parliamentarians joined their government in rejecting a UN proposal to allow Iraq to sell limited amounts of oil to meet urgent humanitarian needs.

France threatened to withdraw its Peacekeepers if a truce isn't extended beyond April. (U.S.) Secretary of State, Warren Christopher denounced the Serbs for refusing to allow the U.S. Ambassador to fly out of Sarajevo, which forced the ambassador to take a perilous land route out of Bosnia, Monday.

April 20, 1995, *Wall Street Journal:*

France issued a 48 hour ultimatum to the UN declaring that French UN Peacekeepers would be withdrawn from Bosnia unless security is stepped up.

For a second day a threat from the Bosnians Serbs to fire upon UN (transport) planes for Sarajevo have forced a plane to turn around.

After holding Barmut for one day, the Russian troops abandoned the Chechen bastion. The acting commander of Moscow's operation was quoted as saying the troops withdrew after encountering rebel fire from the surrounding hills.

April 20, 1995, Die Deutsche Welle:

Chancellor Helmut Kohl called President Clinton's handling of the devaluation of the American dollar unacceptable and that he (Clinton) cannot buy dollars or support the dollar without balancing the budget and balancing international payments. Chancellor Kohl went on to criticize Russian President Yeltsin for lack of leadership.

French elections were characterized by French voters as choosing a man you hate (Balladur) and a man you distrust (Jacques Chirac).

April 21, 1995, Die Deutsche Welle:

Russia accused the BND (German intelligence service) of fabricating a story of Russian nuclear material being smuggled to claim Russia was lax in handling nuclear materials. Russia claims that the BND exported a quantity of plutonium to Moscow and then imported it back to Germany. At that time, several arrests were made (see August 17, 1994, Die Deutsche Welle broadcast) Bonn's Government denies the accusation but Social Democrats say its denial is not convincing.

German Defense Minister, Volker Ruhe, called on Russian President Yeltsin to take a firm hand in setting Russia's political course and strengthening democratic forces after General Alexander Ledbed warned that NATO's further expansion eastward would increase the danger of Russia's isolation and could lead to WW III. Mr. Ruh says further expansion eastward is unavoidable and NATO would not accept a Russian veto against former Warsaw Pact nations for joining (NATO).

The family of Chechen leader, Djokar Dudayev, has requested political asylum from the Ukraine. Members of the Ukrainian parliament have told DDW service that it is too early to say if asylum will be granted but that the Chechen leader himself would not be granted that privilege.

Milovan Djilas who first supported Tito and then opposed him and Communism in Yugoslavia, has died in Belgrade at the age of 83.

April 21, 1995, Swiss Radio:

The UN Security Council has two proposals on sanctions against Serbia. The first by western nations calls for review every 75 days instead of 100 days and applies a border inspection to air space as well. Serbia is accused of supplying ethnic Serbs in Bosnia by air. Russia has put forth a proposal to drop all sanctions against Serbia indefinitely.

Bosnia's warring factions have refused to extend a fragile ceasefire, which expires at the end of this month. Bosnian Prime Minister, Haris Siladjic, after talks with UN Envoy, Yashuchi Akashi, says that it was time for the international community as a last resort to lift the arms embargo against Bosnia. Bosnian Serb Leader, Radovan Karadzic, says after talks with Yashushi Akashi that the Muslims had sabotaged the ceasefire by regrouping and reinforcing their defenses. (Serbs were reinforced by Russian soldiers, supplied with arms, fuel, ammunition, and even had jet fighters and bombers from Serbia and Russia while Bosnia had none. The UN promised Bosnians *Safe Havens* and then UN officers said they have no *mandate* to protect civilians.)

September 21, 1995, Die Deutsche Welle:

Dusan Tadic will become the first defendant in the International War Crimes Tribunal since the aftermath of WW II. The Justice Ministry in Bonn gave the green light for Tadic to be delivered to the United Nations tribunal on the former Yugoslavia, based in The Hague in the Netherlands. Prosecutors in the southern city of Munich where Tadic was arrested last year said they would be handing him over soon but would not give an exact date. Tadic is accused of killing, raping, beating and torturing Croats and Bosnians carrying out a so-called *ethnic cleansing* in Bosnia's Priador region.

Germany's top intelligence official has denied that Bonn's federal intelligence agency faked plutonium smuggling last year (see August 17, 1994, DDW broadcast) to pressure Russia to tighten security within its nuclear industry. In his clearest statement to date, Ernst Schmidbauer said the discovery of almost 12 ounces of weapons grade plutonium at Munich's Airport last August was not stage-managed by German federal agents. Moscow claims the suspected smugglers brought it back to Germany. Bavarian legal officials say they were tipped off that a courier would be on board the Munich bound aircraft with a consignment of plutonium but were expecting a much larger amount – four kilograms.

(A DDW report from **Chris Simon** from Sarajevo): "Undaunted by his failure to get the warring parties in Bosnia to extend this crumbling ceasefire, the United Nations envoy to the former Yugoslavia vowed to return next week and try again. Yashushi Akashi met for two hours Friday with Bosnian President Izetbegovic but to no avail.

A government source said the Izetbegovic stood by Prime Minister Haris Siladjic's flat refusal to renew the ceasefire beyond May first. A defiant Siladjic reiterated his government's view about renewing the truce, saying, 'The international community was interested only in containment, preserving the *status quo* and that is unacceptable.'

A UN spokesman said Akashi will keep the pressure on both the Serbs and the Bosnian Government right up to the very end.

Putting an optimistic spin on the UN's failure to shift the focus from the battlefield to the Negotiating NATO planes *stormed* the Bosnian capital answering a sharp rise in firing incidents throughout the country during the past 24 hours. It is the soldiers in the front lines on both sides in this war about the refusal to accept the ceasefire by their respective leaderships as a green light to increase hostilities.

Friday afternoon, two mortars slammed down into the northeast section of the city. This after an overnight shelling on a Muslim suburb of Sarajevo killed a woman and severely injured her two children.

In Bihac fighting intensified along the northern border with Croatia while north central Bosnia and west of Tuzla, fighting rages with firing incidents not in the 100's but in the 1,000's. **(A smiling) Ashushi Akashi said "The Muslims think they can win, but they can't".**

April 26, 1995, *Wall Street Journal:* Russia's Prime Minister, Chernomyrdin, says fighting in Chechnya will halt May 15 as the Russians in Moscow prepare to receive world leaders for a May 9 Victory Day ceremony.

A Hezbollah suicide bomber crashed an explosives packed car into an Israeli army convoy in south Lebanon, injuring 22 people.

Turkey pulled out 20,000 more soldiers in northern Iraq. Prime Minister Ciller said the troops would return if needed. 12,000 Turkish troops remain in Iraq.

April 28, 1995, *Wall Street Journal:*

Bosnian Serbs battled with (Bosnian) Government on three fronts and a UN spokesman said the fighting was a **possible prelude to a full-scale war.** Serb forces refused to back down over (their determination) about who may land at Sarajevo Airport on UN planes.

May 1, 1995, *New York Times:* Croatia has launched a blitz offensive to retake land held by the Croatian Serbs. Serbs retaliated by sending rockets into Zagreb, killing six people and wounding 200.

May 3, 1995, *Wall Street Journal:*

Serbs fired (cluster bombs) rockets into the Croatian capital of Zagreb after the Croatian Army started its offensive on a Croatian Serb enclave a day earlier. Thousands of Croatian Serbs fled into Bosnia. Bosnian Serb leader, Radovan Karadzic, threatened to send help to the Serbs in Croatia. Meanwhile two hundred UN Peacekeepers are being held by Serbs for use as hostages.

Chechen rebels stepped up hit and run tactics on Russian soldiers. Russia's Ministry of Interior was bracing for a separatist offensive Tuesday (May 3) when world leaders will gather in Moscow.

May 8, 1995, *Wall Street Journal:*

Bosnian Serb mortars slammed into a mainly Muslim suburb of Sarajevo killing at least eight. Serbs also blew up (Catholic) churches in northern Bosnia and tried to set fire to another in reprisal for Croatia's attack on a (Croatian) Serb enclave last week.

May 15, 1995, *Wall Street Journal:*

Battles raged for the fifth day around the Croatian held Grasaje pocket bordering a vital Serb corridor in northern Bosnia.

May 16, 1995, Radio Netherlands: (Carole van den Ring reporting)

The Croatian enclave of Grasaje was under heavy shelling by Serb forces. UN observers say they counted 3,000 explosions within a matter of three hours. According to a spokesman for the Bosnian Croats, the attacking Serbs have been repelled. The Grasaje enclave is being defended by Bosnian Croat units and the Muslim dominated Bosnian Government Armed forces. The town has strategic importance to the Bosnian Serbs because it is close to the narrow corridor linking Serb territories inside Bosnia.

May 16, 1995, Die Deutsche Welle:

The War Crimes Tribunal of the UN in The Hague sustained allegations of genocide against Bosnian Serb leader, Radovan Karadzic, and Bosnian Serb General, Ratko Mladic. The case has been brought by Chief Judge, Richard Goldstone, on behalf of the Bosnian Government. Evidence of Bosnian authorities will be presented before the tribunal. The International Court has initiated its own investigation and accused the two leaders of genocide and crimes against humanity.

May 17, 1995, *Wall Street Journal:*

Five people killed and 26 wounded including two UN Peacekeepers in the worst fighting in Sarajevo in more than a year.

May 17, 1995, Radio Netherlands: (Carole van den Ring reporting)

The Croatian Army launched a major offensive against Krajina Serbs that unilaterally proclaimed independence four years ago.

The United States used its veto for the first time in five years in the UN Security Council to shield Israel from a resolution rescinding its seizure of mainly Arab lands in east Jerusalem and further construction in the occupied territories. Thirteen of the fourteen members on the Security Council voted for the resolution while the U.S. Ambassador (Madelaine Albright) gave the reason for the U.S. veto was that this was strictly an internal affair of Israel (this was not a good enough reason as an abuse of Human Rights and War Crimes committed by Israel).

The Belgrade Government sent a list of eight Dutch mercenaries (fighting for the Croatian Army) to the Dutch Ministry of Foreign Affairs. According to the media reports, their crimes include carrying out summary executions in Serb territory in Croatia. Dutch Foreign Minister, Hans von Mirlo, has passed the list on to the War Crimes Tribunal for the Former Yugoslavia in The Hague. The (Dutch) Justice Department is also being informed of the allegations.

There has been heavy fighting in various parts of Bosnia. In the northwest corner of the republic near the enclave of Bihac, the mainly Muslim Bosnian Government Army captured a town Rihac from the Serbs. UN observers say the Army is trying to drive out the Serb (military) in the region to bring an end to shelling attacks on the enclave. Bihac town again came under heavy shelling from Serb forces on Wednesday. A number of people have been injured. It is yet known how many were hurt.

In addition, heavy fighting continues between Government Forces and Serb Forces around the capital city, Sarajevo. Two UN Peacekeepers were wounded, one Russian and the other French.

Croatian Army is engaged in fighting Serb forces. Hostilities broke out after Serbs shelled Grasaje, a Bosnian Croat town on the border with Croatia. The Croat Army responded by attacking Serb positions.

Boutros Boutros Ghali has suggested UN Peacekeeping Forces in Yugoslavia be reduced and regrouped (the forces can't even take care of themselves as they are frequently taken hostage by the Serbs).

Mary 10, 1995, *Wall Street Journal:*

Hundreds of explosions rocked Sarajevo as the Bosnian Army and rebel Serbs fought for a hill near the capital. Serbian President Milosevic was on the verge of recognizing Bosnia in exchange for lifting international sanctions that are crippling the Serbian economy.

May 23, 1995, *Wall Street Journal:*

Bosnian Serbs broke into a UN heavy weapons depot near Sarajevo and carried off two artillery pieces. Shelling and sniping in Sarajevo left three people dead.

Gun battles raged in Karachi (Pakistan). Dozens of cars were set ablaze and an opposition group shut down the city with a strike, protesting police abuses. At least 25 people were killed, five of them from the security forces.

Sri Lanka's president declares talks with Tamil rebels are dead.

May 30, 1995, Die Deutsche Welle:

The Bosnian Serb Defense Council has rescinded all agreements with the United Nations. The Bosnian Serbs meanwhile have freed six French blue helmet soldiers who had been held hostage near Sarajevo Airport since last Friday.

Russia is to join NATO's Partnership for Peace scheme later this Wednesday, but Russia still opposes the alliance's plan to grant full partnership to the former Soviet satellites states in Eastern Europe. After months of hesitation, Russia's Foreign Minister, Andrei Kozyrev, is to meet with NATO counterparts in Nordwag, Holland, and formally adhere to the 16 nation's Partnership for Peace scheme.

May 31, 1995, *Wall Street Journal:*
While Bosnian Serbs took more UN soldiers hostage B.B. Ghali says to reduce the number of UN troops and regroup, Western nations rushed to bolster the UN Peacekeeping mission   The West is focusing on the American envoy to convince Milosevic to recognize Bosnia in return for lifting sanctions against Serbia.

May 31, 1995, Radio Netherlands (**Jackie Spears** reporting)
Radovan Karadzic has put forth three demands for the release of almost 100 UN soldiers and observers held by Bosnian Serbs. R. Karadzic wants the UN to refrain from using further force demilitarize the UN proclaimed safe havens.
At the NATO summit in the Dutch coastal town of Nordwag, Holland, (Russian Foreign Minister) Andrei Kozyrev said that NATO should play a less dominant role in Europe.
Russian attack helicopters, cruise missiles, and even ballistic (nuclear) warheads were displayed in military parade in Zagreb. The Russians had offered their anti-missile system earlier this year for sale to the United States and it is said to outperform the American Patriot missiles. Also, shown were some domestically made weaponry which included a domestically produced missile with a range of almost 400 kilometers. This is an important new asset,

which changes the regional balance of power. Croatia would be able to hit targets as far away as the Serbian capital of Belgrade. From a political point of view, it was noteworthy that the parade included former members of the Domo Brani, or the home guard of the WW II pro-fascist regime. Although Communist partisans were also present, including President Franjo Tudjman and his chief of staff, Janko Bebetzko, the public parade of the fascist's home guard is bound to be disturbing to Serbs still living in the country. For News line, *Hans Debray.*

June 1, 1995, Radio Netherlands (Spanish language):
The Bosnian Serbs say that if the international community attempts to free the UN hostages by force, there will be bloodshed.

June 1, 1995, Radio Netherlands (English):
Earlier this week, NATO said it did not rule out the use of force in liberating the almost 100 UN soldiers who were captured this last week in reprisal for NATO's air strikes. The Bosnian Serbs want to negotiate for the release of the hostages with the International Contact Group for Bosnia but the United States is opposed to this.

Meanwhile, the U.S. President, Bill Clinton, said he would be inclined to send troops to Bosnia if asked to do so.

Water is in short supply in Sarajevo and even though the streets are dangerous, everybody goes out to collect water whenever possible. Everyone says that everything is going back (to conditions) three years ago and that is no progress in Sarajevo.

(**Harold Dorbas** reporting from Sarajevo): There was some talk about NATO opening up a corridor to Sarajevo to allow convoys to get through. This will take a week to ten days and that such a corridor will have to be done by force.

Everyone in Sarajevo can receive television pictures broadcast by Bosnian Serb television of the UN hostages. The people know that NATO and the UN cannot protect them and that the Bosnian Serbs can do anything they want to do.

June 2, 1995, CNN:

A NATO plane has been shot down 15 kilometers from the Serb stronghold of Banja Luka. The plane is an F-16 but the nationality of the pilot is not known at this time (It was U.S. Captain Scott O'Grady). NATO planes are flying all about there and there are explosions, but it is not known if these explosions are from Serb anti-aircraft batteries or what. It is confirmed that the plane was shot down but the condition of the pilot was not known.

Earlier on CNN, Colonel Charles Taylor of the Strategic Forces Think Tank said that in his opinion, force is the only thing that will change the thinking of the Serbs. He was critical of Slobodan Milosevic and said Milosevic was lying about not supplying fuel and military supplies to the Bosnian Serbs. Taylor said it goes on at night. Former Bosnian desk officer, George Kenny, favored a diplomatic solution, which met the demands of the Serbs and for the UN to get out. (Kenny and four others resigned from State Department in 1992 because the *'hands off* Clinton policy' encouraged Serb atrocities)

June 3, 1995, *Wall Street Journal:*

Lt. General Alexander Ledbed resigned rather than command the 14th Army which ended a 1992 war in Moldavia and made Ledbed a national hero. Speculation is that he will run for president in 1996.

June 5, 1005, *Wall Street Journal:* Ayatollah Khamenei call for defiance of the U.S. at a ceremony marking the sixth anniversary of Ayatollah Khomeni's death.

June 8, 1995, *Wall Street Journal:*
   Serb mortars and tanks pounded Sarajevo just hours after Serbs released 111 UN Peacekeepers.
   Meanwhile, Bosnian troops tried to cut a (Bosnian Serb) supply line linking Sarajevo with Bosnian Serb headquarters.
   In Washington, Defense Secretary, William Perry, and Joint Chief of Staff, General Shalikashvili, spent the day defending administration policy before lawmakers (Congress).
   U.S. Envoy, Robert Frasure left Belgrade after failing to convince Serbia to recognize Bosnia.

June 8, 1995, Radio Swiss International:
   The U.S. House of Representatives voted 318 to 98 to scrap the Bosnian Arms Embargo. President Bill Clinton denounced the Hill (Congress) as "isolationist".
   NATO Ministers expressed support for a quick strike force and also found support for a UNPROFOR withdrawal. Secretary of Defense William Perry said the U.S. would not send ground troops to Bosnia.

June 9, 1995, Radio Netherlands (Carole van den Ring reporting):
   "The UN delegation said Bosnian Serbs have agreed to reopen corridors to allow humanitarian aid to flow into Sarajevo. The U.N delegation is headed by Anne Willem Bligh, from the Netherlands.
   The House Bill to lift the arms embargo against Bosnian Muslims also added a non-binding a provision for a wide-

ranging foreign affairs bill. The measure is aimed at helping Bosnian Muslims defend themselves better.

NATO has given unanimous approval for a rapid deployment force in Bosnia, composed of French, British, and some Dutch soldiers.

June 12, 1995, *Wall Street Journal:*

U.S. pilot Scott O'Grady arrived to a hero's welcome at Andrew's Air Force Base in Maryland. Meanwhile, a U.S. official said that just hours before O'Grady was shot down over Bosnia in his F-16, a Pentagon intelligence agency picked a *tentative* indication that a Bosnian Serb surface to air missile unit was operating in the area.

June 16, 1995, Radio Netherlands:

Speaking from Halifax (Canada) President Clinton said that although he sympathized with the Muslim led Bosnian Government, he could not consider supplying their army with weapons unless the UN pulled out its troops.

June 17, 1995, Radio Netherlands:

According to UN Peacekeeping Force, hostilities in and around Sarajevo subsided on Saturday after Friday's fierce fighting. However, fighting is continuing west of Sarajevo in a town Kisljec where Bosnian Croats have come to the aid of the government's offensive. In addition, fighting has flared up south of Sarajevo for control of a key Bosnian Serb supply route.

The independent Serbian news agency, *Besta,* says there is no chance all 26 UN hostages being released earlier than claimed by President Jacques Chirac. Mr. Chirac made this statement at the end of the G-7 summit conference in the Canadian city of Halifax (Nova Scotia).

The G-7 and Russia made a joint statement calling for the warring parties to stop the fighting and return to the negotiating table. They also called for the international community to avoid helping Iran develop nuclear weapons.

June 19, 1995, *Wall Street Journal:*
 Bosnian Serbs released the last 26 of the 370 UN Peacekeepers detained last month. While the UN agreed to free four Serbs.
 In the capital, Sarajevo, a shell killed seven people and wounded 12 others who were waiting in a line for water.
 Government Forces meanwhile launched an attack on Serb Forces near Tuzla in the northeast.

June 20, 1995, *Wall Street Journal:*
 Bosnian Government Forces battled rebel Serb for land north of Sarajevo that includes key Serb supply routes. Serbs appear to have regained control of a key route captured Friday by the Bosnian Army.
 Russia's Yeltsin said his country wouldn't allow anymore NATO air strikes against the Serbs. (Russia continued to break international treaties, break the UN sanctions against Serbia and the Bosnian Serbs, commit atrocities in Chechnya that were as bad as or worse than Serbs atrocities in Bosnia yet Russia was remained on the UN Security Council and the International Contact Group to submit *peace proposals*;

June 21, 1995, Radio Netherlands:
 Bosnian Serb planes bombed the city of Visoko. There were civilian casualties but the number is unknown. Although the flights occurred within the *no-fly* zone, NATO said it could not respond because of fears that UN Peacekeepers *would be taken hostage.*

June 21, 1995, CNN:

British Minister of Defense, Malcolm Rifkind, said the United States Congress should not undermine the Clinton Government that is cooperating with the UN Bosnian policy.

Mr. Rifkind also said that without the UN Peacekeepers in Bosnia, many thousands more would be dead.

June 21, 1995, *Wall Street Journal:*

Heavy artillery battle erupted around Sarajevo with two civilians killed and seven wounded. In Belgrade, Russian envoy, Vitaly Cherkin, met with Serbian and Bosnian Serb leaders on a peace initiative.

Four hundred French police officers arrested 110 people suspected of supporting the GIA (Group Islamic Algerian) extremists from Algeria. Weapons and documents were seized.

June 22, 1995, *Wall Street Journal:*

Chechen negotiators agreed to a Russian ultimatum to find and arrest Chechen rebel leader, Shamil Baseyev, who led the hostage taking in a southern Russian city. He is a hero to many Chechens.

The UN (Boutros Boutros Ghali) <u>refused</u> to let NATO bomb a Bosnian Serb airfield after two Serb jets bombed a city in northern Bosnia. (Boutros Boutros Ghali was given the authority to stop any NATO punishment of Serbs for breaking any of the prohibitions handed down by the UN or NATO.

(Bosnian) Prime Minister Haris Siladjic accused the UN mission of shirking its duty

An artillery shell killed six people in a Sarajevo suburb today.

June 23, 1995, *Wall Street Journal:*

The Russian parliament passed a non-binding, no-confidence vote condemning the Yeltsin Government action in Chechnya. A second no-confidence vote would be binding.

An artillery shell exploded outside a Sarajevo apartment building killing a young girl and a man.

Clinton aides met with Congressional to discuss a $100 million dollar contribution to a new Rapid Deployment Force (in Bosnia).

June 26, 1995, *Wall Street Journal:*

Serb shelling and sniper fire killed nine people and wounded 30 in Sarajevo.

Bosnian Government troops captured a key hill in an offensive to break the siege of the capital.

June 26, 1996, CNN:

A Bosnian Serb militia is breaking into the homes of refugee Bosnian Serbs living in Serbia and taking men of military age to fight in Bosnia. The refugees say the men are taken away by force but the Bosnian Serbs say the men are volunteers.

June 27, 1995, *Wall Street Journal:*

Bosnia's Prime Minister denounced the UN as an accomplice in genocide for failing to protect his people during 39 months of war. Rebel Serbs pounded the UN patrolled enclave of Srebrenica in eastern Bosnia with the heaviest (artillery) attack this year. (The Dutch show a lackadaisical attitude toward their responsibility at this action and the UN Peacekeepers were too few in numbers to protect the city. Still, UN officials show incompetence in failing to strengthen the UN garrison there against a Serb attack that later resulted in wholesale rape and murder of Muslims in Srebrenica by the Serbs)

An article in the *Wall Street Journal* on Serbian youth says that Serbia is on the edge of a nervous breakdown. Arkan, leader of the Serbian Tigers, responsible for war crimes in Croatia and Bosnia (where they raped and killed thousands) is idolized by Serbian youth and is featured on television talks shows and magazine covers.

June 28, 1995, CNN:

Two explosions rocked the heavily fortified television station in downtown Sarajevo this morning at 9:30, Sarajevo time. One person was killed and seventeen wounded. Glass in nearly all the windows was broken. The building houses international television as well as national television.

June 28, 1995, *Wall Street Journal:*

Two Serb shells hit Sarajevo decapitating an 11 year-old boy and wounding 17 others. Carl Bildt, EU negotiator, says his efforts for arranging peace talks have been fruitless.

June 29, 1995, *Wall Street Journal:*

Bosnia's rival sides refused to compromise on conditions for peace talks. Two Serb shells hit Sarajevo decapitating an 11 year-old boy and wounding 17 others.

January 30, 1995, *Wall Street Journal:*

The UN Bosnian Mission was described as hopelessly inept by Senate Majority leader Dole and House Speaker, Gingrich. In a letter to Clinton, the two said that they oppose U.S. support for a UN Rapid Reaction Military Force.

June 30, 1995, Die Deutsche Welle:

The German parliament voted to send 1,500 troops and two squadrons of Tornado fighters to work with the NATO Rapid Deployment Forces in Bosnia. Serbs and Bosnian Serbs denounced the action by the German Government as reminiscent of Nazi aggression against Yugoslavia in WW II.

July 1, 1995, Radio Netherlands:

In western Slovenia, part of Croatia re-taken by the Croatian Government Forces, Croatians are slowly returning to their homes while Croatian Serbs who remain are fearful, while others have fled this fertile, beautiful land. Four years of wars show the devastation and Croatian farms once farmed by Croatian Serbs have been looted of machinery and house burned by Serbs who have fled the area. Some propose a Marshall type plan for the former Yugoslavia to heal the wounds of war.

The situation in Bihac grows more difficult as no food has entered this so-called *safe haven* for several months. After two people died Saturday of starvation Bosnian Serbs allowed one convoy to go through but the amount of food was only one tenth needed to feed Bihac.

July 2, 1995, Radio Netherlands:

The Bosnian Serbs on Mt. Igman shelled a convoy escorted by French UN soldiers. The French responded with live mortar shells and the Serbs responded by shelling UN Headquarters in Sarajevo.

Dutch Defense Minister, Hans von Mirlo, removed 22 Dutch UN Peacekeepers from the Srebrenica enclave before the Ukrainian troops arrived to relieve them. They were ready for home leave and reassignment.

The Russian negotiators in Chechnya are demanding that Djokar Dudayev, President of Chechnya, resign as part of their peace plan. In return, the Russians say they will remove their pro-Russian Chechen leader before elections are held.

July 3, 1995, CNN:
Great celebrations in Belgrade over Serbia's winning the European basketball championship.
The Bosnian Army has cut a major Bosnian Serb supply route while Serbs attacked a UN supply convoy near Sarajevo and UN troops responded with live ammunition. Serbs sent missiles and mortar fire into UN headquarters in Sarajevo.

July 3, 1995, Die Deutsche Welle:
Germany will send 1,500 troops and two squadrons of Tornado fighters for use in the UN rapid deployment force. Germany will also supply and operate a 1,000-bed hospital in the Croatian city of Split for use in rapid deployment operations.

July 3, 1995, *Wall Street Journal:*
Bosnian Serbs fired a mortar round at the UN headquarters in Sarajevo wounding three UN soldiers when it landed in a courtyard. A guard at the nearby U.S. Embassy was hurt. The rising violence against civilians and UN personnel resulted in 13 civilians and 88 wounded while six people were killed and 16 wounded in Serb-held parts of the city. Sarajevo's mayor said a Bosnian army offensive to ease the Serb siege of the city was exacting a high price in casualties but represented the only hope for his peoples.

July 4, 1995, Radio Netherlands: Carole Van den Ring:
The peace talks in Chechnya are failing over Russia's insistence of a continued Russian military presence. Both

sides accuse the other of breaking the ceasefire.

July 4, 1995: Radio France:

The Croatian government in Zagreb notes there are Croatian Serb troop movements in West Slavonia. The Bosnian government in Sarajevo would like the Croatian government to liberate the Croatian Krajina under Serb control by force to ease the blockade of Bihac.

July 5, 1995, *Wall Street Journal*:

Artillery battles erupted in Sarajevo's suburbs with shells landing near the main UN compound and headquarters of the French peacekeepers. UN expressed concern about a build-up of Croatian forces around two Serb-held enclaves in Croatia. U.S. logistical troops arrived in Croatia to assist a UN rapid reaction force.

July 6, 1995, Radio Netherlands: Carole Van Den Ring:

The UN Security Council agreed to lift the sanctions against Serbia and Montenegro for cultural and international sporting events, a continuation of the lifting of sanctions agreed upon last September in return for Serbia cutting all ties with the Bosnian Serbs. Russia abstained from the voting because of a clause that stated Rump Yugoslavia had to cut all ties to the Bosnian Serb Army.

A food convoy arrived in the Muslim enclave of Bihac for the first times in months. The enclave is cut off from supplies by Bosnian Serbs and Rebel Frikret Abdic's followers.

A Croatian Serb fighter plane bombed a power station in Bihac on Wednesday despite the UN designating the Bihac area as a no fly zone. One person was injured (the UN seldom enforced its 'no-fly zone' order so the Serbs constantly violated it.)

July 6, 1995, *Wall Street Journal*:

The UN said a Serb jet attacked the Bosnian government enclave of Bihac in defiance of a no-fly-zone policed by NATO aircraft. In Geneva, Boutros Boutros Ghali and French President Chirac pledged to press on with diplomatic efforts to end the Bosnian war.

July 7, 1995, *Wall Street Journal*:

Heavy fighting erupted in the UN protected Bosnian enclave of Srebrenica and hundreds of shells hit the town wounding five civilians and forcing hundreds of peacekeepers to take shelter. Shellfire killed two children in a Sarajevo suburb.

July 7, 1995, Die Deutsche Welle:

In Kalinvik south of Sarajevo, Bosnian Serb gunners fired mortars at the helicopter carrying EU negotiator, Carl Bildt and adjacent copter carrying newsmen. Mr. Bildt then flew on to the Croatian city of Split after Serb gunners fired a rocket at the helicopter.

Shelling continues in Sarajevo, Bihac, and Srebrenica. All other fronts in Bosnia were quiet. Bosnian Serbs attempted to break through the middle of the Bosnian government lines at Srebrenica two days ago but were repulsed.

July 10, 1995, *Wall Street Journal*:

Serb tanks advanced on Srebrenica and overran the UN observation post seizing 15 Dutch peacekeepers. The UN threatened NATO air strikes if the attacks continued. A Dutch peacekeeper died Saturday after being shot by a Bosnian soldier as his unit retreated from the UN post seized by the Serbs. A Dutch unit with anti-tank weapons moved to defend the town.

July 11, 1995, *Wall Street Journal*:

Dutch peacekeepers opened fire on advancing Serbs in Srebrenica and the UN threatened to call NATO air strikes on Serb positions. The Serbs responded by demanding all 30,000 Muslims leave within 48 hours.

July 12, 1995, *Wall Street Journal*:

20,000 refugees poured out of Srebrenica toward a UN base three miles north of the city. 30 Dutch peacekeepers were detained by the Serbs and forced the rest of the 450 UN Contingent to flee. Defense Secretary William Perry said the attack raises the question whether the UN force will be able to continue to stay in Bosnia.

July 13, 1995, *Wall Street Journal*:

Serbs rounded up Muslim women and children in Srebrenica and loaded them onto buses. The Serb commander, Mladic, made a triumphant entry into the city and assured Muslims they wouldn't be harmed. One relief spokesman called it a "horrible scene of screaming." UN's Envoy Yashushi Akashi said Peacekeepers wouldn't assist the Serbs in removing Muslims but Mladic was not taking no for an answer.

July 14, 1995, *Wall Street Journal*:

Bosnian Serbs cleared out 40,000 people from Srebrenica and went on a rape and killing spree. About 10,000 refugees were housed in tents on the closed Tuzla airport. Clinton warned that unless the integrity of the UN mission in Bosnia can be restored, "its days will be numbered".

July 17, 1995, *Wall Street Journal*:

Bosnian Serb soldiers were reported within a mile of the center of the Zepa enclave. Serb leader Karazdic said his forces intend to conquer all of the UN protected enclaves between Sarajevo and the border with Serbia. Western military leaders met in London in an attempt to devise a response. Military planners believe a pullout of UN troops will involve a "quick and dirty" airborne retreat. Aid officials prepared for thousands of refugees to join those from Srebrenica.

July 18, 1995, *Wall Street Journal*:
The Clinton administration urged vigorous air strikes and wants allies to focus on breaking the siege of Sarajevo, but does not want to commit ground troops. France is pressing allies to act decisively in Gorazde and proposed the U.S. provide combat and heavy-lift helicopters to fly heavily armed French peacekeepers into the enclave.

July 19, 1995, *Wall Street Journal*;
Bosnian Muslims resisted Serb attacks on Zepa and threatened to use Ukrainian peacekeepers as shields if NATO fails to act. The Serbs say they would shoot the Ukrainians if NATO makes any air strikes against them.

July 20, 1995, *Wall Street Journal*:
The Bosnian Serb army claimed to have captured the UN safe area of Zepa. The U.S. won qualified British support for aggressive air strikes to defend Gorazde.

July 20, 1995, CNN:
A UN spokesman said Bosnian Serb soldiers dressed in the UN Peacekeeper's uniforms used bullhorns to lure Muslim families hiding in forests around Srebrenica to come out. The people who came out were then lined up and shot

by the Serb soldiers.

July 20, 1995, Radio Netherlands;
Demand to leave behind all men from ages 18-55 was unacceptable to the Muslims of Zepa who broke off negotiations with the Bosnian Serbs. The city is completely surrounded and being shelled.

The enclave of Bihac is under attack by Croatian Serbs and renegade Bosnian (Muslims) under the command of Abdic.

A shell hit the presidential palace in Sarajevo where EU representative Karl Bildt is meeting with President Alija Izetbegovic. Another shell landed nearby but no one was hurt.

Moroccan King Hassan V has applied Morocco's entry into the E.U.

July 21, 1995, *Wall Street Journal*:
Fighting resumed around the enclave of Zepa after expiration of a Serb deadline for completion of surrender negotiations with the town's defenders.

July 21, 1995, Radio Netherlands:
NATO says that any Serb attack on Gorazde will meet with NATO air strikes. Russia's Andrei Kozyrev was not in agreement.

Yores Vorhoover accused Serbs of atrocities in Srebrenica. Hundreds if not thousands were murdered.

The International Contact Group is divided over raising sanctions on Serbia if Serbia recognizes Bosnia. U.S. is against raising sanctions, Britain and France for it.

(Bosnian) Foreign Minister Mohammed Sacirby has received promises of arms from several Islamic nations but was unprepared to state what countries would give Bosnia arms.

Five children were killed in Bihac on Friday from Serb shelling.

The attack on Zepa continues. The Serbs say they will use all males taken in Zepa and exchange them for Serb prisoners of war captured by the Bosnian Army.

July 23, 1995, *New York Times:*
Serbs kill two French Peacekeepers. UN threatens punishment from the Rapid Reaction Force.

July 23, 1995, Radio Netherlands: Jackie Spears:
Bosnian government forces have suffered heavy losses in Bihac where a Serb offensive by Croatian Serbs from the Krajina region are attacking along with followers of Abdic.

Speaking from Zagreb, the Dutch commander of the Dutch peacekeeping forces in Srebrenica witnessed a number of murders committed by Serbs after the city fell to the Serbs. The Dutch have pulled out the last of their troops in Bosnia.

On Monday in Grozny, Chechnya, Russian and Chechen leaders agreed upon an exchange of prisoners. The Russians will present their plan for a type of political arrangement Chechnya will have within the Russian nation.

July 24, 1995, CNN:
Eight civilians were killed by the Serb shelling of Sarajevo Sunday. The bloody bodies of a young mother with her baby were shown in the hospital on a slab.

Christian Amanpour gave details on the Serb offensive in Bihac saying that the Serbs have taken 80 square kilometers from Bosnian troops. A British spokesman for the UN said that the rapid action deployment group is in southwest of Sarajevo, ready to strike back whenever the Serbs attack UN peacekeepers. French Foreign Legion and other French and British troops occupy Mt. Igman to protect the road supplying Sarajevo.

July 24, 1995, *Wall Street Journal*:
Bosnian Serbs launched new attacks on the three UN declared 'safe areas' of Bihac, Sarajevo, and Zepa just two days after Western leaders threaten to bomb Serbs if they attack Gorazde. Six civilians and 35 others killed in Sarajevo and two French peacekeepers killed. Top generals from U.S., France, and Britain travel to Belgrade to deliver the Gorazde ultimatum to the Bosnian Serb commander.

July 24, 1995, Radio Netherlands: **Jackie Spears:**
800 British and French troops of the Rapid Reaction Force with light artillery have taken up positions on Mt. Igman. Mt. Igman overlooks the only remaining supply road open to Sarajevo. Last week, two French peacekeepers were killed when Bosnian Serbs opened fire on a UN supply convoy carrying humanitarian aid to Sarajevo. The UN is considering opening a second road to Sarajevo for convoys carrying humanitarian aid.

Heavy fighting continues in Bihac with pressure on all sides from Croatian Serbs, Fikret Abdic's (Muslim renegades), and Bosnian Serbs.

The 470 Dutch peacekeepers that were in Srebrenica have returned to Holland to a hero's welcome. Polish Human Rights investigator Mazowiecki is in Tuzla taking evidence of atrocities committed against the Bosnian civilians by Serbs after Srebrenica's fall.

Russian Foreign Minister Andrei Kozyrev is in Belgrade with Slobodan Milosevic and is calling for the lifting of economic sanctions against Serbia.

Saudi Arabia's government has called upon all Islamic

nations to come to the aid of Bosnia with weapons, food, and humanitarian aid.

July 25, 1995, CNN: Zepa has fallen.
The UN is dispatching UN Peacekeepers to aid in evacuating Zepa.

July 25, 1995, *New York Times;*
Serb General Martic is charged with war crimes for ordering the rocket attack on Zagreb (see: May 1, 1995)

July 25, 1995, ABC-TV;
The War Crimes Tribunal in The Hague indicted the leader of the Bosnian Serbs, Radovan Karadzic, and commander of his army, Ratko Mladic, for the war crime of genocide and crimes against humanity.

July 25, 1995, *Wall Street Journal*;
All 'UN Safe Havens' in Bosnia are under attack except the NATO designated Gorazde. NATO officials in Brussels struggled to agree on details of a more aggressive air strike plan. Talks will continue today.

July 25, 1995, Die Deutsche Welle:
In The Hague today, Judge Goldstone of the War Crimes Tribunal handed down indictments for Serb leader Radovan Karadzic, General Ratko Mladic, and twenty two others for genocide, war crimes, and crimes against humanity against Bosnian Muslim.

July 25, 1995, Radio Netherlands: Jackie Spears:
Croatian troops have taken up positions in Bihac in support of Bosnian Government troops. Some say Croatians are fighting against Serb Croats who have crossed the border

from the Krajina region to overrun the Bihac enclave and join forces with Bosnian Serbs.

Radovan Karadzic and General Ratko Mladic have been indicted in The Hague for genocide, war crimes, and crimes against humanity. Serb Croat leader Milan Markic was indicted for bombing Zagreb.

A continuing report: Germany has received the largest number of Bosnian refugees with 400.000 Bosnians in Germany. Over 1,000 refugees from Zepa have been bused out of Zepa by Serbs who provided the buses. Many from Zepa have fled to the hill where they are hiding. The Bosnian government says the men will fight to the death rather than surrender after the killings and mass murder in Srebrenica after it was overrun two weeks ago. The UN wanted to send UN peacekeepers to protect the 17,000 civilians in Zepa but the Serbs refused to let them in. Only 17 Ukrainian peacekeepers were in Zepa to protect the population.

July 26, 1995, *Wall Street Journal*:

Bosnian Serbs marched into Zepa after more than a week of fighting. Thousands of Muslims fled into the woods of the surrounding hills. The Hague indicted Serb leader Karadzic, his military commander Mladic, and 22 other Bosnian Serbs and Croatian Serbs.

NATO ambassadors were nearing formal agreement on the scope of air strikes to defend Gorazde and in redefining the military command system.

Paris: Police sources voiced suspicions that Algerian extremists were responsible for the bombing of the St. Michel subway station in Paris but they were not ruling out Mid-Eastern or Serb links. (One person died and 30 remain were hospitalized from the bombing).

July 26, 1995, Radio Netherlands: Jackie Spears:

The U.S. Senate voted 69 to 29 to lift the arms embargo against the Bosnians. The bill now goes to the House for ratification. It is not known how the U.S. will arm the Bosnians or if aid will arrive in time before British and French UN Peacekeepers are withdrawn.

UN Secretary General Boutros Boutros Ghali turned over to NATO his authority for halting punitive air strikes on the Serbs.

Russian Foreign Minister Kozyrev obtained a pledge from Bosnian Serbs not to attack Gorazde. Kozyrev said Russia is sending a Russian troop contingent under UN to Gorazde.

Heavy attack (by Serbs) continues against the Bihac enclave in NW Bosnia.

UN Peacekeepers accompanied buses filled with refugees (women and children only) from the fallen city of Zepa to avoid the atrocities committed by Serb forces after the fall of Srebrenica.

Some Islamic nations are calling for all Islamic nations to lift the arms embargo against Bosnia. They are also asking for the members of the Islamic conference to work for a coordinated effort to help the Bosnians. (The vast majority of the United Nations General Assembly opposed the arms embargo).

July 27, 1995, *Wall Street Journal*:

The (U.S.) Senate passes a bill to lift arms embargo against Bosnia 69 to 29. The embargo would be lifted only after the UN peacekeeping force is withdrawn or 12 weeks after the Bosnian Government asks the UN to leave. UN chief Boutros Bourtos Ghali agreed to give up his veto power over aid strikes. NATO and UN military have sole authority to call in NATO air attacks in Bosnia.

July 27, 1995, Die Deutsche Welle:
Bosnian Croats have claimed great success on the battlefield in the enclave of Bihac.
Germany says it will continue to support the arms embargo on Bihac.

July 27, 1995, Radio Netherlands: Jackie Spears:
The UN is deeply worried over hostilities in the Bihac area and Croat Serb controlled Krajina region. Bosnian Serbs have taken more territory around Bihac.
Nearly 4,000 refugees from the fallen 'UN safe area' of Zepa arrived at a tent camp in (Bosnian) government-controlled territory. More are expected. Many Muslim men remained in the forests surrounding Zepa and ignored calls from Serbs to surrender.
(British) Prime Minister John Majors suffered a crushing defeat in the elections in the north of England.

July 28, 1995, *Wall Street Journal*:
The UN Human Rights investigator, Mazowiecki, for former Yugoslavia announced he is resigning over what he called the hypocrisy of world leaders for not fulfilling pledges to protect Bosnians.

July 28, 1995, Die Deutsche Welle:
German opposition party members say that German troops should not be at the disposition of the UN
A combined force of Bosnian Croat and Croat soldiers launched an offensive in western Bosnia, which has halted the Serb drive on Bihac. The Croat advance will cut off supplies to the Croatian Serbs in the Krajina and will surround the Croat Serbs of the Krajina by Croatian forces and Bosnian forces in Bihac.

Interior Minister Manfried Kantor says Germany cannot take more Bosnian refugees and other countries should shoulder the responsibility. There are 400,000 Bosnian refugees in Germany but France has taken only 15,900 and Britain only 7,000.

A 31-year-old Israeli of Russian origin was killed by special German police after he had taken a tourist bus hostage and killed the driver and one of the passengers.

Western European governments denounced the (U.S.) Senate vote to unilaterally lift the arms embargo on Bosnia.

July 29, 1995, Die Deutsche Welle: **Brian Pickering**:

A 31 year old Russian speaking tourist with an Israeli passport took a tourist bus and passengers hostage in Cologne and was killed by Special German police after he shot the bus driver and one passenger.

The Bosnian government has launched an offensive to relieve the Bihac enclave, which is constantly under fire. Croat Serbs and Bosnian Serb leader Karadzic has called for a general mobilization and declared a state of war exists in Bosnian Serb territory (is the man stupid? He started the war years ago)

July 28, 1995, Radio Netherlands: **Jackie Spears:**

The rapid advance of Bosnian and Bosnian Croat troops in northwest Bosnia has taken two Serb occupied towns and threatened the stronghold of Knin. Meanwhile, heavy fighting continues in Bihac.

The Bosnian government has offered to exchange Serb prisoners of war for Bosnian soldiers captured in Zepa.

July 29, 1995, Radio Netherlands:

One third of Croatia is under control of the Croatian Serbs of the Krajina. Ten thousand Croat and Bosnian

Croats are operating in western Bosnia and are poised to invade the Croatian Serb Krajina region.

The economic crisis in Serbia is a result of the economic sanctions which promoted black-market smuggling and created a class of nouveau riche in Serbia. Dirty deals and corruption flourish in Serbia, which has become the money laundering capital of the world.

July 30, 1995, Radio Netherlands: **Marcel Oustings:**
UN's Yashushi Akashi made an agreement with the Croatian Serbs to stop fighting in Bihac.

The Croatian force in Bosnia has taken 700 square kilometers from Bosnian Serbs.

Djokar Dudayev, the Chechen leader, says the peace accords signed Sunday with the Russians are invalid because the Russians used trickery and threats.

The Government of Iraq has announced amnesty for a number of political prisoners.

Musa Abu Marzak, suspected member of the Palestinian Hamas movement, is being extradited to Israel from New York where he was arrested after arriving from Dubai. He has lived in the U.S. for the past fourteen years. Israel suspects he is involved with the Hamas in Israel.

(Croatian) President Franjo Tudjman has demanded the UN station monitors along the Croatian Serb border with Bosnia. He also wants rail and oil pipeline reopened to Croatia from the Croatian Serb Krajina. He rejected the agreement reached by the UN with Croatian Serbs saying the agreement does not go far enough.

Russia is opposed to any expansion of NATO's role in Bosnia.

July 30, 1995, Die Deutsche Welle:
Rebel Croat Serbs have agreed to withdraw from

attacking Bihac. Agreement made in Knin.

Prime Minister Haris Siladjic of Bosnia has called for massive air strikes to protect Bihac. He says more children have starved to death.

Turkish shops and businesses in Germany are being threatened with firebombing by Kurds affiliated with the Kurdish Kommunist Party.

July 31, 1995, CNN;

Karadzic calls the Croat offensive in Bosnia "massive aggression" against Bosnian Serbs.

Within three hours after signing the agreement with the UN to stop their attacks on Bihac, the Croatian Serbs resumed fighting.

Croatian president Franjo Tudjman refuses to meet with the leader of the Croat Serbs calling him a war criminal. The Croatian Army continues to be a threat to the Bosnian Serb army.

Robert Waring, member of Britain's parliament, says there must be a truce to examine the roots of the war and examine diplomatic solutions to end the war there.

July 31, 1995, *Wall Street Journal*:

Croatian Serbs agreed to stop attacking the Muslim enclave of Bihac but there were signs that they were shifting their troops to a new location. Some Croatian Serb fighters were moved to back to Croatian Serb territory where Croatian government forces captured about 270 square miles of land last week. Croatia demanded talks to discuss restoration of its authority in Croat-Serb held land and suggested that war was an option if the Serbs refused.

Serbia's government criticized Croatia's military moves but ignored appeals for help from Bosnian Serb leadership.

July 31, 1995, Die Deutsche Welle:

(UN Envoy) Yashushi Akashi has demanded that Croatia stop its offensive against the Krajina and Croatian Serbs near Bihac. The Bosnian Serbs have threatened that Serbia could be involved. Ratko Mladic, accused war criminal, has said he will ask Serbia for help if the Croatians do not withdraw from territory they have conquered. Over 20,000 Serbs have fled from the area taken by the Croatian army in Bosnia.

(Yashushi Akashi, who demanded that Croatia end its offensive against Krajina and Croatian Serbs, never made demands of the Croatian Serbs stay in Croatia and keep out of Bosnia. Akashi is known for his anti-Bosnian remarks and pro-Serb leanings. The Croat offensive continued and Serbia did not officially enter into the war but had Yugoslav Army units fighting on the Serb side in Bosnia).

Serbs are reported to be moving their troops from the former safe area of Zepa to western Bosnia. Meanwhile, NATO's 16 members have completed plans on their protection of Bihac, which should be operational by the middle of this month.

Of the 500 strong German contingent in Croatia, 300 are medical staff. The 14 Tornado fighters (useful in taking out radar guided anti-aircraft missile sites) are making practice flight now.

Dudayev (Chechen leader) still insists on Chechen independence. Moscow has repeatedly ruled this out saying that Chechnya can have only limited self-determination inside Russia and that its status can be discussed only after Chechens choose new leaders and (hold) elections planned for November.

August 1, 1995, *Wall Street Journal*:

The Croatian army shelled areas within two miles of the Croatian Serb stronghold, Knin. It was the heaviest assault on Knin since the 1991 civil war. Croatian Serbs pledged to pull back on their attack on Bihac then renewed their attack from another direction.

Bullets hit the helicopter carrying UN commander Lt General Rupert Smith as he was flying out of Sarajevo to meet with Serb general, Ratko Mladic. Source of the small arms fire was unclear.

August 1, 1995, CNN:

NATO minister decided on protection for Bihac, Sarajevo, and Tuzla. Secretary General of NATO, Willy Claes, asks all warring parties to stop fighting.

Fighting between Croatian and rebel Croatian Serbs slowed today. Bosnian Serb commander, Ratko Mladic, gathered all Bosnian Serb generals to plan for a counter attack against Croatian army and Croatian Serbs and re-take territory liberated by the Croat army last week.

August 1, 1996, Radio Netherlands:

The Dutch press reports that Moscow told Croatia not to invade the Krajina. But President Tudjman will not only protect the Bosnian Muslims but also to win back the Krajina as it could easily do that.

Radio Netherlands: *Dave Durham*; The NATO Alliance has plans to strike back at any group that attacks them.

Representatives for Croatia and Croatian Serbs will meet in Geneva to resolve their problems.

The Croatian army is set to launch a major attack on Croatian Serbs. Croatian President Franjo Tudjman says a full-scale war could break out if Croatian Serbs continue their attacks on the Bosnia;s Bihac.

August 2, 1995, *Wall Street Journal*:

Serbia's Milosevic, blamed for instigating the wars in

Bosnia and Croatia, and has urged Bosnia's president and the Bosnian Serb commander (Karadzic and Mladic) to make peace.

Chechen leader, Dudayev, fired his chief peace negotiator as Russian and Chechen military commanders issued a joint appeal to Chechnya's rebel forces to disarm and observe a truce.

August 3, 1995, *Wall Street Journal*:

Croatia issued a thinly veiled ultimatum to rebel Serbs who have seized one-third of Croatian territory, demanding Serbs submit to the Croatian government rule or face attack from the 100,000 troops (of the Croatian army).

Saudi Arabia's King Fahd ousted most of his cabinet aimed at reviving the kingdom's oil-dependent economy. The only ministers retaining their positions were those held by Saudi royal princes.

August 3, 1995, Die Deutsche Welle:

120,000 battle-ready Croatians are facing 50,000 Croatian Serbs. The area around the Croatian city of Dubrovnik was shelled by Croatian Serb troops.

Germany was to expel 20,000 Krajina Serb refugees from Germany. This may be delayed because of hostilities in the Krajina.

Bosnian Prime Minister Haris Siladjic was rumored to have offered his resignation. The Bosnian government is facing criticism by the Bosnian people over the losses of Srebrenica and Zepa to Bosnian Serbs this past month.

The August issue of Der Spiegel: The following countries have taken in Bosnian refugees:

Germany 350,000, Norway 11,000, France 15,900. Italy 54,000. Spain 3,700. Britain 7,000, Austria 52,000, Czech 6,730, Greece 150,   Netherlands 45,000, Finland 2,000

Portugal 60. Sweden, 45,000, Slovakia 1,900, Turkey 30,000 Denmark 17,500

August 4, 1995, *Wall Street Journal*:
Prime Minster Haris Siladjic stunned his parliament by offering to resign. He also sought a vote of confidence after the government badly shaken by the Serb capture of Srebrenica and Zepa.

August 4, 1995, CNN:
The Croatian army has launched a full-scale attack on the Krajina Croatian Serbs. Croatian commanders say the war will be over in a matter of days. Yashushi Akashi, UN negotiator denounced the shooting of a Danish UN soldier by a Croat soldier. Serbs have shelled several Croat towns but not Zagreb.

August 4, 1995, Radio Netherlands: Carole Van Den Ring:
General Mladic has resigned as commander of the Bosnian Serb army to command a joint Croat Serb-Bosnian Serb army to oppose the Croatian army. The Croatian army says it will wrap up the war in the Krajina in a short time. Radovan Karadzic has assumed command of the Bosnian Serb army. Croat Serbs fired a rocket into a suburb of Zagreb by no casualties are reported.
Two NATO planes flying over Knin received the radar signal that Croat Serb SAM missiles had been locked onto them and they fired two rockets at the Croat Serb missile site. Results are unknown.
The Bosnian parliament has not accepted the resignation of Prime Minister Haris Siladjic but will consider it in four weeks.
The Croat army has evacuated over 400 UN peacekeepers from the Krajina. One Danish UN soldier was killed when

UN troops refused to abandon their post and came under shelling by Croat forces.

August 4, 1995, Die Deutsche Welle:

The Croatian army claims it has encircled Knin, the Krajina Serb's capital. The town has been hit by over 2,000 artillery rounds. Ratko Mladic is now coordinator between Croatian Serbs and Bosnian Serbs.

The German government has issued a warning to German tourists to leave Croatia and they should avoid the coastal road from Dubrovnik.

August 5, 1995, VOA:

The Croatian commander says all resistance has dissipated and the Croatian Serbs are fleeing into Bosnian Serb territory. Casualties among civilian and military are not known at this time. The Croatian government says that nothing in the Krajina will be as it was before.

General Ratko Mladic has said he resisted a takeover of the Bosnian Serb army and that he is still in control.

August 5, 1995, CNN:

It has taken the Croatian forces 48 hours to take Knin. Croatian flags appeared all over liberated territory and Croatian soldiers were welcomed by the population that remained behind. Croatian forces have captured all interlinking points of the Krajina. Sniping was intermittent and an unknown number of people have died. Celebrations in Zagreb and the Krajina. The Croatian Serbs have nothing to oppose the Croatian army and only interference could change the situation. Yashushi Akashi says refugees (from the Krajina) are being helped to evacuate from a dangerous situation. Akashi seemed upset and accused a Croat soldier of shooting a Danish UN soldier.

Mladic was demoted yesterday but says he won't go. A battle between Mladic and Karadzic is expected.

August 5, 1995, Radio Netherlands: **Carol Van Den Ring**:
Croatian forces have made big gains. Croatian troops joined up with Bosnian troops in Bihac breaking the siege of Bihac.

The death toll is not known but thought to be high. Slobodan Milosevic says he has acted with restraint and offered only humanitarian aid. Croat Serb and Bosnian Serb refugees in Belgrade demonstrated and asked for weapons for them to fight and recover the Krajina.

August 6, 1995, VOA:
Less than 60 hours after the Croat army began their offensive all major cities in the breakaway Krajina have been occupied. The industrial town of Kabatanja was entered today. Serb troops are being surrounded but many staged a tactical retreat into Bosnia. Over 100,000 Croat Serbs are fleeing into Bosnian Serb territory. This is the largest outpouring of refugees in the war.

Bosnian Serb generals are in disarray with some generals refusing to take orders from Karadzic. Mladic is popular among his troops and they support Milosevic. Karadzic and Mladic have been in conflict over the way the war has been conducted. Mladic has refused to step down as commander in defiance of the Bosnian Serb parliament.

August 6, 1995 Radio Netherlands: **Carol Van Den Ring**:
Croatia says the breakaway region of Krajina no longer exists. General Mladic is backed by 18 generals and has refused to resign. Karadzic lost support of Milosevic over his rejection of the International Contact Group's peace plan last year whereas Milosevic support as Mladic.

U.S. Secretary of State Christopher says the loss of the Croatian Serb Krajina may make the Serbs more amenable to a diplomatic solution. However the Krajina Serbs may not be satisfied over the loss of the Krajina where they have lived for the last four centuries and they may seek revenge.

August 6, 1995, Die Deutsche Welle:
Croatia says its military victory has not only recovered its territory but stabilized the region. Chancellor Helmut Kohl says Germany will take many refugees but asks the allies to take a fair share. Rump Yugoslavia asks the UN to force Croatia out of the Krajina.

Another 100 German soldiers were flown to Split where Germany is setting up a hospital as its contribution to the UN humanitarian aid in Bosnia and Croatia.

August 7, 1995, CNN:
As many as 200,000 Croatian Serbs may be on the move out of the Krajina after Croatian forces took control. Croatia has offered safe passage to Bosnia for all Croat Serb soldiers who turn over their weapons.

Bosnian Serb planes bombed five Croatian towns along the border but there are no reports of casualties. (Again there is no response from NATO or the UN over this overt action proving this war has been started and supported by Serbs in Serbia).

Jackie Shymanski reporting: 30,000 to 40,000 refugees are trapped at Topushka (north of Bihac) and can't get into Bosnian Serb territory.

According to an article in the *London Times*, President Franjo Tudjman of Croatia showed a map of how Serbia and Croatia would divide Bosnia. Under the plan, the Croats would get Sarajevo. (See

August 21, 1995 VOA

The Voice of America broadcast states that Richard Holbrooke made a secret agreement with Serbian Prime Minister Slobodan Milosevic to divide Bosnia between Serbia and Croatia.

The Croatian Serb army commander claims that NATO was on the side of Croatia as NATO planes destroyed a Croat Serb anti-aircraft missile site killing all the Croatian Serb soldiers manning the site. He says NATO allowed Croatian planes to bomb Croatian Serbs at will.

Yeltsin called for the UN to place sanctions on Croatia and invited the leaders of Croatia and Serbia to come to Moscow for peace talks.

August 7, 1995, VOA:

Some Croatian Serbs are still fighting, trying to get out of Dvor. 30,000 refugees are trapped on the road outside Dvor. Serbia's UN ambassador calls for sanctions on Croatia. Serbia says it will stay out of the war. Five to six thousand Croat Serb soldiers are trapped at Topuska and negotiating to get out. Croat losses are put at 118 dead and Croat Serb losses estimated at 5,000 to 6,000.

August 7, 1995, Radio Netherlands: Carole Van Den Ring:

At 6 pm today, Croatia declares the Croatian battle is over with (Croatian casualties) 118 dead and some 620 wounded. Croatia apologizes for using Danish UN troops as human shields.

Serb warplanes attacked five Croatian border towns and two were shot down. Red Cross estimates 150,000 (Croat Serb) refugees are in Bosnian Serb territory while 80,000 are trapped in Croatia. Carl Bildt, EU Envoy, says President Franjo Tudjman should be tried as a war criminal. Croatia responded that Carl Bildt has lost creditability.

August 7, 1995, CNN:

Croatia says it will demobilize most of its army while Serbian tanks roll through Belgrade on their way to the Croatian/Serb border of East Slavonia to discourage further Croat liberation of its territory.

August 7, 1995, Die Deutsche Welle: Sue Cox:

Russia has presented a draft to the UN that Croatia is to end all military action within 36 hours or face sanctions. Boris Yeltsin has invited Tudjman and Milosevic to Moscow for peace talks.

Moscow says that Chechen elections may be postponed until next year. He says that Chechnya may have some sort of autonomy but not independence.

August 8, 1995, CNN:

Croatian refugees fleeing the Krajina have reported that Croatian jets fired on columns of fleeing refugees crowding the roads and that Croatian artillery fired at the refugees. They also reported that Croatian soldiers set houses on fire. Five deaths were reported. Some Croat Serb soldiers were reported to have encircled the town of Glina north of Bihac and were continuing to fight.

August 8, 1995, *Wall Street Journal*:

Serbs streaming out of Croatia were trapped and attacked. Fighting continued along the route where Serb civilians tried to make their way to safety, either into Serb-held land in northern Bosnia or farther eastward into Serbia.

Columns of Yugoslav tanks passed through Belgrade for the border with Croatia, threatening to expand the fighting just as Croatia's defense minister declared the war was over.

In one Croatian town, fighting trapped at least 30,000

refugees and in western Bosnia, a column of Serb refugees was apparently attacked by a military jet.

Aid agencies said the Serb exodus from Croatia could total 200,000 people. Columns of cars, trucks, and tractors were strung out along a 140-mile arc in Bosnia en route to Serbia.

August 9, 1995, Die Deutsche Welle (3:00 BMT) **Cameron Morel:**
Banja Luka is where most Serb refugees from the Krajina are headed. Some shelling is reported but it is not known if it came from Croat or Bosnian army artillery.

Slobodan Milosevic has accepted an invitation from Boris Yeltsin and President Franjo Tudjman. The world community welcomes the meeting so long as it does not result to the detriment of Bosnia. (Tudjman said he would not attend unless Izet Izetbegovic was invited).

Radovan Karadzic has written an open letter to Milosevic, criticizing him for allowing the Croatian government to re-take the Krajina and for not coming to the aid of the Croatian Serbs.

August 9, 1995, French TV,
International Channel, Houston, Texas: Bosnian President Izetbegovic traveled to Zagreb where he was decorated by President Tudjman and afterward they discussed cooperation of Bosnia and Croatia and the war criminals of the Croat Serb army now in Bosnia.

Kemal Muftic, top Advisor to President Izetbegovic, said the capacity of the Bosnian Army to oppose the combined Croat Serb Army and Bosnian Serb armies now facing the Bosnian Army is a problem.

August 9, 1995, CNN:

Tudjman says he will not attend the Moscow conference with Yeltsin and Milosevic unless President Izetbegovic of Bosnia attends.

Serb troops around Glina began turning over their weapons to the UN after the UN brokered a truce between the Croats and Serbs. They were being escorted to Bosnian Serb territory.

August 9, 1995, *Wall Street Journal*:

National Security Advisor Anthony Lake is flying to Europe to present a new version of an earlier plan to be backed up by a "more credible threat" if the Serbs fail to sign on. The proposal calls for a UN withdrawal followed by air strikes and lifting the Bosnian arms embargo. Clinton and advisors believe that the Croatian victory over Croatian Serbs may make the Bosnian Serbs more willing to negotiate but State Department officials warn any talk of peace is premature.

August 9, 1995, Radio Netherlands:

Croatian troops set fire to Serb homes in the Krajina, killed livestock and looted. So *normalizing the Krajina* looks more like a scorched earth policy.

In a London restaurant recently, (Croatian) President Tudjman drew a line separating Serbs from Croats that divided Bosnia between Serbia and Croatia. The story so upset (Bosnian) President Izetbegovic and Foreign Minister Mohammed Sacerby that they flew to Zagreb where President Franjo Tudjman calmed their fears. (This is evidence of the secret agreement signed between Milosevic and U.S. Envoy, Richard Holbrooke, See August 21, VOA).

Fran Kirkland: The U.S. has evidence that Serbs committed many atrocities in Srebrenica. Evidence ranges from photos of atrocities to plowed fields indicating mass graves. The Red Cross says it has no evidence of any atrocities.

As the fighting has come to an end in the Krajina, the situation of the fleeing Serb refugees is worsening.

August 9, 1995, Die Deutsche Welle:

Serbia sent planes from Belgrade to Banja Luka to begin an airlift of Croatian Serbs to Belgrade. BBC says its correspondent **John Scoffield** was shot and killed by Croat soldiers. The Croatian government says a Serb soldier shot him.

The International Contact Group has tabled a resolution condemning Croatia for the fighting in the Krajina.

German-made Tornado planes made training flights over Bosnia yesterday. These are the best planes in the world to take out the Russian made SAM missiles in Serb territory.

August 10, 1995, C-Span TV: Senators Feinstein, Spector, and Kerry presided over the Joint Senate hearings on war crimes in Bosnia yesterday. A copy can be obtained from:

    Senate Foreign Relations Committee
    450 Dirksen Building
    Washington, D.C. 20510

August 10, 1995, ABC TV:

U.S. Ambassador to the UN Madeleine Albright will present photos of a mass grave in Srebrenica as evidence of Serb atrocities.

August 10, 1995, French TV International Channel, Houston, Texas:

Croatian soldiers in newly liberated Slunj (Sluny) are shown dancing, drunk, and firing guns in the air. Croatian trucks entering Bihac with medicines are given a cool reception by the residents of Bihac. Several women called the Croats "brothers of the Serbs" and looked the other way as Drunken Croat soldiers rode through the city on trucks and singing while waving bottles of alcohol in the air.

August 10, 1995, CNN:

U.S. National Security Advisor Anthony Lake will meet with British, French, and allies to present a plan to partition Bosnia into two portions, one for Serbs and the other for Bosnian-Croatian Federation.

August 10, 1995, *Wall Street Journal*:

Fighting continued along the route where Serb civilians tried to make their way to safety, either into Serb-held land in northern Bosnia or further eastward into Serbia. Yugoslav tanks along the Serb border with Croatia threatened to expand the fighting just as Croatia's defense minister declared the fighting was over. In one Croatian town, about 30,000 refugees are trapped by the fighting and in western Bosnia a column of refugees was attacked by a military jet. Croat Serb refugees in cars were stoned with windows broken.

August 10, 1995, Radio Netherlands: Grant Kirkland:

The U.S. has presented irrefutable evidence of atrocities committed by Serbs at Srebrenica. An estimated 2,700 are in mass graves and Red Cross estimates 6,000 Bosnian Muslims are missing from Srebrenica.

Bosnian Prime Minister Harissiladjic has rescinded his resignation under pressure from President Izetbegovic. Mr. Siladjic was reportedly disturbed by the actions of the SDS political party.

Moscow is considering unilaterally lifting sanctions against Serbia regardless of the UN and the International community.

Blue Helmets (UN Peacekeepers) have been withdrawn from the Krajina as there is no longer any need for them there.

August 11, 1995, CNN:

(U.S.) President Clinton is expected to veto the bill to lift the arms embargo against Bosnia and hold it until the Senate which adjourns for the summer at the end of today's session. This prevents a Senate override until Congress reconvenes this fall.

The Red Cross says the photos presented by the U.S. to the UN do not represent mass graves (it was later proven the Red Cross lied).

August 11, 1995, *Wall Street Journal*:

U.S. Ambassador to the UN Madeleine Albright presented CIA spy photographs of mass graves as evidence to back up charges that up to 2,700 Muslims were executed by Bosnian Serbs after they captured the UN declared safe haven last month. (The figure was raised to 7,000 after July 2005, when the bodies of the massacred men and boys taken from mass graves and were identified and given proper burial).

Croatian Serbs began arriving into Belgrade at a flow of about 1,000 and hour. Some talked of getting revenge against Croatia for driving them from their homes in the Krajina.

August 11, 1995, Die Deutsche Welle:

About 50,000 Croatian Serbs have reached Serbia. 30 tons of food was flown into Belgrade for the Krajina Serb refugees.

Radovan Karadzic has reversed his decision to remove

General Ratko Mladic as commander of the Bosnian Serb army in the interests of national unity.

The U.S. and Russia have agreed to coordinate efforts to solve the Bosnian war even though their objectives are at times in opposition to the other. Russia will raise unilaterally sanctions against Serbia while opposition from the U.S. Congress to Pres Clinton's Bosnian policy and efforts by Congress to raise the arms embargo, will highlight the differences between the two nations when Anthony Lake and Andrei Kozyrev meet at the Russian Black Sea resort of Sochi on Sunday.

August 12, 1995, Die Deutsche Welle:

The UN Rapid Reaction Force fired 16 mortar rounds into a Bosnian Serb gun position that had fired at a UN position in Sarajevo. Mortar rounds fired by Bosnian Serbs hit Dubrovnik in Croatia and the highway along the coast.

Russia lifted sanctions against Serbia and suspended trade with Croatia.

Croatian Serb refugees in Banja Luka reportedly to committed many atrocities against Bosnian Croats and Bosnian Muslim minorities still living in that city. Murder and looting were some of the charges and expelling minorities by force from their homes.

August 13, 1995, CNN: **Christiane Amanpour**:

The Black Swans are the best-trained and best-equipped fighters in the Bosnian Army. They are recruited from among the Muslims who had been living in what is territory controlled by the Bosnian Serbs and were ethnically cleansed. Many want to return to liberate their cities and villages from the Bosnian Serbs. The Black Swans took heavy casualties this last June when the government tried to lift the siege of Sarajevo. The Black Swans say the Bosnian

Army should not have tried to lift the siege without heavy artillery to support the attack.

Serbs are turning back military age Croatian Serb males at the Serbian border saying these men should stay in Bosnian and fight alongside the Bosnian Serb army.

August 13, 1995, Die Deutsche Welle: **Sue Cox:**

The Al Feram separatist group in Kashmir killed a Norwegian whom they were holding hostage. His body was recovered without the head.

Bosnian government troops are attacking the Serb held city of Donji Vakuf in central Bosnia. Croatian troops are fighting Serb troops firing on Dubrovnik.

President Alija Izetbegovic rejected the U.S. proposal to give the Muslim city of Gorazde to the Serbs in the new American peace plan.

Serbia has told hospitals in Kosovo to expect 16,000 Croatian Serb refugees within the next few days.

August 13, 1995, Radio Netherlands: **Marcel Sniders** (9595 MHz 31 M and 6161 Mhz 49 meters)

The U.S. says that the situation for resolving the war in Bosnia is more amenable because the Krajina was retaken by the Croatian army.

Parts of the American proposed peace plan for Bosnia have been leaked to the press. The proposal calls for 61% of former Bosnia to go to the Bosnian Serbs who will be allowed to unite with Serbia. Muslims would give up Gorazde while receiving land from the Serbs elsewhere. The meeting of White House advisor, Anthony Lake, and Russian Foreign Minister, Andrei Kozyrev, has resulted in little change in their positions on Bosnia and Serbia.

Meanwhile, in Bosnia, the Bosnian Army has launched a ground attack on Donji Vakuf with artillery and reported small arms and machine gun fire.

August 14, 1995, *Wall Street Journal*:
Balkan peace talks resumed amid renewed fighting in Bosnia. Prodded to act after Croatia's re-conquest of its Krajina region from secessionist Serbs, the US, Russia, and European nations began a series of peace talks. The U.S. won Russian support for a set of high-level meetings with the warring parties. Progress on the diplomatic front came as Muslim-led Bosnian government forces pressed forward against Serb-held military positions in central Bosnia. Pres Clinton used his veto to short-circuit a congressional move to end U.S. compliance with the UN arms embargo on Bosnia, saying that such a policy would make the war there "an American responsibility".

An article in the Wall Street Journal says, "top officials of Croatian Serbs and Bosnian Serbs have said they could accept key elements of the U.S. plan. Muslims appear to be renewing their effort to retake territory in Central Bosnia."

The attack on Donji Vakuf appears to be a Bosnian offensive aimed at moving closer to the Bosnian stronghold of Banja Luka to the north. Western officials continued to worry about Croatia's cleanup operation in the former Serb Krajina as angry mobs continued to harass fleeing Croatian Serbs and to destroy property left behind. Croatian military and police forces were unconcerned about the widespread destruction of Serb property. Some said it was in revenge for the attacks on Croat property by Serbs four years ago.

August 14, 1995, CNN: **Christiane Amanpour:**
There are still 60,000 minorities in the Banja Luka area who are now undergoing the latest round of ethnic cleansing by the Bosnian Serbs and the Croatian Serb refugees. This area was once heavily Muslim but Serbs have destroyed over

200 mosques in the area.

The Bosnian Fifth Army in Bihac captured some tanks and heavy weapons from Croatian Serbs and it is poised to sweep out of the northwest enclave where it had been penned up by the combined forces of the Bosnian Serb/Croatian Serb armies as well as Fikret Abdic's Muslim renegades. The combined Croat and Bosnian Armies are now on the offensive with assaults on Serb positions. The war has turned around after the Croatian re-conquest of the Krajina.

The Croatian Army is striking back at the Bosnian Serb army that has been shelling the coastal city of Dubrovnik and the coastal highway from across the border in Bosnia. Attacks on the city's suburbs continue and the Croatian Army has been massing its troops and has threatened to retaliate against the Serbs if the attacks continue.

August 14, 1995, Die Deutsche Welle:

Assistant Secretary of State Richard Holbrooke wants to meet with Bosnian government officials to discuss peace talks.

Russia says it will not allow any acts of terrorism by Chechens (what Yeltsin's plan to terrorize Chechens into submission opened the door for Chechens to commit acts of terrorism outside Chechnya.

August 15, 1995, *Wall Street Journal*:

The U.S. offered the Serbs a chance to change a proposed Bosnia map. Washington officials said the map to divide the former Yugoslav republic could be revised once negotiations begin. The map was rejected by the Serbs last year that would have given them 49% of Bosnia. Serb forces hold over two-thirds of the country. "As we've always indicated, that could be adjusted by agreement of the parties," a White House spokesman said. Also subject to change is the way land is divided among Serbs, Muslims, and Croats.

U.S. intelligence had two un-manned reconnaissance aircraft shot down by the Serbs within the past few days.

August 15, 1995, CNN:

Part of the U.S. peace initiative says that the arms embargo against Bosnia would be lifted and troops from Pakistan, Bangladesh, and Malaysia would join Bosnian forces. While the Bosnian Army would learn to use the new weapons, NATO air strikes would be used to defend Bosnia from Serb attacks.

August 15, 1995, Die Deutsche Welle:

800 Croatian Serb refugees refused to board the train to the mainly Albanian ethnic Serbian state of Kosovo.

From Venice to Brindisi, ten thousand people lined up on the beaches and held hands in a demonstration for peace in Bosnia.

August 15, 1995, Christian Science Monitor Radio (580 Mhz 49 meter)

Dubrovnik'c suburbs have been shelled by Bosnian Serbs from across the border in Bosnia. The Croatian Army commander says that if the attacks do not stop, the Croatian Army will attack. The Croatian Army is massing troops and military weapons in Dubrovnik. Dobrovnik, described as the Pearl of the Adriatic, has never recovered from a shelling it received by the Yugoslav Navy in 1991.

Little is known about Donji Vakuf in central Bosnia since it came under attack last Saturday by Bosnian Government troops. It is believed that territory around the town has been captured by Bosnian troops but that there is still fighting in the city.

UN aid officials in Banja Luka say 500,000 minorities

still live in the area even after four years of murders, attacks, rapes, beatings, and destruction of property. Many people are looking to leave the area.

The peace plan proposed by the Clinton administration is unacceptable to Bosnia because it calls for the surrender of Gorazde to Serbia. As the Croats and Serbs are the two biggest military powers, the (Clinton peace) plan will divide Bosnia between the two.

Croatia is now controlling the forty-mile stretch of oil pipeline that goes through the Krajina and has reopened the 1,000-mile pipeline to Hungary. The pipeline is a good source of revenue for Croatians. Additionally, Croatia is resettling 100,000 Croat refugees in the region replacing Croatian Serbs who fled to Bosnia and Serbia.

Hungarian troops have come into conflict with Croatian Serbs who control the Croatian part of eastern Slavonia. Hungary has been a conduit for arms to Croatia. Serbia has responded by sending troops and tanks to its Hungarian border.

August 15, 1995, BBC: Paul Ward in Belgrade:

UN observers are kept away from the fighting in Drvar but a reported 1,000 Serbs abandoned their positions after an attack by 2,500 Croatian troops. The plan seems to be to link up with the Bihac enclave, to liberate a swath of Bosnian Serb occupied territory.

President Aliev of Azerbaijan foiled an attempted coup against his government. This is the third coup attempt since his election last fall.

Saudi Arabia executed four Turks for smuggling sex stimulants into Arabia. P.M. Tansu Ciller protested the executions and the executions of two Turks the week before but King Fahd has said that they had broken Islamic law and had to pay the consequences.

The issue of Israel's treatment of Egyptian prisoners of war in the 1967 war came to light with the revelations that General Ariye Biro executed 49 Egyptian soldiers (POWs) himself in the   67 war Israel made on its Arab neighbors. He says if he is brought to trial, he will name others who killed even more. (Israel bombed a refugee camp in Lebanon, April 24, 1996. (May 6, 1996, Radio Netherlands reported that Dutch Brigadier General Von Kappen serving with the UN Forces says that Israel bombed the camp intentionally).

August 15, 1995, Radio Netherlands: **Marcel Sniders:**
Croatia has been massing thousands of troops around Dubrovnik for an expected attack on Bosnian Serbs who are shelling the city. Hundreds of Dubrovnik civilians have taken refuge in the bomb shelters in the center of the city.
In Zagreb, Assistant Secretary of State Richard Holbrooke says the U.S. peace plan is more like a discussion paper.

August 15, 1995, Die Deutsche Welle:
The car of the President of European Unity was fired upon as it traveled the road from the airport at Sarajevo to the city.
Croatian troops have renewed their attack on Dvor and expect it to fall soon,
The UN is withdrawing its troops from Croatia beginning with a contingent of 900 Nepalese troops.
Amnesty International is meeting in Ljubljana, Slovenia this week. The conference highlights are rise in the torture, human rights abuses, and murders of journalists around the world. Another concern is the rise of atrocities and abuses against women throughout the world who are defenseless against these crimes.

August 16, 1995, Radio Netherlands: **Marcel Sniders**:

Fighting has broken out around Drvar in western Bosnia with the Croatian Army moving into the area.

The new peace plan contains a division of Bosnia between the Serbs and Croats. The Serbs are refusing to meet representatives of the plan.

August 17, 1995, *Wall Street Journal*:

Truckloads of Croatian troops headed south to protect the medieval port of Dubrovnik from Serb attack. Croat forces also advanced on Serb-held lands in western Bosnia. A U.S. proposal to end the fighting, meanwhile, won initial positive responses.

August 17, 1995, CNN: Christiane Amanpour:

The city of Dubrovnik depends on tourism. Instead of 40,000 tourists at this time of the year there are only 150. The historical architecture of the city has been damaged from shelling over the past four years but the city is doing all it can to repair the damage and preserve works of art.

Assistant Secretary of States Richard Holbrooke is meeting with President Slobodan Milosevic in Belgrade to discuss the new peace initiative by the U.S. and to bring pressure on Bosnian Serbs to sign.

Radovan Karadzic says Drvar must be held at all costs.

August 17, 1995, VOA:

Croatia has doubled its troop strength in Dubrovnik and is ready to push back Serb artillery out of range of Dubrovnik.

Assistant Secretary of State Holbrooke is in Belgrade conferring with President Milosevic on the peace plan. One condition is to treat all warring parties equally. The Bosnian government says it likes some of the proposals but not all.

August 17, 1995, Radio Netherlands:

Croatia wants to expel some 30,000 Muslim refugees from the Krajina to Bosnia. These are followers of Friket Abdic who fled into the Krajina when the Bosnian government took Bihac last year. Croatia considers them traitors and doesn't want them.

The Iraqi army is reported to be very active in the north of Iraq. The US is putting pressure on Jordan to break all economic ties with Iraq and is putting US troops in a state of alert.

Croatia has doubled its troop strength in Dubrovnik.

August 18, 1995, CNN:

Assistant Secretary of State Holbrooke moved peace talks from Belgrade to Zagreb for peace talks with President Franjo Tudjman.

Christian Science Monitor correspondent, David Rohde, said that he had visited the mass gravesites shown in the U.S. spy plane photos and confirmed that the areas were indeed mass graves and that body parts could be seen. He also reported seeing empty boxes of ammunition, which would confirm that there had indeed been much ammunition used recently.

Christiane Amanpour: Croatia has increased its troop strength to 10,000 in face of continued shelling of Dubrovnik. The UN has called for restraint by the warring sides.

August 18, 1995, BBC:

The new Bosnian Serb mayor of Srebrenica says the mass graves outside Srebrenica hold the bodies of those who died in the fighting and were buried in a mass grave to control contagion. He says outside observers are welcome to investigate.

August 18, 1995, Die Deutsche Welle: John Ammon reporting:

EU Envoy Carl Bildt met with Chancellor Helmut Kohl and said that division of territory of Bosnia appears to be the best plan for peace in Bosnia.

President Alija Izetbegovic has tabled a 12-point peace plan that doesn't recognize the territorial integrity of Bosnia guaranteed under the United Nations charter of which Bosnia is a member.

Chechen fighters have frozen talks with Russia after Russia planes made air attacks on Chechen villages. The Russian commander, General Anatoly Romanov said he would investigate the accounts of air attacks on Chechen villages.

August 19, 1995: Houston Post. A photo taken by AP of a deep round hole in the road showed a mine blew the UN armored personnel carrier off the road killing three American diplomats.

August 19, 1995, CNN: Christiane Amanpour:

A UN armored personnel carrier carrying U.S. envoy Robert Frasure to the International Contact Group died along with two other American diplomats. The International Contact Group is trying to get Serbia's Milosevic to recognize Bosnia in return for lifting UN sanctions.

10,000 Croatian troops have massed in Dubrovnik and the city is boarding up historical sites and art treasures to protect them against Serb bombardment. The Croatian Army is expected to push the Bosnian Serb heavy weapons out of range of Dubrovnik.

August 19, 1995: *New York Times:*

Three U.S. diplomats: Robert Frasure, Joseph Krugel, and (Lt. Col) Sam Nelson Drew, are killed when their armored personnel carrier 'slipped' off the Mt. Igman road. (The head of the diplomatic mission, Richard Holbrooke, was in the same convoy but traveling in another vehicle). First reports showed a round hole about a meter in diameter in the road that looked cylindrical and quite deep). General Wesley Clark said he grabbed a fire extinguisher and ran down to try to put out the fire (Armored personnel carriers are designed so as not to catch on fire).

August 19, 1995, Die Deutsche Welle: Richard Williams reporting:
Unconfirmed reports say that Radovan Karadzic has been ousted by the Bosnian Serb military in Pale. This report was from Croatian sources and Bosnian Serbs say this is wishful thinking.

August 19, 1995, CNN:
The NATO Rapid Deployment Group complains it is hampered in getting its equipment and men in place by Bosnia and Croatia.

August 20, 1995 CNN:
Senator Robert Dole says the peace plan is not fair to Bosnians who have only asked to defend themselves. "You can't trust Karadzic, you can't trust Milosevic, and you can't trust Mladic," he is quoted as saying. Senator Richard Lugar (R-Indiana) on the other hand says he supports the Clinton administration's peace initiative.

August 20, 1995, Die Deutsche Welle:
Bosnian Serbs are holding up Ukrainian UN troops from leaving Gorazde. Gorazde is to be protected by NATO air

strikes.

UN soldiers who were in the Krajina say the Croat Army committed human rights abuses in Knin burying bodies of women and children in mass graves and setting fire to Croat Serb homes.

August 20, 1995, BBC:

France kept delivering arms and munitions to the Hutu Army of Rwanda because France didn't want the Tutsi ERP to win. It has been claimed that the Rwanda Hutus massacred over one million Tutsis and that the French were partly to blame.

August 21, 1995, Christian Science Monitor radio:

The U.S. peace initiative has been stalled with the death of the three U.S. diplomats and is not expected to start again until mid-September. The British are planning to withdraw their UN troops around September 16. The U.S. Congress will reconvene mid-September making this an important date in considering the fate of Bosnia. France, however, wants to maintain a high profile in Bosnia. The OIC (Organization of Islamic Countries) does not have alternative plans as yet.

Very little of President Clinton's peace plan is known as these are being kept secret. Trying to understand President Clinton's peace plan is like trying to find a black cat in the dark. One obstacle to the plan is Milosevic's unwillingness to recognize Croatia.

August 21, 1995, VOA (Voice of America):

U.S. Envoy to Bosnia, Richard Holbrooke, has made a secret agreement with Serb leader, Slobodan Milosevic, to divide Bosnia between Croatia and Serbia.

August 21, 1995, Radio Exterior de Espana:

About 1,000 Croatian Serb men refugees of military age were rounded up and deported to northern Bosnia to be inducted into the Bosnian Serb army.

August 21, 1995, Radio Netherlands:

An Algerian suspect in the bombing of the Place d'Etoile in Paris was arrested in Sweden. He is a member of the GIA (Group Islamique Armee) one of the more extreme terrorist groups in Algeria.

August 21, 1995, Die Deutsche Welle: Sue Cox:

Boris Yeltsin has sent his own diplomats to the Balkans to launch his own peace initiative in the Balkan war. He wants a summit of all the leaders involved in the conflict. Croatia's President Tudjman says he will not stop his offensive against Croatian Serbs until Serbia recognizes Croatia.

August 22, 1995, *Christian Science Monitor*: (Correspondent)

David Rohde explained that he was able to examine the mass gravesites near Srebrenica because the Serbs were anxious to admit journalists into their territory to interview Croatian Serb refugees. When he crossed the Border from Belgrade, the crossing guard directed him to go to Pale for permission to proceed further. He was thus able to pass by the mass gravesites and stop to examine them. But when he started to ask questions, the local Serbs became suspicious and hostile. He said he noticed no detention camps but the Serb authorities said hundreds if not thousands of Muslim men were hiding in the hills. Insisted others had made it to Bosnian government territory. The Bosnian government was not talking about those who made it into their territory so it looks like the Serbs had massacred the Muslim men.

August 22, 1995, CNN:

The heaviest shelling and rocket attack in two weeks hit Sarajevo. Eight people were killed and 38 wounded including six Egyptian peacekeepers. The Rapid Deployment Force fired into a Bosnian Serb mortar position after the Serb gunners had fired on UN troops.

The UN continues to evacuate UN peacekeepers from Gorazde while undergoing attacks from Bosnian Serbs. The UN says the attacks do not merit a NATO response. The UN says after the peacekeepers are evacuated NATO, air strikes will be enough to defend Gorazde.

August 22, 1995, *New York Times:*

Serbs shell Sarajevo killing six and wounding 38, including 6 Egyptian Peacekeepers in retaliation for the Bosnian Government shelling a Serb arms factory.

August 23, 1995, CNN:

Serb gunners shelled the runways of Tuzla airport where refugees from Srebrenica were living in tents. UN officials expressed outrage and said the shelling was excessive.

Bosnian Serb gunners shelled Sarajevo yesterday killing four people and wounding 32. The Rapid Reaction Force fired six shells at a Serb mortar, which had targeted UN peacekeepers.

The UN investigator for the Srebrenica massacres, speaking from Switzerland says Serb officials will not let him enter the Srebrenica area to investigate the alleged atrocities. Eyewitness's report hundreds of Bosnian Muslims were lined up by Bosnian Serb soldiers and executed.

August 23, 1995, Die Deutsche Welle and Radio Netherlands:

The three American diplomats killed in the Sarajevo road accident is a temporary setback to the American peace initiative. They will be replaced Sunday by three other diplomats who will resume negotiations for the peace plan (The three diplomats were not killed in an accident but blown up by a Serb mine).

Foreign Minister Mohammed Sacerby says the Bosnian government will give the American peace initiative two months after which the war will escalate.

August 24, 1995, *Wall Street Journal*:

(U.S.) President Clinton named four successors to the three U.S. envoys killed in Bosnia over the weekend. Bosnia's foreign minister said that the U.S. has at most two months in which to broker a peace accord before the parties in the conflict again seek a military solution.

August 24, 1995, Radio Netherlands:

Boutros Boutros Ghali has requested that all but 2,500 UN peacekeepers be removed from Croatia now that Croatia has taken back the Krajina. The 2,500 peacekeepers will be stationed in East Slavonia, which is still occupied by the Croatian Serbs.

All of the Ukrainian peacekeepers have been removed from the UN safe haven of Gorazde. Only 180 British troops remain. The UN says NATO can protect the 60,000 Gorazde inhabitants from the air. There are fears that this enclave will meet the same fate as Srebrenica.

August 27, 1995, Public Broadcast Radio:

Three US diplomats who will replace the three U.S. diplomats are flying to Europe to push the Clinton peace initiative.

The Bosnian Army commander says the outlook for acceptance of the peace plan is not good.

August 28, 1995, CNN:

(Serb) shells slammed into crowded Sarajevo market at noon killing an estimated 22 people and wounding an unknown number. Bosnia's Prime Minister, Haris Siladjic, asks peace talks to be suspended until the UN defines what is meant by *UN protected safe havens.*

August 28, 1995, *Wall Street Journal*:

The leader of the reconstituted U.S. peace initiative warned Bosnian Serbs to join the peace process or face attacks. He said if major progress isn't made in the next two weeks NATO air strikes could be ordered. *Newsweek* magazine said the US is planning a nine-month bombing campaign against Bosnian Serbs to allow Bosnia to build up its forces if the initiative fails. U.S. Envoys are scheduled to meet with Bosnia's president today and with Serb leaders in Belgrade tomorrow.

Croatia is holding back its troops during the peace talks, its foreign minister said, adding the chances of a settlement appear to be good.

August 28, 1995, Radio Netherlands: Carole Van den Ring:

Two mortar shells slammed into downtown Sarajevo killing 38 and wounding 80. Later a mortar hit the hospital where the wounded were being cared for, wounding two more. (Bosnian) President, Alija Izetbegovic, is in Paris for the peace talks. Canada, Italy, and Spain will attend the talks.

French President, Jacques Chirac, has asked for the demilitarization of Sarajevo and the surrounding area.

Meanwhile, the Bosnian Serb parliament in Pale has accepted the idea of a peace initiative.

August 28, 1995, *New York Times:*
The UN has secretly pulled out of the Gorazde *Safe Haven.*

August 29, 1995, *Wall Street Journal*:
Shelling of a marketplace in Sarajevo by Bosnian Serbs killed at least 35. A similar attack over a year ago killed 68. Bosnia's president called for immediate retaliatory air strikes. NATO was meeting to discuss how to respond to the attack which a State Department spokesman described as a crime against humanity. The UN ordered its commanders to take immediate action.

August 29, 1995, CNN:
The UN concluded it was Bosnian Serbs who fired mortar rounds into the crowded market resulting in 36 dead and 86 wounded. The UN said French howitzers would fire at the last known position of the Serb mortars. Foreign Minister Mohammed Sacirby said only if NATO took out all artillery ringing Sarajevo would Bosnia come back to the peace table. One U.S. naval carrier with 50 jets was being moved into the Adriatic but no reason was given.

There is dissention between Bosnian Serb military and Bosnian Serb politicians as well as with Milosevic of Serbia. The Serbs deny they shelled the market place in Sarajevo. Karadzic, who last year rejected the peace plan presented by the International Contact Group, now says he is willing to discuss it. Meanwhile, General Mladic refuses to remove Bosnian Serb artillery from around UN safe havens of Sarajevo, Tuzla, Mostar, and Gorazde.

August 29, 1995, French TV:
   President Izetbegovic had lunch with President Chirac.
   The interim mayor of Srebrenica denies any massacre took place. TV shows the site of the massacres and the bulldozer used to bury the dead. Soil was moved into the bodies. Srebrenica scenes of bombed-out buildings and bullet marked walls were shown. One woman was crying in the streets over the destruction of her country.

August 29, 1995, Die Deutsche Welle:
   Croatia and Serbia agreed to pull their tanks and heavy weapons back 10 kilometers from Croatian/Serb border.
   Explosions east of Sarajevo lit up the night sky as NATO planes hit Serb targets in eastern Bosnia. This was the long awaited NATO retaliation for the mortar attack on Sarajevo last week.
   Another mortar attack today killed a four-year old boy.

August 30, 1995, *Wall Street Journal*:
   An American pilot was killed at a British base when his U-2 surveillance plane crashed after take-off. The plane was assigned to support NATO operations in Bosnia.

Not mentioned in the news media was the dowsing of a French plane attached to NATO that was shot down by a shoulder fired ground to air missile by Bosnian Serbs who captured the two French pilots and subsequent tortured them for two months.

August 30, 1995, CNN:
   More than 60 NATO planes, mostly American, took off from a base in Aviana, Italy and the aircraft carrier Theodore Roosevelt to conduct the largest military operations taken by NATO since its founding. At 2 am Sarajevo time,

explosions lit up the night sky east of Sarajevo as the jets hit military installations and radar sites of the Bosnian Serbs, while the Rapid Reaction Force shelled a heavy artillery piece of the Serbs on a hillside over-looking Sarajevo. NATO sources said targets were destroyed or damaged. Serbs responded by firing mortar shells into downtown Sarajevo. Demands were made for the Serbs to remove their tanks and heavy artillery from within a 20-kilometer area around Sarajevo **as they were told to do so over a year ago**.

President Clinton said he stands by this decision by NATO to make these retaliatory raids against the Serbs. Serb leader, Karadzic, sent a letter to former president, Jimmy Carter, saying the Serbs were willing to consider the peace plan submitted last summer by the International Contact Group. (Milosevic of Serbia had already accepted the division of Bosnia and it was the Bosnian Serbs who had not accepted them).

August 30, 1995, Die Deutsche Welle:

NATO launched air strikes around UN safe havens of Gorazde, Tuzla, Mostar, and Sarajevo on Serb gun positions. The UN told the Serbs to remove their guns from within a 20 kilometers exclusion zone but Serb general, Ratko Mladic, says he will not comply with the UN demand. Bosnian Serbs have agreed to include their armed forces with Serbian leaders in future peace negotiations.

August 30, 1995, CNN Talk Live:

Washington spokeswoman for Bosnian Serbs, **Danielle Sremac**, said it was the Muslims themselves who fired the mortar rounds that killed 37 people and wounded 86 in Monday's attack. She smiled as she said the previous slaughter in January 1994 was Muslims killing their own people to blame the Serbs. (*Sremac smiled when she said "Muslims kill Muslims just to blame Serbs,"* and looked as though she would burst out laughing as she said it).

August 31, 1995, *Wall Street Journal*, p. A-10;

A detailed report by Bosnia's government shows Slobodan Milosevic did not curtail his support of the Bosnian Serbs as he said he would last September. From the beginning of the conflict he supplied the Bosnian Serbs with 512 tanks, 506 armored personnel carriers, 18 transport helicopters, ten high performance military jets, more than 250 mortars, howitzers, and other artillery, and 8,700 tons of fuel.

August 31, 1995, French TV:

Bosnian Serb civilians speak bitterly about a "U.S.-led state terrorism" against Bosnian Serb military targets.

August 31, 1995, CNN:

NATO is searching for the two French pilots downed yesterday over Serb territory. NATO says the air strikes will continue until the Serbs bow to NATO demands to remove their artillery from an exclusion zone 20 kilometers around each UN safe haven. Considerable damage was done to the air defense and military communications systems of the Bosnian Serbs.

Five European monitors reported by the Bosnian Serbs as having been killed in the NATO air strikes but in reality they were kidnapped by the Bosnian Serbs and shown on videotape to be alive when the UN asserted that they might have been murdered by the Bosnian Serbs.

Bosnian Serbs were reported to have kidnapped a *Newsweek* reporter but no information about his safety is available.

Russian president Boris Yeltsin says the NATO air

attacks against Serb military targets are cruel. (But he has no sympathy for men, women, and children killed by Serbs).

August 31, 1995, Die Deutsche Welle:

Albania's President Berishne complains that Serbia is resettling Croatian Serb refugees in Kosovo which is 96% ethnically Albanian.

The German-made Tornado fighters, said to be the best in the world at combating radar directed anti-aircraft missiles, have not been called into use by NATO in the latest air strikes on Serbs.

September 1, 1995, French TV:

A Serbian citizen on the streets of Belgrade calls the NATO strikes on Bosnian Serb military installations a shameful act of the international community against Serbs.

September 1, 1995, CNN:

NATO has halted its air strikes but the Rapid Reaction Force, which operates under different command, is still pounding the heavy artillery surrounding Sarajevo. Some heavy Serb artillery has been pulled out, but an estimated 300 mortars and artillery remain.

September 1, 1995, Radio Netherlands:

Heavy fighting has broken out in the Bihac enclave Friday as the Bosnian Army attempted to break out. Serbs responded by shelling two nearby villages and Bihac town itself.

September 2, 1995, CNN:

NATO has demanded the siege of Sarajevo be lifted and the UN have unrestricted flights into and out of Sarajevo airport as well as removal of all Serb guns from a 20 kilometer exclusion zone around Sarajevo and all other UN declared safe havens.

September 2, 1995, Radio Netherlands **Marcel Oustings**:

NATO has rejected Serb General Ratko Mladic's demands and says it has suspended air strikes to give General Ratko Mladic time to conform to NATO demands. Mladic says he will not conform to any NATO conditions until NATO meets his demands.

On Mt Igman, a Serb mortar fired on a French outpost and the Rapid Reaction Force responded with fire on Serb positions. In the capital, an anti-tank shell exploded in a suburb and the Rapid Reaction Force responded with fire on Serb positions. The UN said it could not determine who fired the shell.

September 2, 1995, Die Deutsche Welle:

NATO said that the Bosnian Serbs can expect resumption of NATO air strikes within hours if the Serbs do not remove their heavy weapons from within the 20 kilometers exclusion zone.

Heavy fighting is reported to have broken out in Bihac between Bosnian government forces and Bosnian Serbs.

September 3, 1995, Radio Netherlands:

The UN Rapid Reaction Force opened another supply road into Sarajevo without asking permission from the Bosnian Serbs. NATO has given the Bosnian Serbs until midnight (7:00 pm CST) Monday to remove their artillery from around Sarajevo and permit unrestricted access to Sarajevo and unrestricted use of Sarajevo airport or expect a resumption of NATO air strikes. General Mladic has so far refused.

Meanwhile, Bosnian Serb guns shelled Bosnian villages around the UN *protected enclave* of Tuzla and shot down a UN unmanned reconnaissance plane in southwest Bosnia.

The Serbs also released the five EU monitors they had kidnapped after the NATO air strikes on Monday. The EU monitors said they were happy to be free as they feared they would be killed when they learned the Bosnian Serbs had announced they had been killed by the NATO air strikes.

September 4, 1995, Radio Netherlands: **Grant Kirkland**:

NATO's deadline for Serb withdrawal of tanks and heavy artillery has expired. NATO has made over-flights of Bosnian Serb occupied territory only for observation and it is not known if air strikes are imminent. General Ratko Mladic came up with his own version for a cease-fire, which NATO rejected.

A five member international commission on human rights headed by Eli Weisel convened in Bonn and stated there was ample evidence of genocide in Bosnia and that President Slobodan Milosevic of Serbia should be indicted along with Dr. Karadzic and General Mladic.

An Italian doctor reported a Dutch UN soldier joined with the Serbs in the gang rape of a 16-yer-old) Muslim girl after the fall of Srebrenica. The girl later committed suicide.

September 4, 1995, Die Deutsche Welle:

Bosnian Serbs have let the NATO deadline pass without removing any weapons from the 20 kilometer exclusion zone. UN Security Council **has been given a report that asks Boutros Boutros Ghali to call Thorvald Stoltenberg and Yashushi Akashi to account.**

September 5, 1996, CNN: **Christiane Amanpour**:

Bombing of Serb targets resumed when NATO ascertained that Serb General Ratko Mladic had not removed any heavy weapons from around Sarajevo. Serb politicians said they were complying with NATO's ultimatum. NATO said this was either a ploy or there was dissention within the Serb leadership but that their patience was worn thin. Ludovica barracks, a Serb munitions depot, was hit and explosions could be heard and smoke seen from Sarajevo. The Serbs say 120,000 Serbs are living in Sarajevo area and fear there might be 120,000 refugees flowing from Sarajevo into the Bosnian Serb territory.

September 5, 1995, French TV:
Bosnian Serbs, rumors are circulating that Serbs captured the two French pilots downed last week. Serbs say other NATO planes were shot at although NATO has said only the one Mirage plane was lost.
Bosnians interviewed on the streets of Sarajevo praised French President Jacques Chirac for getting NATO to do something. One girl said that her cousin had been killed last week and the Serbs were finally receiving just retribution.

September 5, 1995, Radio Netherlands:
French troops of the Rapid Reaction Force on Mt. Igman fired down on Serb positions that were shelling Sarajevo. Serb mortars killed one boy. Russia has condemned the air strikes and claims NATO has taken sides with the Bosnians.
According to the German DPA news agency, NATO air strikes have destroyed a large segment of Serb communications. Serbs claim the air strikes have caused large civilian casualties.
James Cliffhouse, Radio Netherlands correspondent in Bosnia: "It is a Serb tradition to bomb civilians and also to defy ultimatums, then slowly begin to bombard civilian targets again." The so-called peace process is still going on.
President Slobodan Milosevic wants the Bosnian Serbs to stop warring. The Bosnian Government now says it will attend the Geneva peace talks, but now Belgrade says it may

boycott the peace talks.

September 5, 1995, CNN:
Food prices (in Sarajevo) have dropped after UN food convoys reached Sarajevo. People in Sarajevo are relieved to see NATO jets retaliate against Serb guns that have pounded Sarajevo this past year even though the UN had ordered Serb big guns out of the exclusion zone over a year ago.

A Serb water pumping station was destroyed near Lukovica and indignant Serbs complain this was a civilian target. An outhouse was also destroyed. Serb General Mladic said, "The more NATO bombs us, the stronger we get. The U.S. bombed Viet Nam and other places but in the end they run away with their tails between their legs."

September 6, 1995, CNN:
Weather has cleared over Bosnia and NATO plans to step up air strikes on Bosnian Serb military targets as the Serbs have failed to heed a NATO ultimatum to pull back heavy weapons from around Sarajevo.

September 6, 1995, Radio Netherlands: **Marcel Sniders**:
Radovan Karadzic says he will not comply with NATO's ultimatum to withdraw all heavy weapons from around Sarajevo. He demanded an immediate end to NATO air strikes. He said he was in command and that there was no dissention in the Serb leadership.

A Bosnian Croat commander has been accused of destroying a Muslim village and massacring 17 Muslims. He is currently in detention by Bosnian Croat authorities.

September 6, 1995, Die Deutsche Welle: Bosnian Serb leader Karadzic calls NATO air strikes "unscrupulous" For the first times since WW II, the German air force has seen military action with its Tornado fighters taking part in NATO air strikes. Bosnians Serbs claim that 100 civilians have died in the bombings but offer no proof.

September 7, 1995, CNN:
NATO says it will be increasing the number of air strikes until the Bosnian Serbs comply with NATO's ultimatum. Russia's President Yeltsin says NATO has taken sides with the Bosnians and that Russia will have to reconsider its relationship with NATO.

September 7, 1995, Radio Netherlands: **Marcel Sniders:**
A NATO spokesman said that NATO operations will continue. NATO air strikes could have bombed many more targets and damage is not really all that great. Washington says that Russia's contribution to the peace process is invaluable. Russian President Yeltsin says that Russia will have to review its relationship within NATO.

September 7, 1995, Die Deutsche Welle:
(German) Defense Minister Volker Ruhe said the use of German Tornado fighters was not in the retaliation against the Serbs but on reconnaissance flights or coordination with the Rapid Reaction Force.

September 7, 1995, French TV:
NATO officials are not commenting on the French pilots shot down over Bosnian Serb territory because of security reasons. Bosnian Serbs claim the two were "arrested" by farmers and turned over to Serb authorities. One is said to have suffered a fractured leg and both are being closely guarded.
Most of the air strikes originate from Aviani, Italy. The

TV shows Lukovica barracks, which was not abandoned, and shows windows that were broken from the blast when a munitions dump was hit by a NATO missile. The TV also showed where an artillery shell blew up a big concrete bunker, which was deep in the ground.

September 7, 1995, *Wall Street Journal*:
    NATO kept up its air attack on Bosnian Serb positions but (Serb) General Mladic refuses to move his heavy weapons from around Sarajevo. NATO was limiting its attacks to selected military installations so Serbs couldn't say it kept them from withdrawing.

September 8, 1995, CNN (2 AM):
    Russian President Yeltsin went into a rambling rage when asked by an American newswoman about Bosnia. He threatened to send more weapons to Serbia and that Europe would be in flames if the war went against the Serbs. Russia has been in Europe for thousands of years, he said, and Bosnia was a European question to be settled by Europeans.

September 8, 1995, French TV:
    The Rapid Reaction Force did not fire at the Serbs for the first few days after the ultimatum deadline so the Serbs could withdraw. Since then, a thousand rounds have been fired but no assessment of the damage has been made.

September 8, 1995, Radio Netherlands: **Jackie Spears**:
    A diplomatic breakthrough has been hailed in Geneva with the foreign ministers of Croatia, Bosnia, and Rump Yugoslavia agreeing to a confederation of Bosnia to be split 51 % for Bosnian Muslims and Croats and 49% for Bosnian Serbs. No agreement has been reached on how the land is to be divided and no decision taken about Croatia's East

Slavonia, held by Croatian Serbs.

Meanwhile, NATO operations continue against Bosnian Serbs who are still defying the NATO ultimatum to evacuate their big guns from the exclusion Zone around Sarajevo.

September 9, 1995, CNN:

USS Roosevelt sent some sorties with smart bombs to be used on Serb air defense systems around Tuzla, Gorazde, Sarajevo, and Banja Luka. No damage assessment was made. Serb leaders in Pale were angry as they said they were agreeing to comply with NATO demands and the raids took place two hours after they agreed to withdraw their heavy weapons.

The improved Tomahawk has a 1,000 pound payload and is more accurate than missiles used in the Gulf War.

September 9, 1995, Die Deutsche Welle: NATO has fired 13 Tomahawk missiles for the first time at air missile defense systems around Banja Luka. Tomahawk missiles were used because of their accuracy and because weather is of no consequence. This was done after General Mladic rejected (UN) General Janvier's demand to remove Serb guns from around Sarajevo. Artillery positions around Tuzla were also bombed after Serb gunners shelled the city.

Romania joined NATO and will send 450 troops to join NATO command.

By the 5th of October, Chechen fighters will hand over their weapons and Russian troops will begin withdrawing from Chechnya.

September 9, 1995, Radio Netherlands: **Jackie Spears:**

Russia's parliament has urged suspension of Russia's participation in NATO's partnership for peace.

The UN denies its missiles hit a hospital and killed ten

people.

EU's Envoy Carl Bildt said the NATO operations could soon stop if Serbs heeded UN demands.

Croatia's East Slavonia is not covered in the Friday accords and will be dealt with separately.

September 9, 1995, CNN:

Serb Americans demonstrated in Washington and Los Angeles with signs saying Croats and Bosnians supported the NAZIS in WW II and called for an end to NATO bombing of Bosnian Serbs.

The Kashmir separatists have given a reprieve to 2 Britons, 1 German, and 1 American whom they had threatened to kill if India did not release 52 jailed separatists held in Indian prisons.

September 10, 1995, CNN:

13 Tomahawk missiles were launched from the USS Normandy in the Adriatic. Captain Jim Mitchell said they were targeting Serb defenses around Banja Luka which has been quite a threat to NATO. Targets were: General Mladic's HQ, Serb armed forces HQ, main Serb airfield, radar network, and missile batteries of the type that downed American Captain Scott O'Grady's plane. NATO had to act now to get rid of these batteries before Serbs received shoulder-fired missiles.

September 10, 1995, Radio Netherlands Jackie Spears:

13 Tomahawk missiles were aimed at Serb air defenses around the Serb stronghold of Banja Luka Serb defenses around Tuzla.

Chechen fighters agreed to hand over their weapons and Russians agreed to withdraw their troops from Chechnya.

The Taliban militia in Afghanistan denied it received

weapons from Pakistan and Prime Minister Bhutto denied Pakistan has aided the Taliban. Pakistan is closing its embassy in Kabul after it was attacked by a mob and one Pakistani diplomat was killed.

September 11, 1996, Christian Science Monitor Radio:
Bosnian Serbs are threatening to pull out of the peace plan process unless NATO air strikes stop. Washington says the operations will continue as needed.
Bosnian forces captured Serb territory in northern and central Bosnia.
U.S. State Department condemns Israeli settler's attacks on Palestinians. (The settler's terrorist gang is called *Kach).*
The only black bank in South Africa, African Bank, just went into receivership.

September 11, 1995, CNN:
Just as Sarajevo's trams began operating after five months of cessation of operations, due to sniping, a Serb gunman opened fire on one tram wounding eight people.

September 12, Radio Netherlands: Jackie Spears;
NATO has expanded its list of proposed targets. According to U.S. Secretary of Defense, William Perry, planes will now fly with impunity over western Bosnia. American, Spanish, French, and Italian planes have flown in sorties over Bosnia. Washington wants to send stealth bombers for use over Bosnia but Italy is objecting.
Serbs claim there are many children among the civilian casualties resulting from NATO bombings.
Serbian President Milosevic warned EU Envoy Carl Bildt that war, not peace, will result from continued air strikes (He threatened to bomb New York and London at the

beginning of the Bosnia conflict in 1992, if either the United States or the U.K. became involved in Bosnia).

NATO's response is that if the Serbs are serious about peace, they should withdraw their heavy weapons from around Sarajevo.

Bosnian Croat forces have gained considerable territory around Sepovo and several mountains in western Bosnia.

September 12, Die Deutsche Welle:

In raids described as the heaviest yet munitions dumps and military targets around Sarajevo were hit by NATO air strikes.

Bosnian Government forces captured the strategic town of Zornice.

September 12, 1995, CNN:

Bosnian Government troops cut an important supply route of the Serbs and have taken Jajce. Donji Vakuf was captured by Bosnian Government forces.

Five Russian parliamentarians are in Belgrade to verify the civilian casualties caused by NATO bombings of Bosnian Serb military targets and investigate charges of genocide by NATO against the Serbs. They are offering to be human shields against further NATO attacks. The Lukavica barracks were hit by NATO air strikes but they were not the intended target.

September 13, 1995, Radio Netherlands: Jackie Spears:

The UN Security Council has expressed concern over the resumption of fighting in Bosnia. Bosnian Croat forces captured Jajce and the town of Dvor. Tens of thousands of Bosnian Serbs are fleeing western Bosnia for Banja Luka.

September 14, 1995, French TV:

NATO and UNPROFOR do not see eye to eye on continued air strikes against Serb military targets.

Tito's underground bunkers protect the most strategic portions of the Bosnian Serb defenses and are a major bulwark of the Serbs in their aggression in Bosnia. NATO does not want to start a full-scale war and is limiting targets to anti-aircraft missile sites, ammunition dumps, and communication centers.

An offensive by Bosnian Croats and Bosnian Government forces has taken more than 1,500 square kilometers in central Bosnia near Donji Vakuf. This has the Serbs more worried than NATO air strikes even though the territory retaken by the Bosnians is within the limits drawn by the diplomats as the future boundary between the Croat-Bosnian federation and the Serbs. ***The French commentator added that the efficiency of western rockets, bombs, planes, and methods is proven but the efficiency of western diplomacy is still in question.***

September 14, 1995, Die Deutsche Welle:

(U.S.) Deputy Secretary of State, Richard Holbrooke, says that 10,000 Russian troops will be stationed in Bosnia once the peace accords have been signed.

September 14, 1995, CNN:

Deputy Secretary of State Richard Holbrooke says air strikes will be suspended for 72 hours to allow Bosnian Serbs to withdraw their heavy weapons from around Sarajevo. In Moscow, Assistant Secretary of State Strobe Talbott said NATO air strikes have made the situation in Bosnia even worse. (Talbot now heads Brookings Institute).

Serbs allow two roads and the Sarajevo airport to open with a cease-fire around Sarajevo. Even with two roads open, the people of Sarajevo are not free to move in or around Sarajevo. The Serbs have removed only a few big artillery pieces and three tanks but if not all are removed, NATO says it will resume bombing. If the proposed peace agreement is reached, as many as 25,000 U.S. troops could be stationed in Bosnia.

Allied Bosnian and Bosnian Croat forces are gaining ground in northern, central, and western Bosnia. The Croatian Army has given the Bosnian Army some heavy weapons, which has enabled the Bosnian Army to be on a par with the Serb forces.

Serb gunners fired two anti-aircraft missiles at a NATO plane southwest of Sarajevo but the plane was not hit. NATO said apparently the Serb gunners had not received the news about the cease-fire, so NATO did not plan a response.

September 14, 1995, *Wall Street Journal*:

Muslim and Croat forces claimed major gains in a fierce offensive across central and western Bosnia seizing two key towns from Serbs and sending thousands of Serb civilians fleeing. The Serbs offered little resistance and appeared to be pulling back. NATO, meanwhile, launched new air strikes against Serb positions around Sarajevo.

September 15, 1995, CNN:

Allied and Bosnian Croat forces continue to liberate territory in western Bosnia and Serbs appear to be offering little resistance. Some Serb big weapons have been removed from around Sarajevo, but NATO says more must go.

September 15, 1995, Die Deutsche Welle: (0300 UTC) Nigel Tandy:

Eyewitness accounts say three tanks and nine heavy guns have been withdrawn. If the Serbs do not live up to the demand on lifting the siege, bombings will resume.

The Bosnian Government Army is heading toward Banja Luka where 100,000 Serb refugees are reportedly gathering. More territory continues to be liberated in western Bosnia.

September 16, 1995, Radio Netherlands: **Anne Holland Kemp:**
The UN and NATO have given another 72 hours to the Bosnian Serbs to remove their heavy weapons from around Sarajevo.
(**Note:** September 5, 1995, *CNN*) *"People in Sarajevo are relieved to see NATO jets retaliate against Serb guns that have pounded Sarajevo this past year even though the UN had ordered Serb big guns out of the exclusion zone over a year ago."*

September 16, 1995, Radio Netherlands continued)
In Banja Luka, the Serb refugees are leaving in trucks and horse drawn wagons toward Serbia.
In Bangladesh, a second day of strikes and violence has claimed one life. Clashes between pro and anti-government demonstrators continue.

September 16, 1995, CNN:
Bosnian Prime Minister Siladjic and Foreign Minister Sacerby appear positively giddy over the news of continued gains made by the Bosnian Army.
"The fighting goes on," says U.S. Envoy Richard Holbrooke, "whatever its effect is what will be."
Bosnian Serbs admit they have lost much ground. NATO air strikes devastated Serb communications and General Mladic is in a hospital awaiting an operation for kidney stones.

September 16, 1995, Die Deutsche Welle: Nigel Tandy:
200 Serb heavy weapons have been withdrawn from

around Sarajevo.

A government spokesman in Zagreb says the Croat-Muslim offensive aims to liberate all of western Bosnia including Banja Luka.

After five months suspension, Germany has resumed flights into Sarajevo for humanitarian purposes.

September 16, 1995, Sixty Minutes with Mike Wallace:
In interview with Bosnian Serb leader Karadzic says he is protecting Europe from Muslims and their intolerance, torture, and dissection. Says he has seen what they can do to the people. He said Serb soldiers were roasted on spits. He then shows pictures of massacres of Serbs by Muslims. He claims Muslims are responsible for atrocities and that Serbs committed none.

Mike Wallace continued, "In Srebrenica, General Mladic said after the conquest of the city, 'This is going to be a long bloody feast'." (Karadzic didn't reply to Mike Wallace's quoting of Mladic).

In an interview with former U.S. Secretary of State Eagleburger, *Sixty Minutes* he said he wouldn't shake hands with Karadzic who has lied time and time again and responsible for terrible atrocities.

September 17, 1995, National Public Radio (US):
The Serbs have pulled back at least 160 guns out from around Sarajevo and sent them to the front in the north where Serb stronghold of Banja Luka is facing opposition from three fronts. The thirteen cruise missiles only damaged the air defense system around Banja Luka but not the Serbs ability to defend Banja Luka from the ground. The UN said the situation is delicate with the flight of thousands of refugees and the threat of Serbia to enter the war.

The hysterical reaction of Russian politicians last week

ended with the cession of NATO bombings. The Russian posturing of interest to protect their Slavic brothers, the Serbs, appears to be more posturing for Yeltsin's re-elections. Russians are weighing whether they want stability or to seek what they may view as the world's lack of respect and consideration for Russia. Secretary of Defense William Perry says the war in the Balkans seems to be coming to an end and that the Serbs realize a military victory is not possible and the Bosnian Government seems to be acting in good faith.

September 18, 1995, CNN:

The Bosnian and Croat forces now control more than fifty percent of Bosnia. Thousands of refugees are pouring into Banja Luka from western Bosnia as thousands of previous refugees stream out of Banja Luka toward Serbia. The UN says the situation of the refugees a disaster waiting to happen.

UN Secretary General, Boutros Boutros Ghali, has said that UN troops should be withdrawn from Bosnia and replaced by NATO troops under a NATO command.

September 18, 1995, Die Deutsche Welle:

The UN has called upon the warring parties to stop fighting. If Banja Luka falls to the Bosnian or Croat forces, President Milosevic might feel compelled to enter the war on the side of the Bosnian Serbs. The Bosnian Serbs won a concession from NATO to remove only mortars larger than 80 mm and heavy guns larger than 100 mm from the exclusion zone around Sarajevo.

Russia's mothballed submarine fleet has been called a future ecological disaster as dangerous as Chernobyl. The fuel rods and reactors are in such a poor shape there could be a nuclear disaster.

September 19, 1995, French TV:

The Bosnian Army advanced so quickly in its northern and central Bosnia offensive that it captured many heavy weapons and tanks. Bosnian Serbs lost much of it communications capabilities when NATO bombed the Banja Luka area with thirteen Tomahawk missiles. Bosnian and Croat forces now hold more than fifty percent of Bosnia.

Life has reappeared in Sarajevo with food on the shelves, people in the streets, and stores attracting people to buy. Bennaton's has opened a store in Sarajevo with prices the same as Paris and Sarajevo's *jet set* sacrificed food expenditures to buy something fashionable. Children were also openly attending school for the first time in years.

September 19, 1995, *Wall Street Journal*:

The Bosnian Serb losses are so severe that the Serb dominated Yugoslav Army may enter the war in Bosnia.

U.S. Envoy Richard Holbrooke's shuttle diplomacy had already brought hopes of peace, was visibly dispirited after meeting with Serbia's President Milosevic. Gains by Croat forces have rekindled fears among Muslims of being squeezed out by Croats and Serbs.

September 19, 1995, CNN:

British Minister of Defense, Malcolm Rifkind, visited Zagreb and convinced President Franjo Tudjman to halt the Croatian forces from closing in on Banja Luka.

September 19, 1995, Radio Netherlands: (0030 UTC) **Dave Durham**:

The UN says the Bosnian Army has continued to advance into the mountains around Droboyja, Drubar, and

Tuzla.

Presidents Tudjman and Izetbegovic assured U.S. Envoy Richard Holbrooke the Allied Bosnian-Croat armies will not take Banja Luka.

After meeting with Milosevic, Richard Holbrooke said some agreements have been made on a point-by-point basis.

Given until 2000 UTC Wednesday by NATO, Bosnian Serbs say they will pull back their heavy weapons 20 kilometers from around Sarajevo.

September 19, 1995, International Public Radio (US):
The Taliban militia forces are advancing on Kabul on three fronts.

September 20, 1995, French TV:
Bosnian Croat forces are said to have more than 60% of Bosnia under their control. They have halted their advance and will not enter the city (Banja Luka) where 100,000 Serbs have taken refuge.

A French-speaking Serb officer interviewed on French TV says he is from Sarajevo and his family is in Sarajevo. He was born in Sarajevo and hopes the weapons pullback is only temporary. They will return, he insists, because the war started in Sarajevo and must end there. Sarajevo must be divided between Serbs and Bosnians. When asked about bombardment of Sarajevo's civilians he replied, "C'est la guerre".

September 20, 1995, CNN:
Bosnian and Croat forces have advanced to within nine miles of Banja Luka, which has been receiving strong reinforcements.

September 20, 1995, Radio Netherlands:

The UN and NATO say the Bosnian Serbs have removed 250 tanks and heavy weapons from around Sarajevo and NATO. The Serbs have met NATO's demands and NATO will not launch any more air strikes against the Bosnian Serbs.

The Conventional Forces in Europe Treaty will be modified for Russia to allow them more weapons systems. Moscow says conditions have changed since the treaty was signed.

In Dagestan (next to Chechnya), two hijackers have taken a bus and are demanding a million and a half dollars money and a helicopter to take them to an undisclosed location.

September 20, 1995, CNN:

There are unconfirmed reports that President Milosevic of Serbia has sent Serbian militias into Bosnia to bolster the strength of the Bosnian Serbs. (True but covered up by the United Nations monitors).

The Bosnian army has demanded Banja Luka be demilitarized and the city should surrender. But instead the Serbs are digging in.

September 20, 1995, Die Deutsche Welle:

Although NATO has stopped bombing, it could begin again if the Serbs break any of the agreements.

German Foreign Minister, Klaus Kinkel, said that a cooperative Moscow is needed to keep weapons of mass destruction from falling into the hands of organized crime.

September 21, 1995, CNN:

Although the big guns around Sarajevo are silent, sniper fire continues. The Serbs have allowed humanitarian aid convoys to pass but Sarajevo remains without gas or power.

Water is available only at certain spots and people wash their clothes in the river while UN soldiers protect them from sniper fire.

The Bosnian army has halted its offensive while Croatian Army units have retired behind the Croatian border. At Bosanski Nova, Serbs say they have repulsed the Bosnian offensive.

September 21, 1995, Radio Netherlands:
Bosnian Serbs are expelling Muslims and Croats still living in territory under their control.

There were three attempts to rescue the two French airmen downed by a Serb shoulder-fired rocket. On the last rescue attempt, the helicopters were chased away by Serb ground fire and two American servicemen were slightly wounded. The Red Cross is unable to see the French pilots said to be under the *protection* of Milosevic.

September 21, 1995, *Wall Street Journal*:
Prime Minister Tansu Ciller resigned after a party pulled out of her coalition to protest austerity measures. Ciller refused (to order) early elections and will try to put together a new coalition.

Afghanistan's President Rabbani was warned that he has five days to surrender Kabul to the Islamic Taliban militias or face an attack. Taliban, which grew out of a student movement, has made major gains against government forces in western Afghanistan.

September 21, 1995, Die Deutsche Welle:
Russia has failed to get the UN to lift sanctions against Serbia and plans to get a resolution passed that would condemn the Bosnian Government.

Heavy fighting continues in the north around Doboj.

President Izetbegovic says he will agree to a ceasefire when the Serbs agree to demilitarize Banja Luka and restore water, gas, and power to Sarajevo.

September 22, 1995, CNN:

There is a meeting between the Foreign Ministers of Croatia, Bosnia, and Serbia to be held in New York next week but the heavy fighting in western Bosnia between Bosnian Government forces and the Serbs is said to be endangering the peace process.

A Russian electric power station cut off electric power to a Russian submarine base for non-payment of their electric bill. This cut off of the refrigeration for the plutonium rods in the atomic submarines would almost set off another Chernobyl. The base commander forced the electric company to turn the electricity back on or there would have been an atomic meltdown.

September 22, 1995, French TV:

Serb refugees are interviewed. They say Croat soldiers burned houses, destroyed villages and killed livestock without pity. One man says he lost one son near Kupa. His other two sons are with him but they are all living like pigs. He says he is so depressed he says he wants to drown himself. Other Serbs say they lived with Croats and Muslims before and are tired of this absurd war.

Iranian Foreign Minister, Ali Akhbar Velayati, proposed to the French Foreign Minister Herve Charette to help arrange a meeting between the Algerian military government and the Algerian opposition, to bring about peace in Algeria. Charette said he'd "think about it".

September 22, 1995, Radio Netherlands: **Evonne Von Bonavelt**:

Secretary of State Christopher called upon all warring parties in Bosnia to stop fighting. Radovan Karadzic says he won't stop fighting until all the territory lost to the Bosnian Government is recovered.

Seventy towns around Banja Luka have received humanitarian aid.

Bosnian President Izetbegovic presented a four-point demand before they stop fighting. Two of the four demands are the lifting of the siege of Sarajevo and restoring water, gas, and power to Sarajevo.

After the fall of Srebrenica, seven wounded Bosnian men were taken by Serbs from the hospital run by Medicins Sans Frontiers. The seven have not been heard from again. Serbs said they were guilty of "war crimes". A Dutch UN soldier was said to have assisted the Serbs.

September 22, 1995, Die Deutsche Welle:

The Bosnian Army stepped up a three pronged attack on the Banja Luka region from Bosanska Krupa, Bosanska Brod, and Doboj 50 miles east of Banja Luka which controls its supply road. Observers counted 750 grenade and mortar attacks on Doboj.

Serbian President Slobodan Milosevic says he does not want a Berlin wall in Sarajevo. But Bosnian Serb Radovan Karadzic says the division of Sarajevo is unavoidable.

September 23, 1995, Radio Netherlands: **Carole Van Den Ring**:

(Bosnian) Prime Minister, Haris Siladjic, announced the Bosnian Army uncovered a mass grave of 540 Muslims and Croats murdered by the Bosnian Serbs in 1992 near Didic. The grave was discovered last week when this area was liberated from the Bosnian Serbs.

The humanitarian conditions in Iraq have deteriorated

badly these past six months for four million of Iraq's 18 million population. Twenty to twenty-five percent of children under five are malnourished.

The French Embassy has called upon all foreign residents in Kabul to leave the city. The Kabul government has transferred its government to Jalalabad some 30 kilometers east of Kabul.

September 23, 1995, Die Deutsche Welle:

A mass grave, containing the bodies of 540 Croats and Muslims murdered by Serbs, has been discovered near Krasulje.

Bosnian Serbs say they have halted the advance of Croats and Muslims and recovered some territory previously lost to them. With 100,000 refugees in Banja Luka, conditions are said to be terrible. Food is scarce and prices high. 120 elderly are said to have died.

September 23, 1995, CNN:

The Bosnian Army is still advancing in northwestern Bosnia and has taken Sanski Most. Bosnians and Croats have 50.8% of Bosnia under their control.

Croats and Bosnian Serbs exchanged prisoners of war and Croat civilians held by the Serbs.

September 24, 1995, CNN:

It will take billions of dollars to reconstruct Bosnia and Sarajevo once peace has come to that country. Prime Minister Haris Siladjic says that peace will not come without a ceasefire and a ceasefire is not in sight at this time.

September 24, 1995, Radio Netherlands:

Bosnia will not participate in the Tuesday's meeting in New York of ministers of Croatia, Serbia, and Bosnia.

September 24, 1995, CNN:
Heavy fighting is reported south of Banja Luka.

September 25, 1995, Houston channel 51:
Muslim and Croat forces have launched a strong attack on Brcko in northeastern Bosnia, but this supply route on the border of Croatia's East Slavonia is putting up strong resistance.

September 25, 1995, CNN:
Bosnian/Croat forces continue to carve out huge slices of Bosnian Serb territory and heavy fighting is reported south of Banja Luka.

Prime Minister Haris Siladjic has said he will attend Tuesday' meeting in New York with Serbian and Croatian ministers after a U.S. diplomats said they support Bosnia's position that the Serbs are to remain in Bosnia and not be allowed to join Serbia after Bosnia is to be partitioned. The Bosnia Government also demands the demilitarization of Banja Luka and surrounding Bosnian Serb territory.

The Bosnian Government Forces are attacking near Novi Grad in an attempt to cut off the supply corridor to Banja Luka from Serbia, which is still supplying fuel, munitions, and weapons despite Serbia's pledge to stop this military aid last September in return for a partial lifting of UN sanctions against Serbia.

The Rapid Reaction Force in Bosnia gave a demonstration of its firepower, showing guns that never miss targets, and the ability of the Rapid Reaction Force to force a settlement if all sides of the conflict do not agree to a termination of hostilities.

At Al Arish in the Sinai, the bodies of Egyptian P.O.W.'s executed by Israeli soldiers in the Sinai War of 1967 are uncovered (See BBC's broadcast of August 15, 1995). Local residents tell how Israeli soldiers nailed the hands of Egyptian soldiers to palm trees and then used them for target practice. Israel says it will not punish the Israeli soldiers and officers but offers to pay compensation to the families of Egyptian soldiers killed by the Israelis (the War Crimes Tribunal in The Hague still refuses to prosecute Israelis for War Crimes).

Sept 25, 1995, Radio Netherlands:
U.S. Secretary of State Warren Christopher is optimistic that a peace agreement can be reached for Bosnia. Mr. Christopher said the U.S. would oppose any plan that would interfere with the sovereignty of Bosnia. (Bosnia does not exist anymore).

Sept 25, Swiss Radio International:
The UN has appealed to Croatia not to repatriate 100,000 refugees back to Bosnia-Herzegovina, but Croatia has said it will go ahead with the repatriation of Muslim renegade, Abdic's rebels.

September 25, 1995, Die Deutsche Welle:
Germany and Serbia will renew diplomatic relations, which were cut when UN sanctions were imposed on Serbia.

September 26, 1995, *Wall Street Journal:* p. A-18:
A Russian-NATO command structure to police the Bosnian peace, is proposed by Russia. Russian and NATO generals will take turns overseeing the peacekeepers to ensure that "anyone who violates agreements is punished, not just Bosnian Serbs."

September 26, 1995, French TV:

Croatian President Franjo Tudjman concluded a visit with French President Chirac.

September 26, 1995, Radio Netherlands:
Dutch Foreign Minister, Hans Van Meerlo, says the UN bears the blame for the fall of Srebrenica and the atrocities committed by the Serbs after its fall.

September 26, 1995, Die Deutsche Welle: **Nigel Tandy**:
German Foreign Minister, Klaus Kinkel, addressed the UN's assembly of diplomats and said if a breakthrough comes in Bosnia it will be in the next few weeks. Kinkel expressed concern over the non-payment of dues by some UN member nations.

There is to be a ban on the use of land mines. Approximately 16 million land mines are planted around the world, from Central America, Southeast Asia, to Bosnia. The General UN Assembly is strongly condemning their use and manufacture.

The Polish head of UN Rights Commission in Bosnia resigns over the UN's failure ability to act responsibly over the atrocities committed by the Serbs in Bosnia. He is to be replaced by Mrs. Raines.

September 27, 1995, French TV:
Donji Vakuf was taken by Bosnian Government forces two days ago. Serbs blew up their ammunition dumps and left behind tons of trucks, tanks, and equipment as they retreated in a panic. The town of Donji Vakuf had little damage and former residents are rapidly refilling the town abandoned by the Serbs. A few days ago the town was 100% Serb and today it is 100% Muslim.

Shown briefly, General Ratko Mladic says peace in Bosnia can only be through diplomatic negotiations not war (a shift in his position).

September 27, 1995, CNN:
Bosnian Serbs launched a missile carrying cluster bombs against Trovnik, Bosnia, killing two people and wounding ten.
France is negotiating with the Serbs for the return of the two French pilots shot down about August 30 near Pale.

September 27, 1995, Radio Netherlands: **Marcel Sniders:**
Bosnian President Izetbegovic says a truce or ceasefire cannot take place until Serbs de-militarize Banja Luka (the largest city and stop their ethic cleansing and lift the siege of Sarajevo as well as restore gas, water, and electric power to that city.
In Afghanistan, President Bulham Rabbani has offered to hold peace talks with the Taliban movement, which has removed the threat to attack Kabul if Rabbani did not resign. The Taliban hold large areas of western and southern Afghanistan.
China has promised the U.S. it will not build two nuclear-powered electrical generating plants for Iran.

September 27, 1995, Die Deutsche Welle:
Boutros Boutros Ghali said he welcomes the participation of German troops in Bosnia once peace has been restored.
Macedonia is welcomed into the Council of Europe having settled differences with Greece over its entry.
There are 245 US nuclear warheads still remaining on German soil.

September 28, 1995, CNN:
Bosnian President. Izetbegovic appeared on television to

say that Bosnia wants peace but not peace at any price. Bosnians have suffered enough but will continue to fight if necessary.

October 8, 1995, Los Angeles TV news:
NATO responded with an air strike on two Bosnian Serb command posts near Tuzla after a rocket attack on the city that killed 14 civilians and one UN soldier. NATO said six planes delivered laser guided missiles in response to the death of the UN soldier and not over the deaths of the civilians.

October 11, 1995, BBC:
Heavy fighting in Bosnia's north as Bosnians and Croat forces take two towns, Sanski Most (35 kilometers from Banja Luka) and Mrkonjic Grad (35 kilometers south of Banja Luka).
Residents in Banja Luka say the situation is like Saigon and many have packed their bags, ready to leave. Thousands of Muslims and Croats are victims of ethnic cleansing and atrocities are frequent. A Serb official admitted these were occurring but insisted there were only a few. The Bosnian Government says the truce will not hold if ethnic cleansing keeps on. Bosnian guns are within range of Banja Luka.

October 11, 1995, Radio Netherlands: Carole Van den Ring:
The ceasefire has finally gone into effect. 40,000 Serbs have fled from the towns taken by Bosnian Government forces in recent fighting.
Foreign Minister Mohammed Sacirby said in Brussels that further ethnic cleansing will not be tolerated and such actions will break the truce. Mr. Sacirby was in Brussels seeking financial aid on the reconstruction of Bosnia once peace has been secured.

Chechen leaders have avoided further peace talks with the Russians until international observers are brought in to oversee the truce.

October 12, 1995, CNN:
 Ten explosions have occurred around Bosnia after the ceasefire went into effect 12 hours ago. The UN says this is probably due to some Serb commanders not having received news about the new ceasefire. One rocket hit an apartment in Sarajevo just two hours after the ceasefire, but no one was hurt or killed.
 In the north, Serb forces launched heavy attacks against Bosnian Government forces in an attempt to regain Sanski Most that was taken from their forces two days before the ceasefire went into effect.

October 12, 1995, Radio Netherlands: Carole Van Den Ring:
 Fresh fighting has broken out near Sanski Most. Bosnian Croat and Bosnian Muslims have met with UN officials in Sarajevo to work out UN observation of the ceasefire.
 A conference on the inhumane use of weapons has convened in Vienna without achieving a ban on the manufacture and use of land mines, which have caused civilian casualties around the world.
 Washington has stopped development of a laser beam weapon that would blind enemy soldiers.

October 12, 1995, CNN:
 In northern Bosnia near Kokici, territory taken from Bosnian Serbs two days ago, Bosnian Government forces have discovered mass graves of Bosnian civilians massacred by Serb forces this past June (1995).
 The UN has said persons convicted of war crimes at the War Crimes Tribunal in the Hague must be delivered up to

serve their sentences. Any country that harbors war criminals will be subject to sanctions by the United Nations and all its member nations.

October 11, 1995, BBC:
Heavy fighting in the north as Bosnian-Croat forces take two towns, Sanski Most and Masduj Grad before the cease fire is to take effect.

Residents in Banja Luka say the situation is just like Saigon and many have their bags packed and ready to leave. Ethnic cleansing and atrocities are occurring in Banja Luka against Croatians and Bosnians. The Bosnian Government says the truce will not hold if ethnic cleansing keeps on. Bosnian guns are within range of Banja Luka.

October 11, 1995, Radio Netherlands: Carole Van den Ring:
The ceasefire has finally gone into effect. 40,000 Serbs have fled from the towns taken by Bosnian Government forces in recent fighting.

Foreign Minister Mohammed Sacirby said in Brussels that further ethnic cleansing will not be tolerated and such actions will break the truce. Mr. Sacirby was in Brussels seeking financial aid on the reconstruction of Bosnia once peace has been secured.

Chechen leaders have avoided further peace talks with the Russians until international observers are brought in to oversee the truce.

October 12, 1995, CNN:
Ten explosions have occurred around Bosnia after the ceasefire went into effect 12 hours ago. The UN says this is probably due to some Serb commanders not having received news about the new ceasefire. One rocket hit an apartment in Sarajevo just two hours after the ceasefire, but no one was

hurt or killed.

In north Bosnia, Serb forces launched heavy attacks against Bosnian Government forces in an attempt to regain Sanski Most that was taken from their forces two days before the ceasefire went into effect.

October 12, 1995, Radio Netherlands: **Carole Van Den Ring:**

Fresh fighting has broken out near Sanski Most. Bosnian Croat and Bosnian Muslims have met with UN officials in Sarajevo to work out UN observation of the ceasefire.

A conference on the inhumane use of weapons has convened in Vienna without achieving a ban on the manufacture and use of land mines, which have caused civilian casualties around the world.

Washington has stopped development of a laser beam weapon that would blind enemy soldiers.

October 12, 1995, CNN:

In northern Bosnian territory near Kokici taken from Bosnian Serbs two days ago, Bosnian Government forces have discovered mass graves of Bosnian civilians massacred by Serb forces this past June (1995).

The UN has said persons convicted of war crimes at the War Crimes Tribunal in The Hague must serve their sentences. Any country that harbors war criminals will be subject to sanctions by the United Nations and all its member nations.

October 11, 1995, BBC:

Heavy fighting in north Bosnia as Bosnian-Croat forces take two towns, Sanski Most and Masduj Grad before the cease fire takes effect.

Residents in Banja Luka say the situation is like Saigon and many have their bags packed and ready to leave. Ethnic cleansing and atrocities are occurring in Banja Luka against Croatians and Bosnians. The Bosnian Government says the truce will not hold if this ethnic cleansing keeps on. Bosnian guns are within range of Banja Luka.

October 11, 1995, Radio Netherlands: Carole Van Den Ring:
 The ceasefire has finally gone into effect. 40,000 Serbs have fled the towns taken by Bosnian Government forces.
 Foreign Minister Mohammed Sacerby said in Brussels that further ethnic cleansing will not be tolerated and will break the truce.
 Chechen leaders have avoided further peace talks unless international observers are brought in to oversee the ceasefire.

October 11, 1995, CNN:
 Ten explosions have occurred all around Bosnia after the ceasefire went into effect over twelve hours ago. The UN says that some Serb commanders may not have received news about the ceasefire. One rocket hit an apartment building in Sarajevo, but no one was killed. Serbs are launching heavy attacks against Bosnian Government forces that took Sanski Most two days ago in attempts to regain the city.

October 13, 1995, CNN:
 Two mass graves were discovered in territory taken from Serb forces by Bosnian Government forces these past few days. The killings took place near Kokici last June (1995).
 The ceasefire in Bosnia is holding except for northwest Bosnia where heavy fighting is occurring near Snaski Most. Reports are that Bosnian and Croat forces are approaching

Banja Luka. Two villages 12 kilometers south of Banja Luka are abandoned and in flames.

Ethnic cleansing by Serbs is continuing in the area around Banja Luka. Serb forces took away Muslim boys and men from 16 to 60. Nothing has been heard of them. There is concern about their safety.

Two civil suits against Radovan Karadzic have been reinstated in the state of Virginia.

October 13, 1995, Die Deutsche Welle:
Thousands of Serbs have fled their homes in northwest Bosnia. Serb leaders have said the ceasefire will not hold. Both sides accuse the other of breaking the ceasefire.

NATO has approached the German Armed Forces to supply a peacekeeping contingent in Bosnia once peace is established.

October 16, 1995, Die Deutsche Welle:
Andrei Kozyrev said when the peace plan is in effect, Russia will not allow Russian troops in Bosnia to be under NATO commanders.

Donations through UNICEF for nappies (diapers), food, and medicine are needed to supply 100,000 babies in Bosnia whose health will be in danger through this winter.

October 16, 1995, CNN:
The ceasefire is holding but Serbs still have not allowed supplies over the road to Gorazde.

October 16, 1995, Radio Netherlands: **Jackie Spears:**
France and Great Britain are confident the ceasefire will hold in Bosnia.

Former Russian envoy to Yugoslavia, Alexander Zotov, says Bosnian Government Forces threaten the ceasefire in

Bosnia. Estimates are that the ceasefire is holding for 80% of the line.

Libya has withdrawn its application for admission to the UN Security Council. It is currently expelling over a million foreign workers, which it says are illegally in the country. Over 400,000 of these workers are from Sudan, 200,000 from Chad, and the rest are from other African countries. Just how these workers will be transported back to their countries is another matter as no international transportation serves Libya due to the economic sanctions imposed over Libya's failure to deliver the two men accused of masterminding the Pan Am Lockerbee bombing incident.

King Hussein of Jordan is pessimistic about conditions in Iraq between the international sanctions imposed on Iraq and the tyranny of Saddam Hussein.

October 17, 1995, CNN:
President Saparmurrad Niyazov is trying to steer a peaceful course with Russia and avoid the bloodshed that has shattered Tadzhikistan.

President Nazerkhan Bayev has 36% ethnic Russians in Kazakhstan. He says that communism has destroyed religion in his country and he must give the people something to believe in, so he promotes himself as something to fill the void.

Uzbekistan has some 100 different nationalities living within its borders. A newly developed gold mine will soon make Uzbekistan the largest gold producer in the world. Former Vice President Shukrulla Musaidov resigned from the government saying the president has become a despot.

October 17, 1995, *Houston Chronicle* Houston:
The first truckloads of food have finally reached the enclave of Gorazde since the cease-fire has been in effect.

October 18, 1995, Die Deutsche Welle:
The Bosnian Serb military has refused to fire four Bosnian Serb generals as demanded by Radovan Karadzic.

The OECD and German Defense Minister, Volker Ruhe, has warned President Franjo Tudjman, from using force to re-take the breakaway portion of east Slovonia. This matter will be taken up by diplomatic negotiation.

Four Croats have been charged with crimes against Krajina Serbs.

Belgrade and Sarajevo have agreed to open diplomatic missions in each other's capital.

After Bosnia has re-taken considerable territory from the Bosnian Serbs, (Bosnian) President Izetbegovic has said the division of Bosnia proposed by the International Contact Group is not now acceptable to Bosnia. Sarajevo and Belgrade have agreed to establish liaison offices in each other's capital.

October 19, 1995, Die Deutsche Welle:
Russia's ambassador to Belgium is conferring with NATO over Russia's contribution of up to 20,000 Russian troops in Bosnia once the peace is established.

Heavy fighting has broken out in northwestern Bosnia where Serbs have breached the cease-fire in an attempt to gain territory.

Although the Duma wants Foreign Minister Andrei Kozyrev replaced, observers believe that President Yeltsin's statements that he is to be replaced are for public consumption than dissatisfaction with him.

October 20, 1995, Radio Netherlands:
A laser beam weapon to blind enemy soldiers has been developed by the United States (is so powerful it can blind

people even with their eyes closed).

October 20, 1995, *Houston Chronicle* p.26A:
War criminal Zeljko Raznatovic (Arkan) and his men (the criminally insane *Serbian Tigers*) have killed more than 100 people in northwestern Bosnia in the past 30 days. The UN High Commissioner for Refugees received reports of mass killings and rapes by Bosnian Serb forces. The Bosnian Government radio also reported Serbs committed atrocities in Kljus after they took the town in 1992.

October 20, 1995, CNN:
The warring parties in Bosnia will meet at Wright-Patterson Air Base before the end of October.

October 20, 1995, ABC/TV: **Peter Jennings**:
Some of the worst ethnic cleansing of the war is occurring around Banja Luka. Two to three thousand boys and men were taken away and their lives are in jeopardy. Some 6,000 women and children expelled by the Serbs arrived at Zenica.
Previously, Muslims were forced to wear white armbands and white ribbons were placed on their house to identify them as Muslims.

October 21, 1995, Die Deutsche Welle:
Russian President Yeltsin received support from French President Chirac on the stationing of Russian troops in Bosnia and was sympathetic about Yeltsin's concern that neither NATO nor the UN has command over them.
Fighting has stopped in northwestern Bosnia and the ceasefire is holding. Bosnian Government forces and Bosnian Serbs exchanged prisoners. Among the prisoners the Serb exchanged were two Turkish reporters and three

foreign aid workers.

The signing and implementation of peace accord will not automatically lift the UN sanctions against Rump Yugoslavia.

October 23, 1995, Radio Netherlands:

The European Union is having talks on the costs of reconstruction and how the EU can assist Bosnia once peace is established.

October 23, 1995, CNN:

Talks between Serbia, Croatia, and Bosnia seem to have resolved the problem of reintegrating eastern Slavonia into Croatia.

The Bosnian Serb parliament in Pale has said only full integration with Serbia will be acceptable while Bosnia rejects this demand.

October 24, 1995, Radio Netherlands:

The main supply route west of Sarajevo airport has been opened by the Bosnian Serbs to UN convoys. Bosnians will not be allowed to use the road until the Bosnian Government opens up roads for Bosnian Serbs to connect with all their areas.

Dusan Tadic former guard at Omerska camp and the only one of 43 indicted for war crimes that is in custody, will have his judicial process delayed because his defense lawyers are searching for defense witnesses in Bosnia.

October 24, 1995, Die Deutsche Welle: **Grant Kirkland**;

Bonn has approved 4,000 German troops to participate in the UN peacekeeping operations in the Balkans once peace has been signed. Most of the troops will be stationed in Croatia. This is in addition to the fighter squadron under

NATO command and stationed in Italy.

Russian troops put a bloody end to a demonstration in the Chechen capital of Grozny with one killed and four wounded.

October 25, 1995, Radio Netherlands: **Grant Kirkland:**

According to U.S. State Department spokesman Shadduck, the Bosnian Serbs have re-opened numerous "detention" camps in northern Bosnia where they have detained thousands of Muslim men. Bosnian Serbs operated these camps in 1992 and at that time thousands of Muslims were reported killed and thousands of women were raped. The Bosnian Serbs are not allowing foreign observers into the area to investigate the conditions in these camps which are located near Prijedor, Sanski Most, and Banja Luka.

October 25, 1995, Die Deutsche Welle:

Eighteen Russian soldiers were killed in an ambush in Chechnya. Fighting has escalated after peace talks faltered when the Russian commander was wounded in an ambush a few days ago.

Octo0ber 27, 1995, Die Deutsche Welle:

Thousands of Chechens demonstrated in front of the presidential palace in Grozny for independence. The palace is a shell of a building like most of the city of Grozny that received a terrific bombardment by the Russian military last winter. An arms agreement agreed to by the Chechens and Russians at the end of July has yet to be implemented.

October 27, 1995, BBC:

Several thousand Muslim men have been detained by Bosnian Serbs in northwestern Bosnia this month. The UN Refugee spokesman, Spa, said that a teacher who was held in a factory with 350 other men spoke of repeated beatings with an unspecified number of men beaten to death. He escaped when Bosnian Special Forces took Sanski Most. In one instance, a machine gun was used to kill ten men.

About 6,000 Muslims were expelled from around Luka and those who reached government lines described killings, beatings and rapes. Serbian para-military like Zeljko Raznatovic (Arkan) and local Bosnian Serb army units are responsible for the killings (See October 20, 1995, *Houston Chronicle*). The UN says this appears to be a final round of "ethnic cleansing" in an effort to clear out all Muslims from the area. (**At this point a radio-jamming cut in to the BBC broadcast and didn't end until the topic of Bosnia ended**).

October 28, 1995, Die Deutsche Welle:

Over four million Croatians voted today. If President Franjo Tudjman wins the referendum, Croatia will take a strong stand against the Croatian Serb rejection today of the proposal to reunite with Croatia by the breakaway Serbs of East Slavonia.

The Serbs also rejected the timetable proposed by Croatia. Croatia said that if the situation is not resolved soon by diplomacy, they will seek a military solution.

U.S. Envoy Richard Holbrooke says Bosnian Serbs are hardening their stance on the question of territorial division of Bosnia and the division of Sarajevo into a Serb held sector and a Bosnian sector. The Serbs demand a right to secede from Bosnia Herzegovina to join Serbia.

October 29, 1995, CNN:

The *New York Times* reported it had evidence that the Bosnian Serbs murdered 6,000 Muslim men and boys after the fall of Srebrenica this last summer. U.S. State

Department says it has more aerial photos of mass graves in addition to the ones taken last summer.

French soldiers were called into Bosnian Serb territory to remove unexploded NATO bombs that NATO had dropped on Serb munitions and communication centers this past summer.

Assistant Secretary of State Richard Holbrooke said on CNN's "Evans and Novak" that the former UN commander in Bosnia, Sir General Michael Rose was in error in giving a high casualty estimate for any potential UN-NATO conflict in Bosnia. Mr. Holbrooke said, "When the Serbs get out of line, hit them hard and that will be the end of it." (After "Sir Michael" General Rose was knighted he became an ardent supporter of the Serbs - very anti-Bosnian, anti-Muslim).

October 29, 1995, Radio Netherlands:

Parliamentary elections in Croatia give President. Franjo Tudjman's party 48.4%, of the votes which is sufficient for a constitutional change for a Croat-Bosnian federation. Voting was held up in Croatia's seaport city of Dubrovnik because Bosnian Serbs were shelling the city.

October 30, 1995, Radio Netherlands:

Dutch Defense Minister Joris Voorhoeve said the 400 Dutch UN peacekeepers in Srebrenica were too lightly armed to protect the UN safe haven of Srebrenica this last summer. Despite repeated call from the UN peacekeepers in Srebrenica and from the Bosnian Government for NATO air strikes to protect the (Srebrenica) enclave, the UN Security Council turned down all requests for air strikes.

The Dutch soldiers that were in Srebrenica have been returned to the Netherlands where they have been de-briefed on the atrocities committed by the Bosnian Serbs. Documents containing names of those involved and information on the war crimes of mass murder and rape have been turned over to the War Crimes Tribunal in The Hague.

October 30, 1995, Die Deutsche Welle:
   The European Unity expects to allocate 6 billion U.S. dollars for the reconstruction of former Yugoslavia. The EU Envoy to Bosnia, Sweden's Carl Bildt, will be in charge of EU's reconstruction efforts. Any country that does not uphold human rights will not be eligible for EU reconstruction funds.
   The U.S. says economic sanctions will be imposed on any country that harbors war criminals found guilty by the War Crimes Tribunal in The Hague.

October 31, 1995, Radio Netherlands:
   (American) President Bill Clinton has said that the representatives of the warring parties in Bosnia have the best last chance for peace with the meeting in Wright-Patterson Air Base in Ohio.

October 31, 1995, Die Deutsche Welle:
   The government in Sarajevo has raised objections over the choice of Serbian President Slobodan Milosevic to represent the Bosnian Serbs in the Ohio meeting. The objection is based on evidence that Slobodan Milosevic knew and condoned killings and atrocities committed by the Bosnian Serbs after the fall of "Srebrenica UN Safe Haven" last June.
   The Bosnian Government also demands an end to the "ethnic cleansing" and mass murders in the Banja Luka.
   President Fanjo Tudjman's party won 44% of the vote this last election; double that of what the next party received in the election which was 20%. The biggest loss to President Tudjman's party was in Zagreb where his party lost 50

percent of their seats on the city council.

Former Dutch Prime Minister Lubbers is the latest potential candidate for the post of Secretary General of NATO vacated by the resignation of Willy Claes. Chancellor Helmut Kohl of Germany had previously objected to Prime Ministers Lubbers selection because of Lubbers opposition to the reunification of the two Germanys in 1991.

The Ukraine has destroyed 2,000 tanks under the Conventional Forces in Europe treaty signed in 1992.

November 1, 1995, CNN: **Christiane Amanpour** reporting:

Today is the day which all Bosnians honor the dead. Bosnians approached by CNN voiced concern that the peace talks in Ohio would result in the partition of Bosnia. All Bosnians want a whole country while Bosnian Serbs want independence and to join Serbia. After three and a half years, water, gas, and electricity are being enjoyed by the people of Sarajevo.

Over ten thousand people in Sarajevo have died from sniper bullets and the shelling. Of the three people interviewed, they doubted that the world outside Sarajevo could ever understand what it has been like to live under the conditions of no electricity, fuel, or water. "Just try living without water or electricity for one day" advised one of the persons interviewed. Another said that now water has been restored, she takes two or three showers every day.

The Bosnian Government is concerned that Bosnian territory liberated by the Croat Army will be annexed by Croatia.

November 1, 1995, Radio Netherlands: **Dave Durham** reporting:

All three warring parties have hardened their stance on

positions they will take during the peace talks. Meanwhile ethnic cleansing by Bosnian Serbs continues in the Banja Luka region of northern Bosnia.

A German human rights organization has presented a report of misconduct by Dutch soldiers in Srebrenica. The 20 eyewitnesses said that the Dutch UN peacekeepers sold food and medicines that were given free and forced girls into prostitution. (Radio Netherlands was good about reporting all the news and never covered up misdeeds by the Dutch soldiers or anyone).

November 1, 1995, Die Deutsche Welle: **Richard Williams:**
The prosecution of war criminals, the return of east Slavonia to Croatia, the respect of human rights, the recognition of Bosnia as a whole, and peace is what Secretary of State Warren Christopher spelled out for the peace talks. (Bosnia is no longer exists).

The Crimea was officially recognized as an independent republic tied to the Ukraine.

November 2, 1995, Radio Netherlands:
Dutch Foreign Minister Hans Von Mirlo said force may be necessary to implement the peace accords. Much depends upon the command structure of NATO on whether the Netherlands will send Dutch troops to implement the peace plan.

The resignation of Radovan Karadzic and General Ratko Mladic as a step for peace and Serbian President Milosevic apparently has agreed.

November 2, 1995, Die Deutsche Welle:
Mediators on the peace talks for Bosnia in Ohio have presented 4 documents calling for the separation of military

and paramilitary groups, a constitution, and separation of political powers. The return of a few hundred refugees to Croatia and Bosnia was indicated as a demonstration of future cooperation.

If East Slavonia is not returned to Croatia, Croatian President Tudjman says Croatia will take it back by military action.

November 3, 1995, Radio Netherlands:
(Russian) Prime Minister Chernomyrdin has assumed more power of the presidency in view of President Yeltsin's prolonged hospital stay.

Former Dutch Prime. Minister Rud Lubbers appears to be the leading contender for the post of Secretary General of NATO.

November 3, 1995, Die Deutsche Welle:
German President Roman Hertzog has undertaken to remedy the hostile attitude of some groups toward resident minorities living in Germany. He will meet with the leaders of the Islamic community in Germany next month to see what can be done.

German Foreign Minister Klaus Kinkel is in Cambodia on a conference to outlaw the use of land mines. This has become a great concern, as civilians all over the world are the ones who are suffering the most from millions of land mines laid in recent years.

November 4, 1995, Radio Netherlands:
The main supply route west of Sarajevo airport has been opened by Bosnian Serbs.

November 4, 1995, Die Deutsche Welle:
Bonn has approved 4,000 German troops to participate in

peacekeeping operations in Croatia and Bosnia. This will be in addition to the fighter planes stationed in Italy.

A bloody end to demonstrations in the Chechen capital Grozny after Russian troops advanced on demonstrators for independence there.

November 5, 1995, CNN:

David Rohde, a reporter for the Christian Science Monitor, is being held by Bosnian Serbs on charges of illegally entering Bosnian Serb territory. (He saw the empty munitions boxes of the Serbs left in fields where the mass graves were discovered after the fall of Srebrenica).

In (Dayton) Ohio, Serbian President Milosevic objected to the clause in the new Bosnian constitution that prohibits accused war criminals from political office.

November 6, 1995, Univision TV (Spanish news in Houston):

Bosnian Serbs attacked French UN peacekeepers near Mostar.

November 7, 1995, CNN: **Christiane Amanpour:**

8,000 Muslim men and boys are missing after the fall of Srebrenica and there are reports of 5,000 men and boys are missing in northern Bosnia since then and the worst is feared. The Bosnian Serbs insist the mass graves around Srebrenica are those of Muslim man and boys killed in combat. (Srebrenica people gave up their weapons in return for a designation of UN Safe Haven).

From Tuzla, Christiane Amanpour reports atrocities were witnessed by Pouran Suric, who survived, said General Ratko Mladic was in charge of the atrocities even though he assured the thousands of men and boys that they were being exchanged for captured Bosnian Serb soldiers held by the

Bosnian Army and that they would soon be seeing their families. Pouran said they were lined up in rows and warned not to look around, and then the shooting began. He fell to the ground and then the bodies of men behind him fell on him. The Serb soldiers then went among the dead and wounded men calling out "Tell us where you are so we can help you." Then there would be more shots and the groans and moaning stopped.

U.S. space satellite photos taken two weeks before the mass graves were discovered by the aerial photos show hundreds of men in these fields surrounded by Bosnian Serb soldiers.

November 7, 1995, Die Deutsche Welle:

U.S. Defense Secretary William Perry said the U.S. is insisting on a NATO command in Bosnia once a peace agreement is signed. He expected no resistance to NATO forces but there are millions of land mines and a poor infrastructure that could cost some lives.

The German states are requesting the German federal government in share in the cost of maintaining Bosnian refugees in Germany.

November 8, 1995, Radio Netherlands:

U.S. Secretary of Defense William Perry says the 2,000-3,000 Russian troops will be under command of a Russian general who will be responsible to the American NATO Commander in Bosnia, General George Uran.

The U.S. Government says it does not have to share its intelligence with the international community. This was in response to Judge Richard Goldstone of the International War Crimes Tribunal who said the U.S. Government has not responded to his request for aerial photos and satellite photos of the mass gravesites near Srebrenica.

November 8, 1995, Die Deutsche Welle:

German Defense Minister, Volker Ruhe, said the German Armed Forces are ready to participate in the peacekeeping in Bosnia.

November 8, 1995, CNN:

The Bosnian Serb leaders freed American journalist, David Rohde, from charges of illegally entering Bosnian Serb territory as a gesture of "good-will" and released him to Serbia.

November 8, 1995, French TV:

Prime Minister, Alain Juppe, defended his government's record and spoke of France's influence in Bosnia with the creation of the Rapid Reaction Force and the ultimatum for the Serbs to stop bombarding Sarajevo in February 1995.

November 9, 1995, CNN:

A Serb Brigade from Belgrade operating in East Slavonia was accused of murdering 261 non-Serbs in 1991. (This clearly refutes the UN Security Council's statement that the Bosnian Conflict was a Civil War and shows that Milosevic and Karadzic started the war,).

November 9, 1995, Die Deutsche Welle:

Russia has asked the UN to lift sanctions on Serbia so the Russians can deliver natural gas to them this winter.

A Serb brigade from Belgrade murdered 261 non-Serbs in East Slavonia in 1991.

The Council of Europe has admitted the Ukraine and the former Yugoslav republic of Macedonia. The Council stresses the protection of human rights.

November 9, 1995, Radio Netherlands:
The Muslim and Croat members at the Ohio peace talks have signed an agreement to extend their confederation.

Three senior army officers of the Yugoslav Army (JAN) have been indicted for war crimes. This is the first time charges against Yugoslav officers have been made by the International War Crimes Tribunal. Two of the generals are in charge of Serb Army units in Serbia while the other one is in charge of a Serb army unit in Montenegro. (What were Serb units doing in either country if it was supposedly not involved in the wars in either country?)

A U.S. aide compares the destruction of mosques in Bosnia to the destruction of synagogues in Germany in the 1930's. Serbian para-military and Bosnian Serb Army units destroyed over 1,000 of the oldest and most beautiful mosques. (How many synagogues in Gemany were destroyed? Why make this comparison?)

There are concerns (Mr. Tillman Zouk) that the peace talks in (Dayton) Ohio are being rushed through without regard to justice for Bosnians in an effort to make an impact on President Clinton's election chances in 1996.

November 10, 1995, Radio Netherlands:
U.S. opposition to the selection of former Dutch Prime Minister, Rud Lubbers, has created some ill-will among other NATO members. The U.S. said it opposed Mr. Lubbers because he would not be a strong leader with his past action of many compromises.

The accord signed between Croatia and Bosnia calls for a single customs union, a single currency, military cooperation between the two nations, and the reunification of Mostar, now under EU control.

November 10, 1995, Die Deutsche Welle:

German parliamentarian Rita Sussman objected to inviting Iran's Foreign Minister, Ali Velayati, to the upcoming Islamic conference in Bonn over Iranian President Rafsanjani's remarks over the assassination of Israeli Prime Minister, Yitzak Rabin.

November 11, 1995, CNN:
Croatian tank and troop movements are reported headed for the breakaway province of East Slavonia, held by rebel Serbs. Croatia had vowed to re-take East Slavonia by force if diplomatic moves by the end of this month in Ohio fail to restore E. Slavonia.

November 11, 1995, Radio Netherlands (Nov 12, 0030 UTC):
Ex-patriot Algerians flood their consulates in France to cast their vote in Algerian elections.
The Taliban movement is accused of firing the rockets into Kabul that killed 35 people. The Taliban are entrenched in the hills south of Kabul, which they took over this last September.

November 11, 1995, Die Deutsche Welle:
Senior NATO officials have arrived in Bosnia to assess how best to deploy 60,000 NATO troops that will take over from the UN Peacekeepers once a peace agreement is signed.
Dutch, British, and French UN troops in Sarajevo participated in ceremonies observing Armistice Day.
German Foreign Minister Klaus Kinkel has been criticized for canceling the Islamic Conference in Bonn to avoid the issue of Iran's participation in the conference. Israel has been outraged over President Rafsanjani's declaration that Prime Minister Yitzak Rabin's assassination

was divine retribution.

November 12, 1995, Radio Netherlands: **Jackie Spears:**
Croatian and Croatian Serbs have agreed on re-integration. The region will be under UN supervision while under-going this reintegration.

The execution of Ken Saro Wee Eeh in Nigeria (by Nigeria's military) has resulted in EU imposing sanctions against Nigeria.

November 12, 1995, Die Deutsche Welle:
Thorwald Stoltenberg is optimistic war is ending in former Yugoslavia with the accord between Croatia and East Slavonia. 13,000 Croats will be allowed to return to East Slavonia.

November 12, 1995, CNN:
Bosnian Serb leaders Radovan Karadzic and (Serb) General Ratko Mladic say they are ready to step down if accusations of war crimes against them are dropped.

November 13, 1995, Radio Netherlands: (0030 UTC Nov 14)
A group calling itself "Tigers of the Gulf" has claimed responsibility for the bombing of the American mission in Riyadh which killed five Americans and one Filipino. They are demanding all American military withdraw from Saudi Arabia.

Azeris claim the elections in Azerbaijan are fraudulent. The present government is pro-Russian and received military help from Russia in its fight against the separatists Nogorah-Karabagh.

November 13, 1995, Die Deutsche Welle:

The 185 members of the UN (General Assembly) have called into question the existence and need of the fifteen-member Security Council. (It has been a useless, inefficient, and acted contrary to the goals of the United Nations with blunder after blunder in Rwanda and Bosnia that had cost hundreds of thousands of lives).

November 13, 1955, CNN:
Five Americans were killed and 60 wounded in the suspected car bombing of the U.S. military mission in Riyadh.

November 14, 1995, French TV:
Both the "Islamic Movement for Change" and "Gulf Tigers" claim responsibility for the bombing attack on the US military mission in Riyadh. This is the second time since 1991 and the Gulf War the US military in Saudi Arabia has been attacked.

November 14, 1995, Radio Netherlands: **Jackie Spears:**
Croatian President Fanjo Tudjman promoted Teo Viel Blasnic to general one day after the War Crimes Tribunal handed down an indictment against him. Blasnic was in charge of a valley in Croatia where all Muslims were killed or driven away.

President Clinton says that the cost to the U.S. of stationing troops in Bosnia after the peace agreement is reached has doubled to 1.54 billion dollars a year. Mr. Clinton offered to provide 20,000 American troops out of a total of 60,000 NATO troops to be stationed in Bosnia but the Congress may not agree to that.

The peace talks at the U.S. air base in Ohio have apparently hit a snag and are not progressing as smoothly as had been anticipated. (But Assistant Secretary of State

Richard Holbrooke had already gotten Croatia and Serbia to agree to split Bosnia 49 percent for Croatia and 51 percent for Bosnia but Izetbegovic of Bosnia was kept in the dark).

November 15, 1995, Die Deutsche Welle: Russia is not willing to disarm. Defense Minister General, Pavel Grachev, threatened to form a new military alliance with neighboring countries and says its southern frontier is threatened. Russia will not honor its commitment to the CFE (Conventional Forces in Europe) treaty it signed in 1991.t Italy and if these are to be used in Bosnia.

The growth and power of organized crime syndicates from Eastern Europe threatens German and Austrian stability. (Boris Yeltsin has received strong support from Chancellor Helmut Kohl as Yeltsin was to work on keeping Russian weapons of mass destruction from these groups. Germany has given more help to Russia than all other countries).

In a defiant gesture to the International War Crimes Tribunal for the former Yugoslavia, Croatian President Tudjman promoted General Tiomir Blasnic who's accused of massacring hundreds of Muslims in Croatia. One of the rumors coming out of the Bosnian peace talks in Ohio is that Serbs want to exempt Radovan Karadzic and Ratko Mladic from war crimes. Judge Richard Goldstone has threatened to resign if Karadzic and Mladic are exempted.

November 15, 1995, Radio Netherlands: Jackie Spears:

The U.S. has strongly protested the promotion of Gen Tiomir Blasnic by (Croatian) President Tudjman after Blasnic was indicted by the War Crimes Tribunal in The Hague.

November 16, Radio Netherlands: 6125 and 6165 Mhz, 49

meter band, 5:30, 7:30, 10:30 PM CST: English Section, Radio Netherlands, Box 222, Hilversum, Netherlands

The War Crimes Tribunal for the former Yugoslavia announced new charges against Radovan Karadzic and Ratko Mladic for having slaughtered many thousands of Muslims within ten days after the fall of Srebrenica. (**Note:** These massacres were planned to keep Muslims from returning to their homes or reclaiming their property while Serbs can come to Bosnia–Herzegovina without fear of losing their lives).

A foreign intelligence service told Defense Minister Voorhoever that the Serbs are digging up mass graves in an attempt to erase evidence of the massacres committed by Bosnian Serbs.

Croatian President Franjo Tudjman says he is satisfied with the results obtained for his country in the Ohio peace talks.

A Croatian Muslim who served in the Croatian Army is accused of the murder of hundreds of Serbs taken to the War Crimes Tribunal.

November 16, 1995, CNN:

War Crimes Tribunal Judge Richard Goldstone accuses Bosnian Serb leaders Karadzic and Mladic of unimaginable forms of atrocities committed by Serb forces and must be indicted and extradited. He said, "Those who believe peace can be obtained by leaving those political leaders accused of war crimes still in control are mistaken."

U.S. Intelligence files on war crimes are to be turned over to the War Crimes Tribunal in The Hague (The reporter speculated this was prompted by President Clinton's forthcoming election year run for the presidency).

Muslims in Mostar are uncertain if they can trust Croats who want a unified city of Mostar to be the capital of Bosnian Croats.

November 16, 1995, Radio Netherlands:

Charges of planning, instigating, and coordinating crimes against humanity, genocide, are leveled at Karadzic and Mladic.

Bosnian Serbs have not cooperated with the War Crimes Tribunal. A spokesman with the Tribunal says charges and indictments will proceed. The peace talks in Ohio are political and will not affect the judicial process despite rumors the peace is being slowed by the indictments.

November 17, 1995, Radio Netherlands:

Croatian President Franjo Tudjman wants the UN sanctions lifted on Serbia as soon as the peace accords are signed.

Croatia is pressuring some 25,000 Bosnian refugees, followers of Muslim rebel leader Abdic, to return to their homes in Bosnia. (Abdic made the Bihac area prosperous with poultry production but fought alongside Bosnian Serbs against Bosnia). Only 700 of Abdic's followers boarded buses provided by the Bosnian Government to return home. The Bosnian Government says all are welcome in Bosnia except those who have committed war crimes and they will be handed over to the War Crimes Tribunal for trials in The Hague. The Croatians have not allowed international observers into these camps nor have they permitted firewood or fuel into the camps. Living conditions are said to be bad.

November 18, 1995, CNN:

Foreign Minister Mohammed Sacerby says he is willing to step down to allow an ethnic Croat take his place if that will further peace.

November 18, 1995, *Christian Science Monitor*:

The peace talks in Ohio are now described as precarious as on the edge of a knife.

The Bosnian Serbs want an outlet to the Adriatic through the Bosnian-Croat federation.

One point agreed upon is that the Serb leaders, Dr. Radovan Karadzic and General Ratko Mladic are to stand trial for war crimes at the War Crimes Tribunal in The Hague.

November 18, 1995, Radio Netherlands:
One of the problems facing Bosnia is the flight of its most talented and educated citizens who are now refugees in other countries. Sarajevo's half million population is now only 250,000. Teachers have more than double the number of students than before the war. Capital for rebuilding Bosnia will have to be raised.

November 20, 1995, Radio Netherlands: **Ginger da Silva:**
The outcome of the peace accords in Ohio are in doubt because of Serb demands for a widened Posvina corridor near Brcko in northern Bosnia.

November 21, 1995, CNN:
U.S. Secretary of State Christopher created a ruse by telling all the parties at the peace talks in Ohio to re-fuel their planes and get ready to leave in the morning. Then as everyone retired, he sent his aides to the Croatian and Serbian delegates to negotiate. The Bosnian delegates were awakened at three in the morning and were told Serbia and Croatia had signed. Presented with a fait a complis, they signed.

November 22, 1995, National Public Radio (7 AM)
One couple interviewed in Sarajevo says that their village is now in the Serpska Republic and if they will not be allowed to return to their village by the Serbs they should obtain weapons and take the village back.

November 21, 1995, French TV:

President Bill Clinton has forced a Pax American on Bosnia because he needs success in the foreign diplomacy area to get himself re-elected.

Bosnians in Sarajevo expressed their suspicions that the Serbs will not live up to their promises. Belgrade residents showed reserved happiness and President Chirac of France complimented the warring parties on signing the peace accords. France is pressing Serbia for the return of the two French pilots that were shot down over Bosnian Serb territory and stress they should be returned.

Newly elected president of Poland, Alexander Kwasnieski, wants Poland to join NATO and the European Union.

November 22, 1995, Die Deutsche Welle:

Social Democrats say the Islamic world needs a voice in the West. The rescinding of the invitation to Iran over the comment by Iranian pres. Rafsanjani's on Rabin's assassination being God's divine retribution is not sufficient cause for Foreign Minister, Klaus Kinkel, to cancel the Bonn Conference on Islam.

Only Germany and Luxembourg meet EU requirements for a common European currency. The other nations have excessive indebtedness.

November 22, 1995, Radio Netherlands:

All trade sanctions against Montenegro and Serbia have been lifted by the UN Security Council. Russia abstained. If Serbia or the Bosnian Serbs do not live up to the treaty, the sanctions will be re-imposed.

There will be a rotating presidency for the new Bosnian federation.

Holland's largest opposition party has misgivings about stationing Dutch NATO troops in Bosnia.

November 23, 1995, French TV:

The French will contribute 10,000 troops to the NATO peace operation in Bosnia and 1,000 Spanish troops will join the French troops occupying Mt. Igman. The French media portrays the imposed peace accords to the birth of a baby by forceps.

A French newspaper reports that the two French pilots shot down near Pale were "kidnapped" from their Serb captors and are being held in a hunting lodge in the mountains. France insists any peace accord includes the return of the pilots.

The use of napalm was outlawed in 1973 international disarmament conference because it sticks to anything it touches and keeps burning regardless if the target is civilian or military. (Napalm was dropped on Bihac by a Serb plane but it failed to ignite. One of the fighters crashed.)

November 23, 1995, Die Deutsche Welle:

Tanjug News Agency (Yugoclavia) says that President Milosevic summoned hostile Bosnian Serb leadership to Belgrade and that they accepted the Ohio accords even though they claimed Belgrade sold them out by agreeing to a unified Sarajevo. Bosnian Serb news has said that no news about the acceptance of the Ohio accords by the Bosnian Serb leaders has been confirmed in Pale.

U.S. Secretary of Defense William Perry said in Macedonia today that 60 nations have offered to serve under NATO's command in Bosnia once the peace plan is implemented. He said any attack on NATO troops by any one of the warring parties will be met with an immediate response.

The German Institute for Rebuilding has said that all groups concerned in rebuilding Bosnia need to coordinate their efforts so that refugees can be resettled and reconstruction can begin.

November 23, 1995, Radio Netherlands:

Serbia and Bosnian Serbs say the economic sanctions have cost them 150 billion dollars, but EU puts the figure at 50 billion dollars.

One third of Serbia is living below the poverty line. 700,000 have lost their jobs. Fifty percent of the Serbian economy comes from smuggling, stolen goods, and money laundering for organized crime in Russia and the U.S. Most of the smuggling is through Albania and Romania.

In Egypt, the government has closed the fundamentalist Muslim Brotherhood, arrested its leaders and seized its office files. One hundred and sixty members of the Brotherhood were running for office in the elections to be held next week.

November 23, 1995, CNN:

Newest estimates are that AIDS (another killer of people besides war) affects one out of every 92 men age 27-39 in the U.S. Racial breakdown is as follows:

Women 27-39		Men 27-39	
White	1 in 1,667	White	1 in 139
Black	1 in 98	Black	1 in 33
Hispanic	1 in 222	Hispanic	1 in 60

(A story of AIDS began when a Mozambique woman was bitten by a monkey and taken to Paris, France to be treated and the monkey bite gave her AIDS. From France it spread to Haiti and then tainted blood from Haitians sold to blood plasma companies in the U.S.

But a German professor at Leipzig has said AIDS was developed from Icelandic sheep anthrax as part of a biological warfare weapon in the United States. This corresponds to a federal prison to release of prisoners from a Maryland prison six months early if they partook in program to test a *vaccine* back in 1969.

This story of a woman contracting AIDS from a monkey bite is erroneous as the first man to contract AIDS from a woman was a Hong Kong man in 1982. At that time, it was thought that AIDS was only transmitted through homosexual activity and was therefore confined to the Gay Community in America. It remains to be seen just who is responsible for the spread of this disease.

November 23, 1995, Die Deutsche Welle:
Germany wants to repatriate its Bosnian refugees as soon as the peace agreement is signed. With over 400,000 Bosnian refugees, Germany has more than half of Bosnia's refugees.

November 23, 1995, Radio Netherlands:
200 men dressed in Bosnian Army uniforms and firing their weapons in the air, raided a UN supply depot in northern Bosnia. The 80 lightly armed Bangladeshi UN troops did not resist. The raiders took ten vehicles, 2,000 liters of petrol, and food. The Bosnian government says it will investigate.

November 24, 1995, Radio Netherlands:
Bosnian Serbs in Serb suburbs of Sarajevo demonstrate they will not accept Bosnian government rule.
Citizens of Dubrovnik demonstrate against giving Bosnian Serbs a Croatian peninsula in return for Bosnian Serb territory.

November 26, 1995, Radio Netherlands:
Bosnian Serbs attempt to push for renegotiation over the unification of Sarajevo under the Croat-Muslim Federation. Serb leader Radovan Karadzic says any NATO troops attempting to arrest him or any of his men for war crimes will pay with their lives. Arrest warrants have been issued for Dr. Karadzic and the Serb military leader, General Ratko Mladic.
The U.S. says that renegotiations of the peace accords are

out of the question. No U.S. troops will be sent to Bosnia unless the peace agreement is signed by all the warring parties.

November 26, 1995, Die Deutsche Welle:
Serb leader Dr. Karadzic says Serbs in Serb suburbs of Sarajevo will not agree to live under the Croat-Muslim Federation. Sarajevo will become another Beirut and Serb (army) positions will not be vacated until the peace accords are re-negotiated.

November 27, 1995, CNN:
The city of Tuzla remembers the dead young people killed by a Serb shell earlier this year. 71 young Croats, Serbs, and Muslims were having a good time when the Serb shell was fired into the middle of the crowd. The city is now enlarged from the influx of refugees from Srebrenica where 10,000 men, children, and women are still missing after Bosnian Serbs took the town and began slaughtering men and boys. Muslims in Tuzla say everyone is welcome except those with bloody hands.

November 27, 1995, Die Deutsche Welle:
Theo Weigel says that without American participation in the proposed NATO peace force in Bosnia, everything will fall apart. Germany will send 180 men with next week's advance group to set up the NATO force. Later, 4,000 German NATO troops will be stationed in Bosnia. No organized opposition is expected but attacks by uncontrolled extreme elements are possible.

November 29, 1995, Die Deutsche Welle:
The French Government says it is preparing for the signing of the peace agreement in Paris on the 15th of December.

December 1, 1995, CNN:

The Advance Group of American troops for the NATO peacekeeping forces is in Tuzla which has been picked as the command center for American forces.

If Bosnian Serb forces do not surrender their weapons, the Bosnian Government Forces will be given weapons and training commensurate to the Bosnian Serb forces.

December 1, 1995, CNN:

U.S. forces will use Pecs, Hungary for its jumping-off operations to Bosnia. The town of Pecs is looking forward to the influx of American troops, as Hungary wants to draw closer to NATO and Western Europe. The money spent on this operation is also a welcome relief for Pecs.

December 2, 1995, CNN:

In Sarajevo, Iranian Foreign Minister Ali Akbar Velayati and Greece's foreign minister lend the support of their countries to the peace agreement.

Estimates for the reconstruction of Bosnia run as high as 46 billion dollars. Germany says it has given more than any other nation for the reconstruction of Eastern Europe and now wants others to contribute to Bosnia's reconstruction. The EU has spoken about giving 7 billion and the World Bank may be another source.

The U.S. Congress asks Secretary of Defense William. Perry and Secretary of State Warren Christopher just what role Congress is to play in the deployment of U.S. NATO troops in Bosnia if troops are already being deployed. 2,600 U.S. troops will arrive next week and a total of 20,000 troops, or one division, will be a self-contained force.

December 3, 1995, CNN:

The Capital Gang: Katie O'Bierne quoted sources saying the Clinton Administration made a secret agreement with

Russia not to expand NATO in return for Russia's acquiescence on the Bosnian peace accords.

December 3, 1995, Radio Netherlands:
Secretary of State Christopher met in Madrid with Spain's Foreign Minister Javier Solana who has been chosen to head NATO.

The Croat head of the Bosnian-Croat Federation has resigned over the peace agreement because he is to hand over land in northern Bosnia to the Bosnian Serbs that was predominantly Muslim and Croat before the war.

The head of the Bosnian Serb military, Ratko Mladic, says the re-unification of Serbian parts of Sarajevo is unacceptable to him.

December 3, 1995, Radio Netherlands: **Carole Van Den Ring:**
French General Jean Rene Bechelet has been recalled to Paris for critical comments he made about the Dayton Peace Accords. He said that the accords give Serb residents of Sarajevo a choice between a coffin or a suitcase. He also said that the peace accords were pushed through by President Clinton in an effort to improve his bid for re-election next year.

Russia has offered a plan for Chechnya to have a special status within the Russian Federation. The Russians would control the military, currency, and foreign affairs. However, the Chechens want complete independence. Despite the truce, clashes between Russians and Chechens occur daily.

December 3, 1995, BBC:
President Clinton warned Serbian President Milosevic that the Bosnian Serb leaders Karadzic and Mladic had better not compromise the peace accords.

December 4, 1995, CNN:

Young Croats, Muslims, and Serbs of Tuzla have made a memorial to the 71 young people killed by a Serb shelling of Tuzla in July. One girl says she can never forgive Serbs and hates them.

December 4, 1995, French TV:
Chechen rebels blew up a car bomb in Grozny near the Russian Secret Police Station of the puppet government installed by the Russians. Eleven people were killed, 60 wounded, 9 of them critically. The war has been going on for a year now.

December 4, 1995, Radio Netherlands: **Carole Van den Ring**:
NATO Ministers overwhelmingly approve plans to participate in peacekeeping operations in Bosnia. France has not re-joined NATO but will re-enter some military operations. NATO is expected to go ahead with its largest military operation ever after the peace agreement is signed in Paris, December 14. (President De Gaulle kicked NATO out of Paris after French Intelligence learned the Fifth Division of the of the FBI attached to NATO and some in NATO were involved in the attempt on his life in 1962 and in the murder of President John F. Kennedy, November 22, 1963).

December 4, 1995, Die Deutsche Welle:
Chancellor Helmut Kohl will lead the debate on German troop participation (in Bosnia). The opposition party of Social Democrats is expected to approve 4,000 troops stationed September 22, 1963 mainly in Croatia. The Greens Party is divided in opposition.

December 5, 1995, Radio Netherlands: **Carole Van den Ring**
French President Jaques Chirac called Serbian President Milosevic and demanded the return of the two French pilots

captured after they were shot down over Bosnian Serb Territory.

Croat forces burned two villages they were being forced to return to Bosnian Serbs under agreements reached in Dayton, Ohio.

December 6, 1995, French TV:

The Serbian Foreign Ministry said President Chirac should not press the issue of the two downed French pilots as this will have adverse effect on the peace accords.

December 8, 1995, Radio Netherlands:

The European Union office of OSE will oversee the elections in Bosnia nine months after the peace is signed next Thursday, December 14, in Paris.

Chechnya and Russia have reached an agreement that Chechnya will remain within the Russian Federation but handle their own foreign affairs and exports and imports.

December 8, 1995, Die Deutsche Welle:

(British) Prime Minister John Majors opened a conference of forty foreign ministers in London on ways to rebuild war-torn Bosnia once the peace is established.

French Foreign Minister Herve Charette said if Serbia does not return the two French pilots shot down over Bosnian Serb territory, France will take appropriate measures.

December 10, 1995, Die Deutsche Welle:

The deadline set by France for the Serbian and Bosnian Serbs to return the two French pilots has expired. Russian Foreign Minister Andrei Kozyrev has asked the Bosnian Serbs to return the two French pilots shot down over Bosnian Serb territory last August 30. At the same time, Mr. Kozyrev asked that the War Crimes indictments against Radovan Karadzic and

Ratko Mladic be suspended.

December 12, 1995, CNN:
The Serbian Foreign Ministry has said there will be forthcoming news about the two French pilots.

December 12, 1995, Die Deutsche Welle:
Two letter bombs exploded in Graz, Austria slightly wounding one woman and another letter in Vienna, destined for a Croatian, was seized. Right wing extremists are blamed.

Ahmed Sachen, Chechen leader reportedly killed by the Russians, says he is alive and well.

Russian Prime Minister Viktor Chernomyrdin will represent President Yeltsin at the signing of the Bosnian Peace in Paris Thursday. Yeltsin spoke over the telephone for the first time publicly since October 26.

3,000 Bosnian Serbs demonstrate in Sarajevo for a united Sarajevo and for Serbs to remain. But many Serbs have already packed to move to Belgrade. Some say they will burn homes before they leave.

December 12, 1995, Radio Netherlands:
A Bosnian Muslim in the Croatian army was released by Dutch authorities because there were no charges brought against him by the Bosnian Serb leadership.

December 13, 1995, French TV:
After being held as prisoners by the Serbs for 104 days, Lt. Souvignet and Captain Chiffot were reunited with their families at Villiacoublay Air Base in France. Both walked with difficulty from fractures suffered when they ejected from their plane. The day was overcast but both men found their eyes were not used to the light.

The BND (German intelligence) set up controversial

plutonium smuggling sting operation in August 1994. Gerhard Friedreich disputed the Government's denial of the seizure at the Munich Airport was a plan to show a need to continue the intelligence agency's operation.

Karl Spanner, head of Germany's foreign aid, said money is needed for reconstruction in Bosnia.

December 13, 1995, CNN:
A three-foot snowfall created emergency conditions in Sarajevo and Tuzla for civilians and UN personnel.

December 13, 1995, Radio Netherlands:
Turkey has been admitted to the European Customs Union but its record of Human Rights abuses will be monitored.

December 14, 1995, Radio Netherlands: Jackie Spears:
President Milosevic is attempting to reassure the Serbs of Sarajevo to accept the reunification of the city. If war resumes, NATO has said it will retire from Bosnia.

Bosnian Government troops opened fire on a UN French helicopter and Serbs fired some rounds into a hotel and fired one mortar round.

14 Russian soldiers were killed and 30 missing when war broke out again in Chechnya. Dozens of rebels were reported killed.

December 14, 1995, Die Deutsche Welle:
Russians launched attack helicopters against Chechen rebels. 12 Russian soldiers were killed and 30 wounded. Fighting flared and Chechen President Djokar Dudayev said the war was not over but just beginning.

The opposition party accused Germany's intelligence (BND) of engineering the plutonium smuggling plot last August as an electioneering scheme by the government to stay in power.

December 15, 1995, Die Deutsche Welle:
The UN Security Council voted today to hand over peace keeping operations in the former Yugoslavia to NATO's E-Operation.

Germany has set April 1, 1996 as the date to repatriate the more than 400,000 Bosnian refugees living in Germany.

For the second day in a row, heavy fighting is reported in Chechnya. Three cities are taken by the Chechens including the second largest city of the republic.

December 16, 1995, Radio Netherlands: **Jackie Spears**: Heavy winter weather has closed the airport at Tuzla to aircraft bringing in American NATO troops. Next Tuesday's formal turning over of peacekeeping operations by the UN to NATO most likely will be delayed.

December 16, 1995, Die Deutsche Welle:
In Chechnya, for the third day in a row, fighting continues with hundred of Russian soldiers reported killed. Over 50,000 people died in the fighting this last year in Chechnya.

December 17, 1995, Die Deutsche Welle: Chechen fighters were reported to have taken Gudermas, the second largest city of Chechnya.

4,000 Russian airborne troops in Belgrade are being held back by the weather from entering Bosnia.

December 17, 1995, CNN:
Serbs fired a mortar into the Muslim sector of Sarajevo. Sniper fire began.

December 18, 1995, CNN:

The fog has lifted around Tuzla airport and NATO planes with troops and supplies began to arrive after a delay of four days.

A bridge across the Sava River that was destroyed in 1991 (near Brcko) will be replaced by a pontoon bridge by the Americans.

Sniper fire in Sarajevo hit a streetcar wounding a woman whose sight may be lost.

December 18, 1995, Die Deutsche Welle:
A Russian command post in the center of Grozny has over a hundred Russian soldiers pinned down.

Russians claim that the election last Sunday went 85% in favor of their puppet regime (in Chechnya).

The conference to reconstruct Bosnia will reconvene in Vienna in January.

Authorities in Dusseldorf charged a Serb with committing war crimes in 1992 in Bosnia. The man was a resident of Germany from 1979 to 1992 and is being held for the UN War Crimes Tribunal.

December 19, 1995, Radio Netherlands:
Communists had 21% of the vote in Russia's Duma with the *Ultra Nationalists* receiving 11% and Prime Minster Chernomyrdin's *Our Home is Russia* party 10% came in third.

Dozens of civilians have been killed as Russian troops launched an attack on Gudermas against rebel Chechens.

21 people arrested in Holland are charged with smuggling Indians into the U.S. via the Netherlands.

December 19, 1995, CNN:
Lt General Sir Michael Rose handed over the UN mandate to the NATO commander in Bosnia, Admiral Leighton Smith.

The airlift operations into Tuzla are controlled from a

bunker 75 feet below the ground in Ramstein, Germany.

December 19, 1995, Die Deutsche Welle:
Sarajevo's main streets were ablaze with electric lights for the first time since the war began in Bosnia more than three years ago. Electricity came from a plant donated by Germany and designed to work independently without Serb capability to cut off the power.

Germany exports $500 billion annually and is the world's second largest exporter (after China).

December 20, 1995, Die Deutsche Welle: **Gunther Verheugen** Belgrade.
The Serbs in Belgrade are uncritical of Germany's role in Bosnia and eager for German investment. Belgrade's position as regards Human Rights for minorities, specifically the Kosovo Albanian minority (Muslim) is an issue for the Serbs to resolve before investment takes place.

The EU will contribute more than half of the $500 million needed to run the Bosnian government for the first six months. Of this amount, the World Bank will contribute $150 million and the U.S. will give $62 million. In March, another meeting will take place to decide on how to obtain the five billion needed to get the Bosnian economy going again.

December 22, 1995, CNN:
Shots were fired at two planes landing at Sarajevo airport. Admiral Leighton Smith told the UN Commander to find out who fired the shots and to make sure this was not repeated.

December 23, 1995, CNN:
Two helicopters flying near Sarajevo were fired upon,

December 24, 1995, Radio Netherlands:

A British helicopter was fired upon in northwestern Bosnia but not hit.

December 25, 1995, Radio Netherlands:
An American Blackhawk helicopter developed mechanical problems and went down near Serb-controlled Banja Luka.

December 26, 1995, CNN:
Police from Banja Luka surrounded the downed Blackhawk helicopter and offered the American crew hospitality and rooms at the local hotel.

December 26, 1995, Die Deutsche Welle:
Bosnian and Serbian militias are to evacuate 40 positions they hold around Sarajevo by midnight and turn them over to NATO forces. The Bosnian government will take full control of all Sarajevo on March 17.
A French newspaper is publishing accounts that have leaked out of French cabinet meetings about the Bosnian Serb's torture and mistreatment of the two French pilots captured August 30. The men were beaten and endured mock executions and forced to watch the execution of others.

December 27, 1995, CNN:
U.S. Army radar units for tracking artillery and mortar will be placed in Sarajevo to track artillery and mortar fire.

December 27, 1995, Radio Netherlands:
Bosnian and Bosnian Serbs agree to withdraw from 40 positions around Sarajevo just two hours before the deadline.
Prime Minister Tansu Ciller's Center Right True Path Party will join with Motherland Party to form a new government in Turkey. They will not cooperate with the Muslim Welfare Party that got the most votes in the last election and end

secularization in Turkey.

NATO forces in northern Bosnia received assurances that Serbs and Bosnians forces will remove their land mines from that area.

December 27, 1995, Die Deutsche Welle:

The OEC has protested to Moscow that the use of heavy artillery, jet planes and helicopters on civilian areas of Gudermas in Chechnya was tantamount to murder. A URCR truck was able to get into Gudermas with medical supplies and some food.

Russia has said it wants to join in NATO but some readjustment of the organization will have to be made. Kokonirev was selected by the Duma as foreign minister but Andrei Kozyrev may come back to that position even though the Duma labeled him too *"pro-Western"*.

December 28, 1995, Radio Netherlands:

For the first time, U.S.NATO troops moved through Serbia to Bosnia. There were no incidents.

President Clinton removed U.S. trade sanctions against Serbia. He also called for sympathy for Bosnian Serbs living in suburbs of Sarajevo who fear the Bosnian/Croat Federation take-over this coming March.

December 29, 1995, French TV:

General Mladic told Bosnian Serbs to show "love and understanding".

For the first time, the French Government let it be known that several years ago 400 French UN soldiers surrendered to Bosnian Serbs and the troops were abused and beaten. A French Lieutenant and a West African were singled out and subjected to mock executions. The Serbs put a Serb uniform on the Lieutenant and forced him to walk in front of Bosnian lines.

Somehow the Bosnians were aware of what was happening and did not fire. No reason was given why the French (Balladur) Government at the time suppressed this information.

A Turkish fighter plane was shot down over the Aegean Sea by two Greek fighters, according to the Turkish government.

France celebrates 100 years of cinema as 100 years ago today a film of workers leaving a train station was shown publicly in a Paris cafe. Public opinion at that time was that cinema was a 'flash in the pan'.

December 30, 1995, Radio Netherlands:
Admiral Leighton Smith informed the Bosnian Serbs that it is not possible to delay the Bosnian Government takeover of Serb suburbs in Sarajevo. Some Serbs have already left Sarajevo and a few have burned their houses before leaving.

One American soldier was seriously injured with his jeep struck a land mine in northern Bosnia.

All the Yemeni P.O.W.'s and twenty Yemeni civilians, captured when Eritrea took the Harish Archipelago, were returned to Sanaa.

December 30, 1995, Radio France: Radio France:
Admiral Leighton Smith replied in the negative to Serb demands on delaying the turnover of Serb suburbs.

December 30, 1995, CNN:
Busloads of refugees returning to Gorazde were escorted through Serb territory by NATO forces without incident.

January 1, 1996, VH 1-TV, Houston, Texas:
Bosnian Foreign Minister Sacirby hosted U-2's Bono at a New Year's party in Sarajevo. Bono said he will bring U-2 to Sarajevo for a concert this year.

January 1, 1996, Die Deutsche Welle:

A 400 member international police force is to be sent to Bosnia to work in the peace process but none have been sent as yet.

January 2, 1996, Die Deutsche Welle;

Sixteen Muslims were kidnapped by Bosnian Serbs after the Dayton Peace Accords were signed. The Bosnian Government asked NATO to have the Serbs return the 16 people.

January 3, 1996, Houston, Texas, Channel 17:

Dr. Ron Hatchett, graduate of the US Air Force Academy at Colorado Springs, Colorado and Professor at the University. of St. Thomas, friend of Milosevic and Serb propagandist, now labels himself as *"World News Analyst for ABC-TV"*.

January 3, 1996, CNN:

Three Bosnians, a man and two women, were turned over to NATO forces by Bosnian Serbs. The Serbs say they hold no other Bosnians. The Bosnian Government says none of the 3 is from the 16 Bosnians held by the Serbs.

Secretary of Defense William Perry says NATO and IPROFOR have no responsibility to protect Bosnian Muslims.

January 3, 1996, Die Deutsche Welle:

The U.S. Government handed a note to Serbian President Milosevic demanding the release of the 16 Bosnian Muslims seized by Bosnian Serbs. The Serbs say the 16 have been charged with smuggling and will be tried by courts. The Bosnian Government says the kidnapping of the 16 people is terrorism.

EU Administrator for Rebuilding Bosnia, Carl Bildt, arrived in Sarajevo. Mr. Bildt says it is NATO's responsibility to assure the free movement of people in Bosnia and the safety of civilians according to the Dayton Peace Accords.

Croatia, Bosnia, and Rump Yugoslavia are to meet in Vienna Thursday to work on the disarmament issue limiting the number of heavy weapons, tanks, and warplanes. This agreement is to be signed by June 6 or Bosnia is to receive weapons and training commensurate to the other two groups.

January 3, 1996, BBC:

Dr. Maseri, critic of the Saudi Arabian Government, has been asked to leave England. Dr. Maseri arrived in England in 1994 and has been using fax machines to send messages to Saudi Arabia. Great Britain has much money invested in Saudi Arabia and the Saudi Arabian Government demanded Dr. Maseri's expulsion. Britain has offered sanctuary for Dr. Maseri on the Caribbean island of Dominica.

January 4, 1996, Radio Netherlands:

The sixteen people held by Bosnian Serbs were released today. Some said they were kicked and beaten during their detainment.

Bosnian Serbs gave a list of addresses and names of 800 Bosnian Muslim to the War Crimes Tribunal in The Hague. The Serbs said these were snipers that killed 1,000 Bosnian Serbs in Sarajevo.

Russian Defense Minister, Pavel Grachev, said Russia would have to review its agreements for arms limitations and nuclear disarmament if NATO expands eastward.

January 4, 1996, Swiss Radio International:

The Russians say one soldier was killed and others wounded by an explosion in Grozny. Russia says 600,000 Chechens, or half of Chechnya's pre-war population, have been displaced by the war.

January 5, 1996, Die Deutsche Welle:
German physicists have isolated anti-matter which may revolutionize physics.

EU mediators have returned to Chechnya to get the warring parties back to the negotiating table.

The warring parties in Bosnia agree to establish liaison offices in Sarajevo within 10 days.

Two Muslim policemen were wounded by gunfire from the Croat sector of Mostar. Fears are mounting that tensions between Muslims and Croats in Mostar may wreck the Croat/Bosnia Federation.

A gunman wounded an Italian NATO soldier in Sarajevo Thursday and NATO troops returned fire but the gunman escaped.

January 6, 1996, CNN:
A French soldier near Sarajevo was wounded in the foot by an explosion.

British NATO troops fired back after they were fired upon by Serbs in western Bosnia.

January 7, 1996, RN: Carole Van den Ring:
In Mostar, a Croat policeman was shot and killed in a revenge killing of a Muslim. Mounting tensions in Mostar have resulted in many shots fired from both sides.

In Sarajevo, a French plane was fired upon but no great damage done. A Greek plane was fired upon when landing at Tuzla Airport.

January 7, 1996, Die Deutsche Welle:

(German) Foreign Minister Klaus Kinkel will go to Sarajevo to discuss rebuilding Bosnia with President Alija Izetbegovic and Prime Minister Haris Siladjic. Bad weather in Bosnia has delayed his trip.

Hans Koshnick said he will withdraw all plans to rebuild Mostar unless Croats and Muslims stop feuding. Croats want a divided Mostar.

Turkish businesses in Germany have been attacked and a bomb attempt on a Turkish travel agency in Ludwigsburg was foiled as a result of three deaths in Turkish prison riots in Istanbul.

January 8, 1996, Die Deutsche Welle:

Foreign Minister Klaus Kinkel said that Serbs living in the suburbs of Sarajevo have no reason to leave. He also recalled the contribution of Germany in the humanitarian airlift into Sarajevo in ceremonies commemorating the end of the airlift Monday.

Turkish extreme leftists are blamed for the wave of arson against Turkish businesses in Germany as a result of Turkey's crack down on prison riots in Istanbul. A Canadian of Turkish origin was arrested as leader of the leftists.

January 8, 1996, Radio Netherlands: **Carole Van den Ring:**

General Walker expressed disappointment over the Serb movement out of Sarajevo suburbs before the Bosnian Government takes over.

The mounting attacks on NATO troops will be met with heavily armed helicopter gunships in the future.

January 9, 1996, Radio Netherlands: **Carole Van den Ring:**

500 Chechen rebels infiltrated the city of Kizlyar,

Dagestan, and are holding around 2,000 hostages in a hospital. They want to free the women and elderly and have asked Russians for buses. They want Russia to withdraw its troops from Chechnya and to recognize Chechnya and its president, Dudayev.

A streetcar passing through "sniper alley" in Sarajevo was hit by sniper fire and a rifle grenade. One woman was killed and a number were wounded.

Explosions are heard in Serb suburbs of Sarajevo as Bosnian Serbs who do not want to live under Muslim rule set fire to buildings as they leave for Serb controlled territory.

The Turkish Welfare Party, which received the most votes (20%) in the last election, has been asked to form a coalition government. The other Turkish parties have said they do not want to cooperate with the Muslim fundamentalists.

January 9, 1996, Die Deutsche Welle:
In a meeting between Russians and Chechen President Dudayev, and an international news media conference Chechen rebels offered to release women and old people. They want vehicles, an escape passage,

January 11, 1996, Die Deutsche Welle:
No progress has been made in the stand off to release 180 hostages held by Chechen rebels. Russian troops are tightening a ring around the Dagestan village where Russians have blown up a bridge to stop them from leaving.

Bosnian Serbs may be hiding thousands of bodies in a mine in northern Bosnia, near Prijador.

January 11, 1996, Radio Netherlands: **Jackie Spears:**
Rebel Serbs are using a mine in northern Bosnia to hold

thousands of bodies from a detention camp. There are 20 mass graves holding 20,000 bodies Muslims killed by the Serbs.

Chechen rebels have released 20 hostages but still hold over 200. Russian troops, tanks, and helicopter gunships surround them.

January 12, 1996, VOA:

Chechen rebels have been told to release their hostages or face a Russian attack. That would mean some of the hostages would be killed, making a mockery of President Yeltsin who said every hostage's life is precious.

Bosnian Serbs are continuing to flee their suburbs in Sarajevo and some are digging up their dead relatives to take with them.

The Bosnian Croats in Mostar want to divide the city and make their half a Bosnian Croat capital of Herzegovina.

January 12, 1996, Die Deutsche Welle:

The Russian military commander has given the Chechen rebels until 7:30 UTC to lay down their arms and surrender their hostages and then they will guarantee the safety of the Chechen rebels.

January 12, 1996, Radio Netherlands: **Jackie Spears**:

In Russia, the standoff continues. Russians have given the (Chechen) rebels until Monday morning. The hostages have been placed in the position of being human shields if the Russians attack.

(Croatian) Foreign Minister Ejup Granic and (Bosnian Foreign Minister) Mohammed Sacerby met with Klaus Kinkel and Hans Koshnick about unifying Mostar as soon as possible. Mr. Kinkel blames the Croats for the situation in Mostar, which is considered the weakest link in the

Croat/Muslim Federation.

January 13, 1996, Radio Netherlands:
   Mrs. Harawi Ashawri (Christian Palestinian leader) said that Israel is doing everything possible to prevent free elections in the West Bank.

January 13, 1996, Die Deutsche Welle:
   Bosnian Croats and Serbs will exchange 900 POWs.
   Four Norwegian soldiers were injured when their jeep hit a land mine near Maglag in northern Bosnia.
   Croatian Foreign Minister Ejup Granic says Zagreb will bring pressure on Croats to stop hostilities by Croats to Muslims in Mostar.
   NATO HQ in Brussels says 36,000 of the planned 60,000 E-4 troops are in Bosnia now.

January 14, 1996, Radio Netherlands: **Jackie Spears:**
   Officials in Moscow say elite troops have broken the (Chechen) rebel resistance. The rebels deny executing any hostages and say hostages were killed in the shelling and fire from Russian troops.
   The Friday release of hundreds of POWs will be completed Monday. Bosnian Government refuses to release Serb POWs until the Bosnian Serbs give an accounting of thousands of Muslims that disappeared after the fall of Srebrenica.

January 14, 1996, CNN:
   The US will supply retired army personnel to train Bosnians and Islamic nations will supply weapons to put Bosnia on a par with Bosnian Serbs.

January 14, 1996, Die Deutsche Welle:

Most of the Dagestan village where Chechen rebels are holed up is in Russian hands. Russians attacked with gunships, artillery, and tanks.

B'nai B'rith awarded Helmut Kohl its highest award. The B'nai B'rith has a half million members worldwide.

January 15, 1996, Radio Netherlands:
The rebels increased their pressure on Russia by taking 30 Russian workers at an electrical plant near Grozny. No trace of the workers or rebels is found.

Mr. Ogahata opened plans to repatriate 700,000 Bosnian refugees in nearby republics around Bosnia and 700,000 in the rest of Europe, which will take two years.

January 15, 1996, Die Deutsche Welle:
A Turkish ferry bound for Russia was seized in the Bosporus Straits by pro-Chechen gunmen. They said they will free the Turkish passengers but will die with the Russian hostages if Russia does not pull back from Chechnya. U.S. State Dept said Russia must do all it can to prevent further bloodshed in Chechnya but noted that Chechnya is an integral part of Russia.

A German court of North Rhine Westphalia says the Church of Scientology uses violence against its opponents and exploits members and makes members psychologically dependent on it. (Many prominent movies stars are members of the Church of Scientology, which seems to go after wealthy and prominent people and convince them to become members. The founder of the church was assassinated but no one was charged with his murder).

January 17, 1996, Voice of America:
(Bosnian) Foreign Minister Sacerby says Bosnia will not go ahead with the POW exchange unless Bosnia is granted

access to all prison and mass grave sites in Bosnian Serb territory. The U.S. says it knows of hundreds of Bosnian civilians being held in Serbian prisons and supports Bosnia's position.

Pro-Chechen gunmen described as Abkazians took a Turkish ferry and say they will take the ship to Istanbul and release the hostages. They demand Russia pull out of Chechnya and ask for a news conference before surrendering the ship which they have mined with explosives.

January 17, 1996, Radio Netherlands: **Jackie Spears:**
The Turkish news agency reports the hijackers are prepared to surrender if they are allowed to make a statement on Russian policy in Chechnya. A large part of the ship's passengers are Russian.

Russian Tanks and artillery are pounding the Chechen rebels and their hostages in Dagestan. It is doubtful if anyone will survive.

Bosnian Serbs have agreed to stop boycotting the meetings.

January 17, 1996, Die Deutsche Welle:
The Bonn Government voiced concern over the growing violence by the Russian government.

January 18, 1996, Radio Netherlands: Jackie Spears:
Turkey's care-taker Prime Minister Kakeis, said force will not be used against the hijackers and rejected a Russian offer of military help. The ferry will be stopped 15 kilometers before entering the Bosporus because it has been mined with explosives.

Secretary of State Warren Christopher says Russia's integration with European institutions is in jeopardy over its use of force in Chechnya. Popular sentiment in Russia has clamored for a political solution, not a military one.

January 18, 1996, Die Deutsche Welle:
Russian President Boris Yeltsin says Chechens were annihilated after a missile bombardment, 18 hostages are missing. Yeltsin says Moscow must strike at Chechen rebels wherever they are until they are annihilated.

German Foreign Minister, Klaus Kinkel, called upon Russian Foreign Minister Primakov to seek a political solution in Chechnya.

The dispute over the repatriation of POWs threatens to undermine the Dayton Peace Accords and the implementation of reconstruction.

The roads to Pale are choked with Serbs leaving their homes in Sarajevo suburbs.

January 19, 1996, Radio Netherlands:
The Chechen Rebels and 150 hostages are still holding Russian troops back. Russian helicopter gunships circle overhead, and Russian Troops have the rebels penned down. The Chechen rebels are threatening to kill their 150 hostages if the Russians attack.

January 19, 1996, Die Deutsche Welle:
Hostile fire broke out in Mostar between Croats and Muslims with rifle grenades, rockets, and sniper fire coming from both sides. A British vehicle was damaged by a mine in northern Bosnia and an American vehicle was damaged by a mine, but no one was injured.

January 20, 1996, Radio Netherlands: **Marcel Sniders:**
The hijacking of a Turkish ferry is over. No one was harmed. Turkish authorities did not use force.

The Chechen rebels want to negotiate with 37 hostages. 24 hostages were killed in the attack by Russian troops.

Mr. Erbakhan was unable to form a new Turkish government and President Demeral asked Tansu Ciller to try again to form a new government.

In Bosnia, the exchange of prisoners has taken place hours before the deadline.

The sons of Robert Maxwell have been accused of robbing the pension funds of the workers in their father's company but the jury decided there was insufficient evidence. (Maxwell, of Jewish origin was reportedly killed by three Kidon (Mossad Assassins).

January 20, 1996, Die Deutsche Welle:
 Defense Minister Volker Ruhe has charged Russia with using extreme force instead of pursuing a patient outcome in the Chechen hostage situation.

On January 25, 1945, Auschwitz was liberated. Plans are going ahead for celebrations of that event.

Yeltsin confirmed that 130 Chechen rebels escaped the trap set by Russian military on the border of Dagestan after Yeltsin had promised the rebels safe passage to Chechnya.

January 21, 1996, Radio Netherlands:
Bosnian Serb authorities have given permission to inspect suspected mass grave sites. U.S. Envoy, John Shattuck has already visited the sites near Srebrenica where thousands of Muslims were reported to have been massacred.

Haram Muratovic was voted to replace Haris Siladjic as Prime Minister. Mr. Siladjic says the change will weaken Bosnia's position in future negotiations.

Chechen rebels say they will release most their hostages and keep just a few to negotiate for the return of rebels captured by the Russians.

January 21, 1996, CNN;
Lt Colonel Raynor (a British officer in NATO's I-4) says ***NATO is not obliged to protect investigators at the site of Serb massacres of Muslims and Croats.***

January 21, 1996, Die Deutsche Welle:
71 secret caches of weapons were hidden in Austria by the U.S. after the end of World War II. The weapons were to be used in case of a Russian attack on Allied forces in Europe.

The (Bosnian) Muslim SDA party has picked Haram Muratovic and Haris Siladjic resigned when the government limited the number of ministers to six.

U.S. Envoy John Shattuck visited Srebrenica and said there was much evidence of horrible crimes committed against Croats and Muslims. NATO has said it will only carry out aerial observation of the sites but will not protect the investigators.

January 22, 1996, Radio Netherlands:
NATO will dispatch troops to guard the sites of suspected Serb massacres of Bosnians at Srebrenica and Prijador. This is possible because the warring parties have pulled back their troops.

A final exchange of 700 POWs has not yet taken place.

Chechen rebels are still holding 37 hostages in a cellar in eastern Chechnya.

January 22, 1996, Die Deutsche Welle; Nigel Tandy:
Police arrested a 21-year old Lebanese man who lived in the refugee hostel that was set on fire in Leubeck, Germany.

There was wide spread fraud in East Germany at the

time of reunification, estimated to have cost 26 billion DM. Only two billion have been recovered.

Foreign Minister, Klaus Kinkel, said Russia has made great strides to democratize and should be admitted to the EU. He called on Russia to resolve the Chechen Conflict politically not militarily.

January 23, 1996, CNN:
Islamic terrorists are reportedly in Bosnia and NATO troops have been put on high alert.

January 23, 1996, Radio Netherlands:
In Bosnia, 2 Portuguese and 1 Italian were killed in an explosion after carrying a land mine into a NATO barracks.

U.S. troops in Bosnia have been put on high alert after reports that an attack by Islamic terrorists was imminent because of the conviction in the U.S. courts of the New York Trade Center bombing. An immediate call for the removal of all Islamic volunteers from Bosnia has been requested.

Muslims and Croats in Mostar have disagreed over a division of the city. Hans Koshnick, EU administrator for rebuilding the city will most likely make a division of ethnic parts. Mostar was to be the model for rebuilding Bosnia.

The Chechen rebels handed over 42 Dagestani hostages but will hold 14 Russian police until Russia returns the bodies of rebels killed and Chechens captured.

January 23, 1996, Die Deutsche Welle:
The International Red Cross says that 240 POWs are still held in defiance of the Dayton Peace Accords.

The European Council has misgivings over the entry of Russia into the council due to Russian actions in Chechnya.

January 24, 1996, Radio Netherlands:

The Council of Europe has accepted Russia's application for membership despite Human Rights abuses in Chechnya. The council will dispatch a delegation to monitor human rights abuses in Chechnya.

Russian Deputy Secretary, Sergei Krainov, says the expulsion of Polish vice president over espionage activities for Russia is straining relations between the two countries.

A German engineer is said to have supplied Iraq's Saddam Hussein with plans for a plutonium enrichment plant.

France wants to set up talks between Eritrea and Yemen over their dispute for Hamish Islands in the Red Sea.

The siege of Kabul may result in food shortages within two weeks. Kabul is under a cold spell with temperatures as low as -21 F.

January 24, 1996, Die Deutsche Welle:

France and Germany have reaffirmed their commitment for a common European currency.

January 24, 1996, CNN:

The Army Corps of Engineers at Vicksburg, Mississippi, has completed a study of the Sava River showing this year's flood was the worst ever with the river expanding in places as much as 20 miles.

January 25, 1996, Die Deutsche Welle:

The UN High Commission for Refugees says that Germany's plan to start repatriating its 400,000 refugees beginning July 1 is too soon and could create difficulties in Bosnia.

The Council of Europe says that Russia should work for a political solution in Chechnya. Despite its Human Rights abuses in Chechnya, Russia's membership was accepted into the council.

Russia's Foreign Minister Yevgeny Primakov hailed its entry into the European Council as Russia belongs in Europe and can be a bridge between Europe and Asia.

Another journalist has been killed in Russia and President Yeltsin has been asked to investigate.

January 25, 1996, Radio Netherlands:

The former warring parties in Bosnia have signed an accord in Vienna for the inspection of the number of heavy weapons and number of troops in their armies.

Members of a tribe in Yemen have kidnapped 17 French tourists in eastern Yemen and are asking for the release of a tribesman in prison for the kidnapping of an American businessman.

Over 1,000 people were murdered in Moscow last year, half were by professional killers. Oleg Ostinko is the latest journalist murdered in Russia. The western press is asking Yeltsin to personally take charge of the investigation.

January 27, 1996, Radio Netherlands:

Croats and Muslims have released 250 POWs and Serbs handed over 80 civilians but have delayed in releasing 150 POWs because of problems in rounding them up. Croats say they will not release those charged with war crimes.

President Yeltsin expressed strong opposition of any eastward expansion of NATO (Hungary, Poland, Estonia, and Lithuania).

A convoy of 300 trucks arrived in Kabul with food and fuel for 3 weeks. The city has been cut off by guerrilla forces opposing the Kabul government.

January 28, 1996, CNN:

A U.S. Army officer was going about his business in a Serb suburb of Sarajevo was grazed by a bullet. He's back on duty now.

January 28, 1996, Radio Netherlands:
Three British soldiers were killed in northern Bosnia when their jeep hit a land mine. A Swedish IFOR soldier was killed when his vehicle skidded off the road.
The warring parties have exchanged POWs but he Serbs has not returned 150 of their POWs.

January 29, 1996, CNN:
Over 400 POWs were freed over the weekend but the fate of over 900 known POWs has not been clear.

January 29, 1996, Radio Netherlands:
The Egyptian Parliament has rescinded a law whereby a man or wife may divorce the spouse over a difference of political opinion.
Iraq and the UN are having talks over a partial lifting of the UN ban on petroleum exports to help Iraq pay for humanitarian goods.

January 29, 1996, Die Deutsche Welle:
A 150 German Mountain Battalion arrived in Bosnia, the first of 1,400 German troops that will be sent to Bosnia.
Russia's Human Rights Activist, Oleg Koriyev, has voiced concern over freedom in Russia.

January 30, 1996, French TV:
The seventeen French tourists held hostage by Yemeni tribesmen were freed at 6 am today. Pictures on French television showed a jubilant group and their tour bus that were held in eastern Yemen. All appeared happy and well

taken care of. The tribesmen prepared a nice farewell dinner and gave all the tourists gifts. The women in the group said they never once felt afraid and the women of the tribe gave them gifts, kissed them, and cried when they left. All appeared in good spirits by the experience and amused by the attention in the news media. One even dressed in an Arab robe and head dress and was jumping up and down expressing nothing but joy over the experience.

January 31, 1996, Die Deutsche Welle:
The UN has officially ended its mission in the former Yugoslavia and paid tribute to 214 UN Peacekeepers who died there. The U.S. Troops in Macedonia are the only UN force left there.

Serb armed forces left the Sarajevo Serb suburbs which they were obliged to leave Saturday night.

A Sarajevo bridge, blocked during war, is now open.

Russian Human Rights Activist, Sergei Kabalyov, asked western leaders to do more than make protests over Boris Yeltsin's Chechnya policies. The Chechen War saw crimes against humanity and the execution of civilians from order higher up than local commanders.

January 31, 1996, Radio Netherlands (Spanish language)
The last of Islamic volunteers (Mujahideen) have left Bosnia.

The Serbian Parliament in Belgrade said it would take years to investigate the massacres and atrocities committed in Bosnia. (That's no use not to start, but indicates that the Serbs themselves know that the massacres were on a massive scale).

February 1, 1996, Die Deutsche Welle:
NATO Secretary General Solano and German Foreign

Minister Klaus Kinkel met in Bonn and called the operation in Bosnia a success.

A mass grave 90 kilometers north of Sarajevo is being excavated.

A sniper in the de-militarized Serb suburb of Sarajevo was shot dead by NATO French troops who captured another sniper. In the future, no warnings would be given and snipers would be shot.

In Mostar, Bosnian Croats entered a demilitarized zone and surrendered their weapons after NATO planes flew overhead.

Tadzhik rebels launched an attack against CIS "peacekeepers"

February 1, 1996, Radio Netherlands:
170 members of the American Congress boycotted President. Jacques Chirac's address before the U.S. Congress.

NATO Secretary General Solano says the confrontation between Turkey and Greece over the Aegean island threatens peace in Bosnia.

The Netherlands police are abusing laws protecting the rights of citizens in their fight against organized crime.

February 2, 1996, Radio Netherlands: Carole Van den Ring:
Serbs are still holding many Muslim POW's that should have been released.

No one believes NATO can clear 3 million land mines in Bosnia by April. Most believe the number of mines is closer to six million.

Boris Yeltsin is working on a plan for a peaceful solution to Chechnya calling for a partial withdrawal of Russian troops there.

Tadzhik rebels launched several attacks on Russian

troops. Rebels in other Asian Republics are causing serious problems for Russia.

February 2, 1996, CNN:
Near Javica, a mass grave of Bosnian Croats killed by Serbs yielded the bodies of five Bosnian Croats.

February 2, 1996, Die Deutsche Welle:
About 5,000 NATO troops will be brought into East Slavonia, still under Croatian Serb control. Germany has asked for the Bundestag to send Tornado fighters to Bosnia.

The Council of Europe at Strasburg said it will have to discuss Chechnya as it is not an internal problem of Russia (but it is a European problem and concerns the abuse of human rights in Russia which the Russian consider Chechnya is still a part of Russia).

Tadzhik warlords have pulled their forces 35 kilometers back from the capital of Dushanbe. Ashkhabad will be the site of a peace conference between the warring factions. Meanwhile, Tadzhik rebels still launch attacks across the border from bases in Afghanistan.

February 3, Radio Netherlands:
A U.S. soldier was killed by a land mine 40 miles north of Tuzla.

NATO commander in Bosnia, Admiral Leighton Smith, was sure the warring parties will comply with the Dayton Peace Accords. One Serb suburb will not be turned over to Bosnian Government till March.

Tadzhik government troops have created insecurity by revolting.

Polish and Russian intellectuals meeting in Poland quarreled over the eastward expansion of NATO. The Poles were **pro**, Russians **con**.

February 3, 1996, Die Deutsche Welle:
Russian Deputy Defense Minister Andrei Kokosheen warned if NATO extends eastward, it would face a backlash from his country.

February 4, 1996, CNN:
A Jewish settler opened fire on a group of Palestinian school children. There were some fatalities.

The first American soldier to die in Bosnia was killed when his jeep hit a land mine in northern Bosnia near Tuzla.

Land mines are preventing the excavations and investigations of mass graves in Bosnia. The graves appear to contain many bodies.

February 5, 1996, Radio Netherlands:
Thousands of Muslims missing after the fall of Srebrenica are no longer alive.

The Croats, Muslims, and Serbs have to pull back from lines of confrontation according to the Dayton Accords. Croats and Serbs in western and eastern Bosnia have been slow to pull back.

Bosnian President Alija Izetbegovic says the delay permitted the Serbs to hold back from turning their suburbs over to the Bosnian government runs counter to the Dayton Accords.

The recognition of Rump Yugoslavia depends upon Serbia's willingness to turn over Bosnian Serbs accused of War Crimes.

For three weeks, Kabul has been under siege and the situation is becoming perilous for the safety and welfare of the people.

The Minister of police and military has resigned in Tadzhikistan under pressure from the rebelling military.

February 5, 1996, CNN:

Since NATO took over, 8 NATO soldiers have been shot in Sarajevo.

February 6, 1996, Radio Netherlands: **Jackie Spears:**

Assistant Secretary of State Richard Holbrooke has called off a trip to Greece and Turkey after Greece said it would not meet with him.

A senior Bosnian Serb says the men, women, and children, missing after the fall of Srebrenica, are no longer alive.

A Bosnian Serb general was arrested by Bosnian forces after he strayed into their sector. The general and other Serb officers were on their way to a meeting with NATO officers.

February 6, 1996, Die Deutsche Welle:

Richard Holbrooke said the role of NATO in Bosnia will greatly influence Europe's future.

Croat sources in Zagreb say another mass grave has been discovered in Malagjab.

February 6, 1996, French TV:

The *rumors of atrocities in Bosnia are realized as truth as the mass graves reveal atrocities of the Serbs.*

Only one of the 52 indicted Serbian war criminals is in custody. Claude Jorda of the International War Crimes Tribunal shows shelves of investigative material (Omerska files shown). Reporters are being kept from the sites of the mass graves by armed Bosnian Serbs (but the gruesomeness was that Serbs said the mass graves of Muslims killed in the fighting when Srebrenica Muslims gave up all weapons with the promise of UN protection, and the Dutch UN forces simply gave way to the Serbs.

A young girl told of girls 10 to 12, being taken from buses by Serb soldiers never to be seen again.

February 7, 1996, Radio Netherlands: Jackie Spears:

Even though not on the list of indicted War Criminals, the International War Crimes Tribunal has asked the Bosnia Government to continue holding Bosnian Serb General, Alex Krosvic, and a colonel until they can complete an investigation into possible war crimes.

Mostar Croats have cut all relations with the E.U. and attacked the car of Hans Koshnick in Mostar. The Croats are against unifying the city and demand the city be divided.

German Foreign Minister Klaus Kinkel got on the phone and called President Franjo Tudjman to calm his fellow Croats in Mostar. The major problem in Mostar is the powerful Herzegovina Mafia that operates worldwide which had given Tudjman its support when he sought it before.

February 7, 1996, French TV:

A UN War Crimes investigator, Mrs. Rehn, says that despite the Dayton Peace Accords, the rapes, violence, and killing continue.

February 8, 1996, Radio Netherlands: Jackie Spears:

The U.S. is sending Richard Holbrooke to Bosnia to avoid continuing problems with Dayton Peace Accords raised by the Bosnian Serbs since the arrest of a Bosnian Serb general and colonel for suspected war crimes.

In Grozny, 2,000 people demonstrated against Russian troops in Chechnya. Yeltsin denies he is withdrawing any Russian troops from Chechnya. No force was used against the demonstrators who have erected barricades in the streets.

The Council of Europe has officially accepted Russia's membership and it will be the 59th member. There are misgivings over Russia's membership because of its crimes against humanity in Chechnya.

February 8, 1996, CNN:
The Croat Mayor of Mostar says any federation between Muslims and Croats will be temporary, as it cannot last.

February 8, 1996, BBC:
The International War Crimes Tribunal is mediating over the arrest by Bosnian forces of a Bosnian Serb general and colonel suspected of war crimes.

February 8, 1996, Die Deutsche Welle:
Twelve Turkish police are being held for the killing of a Turkish journalist. **Journalists Without Frontiers** has made a complaint and asked for an investigation by the Turkish Government.

The military leadership of the Bosnian Serbs has broken off communications with NATO and the Bosnian Gove.

Judge Richard Goldstone says the Bosnians have the right to pursue suspected war criminals.

180 armored vehicles were discovered hidden along the boundary between Bosnia and Bosnian Serb territory.

February 24, 1996: Radio Netherlands:
A car bomb exploded in the Algerian capital killing one person.

Demonstrations in Bahrain for democracy and an attempted coup in Qatar along with King Fahd taking the throne in Saudi Arabia, mark the end of Ramadan celebrations for Muslims in the Middle East.

Despite assurances for their safety, the two sons-in-law of Saddam Hussain were killed upon their return to Iraq.

Holland will donate $50 million for rebuilding Bosnia.

February 24, 1996, Die Deutsche Welle:

EU administrator of Mostar, Hans Koschnick will resign at the end of July. He says a new EU administration should take over in Mostar.

French Lawyer and Nazi hunter, Sergei Karsfeld, speaking from the Bosnian Serb city of Pale called upon Radovan Karadzic and Ratko Mladic to surrender themselves to the International War Crimes Tribunal. The lawyer was then picked up by Bosnian Serb police and after questioning him for two hours was compelled to leave.

Bosnian Serbs are abandoning their suburbs in Sarajevo en masse. Bosnian Serb army vehicles are being used to move them to Bosnian Serb territory. On Friday, Vokoi Serf, the first of five Serb suburbs to be handed over to the Bosnian Government was concluded.

February 24, 1996, ABC-TV:

(Bosnia) Food has become more abundant but 1/3 of all apartments and apartment buildings and 1/2 of all streetcars need repair or replacement. People have no work and it will take three billion dollars annually over the next ten years to rebuild Bosnia.

February 25, 1996, Die Deutsche Welle:

Libya is about to open an underground chemical weapons factory located in a mountain 90 kilometers south of the capital. It was built with the help of German and Austrian engineers.

February 26, 1996, CNN-TV:

EU administrator for Mostar Hans Koschnick has handed in his resignation and will stay until a successor replaces him.

February 27, 1996, Die Deutsche Welle:

The UN has lifted all sanctions against the Bosnian Serbs after their military completed the military pullback from their positions in accordance with the Dayton Peace Accords.

February 28, 1996, CNN:

People in Sarajevo have resumed a normal life. Serbs continue to move out and say the wounds are too deep although the Muslims say the Serbs are welcome to stay. Children are shown using sleds on hillsides and enjoying themselves. On the Serb side, Serbs enjoying the ski slopes say Bosnian Muslims had better not come there to ski.

The War Crimes Tribunal says their efforts to investigate war crimes in the former Yugoslavia are hampered because they have no vehicles even though the UN in Sarajevo has many unused vehicles parked in their vehicle compounds.

Ilidjic is the next Serb suburb to be turned over to the Bosnian/Croat federation.

February 28, 1996, Radio Netherlands:

Bosnia and the former Yugoslavia have lost their right to vote in the UN because they have not paid their dues for several years.

Bosnian Serb General George Jujic and Colonel Alexei Kaganovic are still held by the International War Crimes Tribunal while investigations are going on.

February 29, 1996, Radio Netherlands:

War Crimes Tribunal Judge Richard Goldstone returns to South Africa and Canadian judge Louise Arbor will take his place.

March 1, 1996, Radio Netherlands:

General George Jujic, held in The Hague for the past two weeks had been indicted by the War Crimes Tribunal. Colonel Alexei Kaganovic who is held along with him had not been indicted.

March 1, 1996, Die Deutsche Welle:

Judge Goldstone said that General Jujic has been accused of crimes against civilians.

March 2, 1996, Die Deutsche Welle:

German forces in Croatia successfully have carried out fourteen convoys.

Chancellor Helmut Kohl says that a seat on the UN Security Council is a remote goal for Germany.

March 2, 1996, Radio Netherlands:

Mesut Yilmas of the Motherland Party and Prime Minister Ciller of the True Path Party have formed a coalition government in Turkey.

March 4, 1996, Radio Netherlands: Jackie Spears:

In Russia, some 20 parties have formed a coalition to support Zugonov, the Communist Party candidate.

The Whitewater investigation is over whether the Clintons used those funds to finance his 1992 presidential campaign.

The arrested Bosnian Serb General George Jujic challenged the War Crimes Tribunal on charges of shelling Sarajevo saying all the Bosnian Serb generals should be on trial.

March 4, 1996, Die Deutsche Welle:

Thousands of Chechens fled a Russian attack on their

village.

George Jiujujic said he had nothing to answer to as any Bosnian Serb general could be charged with the same. (Just because a hunter can't get all the ducks doesn't mean he should stop duck hunting).

Any recognition of Rump Yugoslavia must be tied to Human Rights.

Germany will continue with 40 Tornado fighters in Bosnia in spite of IFOR reduction in aircraft.

March 5, 1996, CNN:

Serbs burn and loot as they move out of the Sarajevo suburb of Hadzici.

Czech soldiers serving under the UN in Bosnia raped an American woman soldier. The number of Czech soldiers is not known.

March 5, 1996, Radio Netherlands:

Mohammed Javad Zarif, Deputy Foreign Minister of Iran, ***says Iran has nothing to do with suicide bombings or terrorism anywhere in the world.***

The (Chechen) village of Cienovodsk was under bombardment by the Russian Army and is in flames and smoke. Rebels kill three Russian soldiers.

Muslims and Croats in Mostar want an extension in the scheduled reunification under the Dayton Peace Accords.

Prime Minister John Majors is being criticized for expelling Saudi critic, Mohammed Mosari to Dominica because there is no security for the safety of Mosari there.

March 5, 1996, Die Deutsch Welle:

German President Roman Herzog said Russian leaders should get involved in NATO and not look at NATO's eastward expansion as a threat to Russia.

The European Unity has extended its authorization to stay in Mostar until the end of 1996.

Civilian duties will be part of NATO's duties in Bosnia.

Funds for reconstruction to the warring sides in the former Yugoslavia will be paid only to those respecting human rights.

Salman Radiyev, the leader of Chechen rebels in the border village of Chechnya and Dagestan, was shot in the head by an assailant.

March 6, 1996, Radio Netherlands:

The Russian Army has launched a massive counter-offensive against the Chechen rebels in the capital of Grozny.

Many people have been killed by Russian cluster bombs but the rebels are holding out in the strongest attack in over a year.

March 6, 1996, Die Deutsche Welle:

In Chechnya, rebels have launched an offensive and control three suburbs of Grozny.

Soldiers in IFOR in Bosnia are to perform more humanitarian and civilian tasks. They had asked some Croat police to leave a police station they illegally occupied in one of the Serb suburbs.

The CIS wants to modernize and improve air defenses in its southern regions, especially Armenia and Tadzikistan.

March 7, 1996, Radio Netherlands: **Jackie Spears**:

Palestinian leader Yassir Arafat has called for an international summit on terrorism.

In Belgrade, a 24 year-old Bosnian Serb is arrested for war crimes and will be turned over to the War Crimes Tribunal in The Hague.

Russians report that 70 Russian soldiers have been killed and 170 wounded and the rebels have been driven out, but no independent sources confirm this.

Aviation parts bound for Iraq have been seized in Jordan.

Mrs. Ciller will return to the cabinet with Mesut Yilmas as Prime Minister in Turkey (Motherland and True Path Parties)

March 7, 1996, Die Deutsche Wells:
A Human Rights Council has been set up in Sarajevo with 4 representatives from the Bosnian Government and 2 by the Serbs.

Vice President Dieter Lau says the 4 billion Deutschmark loan to Russia is tied to human rights condition, otherwise it might be interpreted as aiding the campaign to re-elect Boris Yeltsin.

March 8, 1996, ABC-TV:
A Western reporter in Belgrade came across a 24 year old Bosnian Serb soldier who deserted from the Bosnian Serb army after he was forced to participate in massacres in Srebrenica.

In Tuzla, International Women's Day was the scene of a march by thousands of women whose husbands and fathers are missing after the fall of Srebrenica and feared to be massacred.

March 8, 1996, Radio Netherlands: **Jackie Spears**:
Fighting in Grozny has been pushed into the suburbs.

Iran's President Ali Akhbar Rafsanjani warned the Iranian people that Israel and the U.S. are waging a propaganda war against Iran.

Bosnian Serb soldiers murdered one thousand two

hundred Muslim men the day after Srebrenica was taken from 400 Dutch soldiers. A Bosnian Serb soldier, Drazen Ardemovic was arrested by Serb authorities after he gave an interview to a western reporter. The War Crimes has asked Serbia to turn him over to them. Ardemovic named two Bosnian Serb officers that the War Crimes Tribunal wants to question about the massacres near the town of Potochari. Noel Gerard of *Le Figaro* said Ardemovic told him that groups of ten Muslims men were led away to be shot. Over 1,200 were put in a hole and shot.

The UN Dutch troops surrendered to the Bosnian Serbs and abandoned the Muslims to the Serbs. **Ardemovic deserted from the Bosnian Serb army because his commanding officer, Major Milar Aramovic, was cruel. Aramovic was given 12 kilos of gold and other valuables, which he kept for himself.** Judge Goldstone said that if Ardemovic gave full evidence and showed he had no choice to disobey orders he most likely would not be prosecuted. *The two Bosnian Serb officers being sought can implicate Radovan Karazdic and Ratko Mladic with the massacre.*

After his interview with the reporter from *Le Figaro*, Ardemovic was arrested by Serb police in Belgrade. Ardemovic's wife and Gerard went immediately to the U.S. Embassy where they made a report to U.S. State Department in hopes of protecting his life.

Unless international aid to Bosnia is doubled, there is little possibility to resettle Bosnian refugees quickly as the infrastructure of Bosnia has been disrupted or destroyed.

The Russian Army has thrown a blockade around a Chechen village and no one can enter or leave while they are mounting a massive bombardment. 7,000 remaining villagers have taken shelter in their cellars. The Russians do not want anyone to know what they are doing to the villagers and are keeping all westerners at a distance.

March 9, 1996, Radio Netherlands: **Jackie Spears:**

Hamas says it will resume suicide bombings because of attacks launched against it by Israel and the Palestinian police.

In Belgrade, thousands demonstrated against the government of Slobodan Milosevic claiming he is responsible for the war in former Yugoslavia. The demonstration was organized by the two opposition parties and call for new parliamentary elections.

In western Algeria, a train was ambushed and many were killed.

Almost three months after the Dayton Peace Accords, cross ethnic conflicts are rare. Restoration of justice is necessary to re-integrate the country. Belgrade should be pressured to recognize Croatia, Bosnia, and Macedonia. The peace is shaky and the pace is slow.

Carl Bildt is the international mediator for EU's plan for (Bosnia's) reconstruction.

March 9, 1996, Die Deutsche Welle:

In Bosnia, NATO has sent in fire fighters to fight fires started by gangs of Serb arsonists. Two Serbs who refused to join the Serb exodus are reported missing.

March 11, 1996, Radio Netherlands: Dave Durham:

The U.S. says it will make available about $100 million to the Croat-Muslim army. Despite some NATO criticizing the move as leading to a possible widening of the war in Bosnia, the U.S. says that this will stabilize the region.

Croatia and Rump Yugoslavia have agreed to reopen railway and highway links with each other in normalizing relations.

March 11, 1996, Die Deutsche Welle:

According to television reports, Russian planes bombed the village of Barmut, cut-off since the end of February from outside contact. Some 200 Chechen rebels hold 80 Russians soldiers hostage and threaten to kill them unless the bombings stop.

Serb extremists and arsonists forced Serbs out and looted and set fire to the fourth suburb to be handed back to the Muslim-Croat Federation in an attempt to use the news media to show that Serbs are un-willing to live with Muslims.

Germany's Deutsche Bahn has worked out an agreement with Trans-Siberian Railways for joint cooperation in the future.

March 12, 1996, Radio Netherlands:

Bosnians celebrate the taking over the suburb of Ilydzic. Only one suburb remains to be reunified with Sarajevo.

Authorities in Serbia are willing to let War Crimes Tribunal talk to the two witnesses who were part of the massacres in Srebrenica. One of them was a soldier who gave evidence to French reporter of *Le Figaro*. John Shattuck of U.S. State Dept. met with Slobodan Milosevic and said he is sure Serbian authorities would hand the two over to the War Crimes Tribunal. At the time of their arrest it was suggested that the Serbian police wanted to get them before they could disclose information sensitive about Serbia.

March 12, 1996, Die Deutsche Welle:

The Muslim-Croat Federation has taken over the Serb suburb of Ilydzia. Serb gangs set fire to the suburb determined to leave nothing to the Muslim-Croat federation.

Fighter planes, land mines, and weapons ban on Serbia

is still in effect despite Russia's lifting of economic sanctions on Serbia.

March 13, 1996, Radio Netherlands:
   Bosnia has been declared eligible to join the World Bank and may draw up to $450 million over the next four years.
   According to Russian soldiers involved in the fighting in Chechnya last week, over 400 Russian soldiers and Chechen police siding with the Russians were killed. Russia reported only 70 killed.

March 13, 1996, Die Deutsche Welle:
   Germany's Foreign Minister said the Muslim/Croat Federation had too few police to do the work and 3,000 more were needed.
   Ilydiza was set on fire Saturday. Fire fighters were unable to enter the suburb to fight the fires. Bosnia is unable to use civilians serving with E.U. to collaborate or cooperate (with the Bosnian Government). The international police force is too few in number.

March 14, 1996, French TV:
   The anti-terrorism summit in Sharm Al Sheik between anti-Islamic nations led by the U.S. President Clinton and the Arab and Muslim nations agreed on peace but there was no convergence of thought on how to combat terrorism. Simon Peres and Yasser Arafat never met but went in different directions. French President Jacques Chirac offered economic help to Palestinians as a way to improve their economic situation. Food and medicines are in short supply.
   Meanwhile, President Clinton attended an Israeli security cabinet meeting in Jerusalem and rode on a Jerusalem bus.

(To show Israel was safe for tourists. He rode the bus a couple of blocks then got off).

Spy satellite photos of Palestinian terrorist training camps were given by the U.S. to Israel. (Didn't the U.S. Government previously say it does not have to share its intelligence with the United Nations?)

March 15, 1996, Radio Netherlands:

Israel has arrested over 1,000 suspected Hamas members. The UN Security Council lifted its embargo on small arms to the former Rump Yugoslavia but the ban sale of heavy weapons is still in effect.

Military aid to the Muslim/Croat Fed is under discussion in Ankara, Turkey. The European Union opposes the U.S. aid of $100 million for training the Muslim/Croat Army as ethnic feelings are still inflamed.

March 15, 1996, CNN:

Russian President Boris Yeltsin has come up with another plan to end the war with Chechnya. Unless he comes up with a plan to give Chechnya autonomy, the Chechens will not stop and the Chechens are fighting very well (Judy Woodruff in an interview with Allen Weinstein, Center for Democracy).

An American solider was shot in Tuzla when he stopped a suspicious acting man.

March 15, 1996, Radio Netherlands: **Carole Van den Ring**:

Iran's Cabinet Minister of Intelligence and Security Affairs, Ali Falayan, is being sought by a warrant from a high court in Germany for involvement in the assassination of three Kurdish exiles and their translator in a bombing of a cafe in Berlin.

At the International Conference on Rearmament of Bosnia in Ankara, Turkey, Turkey has offered $2 million and the U.S. $100 million but attending EU members opposed any re-armament of Bosnia without reciprocation. (This is not re-arming Bosnia as it never had enough arms and a count of weapons made on both sides revealed that Serbs hid 180 heavy weapons and tanks in one instance).

Ministers of the International Contact Group will meet in Moscow next week and minister from Croatia, Serbia, and Bosnia will be in attendance to give assurances they will abide by Dayton Accords.

A bus carrying immigrant foreign workers from Yemen over-turned in Saudi Arabia killing many.

Russia says it opposes Poland's membership in NATO.

March 15, 1996, Die Deutsche Welle:
The E.U. says it will not help build a Bosnian Army but will provide money for reconstruction.

A German soldier wounded near Sarajevo by a land mine became Germany's first casualty in Bosnia. He was evacuated to a German field army hospital.

Russia's Foreign Minister, Yevgeny Primakov, stated Russia's guarantee for Poland's security if it rejected NATO membership. Russia's plan to cut a highway across northeastern Poland has raised fears in Poland about Russia's intentions.

March 16, 1996, Radio Netherlands:
Yasir Arafat accused Iran of being behind the Hamas acts in Israel. (Ayatollah Khomeini invited Yasar Arafat to Iran and then kicked him out with Israel's Mossad coming back to Iran).

Russia says the International Contact Group convened by the U.S. in Geneva is not necessary and will not attend.

Boris Yeltsin says the Duma's annulling of the 1991 accords to dissolve the Soviet Union is unconstitutional.

March 16, 1996, Die Deutsche Welle:
Boris Yeltsin strongly condemned the Duma's annulling of the 1991 treaty disbanding the former Soviet Union.

A German High Court ordered the arrest of Ali Falayan who is said to have ordered the murder of 3 Kurdish dissidents and their translator in a bomb attack in Germany.

Der Spiegel says that two German ministers cannot agree on which is to pay for the 180 international police in Mostar and thus Germany is not living up to the Dayton Peace Accords.

March 17, Radio Netherlands: 2330 UTC (530 CST)
In Bosnia, IFOR troops freed residents trapped in a flaming apartment and arrested Serbs starting fires. 22 separate fires were started in the last Serb suburb to be turned over to the Bosnian Government and Serb fire fighters refused to fight the fires saying anyone left behind was a traitor. A Sarajevo fire fighter group that came to aid in putting out fires was subjected to a grenade attack.

March 17, 1996, Die Deutsche Welle:
Boutros Boutros Ghali will attend the fifty-second Human Rights Commission in Geneva. The 53 member states say the commission lacks money making it difficult to operate.

Germany is Iran's principal trading partner.

March 18, 1996, Radio Netherlands:
The Geneva convening of the International Contact Group is because of an increasing number of violations of the Dayton Peace Accords by the Serbs such as failure to

release all POW's and lack of cooperation with the Muslim/Croat Federation (this *lack of cooperation is unspecified* which is typical of the UN)

March 18, 1996, Die Deutsche Welle:

Balkan leaders have reaffirmed to adhere to the Dayton Peace Accords and release all POWs. Also discussed was a twelve-point plan to stabilize the shaky peace in Bosnia and the reunification of Mostar.

Hundreds of Iranians demonstrated in front of the German Embassy in Tehran over the arrest warrant issued by the German High Court for the Internal Security and Intelligence Minister Ali Falayan.

March 20, 1996, Radio Netherlands:

Russia will open a liaison office with NATO in Brussels although it remains opposed to NATO's expansion eastward.

The War Crimes Tribunal has opened a case of three Serb generals in Vukovar, Croatia, 261 patients were taken from a hospital and killed. This was the beginning of ethnic cleansing in the former Yugoslavia.

Vladomir Zhirinovsky wanted to go to the War Crimes Tribunal to defend the Serb generals accused of War Crimes but the Tribunal said Zhirinovsky's presence was not needed.

Thousands have fled western Chechnya under an onslaught of Russian troops. Shamasky has been under siege and 600 villagers were killed last week. The Chechen rebels sent a message to Boris Yeltsin accusing Russian soldiers of shooting innocent civilians.

The U.S. will deliver the $361 million in planes and missiles to Pakistan after blocking exports for three years over suspicion Pakistan was developing an atomic bomb.

March 19, 1996, Radio Netherlands:

Boris Yeltsin and Georgian President Schevardnadze are to meet over the continued instability in the southern Caucasus region of the former Soviet Union over Armenia with Azerbaijan and Abkazia with Georgia: and the fighting in Chechnya.

March 20, 1996, Radio Netherlands:

Russia opened a liaison office with NATO in Brussels although it remains opposed to NATO's expansion eastward.

The War Crimes Tribunal is investigating the atrocities in Vukovar, Croatia, where ethnic cleansing was started with the massacre of 261 Croatian men. Three Serb generals are accused.

Valdimir Zhirnovsky was refused a visa after the War Crimes Tribunal said that the presence of Russian parliamentarian was not needed to defend Serbs accused of war crimes in Croatia and Bosnia.

Thousands have fled western Chechnya under the onslaught of a heavy Russian Army attack. Shamasky was under siege for weeks and 600 villagers were killed last week. The Chechen rebels sent a message to Boris Yeltsin accusing Russian soldiers of killing unarmed civilians.

The U.S. finally agreed to the export of $361 million in missiles and planes Pakistan had purchased. The exports were blocked for three years because Pakistan was accused of developing an atomic bomb.

Three Bosnians (two Muslim and one Croat) have been arrested for War Crimes.

March 19, 1996, Die Deutsche Welle:

The Sarajevo suburb of Grabaviza is the last Serb Suburb to be re-united with Sarajevo. Only a few thousand

Serb residents remain in it.

Austria arrested two Bosnians for War Crimes against Bosnian Serbs.

March 19, 1996, National Public Radio (U.S.):

A Serb woman gave warning to IFOR troops about a booby trap set in an apartment next to hers. A bomb squad found a hand grenade was wired to go off when the door was pushed open.

March 20, 1996, Die Deutsche Welle:

U.S. Secretary of State, Warren Christopher, reassured NATO will expand eastward as planned despite Russia's opposition.

Barmut and Shamasky are under heavy attack by Russian troops, which are being reinforced.

The Bosnian capital is now reunified and de-militarized according to the Dayton Peace Accords with the pull back of the Muslim/Croat Federation troops.

Amnesty International has asked President Jacques Chirac to issue a condemnation of China's abuses of human rights.

German magazine, *Das Bild,* says Iran funds Hamas fighters with $30 million a year. President Rafsanjani met with Hamas in Kerman.

March 21, 1996, CNN:

U.S. Ambassador to UN Madeleine Albright's car was stoned in Vukovar which is scheduled to go back to Croatia under the Dayton Peace Accords. Vukovar was the scene of the first atrocities of the war. Serbs are not allowing the War Crimes Tribunal access to Vukovar.

March 20, 1996, Radio Netherlands:

Yeltsin met with NATO's Secretary General Solano over Moscow's alarm and resistance to NATO's eastward expansion.

Angry Serbs in Vukovar stoned Madeleine Albright's motorcade in Vukovar. Serb police did nothing to protect her motorcade as Serbs shouted anti-Croat slogans.

The honorary ambassador of Sri Lanka has been held after a sale of babies from Sri Lankan women who were raped and held captive until the babies are born. The babies are sold for $250,000 each.

The Dutch ambassador to France delivered a note of protest over French criticism of the Netherlands open drug laws.

March 21, 1996, Die Deutsche Welle:

Bulgaria has requested to see how Germany can modernize its financial sector. President Roman Herzog offered German support to Bulgaria and other eastern nations if any decide to join NATO.

Turkey has said it will give more rights to Kurds and lift its ban on Kurdish language.

Madeleine Albright appealed to the War Crimes Tribunal to hunt down all war criminals.

March 22, 1996, ABC-TV:

UN Ambassador Madeleine Albright toured the site of last year's massacres near Srebrenica. Drazen Ardemovic described the massacres and the farm is identified with the machines used to cover the bodies.

Admiral Leighton Smith says NATO is keeping the sites of the massacres under observation.

March 22, 1996, Radio Netherlands.

For the first time, three Muslims and Bosnia Croat were

indicted by the War Crimes Tribunal in The Hague.

UN reporter Elizabeth Wren says 3,000 Muslim men were killed and the number could be much higher.

Turkey says it will deal more humanely with its Kurdish minority.

March 22, 1996, CNN:

An American soldier was killed in a vehicle accident on the bridge crossing the Sava River.

(U.S.'s) UN Ambassador Madeleine Albright presented aerial photos of mass graves in Bosnia. She said, "Scores of people must have known of these atrocities."

Eleven mass gravesites are under investigation in the five former Serb suburbs of Sarajevo turned over the Bosnia govt. Four of the mass graves are in Gerbaviza.

Christian Cartier of the War Crimes Tribunal spoke of a camp run by Bosnia and the indictments of 3 Muslims and one Bosnian Croat for War Crimes.

March 23, 1996, Die Deutsche Welle:

Germany has issued a warrant for the arrest of Abdullah Ursalan, leader of the banned PKK Kurdish communists who is in Syria.

Hamburg inspectors found detonators and explosives in a shipment destined for Iran. The detonators were labeled "irrigation regulators".

The Bosnian Government set 109 Serb POWs free but still holds dozens near Tuzla. Serbs have not set any of their POWs free.

Mar 24, 1996, Radio Netherlands:

Former Minister of Agriculture, Buzamil Buluyev, is sentenced to death in Azerbaijan for plotting a coup against the government.

General Tiomir Blasnic, commander of the Bosnian Croat Army when 1,000 Muslims were slain in a village, is indicted by the War Crimes Tribunal. Blasnic says he did no wrong.

March 24, 1996, Die Deutsche Welle:
Russia Army is shelling and bombing western Chechen villages while Russians in Grozny are bracing for an attack by Chechen rebels. The Russian Army delivered an ultimatum to 500 rebels in western Chechnya to surrender.

March 24, 1996, CNN:
200 POWs remain in detention camps despite assurances to release all. Bosnia has fulfilled some of its assurances but the Serbs have not.

March 25, 1996, Radio Netherlands: **Jackie Spears**:
The E.U. has extended trade relations to Belorussia.
Bosnian Croat General Tiomir Blasnic is refusing to surrender to the International War Crimes Tribunal.
Bosnian Serb General George Jujujic complains about conditions of his arrest especially his handcuffing from prison to the court in The Hague. (He died in Sarajevo, May 19, 1996 from cancer).
Indian troops are massing around a Muslim shrine in Srinajir where some 20 Kashmiri separatists have taken refuge.

March 25, 1996, Die Deutsche Welle:
The Czech Republic, Hungary is the 2nd country to accede to the European Commission.
Greece wants to take Turkey to the International Court over a dispute of a deserted island in the Aegean Sea.
The European Court of Human Rights has ordered

Turkey to pay indemnification of $8,000 each to two men held too long before charges were carried into court.

March 25, 1996, CNN:
First Lady Hilary Clinton visited U.S. troops in Bosnia.

March 26, 1996, Radio Netherlands:
(Russian Defense Minister) Pavel Grachev says the attacks on Chechen rebels will stop when President Boris Yeltsin comes up with a peace plan.

200 bomb attacks in Bahrain this past year are the result of the arrest of a Shia clergyman.

Sudan accused Ethiopia of aiding Sudanese rebels in southern Sudan. Ethiopia denies the charges.

March 26, 1996, CNN:
For months, NATO has been accused of going slow because it fears "mission creep" (slow changes not in the original Dayton Accords). There has been a recent change as the military has started improving roads, clearing land mines, and improving hospital are as civilians in charge of these operations have failed to do anything.

March 25, 1996, Die Deutsche Welle:
The customs union between Turkey and the E.U. in January is being attacked by Greece.

Speaking before the Polish parliament, Queen Elizabeth called upon the eastern bloc nations to join NATO.

March 27, 1996, Radio Netherlands:
German Foreign Minister, Klaus Kinkel, called off a meeting with the Muslim/Croat Federation because there is not enough good-will in the federation to permit cooperation.

UN monitoring of Iraqi build-up of chemical weapons and weapons of mass destruction is through sanctions on Iraq which will continue.

March 27, 1996, Die Deutsche Welle:
Surviving Croat witnesses from Vukovar told of brutal treatment at the hands of Serbs. Most captives were murdered. 261 Croats were killed and three Serbs are being sought.
Muslim/Croat Federation police in Sarajevo are failing to cooperate with the International police. They are holding a UN translator who was attempting to negotiate between them and the UN

March 28, 1996, CNN:
The Muslim/Croat Federation is in danger of collapse from internal differences.

March 30, 1996, (Sat) Radio Netherlands: Carole Van den Ring:
Croat General Tiomir Blasnic will turn himself over to the War Crimes Tribunal in The Hague on Monday to face charges of massacring 1,000 Bosnian Muslims. He and six other Croats will be the first Croats tried.
Belgrade handed over two Serb officers who will testify to the guilt of Radovan Karadzic and General Ratko Mladic in massacres.
Defense Secretary, William Perry, says IFOR will crack down on illegal checkpoints using force if necessary to remove these roadblocks.
1,000 Albanians of Kosovo demonstrated in Bern, Switzerland for an independent Kosovo, which is under Serbian control.
Hamas has said it will avenge the deaths of two

Lebanese civilians killed in a shelling by Israeli artillery. Prime Minister Simon Peres said the shelling was a mistake. Mr. Peres will travel to Qatar and visit neighboring Oman Tuesday.

Human Rights are unknown in Iran according to UN Human Rights Commissioner Maurice Capricorn.

The Bangladesh parliament is dissolved after the resignation of Prime Minister, Zia Khalida. It is not clear is she will have a post in the new government.

Tamil Tigers launched an attack on Sri Lankan naval forces.

Hezbollah fired two rockets into northern Israel to avenge the deaths of two Lebanese.

March 30, 1996, Die Deutsche Welle:

Russian President, Boris Yeltsin, is to present his peace plan on Chechnya on TV Monday. The plan has been kept under wraps for two weeks while Russian forces shelled and bombed Chechen villages.

Kurdish PKK leader, Abdullah Ursulan, living in Syria threatens to create terrorism all over Germany and Turkey.

Croat fascists control the media in Mostar and so the media has become fascist. The goodwill of the international officials in Mostar comes up against the reality of deep wounds.

Hungary was the main crossroads for smuggling into Serbia when it was under UN sanctions. Now the sanctions are lifted against Serbia, smuggling turned into a black market business with sales and services going unreported

March 31, 1996, Radio Netherlands;

Despite Boris Yeltsin's order to stop military action (in Chechnya), shelling continues as Russian General Genadi Cherchenov says it is impossible to stop all at once. Yeltsin has ruled out independence but will discuss with Chechen leader Djokar Dudayev what type of autonomy Chechnya will have.

Fifty (Serb) checkpoints have been removed by IFOR and vigorous action will be taken against other illegal checkpoints, says (U.S. Secretary of Defense) William Perry. He says the military aspects are working well in Bosnia but the political aspects are not. All NATO will leave after one year and no extension will be given.

Admiral Leighton Smith, head of NATO in Bosnia says NATO will not hunt down war criminals, as it doesn't have that mandate.

March 31, 1996, Die Deutsche Welle:
According to Russian news agencies, the ceasefire is in effect but artillery can still be heard. Russian General Cherchenov, says it's impossible to stop all the firing at once.

Muslim and Croat politicians have agreed to strengthen the federation. The Croats pledge to pay taxes into a common treasury.

EU administrator for Mostar, Hans Koschnick, finished his assignment in Mostar. He said the IFOR mandate could be extended two years.

April 1, 1996, Radio Netherlands:
Croatian General Tiomir Blasnic charged with massacring hundreds of Muslims in December 1993 surrendered to The Hague.

Bosnia/Herzegovina has officially joined the World Bank and received a $270 million loan to rejuvenate agriculture, sanitation and water, and the infrastructure of Bosnia.

President Clinton asks the Chechen rebels to accept

Boris Yeltsin's offer of a peace. Yeltsin says full independence was out but autonomy is to be worked out.

Eastern Europe is experiencing a period of great economic growth according to the European Bank for Reconstruction and Development.

Chechen rebels claim the Russian military is stepping up military operations in Chechnya.

April 1, 1996, Die Deutsche Welle:

German Agricultural Minister, Joachim Burkhardt, said an aide to Djokar Dudayev reported the Russians are still attacking with air and artillery despite Boris Yeltsin's ceasefire.

Croatian General Tiomir Blasnic flew to The Hague and was taken into custody by the War Crimes Tribunal.

Guaranteed loans to Bosnia by the World Bank for DM 110 million were given and Bosnia will seek US$1.8 billion of the promised five billion by the U.S.

April 2, 1996, Die Deutsche Welle:

EU diplomats have arrived in Tehran to get a stronger statement from Iran condemning international terrorism. Germany has already said it will not break diplomatically with Iran.

Dudayev said he will meet with Russian leaders for peace talks after all Russian troops have left Chechnya.

PKK leader Abdullah Ursulan made death threats against Chancellor Helmut Kohl and Foreign Minister, Klaus Kinkel. He said he will send suicide bombers to Germany causing officials to beef up German security.

Bosnia's humanitarian award was given to German Chancellor Helmut Kohl for recognition of Germany's acceptance of 400,000 Bosnian refugees. Posthumous awards were also given to the three American diplomats killed in 1995.

April 2, 1996, Radio Netherlands:
Two War Crimes Tribunal investigators are in Srebrenica to ascertain which mass graves will be investigated first. Actual digging is expected to start mid-April.

Croats released 15 Serb POWs and Serbs freed 7 Croat POWs. The warring parties still hold several dozen POWs despite the deadline for release of all POWs.

Djokar Dudayev has responded cautiously to Moscow's peace plan but says he believes the Russians want complete capitulation and are not sincere about working for peace. He mentioned Mikhail Gorbachev as a possible negotiator.

Russian and Belarus have joined in a common defense, monetary, and diplomatic union.

April 3, 1996, ABC-TV:
UN War Crime Tribunal has begun taping around the scenes of mass graves in Bosnian Serb territory. Already it appears the graves have been disturbed in attempts to hide the enormity of the massacres.

April 3, 1996, Radio Netherlands:
If Belgrade does not turn over three Serb officers charged with massacres to the War Crimes Tribunal, the UN Sanctions against Belgrade can be re-imposed.

Colonel Alexei Kramanovic was flown to Sarajevo from The Hague after being released by the War Crimes Tribunal for lack of evidence.

Russia is keeping its export of arms secret because this brings in hard currency and Russia doesn't want international controls to be imposed, which may limit this source of money.

April 3, 1996, The Internet. The Air Force plane carrying Secretary of Commerce Ron Brown crashed on approaching the airport at Dubrovnik, Croatia. First reports said there was an explosion like a missile had hit the plane.and parts of the plane were strewn across sven miles before crashed. The official American Clinton White said the area was hit by the worst storm in a decade. But the weather report at Dubrovnik International Airport stated that visibility was more than five miles and Brown's plane crashed just two miles from the /airport.

The only survivor was an Air Force flight attendant, Sgt. Shelley Kelly, who was walking among the wreckage when rescuers came. She was put on a medical helicopter but dead on arrived at the hospital of a broken neck. The next day, the air controller at Dubrovnik Airport was said to have *committed suicide.*

An observer at the scene of the crash said there appeared to be a bullet hole in the top of Commerce Secretary Ron Brown's head. **No autopsy was allowed.** Some have suggested a thermite bomb was placed on the aircraft and it exploded on approach to the airport or it was hit by a Serb missile as it passed over Serb artillery on its approach which would account for parts of the plane scattered for seven miles on its approach to the airport).

April 3, 1996, Die Deutsche Welle:
Rescue troops have found some bodies of the 35 people on board the plane carrying Secretary of Commerce Ron Brown. There were reports of hostile activity in the area before the crash.

The War Crimes Tribunal accused Rump Yugoslavia of non-cooperation and of sheltering war criminals. The Tribunal will petition the UN to re-impose sanctions against

Rump Yugoslavia.

The EU Commission visiting Iran was unable to get neither a condemnation of Hamas nor a promise to stop supporting terrorists.

The president of Tartarstan, Shah Imjef, says he is willing to negotiate a peace between Chechnya and Russia.

April 22, PBS-TV: McNeil-Lehrer Report:

The Clinton administration is said to be seeking a policy of not making things better but keeping them from getting worse. This administration is (said to be) extremely supportive of Israel.

April 22, 1996, Radio Netherlands: Carole Van den Ring:

Defense lawyers for Bosnian Serb General George Juijujic say they won't accept a medical release from the International War Crimes Tribunal but demand a trial to clear the general's name. The general is suffering from fatal cancer of the pancreas and is being allowed to return home to die among family.

About 50,000 people, mostly refugees, are in Shalee, Chechnya, surround by Russian troops who will not let food or water in. The village is expecting an immediate attack by the Russian Army.

April 22, 1996, Die Deutsche Welle:

EU membership or aid to Rump Yugoslavia (Serbia and Montenegro) depends upon that nation's adherence to Human Rights.

The first contingent of 85 German police to monitor the police force of Bosnia has arrived in Zagreb.

April 24, 1996, Radio Netherlands: Carole Van den Ring:

Russian aircraft killed Chechen rebel leader, Djokar

Dudayev with a bomb that homed in on his satellite telephone. (When he had his mobile phone repaired, the Russians had a homing device installed in his telephone which they used to locate him and blow him up when he used the phone). The new leader, Zelin Khan Adenbayev, says Dudayev's death will be avenged.

Charges of shelling Sarajevo are accusations against General George Juijujic by the War Crimes Tribunal. The general was granted a provisional release and is not expected to live much longer (fatally infected with cancer).

Former Prime Minister (Turkey) Tansu Ciller is being attacked by Israel for her nationalization of a private business. This is putting the new coalition government of Turkey under danger of collapse (this news was on the 6:30 pm broadcast but omitted in the 7:30 broadcast. Why Israel should object to nationalization is unclear).

General Franklin Von Kappen says the UN is investigating the bombing of a refugee camp in Lebanon by Israel. Von Kappen visited the camp and found the scene "troublesome". He said it was one of the worst sights he had ever seen.

April 25, 1996, Public Broadcast Service:
General George Julwan says the initial stages of the peace accords have produced more refugees than fewer with the exodus of Serbs from Sarajevo's suburbs. The greatest war criminals, Radovan Karadzic and General Ratko Mladic are still free.

The War Crimes Tribunal is starting investigation of war crimes. Everyone believes War Criminals must be prosecuted before the healing process can begin.

. Over 250,000 Bosnian men died in this war and there is no help for the widows or orphans.

David Rohde (of Christian Science Monitor) said the

photos he had taken of piles of clothing at the scene of the Srebrenica massacres show large numbers of bodies are missing from the mass graves. Apparently Serbs have cleaned up the mass grave sites as the heavy cloud cover could have kept NATO surveillance planes from observing this cleaning up. General Mladic was seen at three of the execution sites.

April 25, 1996, Radio Netherlands:
Serbia and Bosnian Serbs are hindering the War Crimes Tribunal investigation. Antonio Kazizi says the Serbs are not cooperating and say the Tribunal is a "paper tiger". If there is no improvement, he wants all aid suspended to these countries.

General Jiujujic has arrived in Sarajevo (he dies 24 days later).

Bosnian Serb authorities are preventing Muslim refugees from returning to their homes in Bosnian Serb territory. The Serb line is becoming solidified, as the Freedom of Movement guaranteed under the Dayton Peace Accords is not being supported by IFOR.

Yeltsin signed an agreement with China for greater cooperation. Russia and China seek to offset what they say is Western domination of the world after the collapse of the Soviet Union. Russia supports China's Tibet and Xinjiang policy and China supports Russia's Chechen policy

India's VJP party has adapted a platform supporting India's creation of an atomic bomb.

Zelin Khan Adenbayev, the new Chechen rebel leader, says the death of Djokar Dudayev will be avenged.

April 25, 1996, Die Deutsche Welle:
The refusal by Serb authorities to allow Muslims and Croats to return to their former homes is creating a strain on

the peace in Bosnia.

A Bosnian-Croat police force is to be set up before September.

Bosnian Croat General Tiomir Blasnic was turned down on his request for release, as the charges against him by the War Crimes Tribunal are too severe.

April 26, 1996, Radio Netherlands:

A Russian passenger train was derailed by an explosion ten miles east of Grozny killing a number of people. The exact number of dead is not known. The Chechen rebels say they will avenge the death of Djokar Dudayev.

April 28, 1996, Radio Netherlands:

The Black Sea Conference between Greece and Turkey met in Bucharest, Romania, to discuss their differences over islands in the Aegean Sea. Another meeting is scheduled for Berlin in January.

Indian elections have claimed the lives of sixteen people. 12 were killed in a bomb explosion NE of New Delhi. Six hundred million people are registered to vote in India.

April 28, 1996, BBC:

Bosnian Serb authorities continue to block repatriation of Bosnian Muslims in Bosnian Serb territory while IFOR says its first mission is to preserve peace in Bosnia. The Serbs feel that large numbers of Muslims would decrease their claim to territory under their control.

In Chechnya, seven Russian soldiers were killed in Grozny while 120 rebels captured a police station in Argun. Djokar Dudayev's widow, a Russian, wants safe passage to Moscow to meet with Yeltsin hoping to avoid more bloodshed. She says that after the period of mourning is over, the separatists will mount many more attacks.

April 29, 1996, Radio Netherlands: (Spanish language)

Dutch Foreign Minister Hans Von Mirlo, met with leaders of Bosnia and Croatia. He said the country lacks internal communications that would permit elections by the time of the September deadline for free elections in Bosnia.

Near Lahore in Pakistan, 30 people were killed when an explosion ripped a bus apart. The number of dead may rise.

April 29, 1996, Radio Netherlands: (Dave Durham);

200 Serb civilians attacked a bus carrying Muslim families who were returning to their villages now under Serb control to visit family graves. The bus was escorted by French tanks which were then used to turn the bus around and head back to Bosnia.

Mr. Van Mirlo said scheduled elections in Bosnia should be held even though it may be impossible for everyone to return to their home city to vote.

The Israeli incursion into south Lebanon resulted in one billion dollars in damages and 160 Lebanese citizens killed.

The Bosnian government wants the International Court of Justice in The Hague to condemn Serbian leaders of being directly and indirectly involved in the genocide in Bosnia because **Bosnian Serb officers were on the payroll of Belgrade**. Bosnia is asking for indemnification from Serbia. (The Court of Justice denied Bosnia's claims).

Chances of Russia bringing peace to Chechnya or resolving the conflict before elections in June are considered nil.

A Yugoslav journalist from Banja Luka in 1991-92 said her reports of Serb meetings at which Serbs were exhorted to violence against Muslims were suppressed at that time by the news media.

Carl Bildt backs a centralized TV station in Bosnia, which is opposed by Mark Thompson who says this will attract journalists from the old established news media outlets and will be a disaster.

April 29, 1996, Die Deutsche Welle:
U.S. Secretary of Defense William Perry has refused to rule out the use of force to take out a suspected chemical weapons factory in Libya.

April 30, 1996, Radio Netherlands:
In response to the Muslims killed yesterday when attempting to visit family graves in Serb occupied Bosnia. EU Administrator Carl Bildt called for the three groups in Bosnia to meet in Sarajevo and sign an agreement reiterating the freedom of movement, part of the Dayton Peace Accords.

Hamas attacked the pro-Israel South Lebanon Army. ***102 people were killed last week when Israel shelled a refugee camp.***

May 1, 1996, Radio Netherlands:
Dutch Foreign Minister Van Mirlo said pressure should be put on Milosevic to remove Serb leaders Karadzic and Mladic who are still holding power and thus not subject to NATO capture.

The Dayton Peace Accords states all refugees must return to their hometowns to register for up-coming elections. Serbia released five Muslims who fled into Montenegro and Serbia last summer after General Mladic and the Bosnian Serb army rolled over the UN Safe Havens. Sarajevo will release 6 of 11 Serbs held on suspicion of War Crimes and Pale will release 2 Muslims.

At the International Conference on Controlling Land Mines, Pakistan raised objections to the clause on export and imports of mines.

In the UNCTAD Conference in South Africa, the world's 30 poorest countries want their foreign indebtedness canceled as this indebtedness absorbs most of their exports now.

May 1, 1996, Die Deutsche Welle:
The Russian Communist candidate for president, Gennady Zhuganov, says he will win the Russian elections in June.

German parliamentarian, Borschlager, says Germany will go ahead with the repatriation of 320,000 Bosnian refugees starting in July even if it has to be done by force.

Albania wants IFOR forces in Albania.

May 3, 1996, Die Deutsche Welle:
Federal and State authorities have agreed on July for the repatriation of Bosnian refugees but not on the date.

May 4, 1996, Radio Netherlands:
Fighting in Chechnya continues with the arrest of the leader of the Russian supported Chechen government, weakening that group more.

Israel insists Jerusalem will remain its undivided capital.

Mohammed Adid was shot by 3 men outside the capital Algiers.

On Tuesday, Dusan Tadic will be the first accused War Criminal to be tried. Tadic is accused of murder and rape. Rape formed a part of the ethnic cleansing in Bosnia and ii will be a new stance for international law as an issue of war crimes.

May 4, 1996, Die Deutsche Welle:
The three Baltic States met on the Swedish island of Gottland to agree on ways to cooperate in fighting the

Russian Mafia and work together to join the EU.

Chechen rebels attacked Russian headquarters in Grozny killing one of the defenders.

Kurdish PKK leader Ursalan said he never threatened violence against Germany. (He denied that the PKK planned to assassinate German Chancellor, Helmut Kohl, and to start a wave of terrorism in Germany).

HIV infections in Germany are declining. But HIV infection among women doubling with 4,000 cases reported.

NATO forces in Bosnia have faced one of the worst days Monday when one Muslim was shot, one blown up by a land mine, and one was stoned to death as he visited a family grave site in Serb territory.

Rumors of Chechen sabotage abound in Russia as the new Chechen leader, Azebanyev, vows to continue the fight.

Privatization and the expanding markets of Eastern Europe threaten Germany's labor force which is the most efficient and the most expensive in the world (with all of its benefits).

The Islamic Party of Turkey charge of corruption against former Prime Minister Tansu Ciller has almost split the new coalition government of the **Motherland** and **True Path Parties**. Prime Minister Yilmas is able to rule only with the support of the DSB.

May 6, 1996, PBS-McNeil Lehrer Report:
People in Belgrade laugh at the subject of war crimes. Belgrade does not recognize the War Crimes Tribunal and gives sanctuary to Serbs charged with War Crimes. As witnesses prepare documentation they must hide for fear of their lives from those whom they accuse.

Judge (American) Gabrielle Kirk McDonald of the War Crimes Tribunal says it takes only one case to make a precedent.

May 6, 1996, Radio Netherlands:

Israeli Brigadier General Goma Harrow said the Israeli bombardment of a UN camp and a refugee camp was due to out-dated maps. Dutch General Von Kappen says Israel did it deliberately.

Bosnian Serb Dusan Tadic, awaiting trial for War Crimes says he will go on a hunger strike if witnesses in Bosnia who can prove his innocence are not allowed to testify by satellite communications.

U.S. Ambassador to Bosnia, John Kornblum, says Serbia and Bosnian Serbs should have their funds restricted for not cooperating with the free passage guarantees of the Dayton Peace Accords.

May 6, 1996, Houston, Texas Channel 51:

Chechen separatists shot down a Russian plane and are attacking (the Russian military) in several areas.

May 6, 1996, Die Deutsche Welle:

Gennady Zhuganov criticized Western nations for favoring only one Russian candidate, Boris Yeltsin.

Germany plans to be the foremost nation in DNA studies by the end of this century.

May 7, 1996, Radio Netherlands:

The UN report on the Israeli shelling of a refugee camp in southern Lebanon was said to be deliberate. Major General Van Kappen and (UN) Secretary General Boutros Boutros Ghali support the report. The U.S. government and Israel are raising objections.

Defense lawyers for accused Serb war criminal, Dusan Tadic, say they do not refute the accounts of horrible crimes committed in Serb detention camps against Muslims but say

Tadic is innocent and the witnesses are mistaken.

A road from Zagreb through eastern Slovenia to Belgrade has been re-opened. This is a step toward normalizing relations between Croatia and Serbia.

May 8, 1996, Radio Netherlands:

Musa Maril Asook, a suspected Hamas member, was extradited from the U.S. to Israel.

There are over 5,000 cases of fraud with 1.4 billion dollars involved in Europe, mostly out of Rotterdam.

A Bosnian Muslim, Gennady Veradic, has been handed over to the International War Crimes Tribunal in The Hague.

Bosnian officials say that without Iranian weapons and supplies, it would not have survived the war. The U.S. knew about the supply line but was not involved.

May 10, 1996, Radio Netherlands:

The U.S. has decided not to impose sanctions on China for selling atomic weapons grade material to Pakistan.

May 12, 1996, Radio Netherlands:

The Israeli military has launched air raids against Hezbollah in south Lebanon in violation of the truce signed by Hezbollah and Israel to stop all attacks on civilians.

Egypt, the PLO, and Jordan have signed an agreement to work against Hamas.

May 12, 1996, Die Deutsche Welle:

Tadzhik rebels have killed some Russian soldiers near Dushanbe.

The capital of Grozny and villages around the city are under attack by Chechen rebels opposed to the pro-Russian Chechen govt.

The 16-day attack by Israel on south Lebanon has resulted in the destruction of 400 million in materials (damage to buildings, highways etc.) and unknown losses to the economy in lost wages, tourism, etc.

May 13, 1996, Radio Netherlands:
Israeli helicopter gunships fired on suspected Hezbollah targets in south Lebanon.
EU vows to push ahead with May 31 elections in Mostar. The Muslim Party in Mostar says election rules discriminate against non-Croats.

May 13, 1996, Die Deutsche Welle:
German Defense Minister, Volker Ruhe, says Poland will be the first East European nation to enter NATO and NATO will continue to expand eastward.
Four German engineers have gone on trial for their part in aiding Iraq make mustard gas.
A group of EU ministers have met to underpin support for Boris Yeltsin in next month's Russian elections.

May 14, 1996, Radio Netherlands:
The Bosnian and Croat leadership in Bosnia have agreed to merge their armies as well as unify their monetary and taxation within three years as required by the Dayton Peace Accords (in order to receive) for financial assistance.
The EU is concerned about Croatia's application for membership with its lack of democratic reforms, its return refugee policy, lack of Human Rights, and its non-cooperation with the War Crimes Tribunal.
Russian Interfax news agency said Chechen rebels released 32 Russian construction workers while Russians killed 50 Chechen rebels in an attack on Widomer.
The Turkish Army killed 35 Kurds after entering Turkey

from Iraq.

May 14, 1996, Die Deutsche Welle:
Even though EU has said Croatia's membership is necessary, the Council of Europe suspended Croatia's application for an indefinite period. Croatia's lack of democratic reforms and non-cooperation with the War Crimes Tribunal was given as the reason.

NATO will admit eastern European nations before NATO's 50th anniversary, May 15, 1999. German Defense Minister, Volker Ruhe, says that Poland is expected to be the first.

May 15, 1996, Radio Netherlands: **Jackie Carver** reporting:
NATO has agreed to a restructuring of its command by creating a combined field force: with one force created to be ready at a moment's notice. This plan is to be ratified this June at a meeting of all NATO ministers.

Israel has completely sealed its borders with autonomous Palestinian territories and Gaza Strip. The move is to forestall terrorists' attacks.

Serb leader Radovan Karadzic dismissed co-prime minister Kasajic as damaging the Serpskaya Republic (Bosnian Serb) after Karadzic said Bosnian Serbs should comply with Dayton Peace Accords.

Tansu Ciller, of the True Path Party, believes a new vote of confidence should be held on Prime Minister Yilmas' government. Speaker of the Turkish parliament, Kalimay, says no need for elections.

May 15, 1996, Die Deutsche Welle:
The UN High Commission for Refugees has called upon Europe to formulate a common policy for political asylum seekers.

Self-appointed President Karadzic's move to sack his Prime Minister Kasajic was criticized by European leaders. Mr. Kasajic's moderate approach angered Serb hard-liners.

May 16, 1996, Die Deutsche Welle:
German Foreign Minister, Klaus Kinkel, revived talks with Belgrade and offered Rump Yugoslavia help in getting international recognition if it would stop sheltering war criminals and comply with the Dayton Peace Accords.

May 17, 1996, Die Deutsche Welle:
The Bosnian Government has given its permission to the extradition of two Muslims accused of War Crime. No date has been set on turning over of the men to the Tribunal in The Hague.
On Friday, Goran Lacic pleaded not guilty at the tribunal saying his was a case of mistaken identity.

May 17, 1996, Die Deutsche Welle:
Chancellor Helmut Kohl promised Turkey's Prime Minister Yilmas to help Turkey get into the European customs union. Greece is still opposing Turkey with its veto.
German Foreign Minister Klaus Kinkel said Belgrade has agreed to the return of 120 Serb asylum seekers.
Chechen rebel leader, Zelimkhan Yandarbiyev, says Chechens are continuing to resist Russian attacks. Chechen rebels dug in at the former Barmut military base are resisting an all-out offensive by the Russian military.

May 18, 1996, Radio Netherlands:
Tanjug news agency of Yugoslavia reports that Radovan Karadzic has handed over the power to Berliano Plasic. The Bosnian Serb parliament confirmed the dismissal of Prime

Minister Kasajic has accepted his sacking.

Boris Klicovic is the new Bosnian Serb foreign minister and says he will take a harder line than his predecessor.

Prime Minister Suleiman Demirel of Turkey was the target of an assassin over the new Israel-Turkey military cooperation.

May 18, 1996, Die Deutsche Welle:

Turkey's Prime Minister Demirel survived an assassination attempt in Ismet, Turkey, but several others were wounded.

Russia has offered Ukraine $450 million for the demolition of its atomic warheads.

The new Bosnian Serb Prime Minister Klicovic, who replaced (Bosnian Serb) Prime Minster Kasajic dismissed by Karadzic, said there is no need to extradite Radovan Karadzic or General Ratko Mladic to the War Crimes Tribunal in The Hague.

May 19, 1996, Radio Netherlands: **Carole Van den Ring**:

The Bosnian Serb parliament decided to hold a referendum on Serb leader Radovan Karadzic and end rumor's of his resignation. Even if Karadzic resigned, he would remain a political force. Mr. Karadzic is accused War Criminal and subject to arrest if he ever travels outside Bosnian Serb territory.

Bosnian Serb General Djorje Jiujujic has died. He was in charge of Bosnian Serb army logistics and accused of shelling Sarajevo.

The Palestinian police have been accused of corruption and arbitrary arrest and of raising psychological fears among Palestinians.

May 19, 1996, Die Deutsche Welle:

In Pale, the new Bosnian Serb prime minister told EU's Carl Bildt that Radovan Karadzic has not resigned.

May 22, 1996, Radio Netherlands:
The U.S. warned (Serbian) Prime Minister, Slobodan Milosevic, that if Radovan Karadzic and General Ratka Mladic were not removed from their positions of power, the U.S. would see that sanctions against Serbia were re-imposed.
40 Russian soldiers were killed outside the village of Barmut in hand to hand combat when Chechen rebels left the village to attack the Russian lines. No mention of how many casualties among the (Chechen) separatists.

May 22, 1996, Die Deutsche Welle:
Chancellor Helmut Kohl will meet in Washington to discuss Bosnia with President Clinton and Republican Presidential candidate Bob Dole.
NATO Secretary General Javier Solano said that IFOR troops have finished with the first part of their mandate and will concentrate on the capture of War Crimes Criminals at checkpoints, especially Radovan Karadzic and Ratko Mladic. Solano is in Turkey for talks with President Demirel on differences between Turkey and Greece.

May 22, 1996, *Houston Chronicle:*
Bosnian Vice President, Ejup Ganic, warned that Bosnian Muslims will boycott the September elections because the Serbs are not honoring the Dayton Peace Accords and. are keeping out the returning Bosnian refugees from returning to their former home villages.

May 23, 1996, Die Deutsche Welle; Cameron Morel reporting:

Chancellor Helmut Kohl and (American) President Bill Clinton met in Milwaukee today and agreed that the IFOR peace force will be withdrawn as planned at the end of the year.

A Russian military officer says they captured Barmut, the former Soviet missile base and stronghold of the Chechen rebels. The Russians say they lost 21 soldiers and killed 120 rebels. Barmut was under heavy Russian aerial and artillery bombardment for days. Boris Yeltsin will meet with Chechen rebel leader, Zelimkhan Yanderbiyiev, in Moscow. Resolving the Chechen dispute is the main problem.

May 24, 1996, Radio Netherlands:
Russian troops have captured the last Chechen stronghold, Barmut, and the Chechen supply corridor from Ingushtia. Moscow says Chechen independence will not be on the conference table in Moscow.

A crisis in the Turkish coalition government as Prime Minister Yilmas and Tansu Ciller charge each other with corruption.

In Albania, a high court has sentenced to death three officials of the former communist regime.

May 25, 1996, Radio Netherlands:
Boris Yeltsin confirmed he will meet with Chechen rebel leader Zelimkhan Yanderbiyev on Monday. The Russian Army is keeping up its attacks on the rebels.

5,000 demonstrate in Tehran for stricter adherence to Islam.

The exiled king of Bulgaria returned to Bulgaria for the first time in 50 years after he was banished by the communists in 1946.

May 25, 1996, Die Deutsche Welle:

French President, Jacques Chirac, has ordered the arrest of Radovan Karadzic. No mention of what measures would be taken. As for the withdrawal of IFOR troops in December, there are no plans on how the peace will be kept.

May 27, 1996, Radio Netherlands:
The Russian Government and Chechen separatists have reached a truce/ceasefire. On Thursday, there will be discussions on the form of government for Chechnya.
President Kuchma of Ukraine dismissed Prime Minister Marchuk who will be deputy minister.
The True Path (Tansu Ciller) and Islamist Welfare Party are to vote for a no-confidence in Prime Minister Yilmas' coalition government.
Opposition parties in Albania claim fraud in the last election and are to demonstrate Thursday against Bereshna's election.

May 27, 1996, Die Deutsche Welle:
The Welfare Party is expected to support the True Path Party for a new coalition government.

May 29, 1996, Radio Netherlands:
UNHCR reports the Bosnian Serbs are in defiance of the Dayton Peace Accords and are continuing their ethnic cleansing by expelling minorities (Muslims and Croats)..
French General Bernard Hensfort (sp?) refused to call for a NATO air strike to support Dutch troops in Srebrenica last summer in return for some UN troops kidnapped by the Serbs.

May 29, 1996, Die Deutsche Welle:
Boris Yeltsin gave out a draft of the proposed peace settlement giving Chechnya control over its resources and limited autonomy.

Albanian leader Bereshna received 95% control over Albania's parliament. Outsiders and opposition leaders say election was rigged.

German Foreign Minister, Klaus Kinkel, arrived in Tashkent, Uzbekistan.

German Company Deutz is having repercussions over charges of falsified documents in Saudi Arabian Operations.

May 30, 1996, Bloomberg TV:

A powerful homemade bomb was defused by the Russian military in southeastern Chechnya just hours before Chechen rebel leader, Zemilkhan Yanderbiyev was scheduled to visit. Autonomy talks for Chechnya will resume Sunday in Moscow.

(Identified as Croat in May 31, 1996, Die Deutsche Welle) Bosnian Serb, Drazen Ardemovic is in The Hague charged with participating in the massacre of Muslims after the fall of Srebrenica last summer.

The Muslin-Croat Army will be trained by a private U.S. Company.

Belgrade accuses Zagreb of holding hundreds of Serbs prisoners despite accords signed in Zagreb last April.

May 31, 1996, Bloomberg TV:

A Bosnian Croat pleaded guilty to participating massacres after Srebrenica's fall last summer.

U.S. Ambassador to Bosnia, Kornblum, is making a tour of Balkan capitals asking (for their support) for the removal of Radovan Karadzic and Ratko Mladic from power.

May 31, 1996, Radio Netherlands:

The Chechen separatists insisted on a military escort for their safety. They also criticize continuing Russian attacks on Shaliney.

May 31, 1996, Die Deutsche Welle:
About 100 opposition leaders in Albania have begun a hunger strike against Saleh Breshna's Government.
At the War Crime Tribunal, Croat Drazen Ardemovic, who served in the Bosnian Serb army, pled guilty to participating in the massacre of hundreds of Muslims after the fall of Srebrenica last summer.

June 1, 1996, Radio Netherlands:
Bosnian Serb vice president Belyma Prabsic says Karadzic is still in command but she will represent Bosnian Serbs at talks with the International Contact Group in Geneva. Secretary of State Warren Christopher says that Serb President Slobodan Milosevic should remove Karadzic and Mladic from power.
The former Warsaw Pact nations have given Russia 3 years to comply with the CFE treaty even though Russia has breached the treaty with serious violations.
Tensions are high between Chechens and Russians in and around Shaliney with each charging the other of breaking the truce first. The Russians have dropped a net around the town. Russian troops are continuing to engage Chechen rebels in southeast Chechnya.

June 1, 1996, Die Deutsche Welle:
The former Warsaw Pact nations have given Russia three more years to reduce its weaponry from around its border regions and adhere to the CFE Treaty by reducing its heavy tanks and artillery.

June 2, 1996, Die Deutsche Welle:
Secretary of State Warren Christopher said sanctions

against Serbia should be re-imposed as Slobodan Milosevic has not done all he can to force Radovan Karadzic from his position of power.

Tansu Ciller's True Path Party will not support Prime Minister Yilmas in a new election.

International observers of last week's elections in Albania said there was wide spread fraud and intimidation of voters.

There is fierce fighting between the Taliban movement and President Rabbani's Government. The Taliban student movement has surrounded Kabul for several months now. (The U.S. supported the Taliban and after the Taliban took over in Afghanistan, Osama bin laden of the Mujahideen trained volunteers in Afghanistan helped raise money for the Taliban Government of Afghanistan with donations from other Arab nations, mainly from the Trucial States).

June 4, 1996, Fox TV:
The International Contact Group and Russia have called upon Slobodan Milosevic to have Radovan Karadzic step down from power, but Russia said that Karadzic should not be tried as a war criminal.

Bosnian Croat Drazen Ardemovic said he participated in the Srebrenica massacres because he was told, "if any of you feel sorry for these men, you may line up with them."

June 4, 1996, Radio Netherlands:
NATO ministers have opted for a greater European role, especially in the formation and deployment of a rapid deployment force.

At the Habitat Conference in Istanbul, the non-aligned nations said that housing should be made a "civil right".

Russia reached an accord with Azerbaijan, Armenia, and Georgia to stop religious intolerance and keep the peace.

Iraq is to use the proceeds from oil sales to alleviate severe food and medical shortages. $80 million is presently needed as the money from the oil sales is being delayed.

The Turkish parliament will hold elections Saturday for a new prime minister.

Bahrain has accused Iran of backing the Hezbollah in an attempt to overthrow the Bahrain Government.

June 4, 1996, Die Deutsche Welle:

NATO ministers in Berlin plan for its expansion eastward. Yevgeny Primakov of Russia says Russia should enter before any other eastern European nation, but Poland, Hungary, and others are pressing to enter before Russia.

There are further violations between Chechen and Russian forces. It is unclear if there will be a meeting Tuesday.

Russia has canceled its partial withdrawal in Chechnya.

June 5, 1996, Radio Netherlands:

Iraq's return to the international oil market will likely be one of the most important topics at the OPEC meeting in Vienna. Profits are to go to food and medicines.

Prime Minister D.V. Gowda says India will retain its option to make nuclear weapons until universal nuclear disarmament is agreed.

Jamu and Kashmir are to receive the greatest autonomy within India's government.

Ashud Abiola, opposition leader in Nigeria, is assassinated. He was widely considered to have won the 1993 elections in Nigeria.

June 5, 1996, Die Deutsche Welle:

Chechen rebels warn they will continue to war is Russia rejects three-point proposal: i.e. Russian troops must be withdrawn and elections on autonomy held.

Prime Minister Yilmas resigns in Turkey.

Losses over the sale of cement plants to Saudi Arabia has sent German firm Deutz into reformation of the company.

June 6, 1996, Die Deutsche Welle:

The E.U. Mission to Reconstruct Communications in the former Yugoslavia will help if Human Rights are guaranteed.

The Russian-Chechen Separatists talks ended without agreement.

War Crimes investigators have discovered another mass grave in eastern Bosnia where perhaps 2,700 Muslim men and boys were murdered. One body had hands bound with wire and another with shoelaces. Ratko Mladic was said to be present. The task of arresting Mladic will be much easier with IFOR troops entering Bosnian Serb territory with War Crimes investigators.

June 7, 1996, Radio Netherlands:

President Demirel of Turkey has asked the Islamic Welfare Party to form a new government.

OPEC nations have agreed to freeze and reduce their production to allow Iraqi oil to enter the international market.

Today was to have been the start of the disarmament conference by Bosnia, Croatia, Bosnian Serbs, and Rump Yugoslavia according to the Dayton Peace Accords. This has been postponed because Bosnia and Croatia object to the final wording of the treaty, which gives Bosnian Serbs equal status.

June 7, 1996, Die Deutsche Welle:

In Vienna, six former Communist nations met with Austria, Germany and Italy for assistance in reintegrating their countries with the rest of Europe.

Accused Nazi War Criminal, Karl Hass, fell from a window in Italy.

June 9, 1996, Radio Netherlands:

The Russians do not want Chechens to take part in Russian elections. There has been no agreement on the withdrawal of Russian troops, which is one of Chechnya's three conditions.

Police in Split, Croatia, arrested Slako Arsofsky for the War Crimes Tribunal. He is accused of taking part in massacres of Muslims.

June 9, 1996, Die Deutsche Welle:

Former Prime Minister Tansu Ciller has rejected her party's recommendation to form a coalition with the Islamic Welfare Party.

Chechens say the Russians have agreed verbally to withdraw all troops before August 30, but the Russians disagree.

Goodman of the EU was excluded by the Russians who claimed he was won over to the (Chechen) rebel side.

Coalition police arrested in Split, Croatia one of the nine Croats accused of War Crimes. The 36-year-old Slako Arsofsky is accused participating in massacres of Muslims in Lasar Valley.

June 10, 1996, Radio Netherlands:

(Jackie Spears reporting) Russians and Chechens have reached an agreement whereby Russian troops will withdraw by August 30 and remove their roadblocks from around Chechen villages. It is not clear if Chechen rebels will be disarmed.

Slovenia has officially applied to join the EU

Anti-Semitism appears to be decreasing everywhere but Sweden.

June 10, 1996, Die Deutsche Welle:

German Finance Minister, Gunter Rechsalt, is in a Berlin hospital with malaria contracted on his African trip last month. (Put to sleep and treated with highly potent medicines he was cured of malaria).

June 11, 1996, Radio Netherlands: Jackie Speer reporting:

There is no end to the deadlock over Bosnia's objections to Bosnian Serbs being referred to as Serpskaya Republic in the disarmament treaty to be signed.

The first witness against Dusan Tadec, who is accused of torturing, murdering, and raping inmates at a camp in Bosnia, will testify incognito to protect him and his family from retaliation.

An explosion ripped through a subway car in Moscow killing three.

Police defused a one-kilo TNT bomb in the toilet of the Honduran legislature in Tegucigalpa. An unknown guerrilla group claimed responsibility.

The UN has come out publicly against re-imposing sanctions against Serbia or the Bosnian Serbs.

June 12, 1996, Public Broadcast Radio:

Secretary of Defense William Perry says the Dayton Accords are not on schedule which means the NATO pull-out in December might be delayed. Mr. Perry says this is only speculation.

June 13, 1996, Die Deutsche Welle:

Chief of the War Crimes Tribunal, Antonio Cacefi, said the Bosnian Serbs are not cooperating and some sanctions should be re-imposed. He wants Serbs to deliver Radovan Karadzic and other Bosnian Serb criminals to The Hague. Bosnia is sending three Muslims accused of war crimes. The International Conference in Florence, Italy is unwilling to re-impose sanctions and says mid-September elections will take place according to the scheduled Dayton Peace Accords.

June 14, 1996, Radio Netherlands:
The 180 nations participating in Habitat Conference in Istanbul have recognized adequate housing is a human right.

The Conference on Bosnia attended by ministers from 40 countries, stopped short of placing sanctions against Bosnian Serbs. It was desirable that Mr. Karadzic step down, as per Dayton Peace Accords, but not necessary as a prerequisite for elections.

The disarmament treaty for all Bosnian signatories was signed today by all participants who signed the Dayton Peace Accords.

At The Hague, a witness directly accused Dusan Tadic of stabbing two police officers to death after they surrendered to Serbs.

Russia will have liaison officers stationed in NATO HQ and NATO will have liaison officers stationed in Russian military HQ.

June 14, 1996, Die Deutsche Welle:
The International Conference asked for stepped up efforts for the arrest of Radovan Karadzic. The leader of the conference will travel to Belgrade to push Milosevic to arrest Serb war criminals.

Russia and Germany have signed an agreement for

closer cooperation in sharing military technology.

June 14, 1996, Die Deutsche Welle:
The International Conference in Florence renewed calls for the arrest of Karadzic and Mladic. Antonio Cacefi, Chief Justice of the War Crimes, said if Serbia were barred from attending the Olympic games in Atlanta, this would be enough to get the Serbs to cooperate.

EU's Carl Bildt says that even though elections will be set for September, Karadzic will have the upper hand. It is clear the international community does not have the stomach to press for the arrest of Karadzic and Mladic.

Karadzic avoids roadblocks manned by IFOR troops and says his territory is "his country". IFOR does not want to confront Serb forces.

June 15, 1996, Die Deutsche Welle:
A powerful bomb exploded in Manchester, England, injuring hundreds. (Manchester is home to thousands of Muslims in England).

Thousands of Kurds demonstrated in Hamburg over Ankara's policy against the Kurds in Turkey.

German Foreign Minister, Klaus Kinkel, signed an arms agreement in Florence limiting arms of all belligerents in the former Yugoslavia.

On paper, the Chechen conflict shows how difficult it is to solve all problems. A convoy carrying Chechen and International negotiators was halted twice due to explosions.

One third of all air traffic in the world is in Europe, but Europe has only 10% of all the accidents.

June 16, 1996, Radio Netherlands:
Turkey and Syria are massing troops on both sides of their common border. Syria claims Turkey is aiding

political opposition and building dams on the Tigris and Euphrates. Turkey claims Syria is aiding Kurdish rebels in Turkey.

June 16, 1996, Die Deutsche Welle:
The Russian Far East reports first with 29 million votes (40% of Russia's voters), giving Yeltsin 34%, 32% for Zhuganov, and 15% for General Lebed, 7% for Zhironovsky and 0.57% for Gorbachev.
Polls in Chechnya were closed by threats from Chechen rebels.

June 17, 1996, Radio Netherlands: Carole Van den Ring reporting:
Russian General Alexander Ledbed has come out against the Communists but declined expressly to support Yeltsin.
The Bosnian Serb, Vordan Ladic, handed over the War Crimes Tribunal in mid May, is released as he was the wrong Ladic.
The International Federation of Human Rights has criticized France's treatment of foreigners.
23 new countries have joined the disarmament conference.

Jun 17, 1996, Die Deutsche Welle:
Germany's Finance Minister, Volker Ruhe, is in Croatia and Bosnia to inspect German IFOR troops. No decision to extend IFOR's mandate will be taken until after elections in September.
Vordan Ladic released by the War Crimes Tribunal was the wrong man.

June 18, 1996, Radio Netherlands:
The UN accused 50-60 Bosnian Serb women in Banja

Luka of taking two OECE officials prisoner after they demonstrated about relatives they say were taken prisoner during the war. This may have been a ploy by Radovan Karadzic to embarrass Banja Luka's mayor who is running against Karadzic in September's elections.

Intimidation of Muslims by Serbs has grown over the last month. The level of violence is show when President Izetbegovic was beaten over the head by a Muslim. These threats and violence have been directed against Muslims and this is the first time international diplomats were involved.

June 18, 1996, Die Deutsche Welle:
Two Bosnian Muslims appeared before the War Crimes Tribunal extradited by their own country. Both deny their guilt.

June 19, 1996, Radio Netherlands: **Carole Van den Ring** reporting:
The International War Crimes Tribunal says the Bosnian Serb War Crimes Tribunal in Pale is not legitimate. The Bosnian Serb Tribunal is expected to exonerate War Criminals Radovan Karadzic and Ratko Mladic.

In inquiry is being made over the failure of the UN to protect Srebrenica in July 1995.

UN Secretary General Boutros Boutros Ghali has decided to seek a second five-year term as head of the UN

In Bangladesh, the Arami League with 148 seats out of 300 has just failed to win a majority. The Nationalists won 118 seats.

Cholera has broken out in the northern Nigerian state of Kalaba.

June 20, 1996, Bloomberg TV:
Turkish parliament rejects charges of corruption against

former Prime Minister Ciller.

Bosnian Serbs set up their own War Crimes Tribunal. (I'll bet there were no convictions).

June 20, 1996, Radio Netherlands: Carole van den Ring reporting:

Bosnia's general elections will be held September 14. OECE has the task of over-seeing the elections. Radovan Karadzic has said he will be a candidate.

Genady Zhuganov says democracy is in peril in Russia because Yeltsin is losing control. Mr. Yeltsin sacked his bodyguard who was accused of intending to sabotage the run-off elections.

June 20, 1996, Die Deutsche Welle:

Three top senior Russian officials were sacked by Yeltsin.

The EU parliament has advised Albania to nullify its last elections, which were considered irregular.

June 21, 1996, Radio Netherlands:

Under the Dayton Peace Accords, all displaced persons will have a right to return to their former homes.

A joint European Police Organization will be under The Hague Court, as envisioned at the E.U. summit in Florence.

Prime Minister Ciller's True Path Party in Turkey is considering a coalition with the Islamic Welfare Party.

June 22, 1996, Radio Netherlands:

12 prospective member nations of the EU have attended the Florence Conference.

The leaders of Arab countries are meeting behind closed doors. They call upon Israel to recognize the Palestinian State, return Golan Heights, and return to the peace process.

General Ledbed is in favor of Chechen independence and allowing the Chechens to choose for themselves. July 3, 1996, is set for the run-off election between Yeltsin & Zhuganov.

22 million in sub-Sahara Africa are facing starvation. The international community cannot meet the needs due to dwindling grains reserves, smaller expected grain crops, and higher prices for grain.

June 22, 1996, Die Deutsche Welle:
Yeltsin arrived in Kalingrad for the dedication of an Orthodox cathedral. He said the eastward expansion of NATO alarms both the people of Belarus and Russia.

According the German intelligence (BND), crime syndicates are buying up companies and banks in many countries to launder money.

June 24, 1996, Bloomberg TV:
Chechens and Russians are exchanging lists of prisoners and missing soldiers.

June 24, 1996, Radio Netherlands:
In the early part of the Bosnian war, Muslims captured were taken by bus outside Sarajevo and killed in cold blood by Bosnian Serbs. Forensic investigators are now excavating the mass graves.

Rob Yamacher of Switzerland has re-worded the nuclear arms limitation treaty to address the objections raised by India.

(Israeli) Prime Minister, Netanyahu, says Jerusalem will remain the undivided capital of Israel, which will nullify any proposal that East Jerusalem will be the capital of the Palestinian State.

More than 1/5 of the world's population lives on a dollar a day.

30 Bosnian Muslims were expelled from their homes in Banja Luka suburb of Ubanja, the worst ethnic cleansing since the Dayton Peace Accords. Bosnian Serbs surrounded the houses then went in, beat up the families, expelled them. Ethnic cleansing continues. There are still significant numbers of Muslims and Croats in the Banja Luka region.

Tesla region in Bosnian Serb territory also had some expulsions but IFOR increased its presence there and it stopped.

June 24, 1996, Die Deutsche Welle:
Russian Communist candidate for president, Genady Zhuganov has called for a national peace pact and a coalition government. Yeltsin says crime fighting and peace in Chechnya are of primary importance.

Three Kurdish Hadeb leaders were ambushed by 8 assassins as they traveled in a car. The Hadeb is working for Kurdish independence.

June 25, 1996, Bloomberg TV:
Yeltsin fired more top generals close to former Defense Minister, Pavel Grachev.

A mass grave in Bosnia yielded 47 bodies.

UN destroys a biological warfare plant near Baghdad that produced botulism, anthrax, etc.

June 26, 1996, Bloomberg TV: www.bloomberg.com :
The War Crimes Tribunal will see the first evidence against Radovan Karadzic and Ratko Mladic.

North Korea sold scud missiles to Egypt. Calls are made for sanctions against Egypt.

80% of 1,272 women in prison suffer from mental

disorders of some kind.

June 27, 1996, Die Deutsche Welle:

Radovan Karadzic, leader of the Bosnian Serbs, has threatened to run unless Serbs receive certain commitments. E.U. representative Carl Bildt says no special deals will be given to the Serbs.

The War Crimes Tribunal will hear evidence on Radovan Karadzic and Mladic. Karadzic says he doesn't recognize the tribunal at The Hague but has sent a Belgrade lawyer to represent him.

The Tribunal has issued indictments for 8 more Bosnian Serbs for the imprisonment and rape of Muslim women in 1991, 1992, and 1993. This is the first time rape has been classified as a war crime.

June 29, 1996, Radio Netherlands:

E.U. representative Carl Bildt calls for the removal of Radovan Karadzic before Monday. The E.U. endorses the removal of Karadzic.

A Hutu rebel leader in Rwanda has offered $1,000 for the head of every American and $10.000 for the head of the American ambassador.

The Chechen rebels have voiced their demands to replace the pro-Russian Chechen puppet government, declare the last elections null and void, and re-adjust the Russian negotiators with the rebels.

A hundred Bosnian Serbs arrived in Mostar to vote in elections there. About 20,000 Bosnian Serbs were expelled during the war.

A Bosnian Croat indicted by The Hague had immigrated to the Netherlands and died there last year. He was involved in attacks on Muslim villages in 1991 and 1993.

Much of G-7's talks with Russia this past week were

about Bosnia and what to do with Radovan Karadzic.

June 29, 1996, Channel 51 (CNN)
Prime Minister John Majors said that if Radovan Karadzic does not remove himself from power, swift action to re-impose sanctions on the Bosnian Serbs will be made. The Russians were in agreement.

June 29, 1996, Die Deutsche Welle:
(Russian) Prime Minister, Viktor Chernomyrden, partook in all G-7 talks. Chancellor Helmut Kohl said he hopes that G-7 will soon become G-8 by including Russia.

Bosnian Serbs were told specifically that Radovan Karadzic has to step down or sanctions would be re-imposed. German Foreign Minister Klaus Kinkel and EU's Carl Bildt said Bosnian Serbs would receive no reconstruction money until that happens.

Nechman Eberkhan is the new prime minister of Turkey's coalition government of the Islamic Welfare Party and the True Path Party of former Prime Minister Ciller. The Islamists said they would continue with the secular government policy of Ataturk.

June 30, 1996, Radio Netherlands:
The International Community is skeptical that Karadzic handed over his power to Biljana Blasic.

In Mostar, no serious incidents were reported between Croat and Muslims. A high voter turnout for the elections was reported.

In eastern Turkey, 9 soldiers were killed and 30 wounded in an attack by the PKK rebels.

Sheik Ahmed Sahoon, 89, was shot in the head as he prayed in Mosque in Algiers, Algeria. The Sheik was an Islamic leader. The assassins are thought to be Islamic extremists.

June 30, 1996, Die Deutsche Welle:
Karadzic's handing over of his power is called a charade by UN observers.
Elections in Mostar passed peacefully despite fears of violence.
Turkey's coalition government is being opposed by some of Tansu Ciller's True Path Party, which disagreed with her cooperation with the Islamic Welfare Party.

July 2, 1996, Radio Netherlands:
The U.S. warned that the Serb Democrat Party will not be allowed to participate in the September elections if Radovan Karadzic is ruling the party. His party urged him to run in the September elections.
The UN has been asked to stay on in Mostar. In last week's elections, the Bosnian Muslim Party won 48% and the Bosnian Croats 45%, but the crisis of ruling the city has not been resolved.
Amnesty International urged the International Community to make money available to identify bodies in mass graves near Srebrenica.

July 2, 1996, Die Deutsche Welle:
The War Crimes Tribunal in The Hague will continue taking evidence against Radovan Karadzic and Ratko Mladic (but there will be no trial as The Hague will not try anyone *in absencia*).
Today witnesses gave evidence that the order for the systematic rape of Muslim women came from the Serb leadership.
The German High Court ruled that those who were slave laborers in World War II could sue individually.

July 3, 1996, Public Broadcast Radio (U.S.):
NATO and the UN have ruled out capturing accused war criminals Radovan Karadzic and General Ratko Mladic and will not impose economic sanctions on Serbia or on the Bosnian Serbs

July 7, 1996, Radio Netherlands:
War Crimes Tribunal prosecutor, Mark Harmon, has asked for arrest warrants of Karadzic and Mladic. He accused Serbia and the Bosnian Serbs of failing to live up to the Dayton Peace Accords.

(In Russia) Viacheslav Tekamerov says he will take appropriate steps if Chechen rebels do not turn over Russian prisoners.

July 10, 1996, Public Broadcast Radio:
War Crimes Tribunal Justice Jorda issued arrest warrants for Bosnian Serb Radovan Karadzic and General Ratko Mladic. Interpol was also notified. The UN Security Council was advised that Serbia, Montenegro, and the self-styled Republic of Serbia (Bosnian Serb territory) are not cooperating with the War Crimes Tribunal.

Newly elected Russian president Yeltsin says the War Crimes Tribunal in The Hague is not legitimate.

July 13, 1996; Radio Netherlands:
An American woman working with the U.S. Embassy in Sarajevo was shot in the back yesterday by a gunman following the car her husband was driving. The car in which the gunman was riding disappeared after the shooting. The woman is in stable condition in a Sarajevo hospital.

July 13, 1996, Die Deutsche Welle:

German Finance Minister, Theo Weigel, told Bosnian Serbs they will get no money for reconstruction until they cooperate with the War Crimes Tribunal and turn over accused Serb war criminals. Serbs are arguing about the legitimacy of the War Crimes Tribunal to try them.

July 30, 1996, Die Deutsche Welle:
Radovan Karadzic sent Marko Omerska, Attorney General of the Serb Government to lodge accusations of War Crimes against President Alija Izetbegovic to the War Crimes Tribunal. The Tribunal said the accusations had no evidence introduced and rejected the accusations.

August 2, 1996, CBS-TV:
Radovan Karadzic appears to still be in control in Bosnian Serb territory despite the papers he signed relinquishing his political powers. Ambassador Richard Holbrooke said that Karadzic knew what he was signing and had again shown his word was worthless.

August 14, 1996, Die Deutsche Welle:
Former Prime Minister Tansu Ciller asks Greece to halt provocations by demonstrators in Cyprus as another one is shot climbing a flagpole to tear down the Turkish flag.

August 15, 1996, Die Deutsche Welle:
Shots were fired at Minister of Security, Alexander Lebed, as he arrived in Chechnya to hold talks with rebel Chechens. Ninety percent of Grozny is held by the rebels. One group of refugees fleeing the city was attacked by Russian soldiers and some killed.

August 16, 1996, Die Deutsche Welle:
A Croat mayor was selected in Mostar and the elected mayor, a Muslim, will step down to be deputy mayor after

EU threatened to pull out its reconstruction forces if both sides did not agree.

August 16, 1996, Radio Netherlands:
A NATO inspection team last week was to inspect a Serb weapons depot was told that its guide would be General, Ratko Mladic, whose arrest on sight warrant was issued by the War Crimes Tribunal in The Hague. Rather than confront General Mladic, the NATO inspection team withdrew until the Serbs provided a different guide.

August 17, 1996, Radio Netherlands:
A report out says terrorism is being financed out of Saudi Arabia and Persian Gulf States by wealthy individuals, not Iran, Iraq or other nations named by the U.S. as sponsors of terrorism.

August 18, 1996, Radio Netherlands:
OSCE has decided to postpone municipal elections in Bosnia until next April or May due to irregularities. But elections for president and legislation will be held in September.

What is Terrorism?

Terrorism is to spread terror among a civilian population and induce fear that will destabilize a government. The first terrorists in history were the Zealots of Jesus time who wanted to create a pure Jewish state and were terrorizing non-Jews to leave Palestine. They called themselves the *sons of Light* and the precursors of Zionists today.

The next known terrorists were the *Assassins* founded by Hasan ibn Sabah who studied at the *House of Wisdom* run by the Fatamid rulers of Egypt. From his studies at the House of Wisdom, Hasan ibn Sabah it appears to have learned mind control techniques which he used on young Ismaili men he invited to his villa. There he subjected to a program of drugs, sex, alcohol, and mysticism to make them into *fida*. *Fida* were trained to accept death on orders of the *Grand Master*.

A few years later in 1119, the Knights Templar was founded in Jerusalem with the same designation of lodges and *Grand Master*. While the first group was drawn from Ismaili Muslims the Knights Templar were Catholic Christian but both cooperated in fighting Muslims and both dedicated to the destruction of Islam.

Around 1252, a great Mongol Army invaded Persia's province of *Korasan* which provided the drugs used by the Assassins in their mind control. Khorasan is the invasion route into India, the British wanted to take it from Persia (Iran) to keep Russian from invading and annexing Khorasan to Russia which would allow them to India.

Communism was created in the late 1700's in Russia by the Khazar Jews, a Central Asian Tribe north of the Caspian Sea and lived off of raiding caravans crossing their land with trade between Europe and China. Their leaders converted to Judaism around 809 AD.

When the Russians took over their territory there was persecution of the Jews called Pogroms which were not anti-Semitistic but the result of the Jewish money-lenders. But the Khazar Jews were told it was their religion that caused their persecution, and so they endorsed Communism that was created to destroy ALL religions and create a One World Government under them.

Formulating Communism from theory into practice, Karl Marx considered Communism the ultimate step upward in Man's Evolution using Darwin's idea of the Origin of the

Species. He advocated using violence to hasten the goal of a One World Government under Communism and terrorism was a major part of this world domination.

Coming to more recent times, o\n August 22, 2005, His Excellency, the Prime Minister of Pakistan, Mr. Azziz, was visiting Hong Kong and his host asked him to talk about terrorism in Islamic nations. There was never any terrorism by Muslims before the 20th Century. Mr. Azziz expressed that terrorism is not something Islamic but is an outgrowth people who feel disenfranchised and unprotected. By silencing Muslims underground *Vigilante Groups* developed to protect Palestinians that became known as *Hezbolla, Hamas, Al Fatah, and other groups.*

When President De Gaulle offered to make France a meeting ground between East and West, French bankers created a financial crisis (financial *terrorism?)* that resulted in his losing confidence in the French Parliament and he was taken out of power. Terrorism is not the result of people who "are jealous of other people's freedom," as stated by Mr. George W. Bush.

The author says he found Bosnian Muslims accepted others of a different religion. Orthodox and Catholic Churches were never bombed or set on fire while more than a thousand mosques were burned and destroyed by the Serbs as well as some Catholic churches. Croats and Muslims made no threats to bomb and/or make terrorism in the United States and England as was done by Serb leaders who also threatened the life of Pope John Paul II on his plan to visit Sarajevo.

The Koran does not advocate killing non-Muslim and the Koran specifically states that Muslims are to gain converts by example, not forced conversion. Muslims never forced Christians to spit on the cross or step on a picture of Jesus such as Masons have in their initiation where they have initiates spit on the cross because Muslims would force suspected Christians to do that.

In the first place, Jesus is considered a Prophet by Muslims just they consider Mohammed as a Prophet. Muslims say both men were divine men who heard the words of God and spoke with God.

In the United States, the first terrorists were the KKK that was created from vigilantism to protect Southerners from the terrorism created by the Carpetbaggers. To stop this terrorism, Lt. General Nathan Bedford Forrest created the Invisible Army that he formed from his old cavalry officers from the Civil War. That later became the KKK, Christian in origin but designated as a terrorist organization by the US Congress in 1867.

Stalin used State Terrorism to hold power in Russia. He had millions of Russians killed and used Beria who ran the KGB (NKVD) to spy on people. In 1953, Stalin was planning to create six huge concentration camps in Central Asia to hold all Russian Jews. But before the plans were put into execution, Stalin suddenly died in his Dacha outside Moscow.

The **Black Operations, False Flags,** or just **Black Ops** which is a terrorist act made to blame on others like the CIA did in the overthrow of Iran's democratic government of Dr. Mossadegh. In 1953, workers in Tehran's Bazaar were told they would be paid hundred dollars each to stage 'a communist demonstration which was to be part of a movie. They were shown leaving the Bazaar so happy at being 'movie stars' and getting so much money. They went to their death as another group was waiting to attack them as Communists and they died at the hands of "Iranians angry that Prime Minister Mossadegh was not controlling the Communist. The Iranian military then declared Martial Law and arrested Dr. Mossadegh, all done to get control of Iran's oil.

In 1978, the CIA borrowed British MI6's control of the Ikhwan (Muslim Brotherhood) to recruit Muslims create a *Muslim Foreign Legion* called the *Mujahideen* to help their brothers in Afghanistan fight 'atheist Russians'.

After Ayatollah Khomeini cut off Iran's natural gas to the Russians that the Russian economy took a dive. The exploitation of northern Afghanistan's huge reserves of natural gas by the Russian would have given them a cheap source of energy. The CIA sought to deprive the Russians of this Afghan gas by using this Muslim Foreign Legion to kick the Russians out of Afghanistan. That Muslim Foreign Legions became the Al Qaida because these Mujahideen became angry that the West and UN permitted these massacres and atrocities against peaceful and innocent Bosnians.

On April 19, 1995, Timothy McVeigh, who had been awarded the Bronze Star in the Gulf War wrote his sister from Ft. Bragg Special Forces training, that he and nine other men, were selected by the CIA to do ***drug trafficking*** and ***government sanctioned assassinations.*** Those letters were seized by the FBI who threatened his sister with prison if she ever revealed the contents of the letters.

When the Murrah Building blew up people heard explosions coming from inside the building. This was corroborated by seismic records showing there were explosions inside the Murrah building at nearly the same time as Timothy McVeigh's truck bomb went off.

Steven Emerson, an anti-Muslim spin doctor, and Dr. Ron Hatchett (graduate of the U.S. Air Force Academy at Colorado Springs, Colorado), took to the news media of major television networks as ***experts on terrorism*** to say the Bombing of the Murray Building in Oklahoma City was the work of Muslim extremists. President Clinton also said on

TV this terrorism was the work of Muslims. This all changed when the Oklahoma State police revealed they had taken the *Oklahoma City Bomber* in custody on an automobile license violation. He was Timothy McVeigh, a Bronze Star recipient, hero of the Gulf War, and worked for the CIA, hidden from the public by the FBI.

A month after **9-11,** in **October 2001** there was the **anthrax scare** which was blamed on Saddam Hussein until a DNA analysis showed the anthrax came from a biological warfare laboratory in Maryland just outside Washington, D.C. Then blame was put on an Egyptian scientist who quit working there six months before. When he was cleared, suspicion was pointed at a Jewish American scientist working but the investigation stopped and years later, when one of the workers died a natural death, the blame was put on him.

The Secretary of Senator Tom Daschle was the first person to die from opening an anthrax laden letter address to the Senator. Senator Daschle was Senate Majority Leader of a Democratic Senate and from South Dakota. He previously worked for Senator James Abourezk, the first Arab American to be elected to the Senate. Then Senator Leahy's secretary died from an anthrax-laden letter and then others not related to political officials but looked to be picked at random.

Senator Daschle opposed President Bush's demand that Congress give him expansive powers, *not only overseas but inside the United States.* Congress denied his request for eavesdropping on emails and wire-tapping as that would violate the Constitution. Mr. Bush retorted, "The Constitution is nothing but a Goddam piece of paper."

A test of the ability for the USS Normandy to distinguish between *friendlies and unfriendlies* was arranged to take place over Long Island Sound. The tragedy of that test was revealed in the book *The Downing of TWA Flight 800,* which documented the real cause of the plane going down was the test missile that hit the plane instead of being destroyed. Only one book store in America carried the book which was the Virgin Bookstore at Caesar's Palace in Las Vegas.

French Intelligence found out about the test that went wrong and President Jacques Chirac was furious as some French citizens were on board the plane. It was not an empty fuel tank that caused the plane to split apart but a missile shot up from the USS Normandy.

Boeing took the blame and was rewarded with government contracts while TWA employees saw that when they told the truth their company, TWA, was destroyed.

There were courageous Serbs who opposed Milosevic even though Milosevic's goons beat them and their lives were endangered.

If Bosnia had been allowed to defend itself **there would have been <u>no war,</u> no massacres, and no campaign of rapes. The Truth of this statement is shown that when Iran supplied weapons to both Croatia and Bosnia, the war quickly ended.**

Bosnians was a member of the UN and had the right to defend itself. Kosovo was next and the German contribution to the occupation forces was the most commendable. The Germans maintained a warehouse full of building materials. Any Serb or Albanian who had his home destroyed could go there and get anything he needed to repair his home. The American program was to hand out plastic sheeting, nails, and wood, make one room to live in and rebuild with their own money.

In Kosovo, two Serbs driving a Yugo shot a young German soldier. The German unit responded quickly and killed the attackers. The Serbs were stupid as these young

Germans never knew Hitler, were never in the fighting in Bosnia. They did it to show off and they paid for it.

No Weapons of Mass Destruction were found in Iraq. Saddam Hussein had cyanide gas and used it against Iraqi Kurds. He used mustard gas on Iranian soldiers during the Iran-Iraq War of 1979-86 and no one objected.

President George W. Bush got the War Crimes Tribunal to exempt all Americans on a year by year basis. Charges of War Crimes from the 1991 Gulf War against Americans were given immunity after the United States threatened to cut military aid to many countries as well as threats to pull out of NATO or cut American contribution to NATO.

Bios of People and War Crimes Indictments

Abdic, Friket millionaire from chickens exported to EU, he sided with Serbia, raised his own army to fight Bosnia in his area around Bihac.

Albright, Madelaine, U.S. Ambassador to the UN, born in Prague, Czechoslovakia, 1937. As a baby, she and her family fled to London in 1939 when the Germans marched into Prague. They returned to the Czech capital in 1945, when Madelaine was eight and learned several relatives had died in concentration camps.

After WW II, her father returned to Prague where the Communist administration expropriated a luxurious first-floor flat at 11 Hradsanke Street owned by Karl Nebrich, an Austrian industrialist. Although Nebrich was never a member of the Nazi Party the new Communist administration in Prague who assigned the apartment to

Madelaine's father for his services to the Czech Foreign Ministry.

The Times of London, March 30, 1999 carried a story that a surviving daughter of Karl Nebrich learned in 1996 after Madelaine spoke of her happy childhood memories there that her father, Josef Korbel, a stole millions of dollars' worth of art and furniture from the flat and took it to America when they immigrated there.

The surviving daughter of Nebrich, Doris Renner, recalled that Josef Korbel argued he was entitled to these works of arts and furniture for having lost everything to the Nazis. "All his relatives died in concentration camps," Doris Renner said last week from her home on Lake Wolfgang near Salzburg. "That is very sad. But it doesn't justify him taking everything from us."

Aramovic, Milar, a Major in the Bosnian Serb Army and a Jew. He was in charge of the men who he ordered to kill 8,700 men and boys after the fall of Srebrenica and was paid 12 kilos of gold to do it. Judge Goldstone on the Internatioanl War Crimes Tribunal dismissed the charges of mass murder and genocide as Amarovic said he was under orders.

Arkan: Real name Zelko Raznatovic, an international criminal of the Serbian Mafia, formed his 'volunteers" of criminally insane Serbian paramilitary he called the *Serbian Tigers*. Starting in 1991 with the massacres of Christians in Eastern Slavonia (the part of Croatia next to Serbia) he continued his killing spree of torture, rape, and murder in Bosnia on April 6, 1992. His name has never appeared on the list of War Criminals issued by The Hague in 1996. He was a hero to Kosovo Serbs (Croatian Serbs that fled from Croatia when the Croatian Army liberated its own territory were sent to Kosovo to make trouble. They chose Arkan for their representative in 1998. He was killed in a Belgrade hotel on January 15, 2000.

There are two stories about who killed him. The first one is that the Serbian Mafia murdered him and the second story is that he was murdered by Serbia's Secret Police because they wanted his lips sealed about other Serbs who were involved in War Crimes in Bosnia and Croatia. After Arkan's murder, his widow, a former pop star of Yugoslavia, moved in with Arkan's Serbian Mafia boss.

Balladur, Eduard, Iranian-born Christian and French Prime Minister suppressed the news of torture and abuse of French Peacekeepers taken hostage or captured by the Serbs like the two French pilots shot down and taken prisoner by Bosnian Serbs. Later in the war after two French UN Peacekeeping soldiers were shot in Sarajevo, Balladur quickly said he had definite evidence it was Muslims who shot them. But the UN said it was Serbs who killed them and threatened to punish the Serbs with the Rapid Reaction Forces (July 25, 1995, *New York Times*). In1996, Balladur lost in his election bid for the presidency to Chirac.

Chirac, Jacques, President of France, replaced Mitterand. He wanted all UN Peacekeepers armed and able to protect themselves from Serb kidnappings and sniping. His ideas were the best among all the leaders of NATO nations and French troops assigned to Bosnia were the most effective bringing peace to Bosnia after Balladur stepped down.

Christopher, Warren Minor, U.S. Secretary of State under Bill Clinton, was born in 1925 in Scranton, North Dakota.

He studied law at Stanford Univ. (1946-49) and was a clerk to Supreme Court Justice William O. Douglas (1949-50). He was in private practice before being appointed as deputy attorney general under President Lyndon Baines Johnson (1967-69) and Deputy Secretary of State under President Jimmy Carter. He was chief American negotiator in the 1981 talks on the Iranian hostage crisis. Appointed Secretary of State (1993-97) by President Clinton, Christopher worked hard to get Arab-Israeli peace.

Previously, he chaired the Independent Commission on the Los Angeles Police Department after the trials in which the LA police charged in beating Rodney King were exonerated. The resulting riots in Los Angeles were the worst in American history.

His performance in the Bosnian Conflict was always wavering as he waited for orders from President Clinton. He wrote his memoirs, *In the Stream of History* (1998) and *Chances of a Lifetime* (2001).

Clark, Wesley, was born in Chicago, Illinois, December 1944 to Venita and Benjamin Kanne. His father died when he was a child and his mother moved to Rock Island, Illinois, where they lived with his grandparents until the mother bought a small house with the help of Veteran's benefits from his father's service in the military. She later remarried, and Clark took the name of his stepfather.

Entering West Point when he was seventeen, he later received a Rhodes Scholarship (like Clinton and Strobe Talbott) and passed his Oxford exams two years later. When the three diplomats traveling in an armored personnel carrier were trapped inside the burning vehicle after it 'slipped' from the road, Clark grabbed a fire extinguisher and tried to put out the fire. He blamed Milosevic for their deaths but it was more likely the murderous Mladic who murdered them and with whom he horsed around as you can read from below.

From the *New Republic, April 21, 1997.* Headline of the article reads: **General Clark, Who Fraternized with Mladic, to Head NATO**

"Bill Clinton last week nominated General Wesley Clark to lead NATO and America's forces in Europe." If the president was trying to remind the public about the lack of seriousness with which his administration has taken war crimes in Bosnia, this is a fine choice because on August 27, 1994, Clark, then director of strategy, plans and policy for the Joint Chiefs of Staff, met in Banja Luka with Ratko Mladic, the bloodstained military leader of the Bosnian Serbs.

"The State Department had advised against the meeting, on account of Mladic's well-documented war crimes in Gorazde, Srebrenica and Sarajevo. Still, Clark and Mladic had a jolly time. Mladic gave Clark some plum brandy and a pistol with a Cyrillic inscription, and the two merrily swapped military hats. What do you do with a man with that kind of moral cloudlessness? Promote him," end of article.

Clark was unsuccessful to win his party's nomination to run in 1992 presidential elections. He is now retired.

Clinton, William "Bill" Jefferson, President of the United States 1992-2000, scandals and violence marked his presidency. In the case of Ruby Ridge, Idaho, an FBI sharpshooter shot and killed the wife of the man they were trying to arrest.

On April 19, 1993, just three months after taking office, the new Attorney General Janet Reno gave the FBI permission for a gas and tank attack on the David Koresh's Branch Dravidian compound at Waco, Texas, after publicly showing letters dated April 9 and 10, from a defiant David Koresh. On April 14, Koresh wrote a letter to say he was willing to allow inspection of the compound after an army tank was used to smash motorcycles and cars outside the compound. Extremely loud music was played day and night and floodlights played on the buildings every night, all to induce nervous anxiety and a nervous breakdown. Janet Reno gave the order to set the wodden compound on fire and it burned to the ground in a five minutes killing 86 men, women and children. Reno said it was necessary as Koresh who she said was sexually abusing the children.

On July 20, six months after President Clinton was sworn in as president, his legal advisor, Vincent Foster, was found dead in Ft. Marcy Park. Boxes of files and documents were removed from his office before the Police sealed it. He had an appointment with Mr. Clinton the next day to give his resignation. Louis Freeh, made head of the FBI that day, ruled hid frsth was a suicide. Mr. Foster had said Foster was Catholic and suidice is condemned as a sin.

A year later, the Oklahoma City Bomber, Timothy McVeigh, blew up the Murray Building in Oklahoma City (see: pages

Another cover-up was TWA Flight 800, July 17, 1996, three months before Mr. Clinton faced his second election as president of the United States. An investigative reporter and former policeman, James Sanders has written a very good book. ***The Downing of TWA Flight 800.*** Sanders wrote in his book that the plane was knocked out of the sky by a test to see if a rocket from the USS Normandy could tell friendly from *unfriendly* aircraft. Many navy ships were in the area along with the USS Normandy that fired the missile.

When the first news reports came out there were eye witnesses saying they saw a small plane crash into the Boeing Jumbo Jet over Long Island Sound. The small plane was the rocket. The test was a failure and 230 people died. TWA employees did not keep quiet, which is why TWA no longer exists.

The USS Normandy was used extensively in 1999 against Serbia over the US and UN demand that Serbia get out of Kosovo Province and the Danube River cannot be used through Serbia today because of bridges that were destroyed by missiles from NATO forces.

After airport security was 'beefed up' all around America on September 11, 2001, four Jumbo Jet Boeing plane were "high-jacked". The NORAD installation inside Peak's Pike at Colorado Springs, Colorado, has since 1970 the technology to take over all 4,000 airplanes in the air over the U.S. but on this day it failed.

On September 11, 2001, after the planes crashed into the WTC towers, a group of five men in an apartment building parking lot in New Jersey, across the river from the WTC, were celebrating. A lady saw the men giving other high fives and wanting their photos taken with the burning twin towers in the background from her apartment window. She called the police to tell about five 'Middle-Eastern looking men" celebrating and the five were picked up and identified as Israeli *students*. The Israeli Ambassador explained that the five were just 'immature'.

After being held for three months, they were put on an airplane and send to Israel without anyone having a chance to interview them. Nine months later, on July 17, 2002, Egyptian Air flight 587 crashed into Long Island waters after taking off from JFK Airport in New York. Bernard Loeb of the National Transportation Safety Board said it was an accident. On board were 33 Egyptian officers, some with their wives and children. The blame was put on a co-pilot, Jamil Al-Batati, who NTSB said committed suicide. Question is whether the Mossad did the 9-11 and Egyptian

Air Flight 587? An Egyptian pilot familiar with JFK Airport said that employees in the cargo area were known cocaine, heroin, and morphine addicts, yet nothing was done about tightening security after 9-11.

These things tie in with the NTSB also targeting Presidential Airlines, which was flying from Long Beach, California to Houston, Texas and to Atlanta, Georgia, which was targeted by NTSB because it was a business started up by

Concerning Mr. Clinton and his affair with Monica Levinsky there are two stories. Knowing Mr. Clinton's proclivity for women he was set-up for blackmail by Israel because: 1. Mrs. Clinton suggested that Israeli settlers return land they confiscated from Palestinians, or 2. Mr. Clinton was not adhering to Israel's orders for him to invade Iraq and dispose of Saddam Hussein who was shipping arms to Palestinians for their defense against Kach, a terrorist group organized by Meir Kahane, who also founded the JDL terrorist gang in America. Kahane previously worked for the FBI doing security clearances with Robert Strauss who later became Chairman of the Democratic Party.

As for Hillary Clinton, there was no impropriety in her building a one thousand dollar investment in commodity futures to a handsome 100,000 profit on the advice from Mr. Tyson. This money was lost in an investment scheme called 'Whitewater',

Two months after Waco, Mr. Clinton's White House legal advisor and lifelong friend from Hope, Arkansas, Vincent Forster, was found dead on the Washington Parkway not far from CIA headquarters. The FBI ruled his death a suicide. As legal advisor to the White House. Mr. Foster would have counseled Mr. Clinton about the attack on the Branch Dravidian Compound. Mr. Foster also handled the Whitewater Papers that were under subpoena which then disappeared from Foster's office. A maid in the White House found the Whitewater Papers three years later in Mrs. Clinton's bedroom.

In 1988, Jewish organizations pressured the FBI to name the Number One terrorist organizations in the U.S. and when the FBI named Rabbi Meyer Kahane's JDL the Jewish organizations asked for the FBI to rescind that designation, which it did. Then under the presidency of Mr. Clinton the JDL's terrorism grew bigger and bigger.

These happenings have been included to show: 1. Mr. Clinton had a lot of problems unrelated to Bosnia, 2. There were cover-ups for all the above errors, 3. He showed no support for the Bosnian Muslims, 4. He continued the policies of demonizing the Muslim nations of Iran, Iraq, and Libya as previously done under presidents Carter, Reagan, and George H. W. Bush, 5. Mr. Clinton tried to keep a lid on atrocities ordered by Yeltsin Russia against Chechens, 6. Kept silent about provocations by Israel against Palestinians, 6. Maintained a policy of destabilizing oil and gas exporting nations such as Indonesia, Philippines, Nigeria, and Algeria.

Grachev, Pavel, Russian Minister of Defense ordered atrocities against Chechens. Removed from office as Russian Minister of Defense on charges of corruption he has never been brought to trial or punished for those charges. It was Grachev who broke UN sanctions imposed on Bosnian Serbs and Serbia and supplied 3,000 elite Russian troops to fight on the side of Bosnian Serbs. He supplied SAM 11 anti aircraft missiles, heavy artillery, helicopters and other military equipment to Bosnian Serbs, Serbia, and Montenegro breaking the UN weapons ban on the former Yugoslavia. All evidence points to Grachev as being the major financier of the Serbs in their war on Bosnians.

Holbrooke, Richard, graduated of Brown University, 1962, held many top positions but seldom more than a year before changing to another top position. (In 1981, consultant to Lehman Brothers one of the banks that founded the Federal Reserve Bank, established in 1913 and owned American Express). He was U.S. Ambassador to Germany and awarded the Grand Cross of Merit. In 1999, he was appointed **permanent** U.S. Ambassador to the UN by President William Jefferson Clinton, (only lifetime appointments by the U.S; Government are Supreme Court judges and must be approval by the U.S. Congress.

Mr. Holbrooke signed a secret agreement with Slobodan Milosevic to divide Bosnia between Serbia and Croatia (VOA August 23, 1995).

Izetbegovic, Alija, born in Bosanski Sumac, Bosnia, August 8, 1925, died October 19, 2003. Political rival Frikert Abdic, a multi-millionaire from Bihac. Izetbegovic was imprisoned for several years because of his religious beliefs. It is said that he advocated a hard line Islamic approach but there is no evidence to back up this claim and it appears that *Spin Doctors* or *Disinformation Specialists* are now using the Internet to twist the truth.

Karadzic, Radovan, President of Republika Srpska during after Yugoslavia broke up in 1991. Accused of violations of the laws or customs of war and ordering atrocities, he was arrested 21 July 2008 and extradited to the Netherlands where he is on trial in the UN Detention Unit of Scheveningen. He worked in a private clinic in Belgrade under the alias of Dr. Dragan, David Dabic, and he served time for fraud before being elevated to President of Bosnian Serbs. Using various aliases he traveled around Europe and was captured posing as a doctor of herbal holistic healing in Belgrade.

Richard J. Goldstone, Prosecutor of the International Criminal Tribunal for the Former Yugoslavia, Charges:

THE ACCUSED RADOVAN KARADZIC born on 19 June 1945 in the municipality of Savnik of the Republic of Montenegro, and served from May 1992 as the president of the Bosnian Serb administration in Pale.

SUPERIOR AUTHORITY : RADOVAN KARADZIC

1. RADOVAN KARADZIC was a founding member and president of the Serbian Democratic Party (SDS) of what was then the Socialist Republic of Bosnia and Herzegovina. The SDS was the main political party among the Serbs in Bosnia and Herzegovina. As president of the SDS, he was and is the most powerful official in the party. His duties as president include representing the party, coordinating the work of party organs and ensuring the realization of the programmatic tasks and goals of the party. He continues to hold this post.

2. RADOVAN KARADZIC became the first president of the Bosnian Serb administration in Pale on or about 13 May 1992. At the time he assumed this position, his *de jure* powers, as described in the constitution of the Bosnian Serb administration, included but not limited to, commanding the army on the Bosnian Serb administration in times of war and peace and having the authority to appoint, promote and discharge officers of the army.

3. In addition to his powers described in the constitution, RADOVAN KARADZIC'S powers as president of the Bosnian Serb administration were augmented by Article 6 of the Bosnian Serb Act on People's Defense which vested in him, among other powers, the authority to supervise the Territorial Defense both in peace and war and the authority to issue orders for the utilization of the police in case of war, immediate threat and other emergencies. Article 39 of the same Act empowered him, in cases of imminent threat of war and other emergencies, to deploy Territorial Defense units for the maintenance of law and order.

4. RADOVAN KARADZIC'S powers are further augmented by Article 33 of the Bosnian Serb Act on Internal Affairs, which authorized him to activate reserve police in emergency situations.

5. RADOVAN KARADZIC exercised the powers described above and dealt with internationally as the president of the Bosnian Serb administration in Pale participated in negotiations and agreements on cease-fires and humanitarian relief that have been implemented.

Majors, John, Prime Minister of Britain said that if he allowed the arms embargo against Bosnia to be lifted, his government would fall. When Majors trip to Moscow that the *most hated man in the West* was to meet with the *most the most man in the East* (Yelsin). Both committed was crimes,

Mladic, Ratko, born on 12 March 1943, in the municipality of Kalinovik, Republic of Bosnia and Herzegovina is a career military officer and holds the rank of general in the Bosnian Serb armed forces. On or about 14 May 1992 to the present, he has been the commander of the army of the Bosnian Serb administration.

1. RATKO MLADIC was, in 1991, appointed commander of the 9th Corps of the Yugoslav People's Army (JNA) in Knin in the Republic of Croatia. Subsequently, in May 1992, he assumed command of the forces of the Second Military District of the JNA which then effectively became the Bosnian Serb army. He holds the rank of general and from about 14 May 1992 to the present, has been the commander of the army of the Bosnian Serb administration.

2. RATKO MLADIC was the leader on negotiating, *inter alia*, ceasefires and prisoner exchange agreements; agreements relating to the opening of Sarajevo airport; agreements relating to access for humanitarian aid convoys; and anti-sniping agreements.

3. All acts or omissions herein set forth as grave breaches of the Geneva Conventions of 1949 (hereafter "grave breaches") recognized by Article 2 of the Statute of the Tribunal occurred during that armed conflict and partial occupation.

3. In each paragraph charging crimes against humanity, crimes recognized by Article 5 of the Statute of the Tribunal, the alleged acts or omissions were part of a widespread, systematic or large-scale attack directed against a civilian population.

4. The term "UN peacekeepers" used throughout this indictment includes UN military observers of the United Nations.

5. The UN peacekeepers and civilians referred to in this indictment were, at all relevant times, persons protected by the Geneva Conventions of 1949.

6. The accused in this indictment was required to abide by the laws and customs governing the conduct of war, including the Geneva Conventions of 1949.

CHARGES

7. The charges set forth in this indictment are in three parts:

Part I of the indictment, Counts 1 to 9, charges a crime of genocide, crimes against humanity and crimes that were perpetrated against the civilian population and against places of worship throughout the territory of the Republic of Bosnia and Herzegovinia.

Part II of the indictment, Counts 10 to 12, charges crimes relating to the sniping campaign against civilians in Sarajevo.

Part III of the indictment, Counts 13 to 16, charges crimes relating to the taking of UN peacekeepers as hostages.

PART I

COUNTS: 1-2 (GENOCIDE) (CRIME AGAINST HUMANITY)

8. RADOVAN KARADZIC and RATKO MLADIC, from April 1992, in the territory of the Republic of Bosnia and Herzegovina, by their acts and omissions, committed genocide.

9. Bosnian Muslim and Bosnian Croat civilians were persecuted on national, political and religious grounds throughout the Republic of Bosnia and Herzegovina. Thousands of them were interned in detention facilities where they were subjected to widespread acts of physical and psychological abuse and to inhumane conditions. Detention facility personnel who ran and operated the Omarska, Keraterm and Luka detention facilities, among others, including, but not limited to Zeljko Meakic (Omarska), Dusko Sikirica (Keraterm) and Goran Jelisic (Luka), intended to kill Bosnian Muslim and Bosnian Croat people as national, ethnic, or religious groups deliberately inflicted upon them conditions intended to bring about their physical destruction. The conditions in the detention facilities, which are described in paragraphs 20-22 hereunder, are incorporated in full herein.

10. RADOVAN KARADZIC and RATKO MLADIC, between April 1992 and July 1995, in the territory of the Republic of Bosnia and Herzegovina, by their acts and omissions, and in concert with others, committed crimes against humanity by persecuting Bosnian Muslim and Bosnian Croat civilians on national, political and religious grounds. As set forth below, they are criminally responsible for the unlawful confinement, murder, rape, sexual assault, torture, beating, robbery and inhumane treatment of civilians; the targeting of political leaders, intellectuals and professionals; the unlawful deportation and transfer of civilians; the unlawful shelling of civilians; the unlawful appropriation and plunder of real and personal property; the destruction of homes and businesses; and the destruction of places of worship.

11. As soon as Serb military forces from in Bosnia and elsewhere in the former Yugoslavia began to attack towns and villages in the Republic of Bosnia and Herzegovina, thousands of Bosnian Muslim and Bosnian Croat civilians were systematically selected and rounded up on national, ethnic, political or religious grounds and put in detention throughout the territory occupied by the Bosnian Serbs. These facilities include, but are not limited to:

Detention Facility -- Dates of existence

Facility		Dates
Omarska --		May- August 1992
Keraterm --		May- August 1992
Trnopolje --		May -December 1992
Luka --		May -July 1992
Manjaca --	Summer	1991 to December 1992
Susica --	June	1992 - September 1992
KP Dom Foca --		April to mid-1993

12. Many of these detention facilities were staffed and operated by military and police personnel and their agents, under the control of RADOVAN KARADZIC and RATKO MLADIC. In addition, Bosnian Serb police and military interrogators had unfettered access to all of the detention facilities and operated in conjunction with the personnel in control of these detention facilities. These facilities and personnel include, but are not limited to: Detention Facility -- Commander -- Guards

Omarska -- Zeljko Meakic (police) -- police/military
Keraterm -- Dusko Sikirica (police) -- police/military
Trnopolje -- Slobodon Kuruzovic (military) -- police/military
Luka -- Goran Jelisic (police) -- paramilitary
Manjaca -- Bozidar Popovic (military) -- military
Susica -- Dragan Nikolic (military) -- military
KP Dom Foca -- Milorad Krnojelac -- military

13. Thousands of Bosnian Muslim and Bosnian Croat civilians, including women, children and elderly persons, were detained in these facilities for protracted periods of time without judicial process and were detained, in large measure, solely because of their national, religious and political identity. The conditions in the detention facilities were inhumane and brutal. Bosnian Serb military and police personnel in charge of these facilities, including Dragan Nikolic (Susica), Zeljko Meakic (Omarska), Dusko Sikirica (Keraterm) and other persons over whom they had control, subjected the civilian detainees to physical and psychological abuse, intimidation and maltreatment. Detention facility personnel, intending to destroy Bosnian Muslim and Bosnian Croat people as national, ethnic or religious groups, killed, seriously injured and deliberately inflicted upon them conditions intended to bring about their physical destruction. Detainees were subjected to and/or witnessed inhumane acts, including murder, rape, sexual assault, torture, beatings, robbery as well as other forms of mental and physical abuse. In many instances, detained women and girls were raped or taken out of detention centers, raped or otherwise sexually abused at other locations. Daily food rations provided to detainees were starvation rations. Medical care for the detainees was

insufficient or non-existent and the general hygienic conditions at these centers were grossly inadequate.

TARGETING OF POLITICAL LEADERS, INTELLECTUALS AND PROFESSIONALS

14. Persns singled out for persecution by the Bosnian Serb military, Bosnian Serb police and their agents, under the direction and control of RADOVAN KARADZIC and RATKO MLADIC, were political leaders and members of the Bosnian Muslim political party, the Party for Democratic Action (SDA), and Bosnian Croat political party, the Croatian Democratic Union (HDZ), from the cities of Prijedor, Vlasenica, Bosanski Samac and Foca. In many instances, lists identifying leaders of the SDA and the HDZ were provided by the SDS to leaders of the Bosnian Serb military, police and their agents. Using these lists, Bosnian Muslim and Bosnian Croat political leaders were arrested, interned, physically abused and, in many instances, murdered. Some local SDA leaders who were persecuted because of their political beliefs include, but are not limited to, Muhamed Cehajic (Prijedor), Sulejman Tihic (Bosanski Samac), and Ahmet Hadzic (Brcko).

15. In addition to persecuting Bosnian Muslim and Bosnian Croat political leaders, the Bosnian Serb military, police and their agents targeted Bosnian Muslim and Bosnian Croat intellectuals and professionals in many towns and villages including Prijedor, Vlasenica, Bosanski Samac and Foca. Individuals persecuted include Abdulah Puskar (academic), Ziko Crnalic (businessman) and Esad Mehmedalija (attorney) from Prijedor; Osman Vatic (attorney) from Brcko.

DEPORTATION

16. Thousands of Bosnian Muslims and Bosnian Croats from the areas of Vlasenica, Prijedor, Bosanski Samac, Brcko and Foca, were arbitrarily interned in detention facilities maintained by the Bosnian Serb military, police and their agents and unlawfully deported or transferred to locations inside and outside of Bosnia and Herzegovina. In addition, Bosnian Muslim and Bosnian Croat civilians, including women, children and elderly persons, were taken directly from their homes to be used in prisoner exchanges by Bosnian Serb military and police and their agents under the direction of RADOVAN KARADZIC and RATKO MLADIC. These deportations were not conducted as evacuations for safety, military necessity, or any lawful purpose and were targeting Bosnian Muslim and Bosnian Croat civilians to reduce or eliminate Muslim and Croat populations.

17. Beginning in July 1992 through to July 1995, Bosnian Serb military forces, under the direction and control of RADOVAN KARADZIC and RATKO MLADIC, unlawfully fired on civilian gatherings that were of no military significance in order to kill, terrorize and demoralize the Bosnian Muslim and Bosnian Croat civilian population. These incidents include, but are not limited to the following:

Location/Type of Civilian Gathering - Municipality - Date - Casualties

Location (Type)	Municipality	Date	Casualties
Sarajevo (picnic)	Sarajevo	03/07/92	10
Sarajevo (airport)	Sarajevo	11/02/93	4
Srebrenica (playground)	Srebrenica	12/4/93	15

Dobrinja (soccer game) Sarajevo - 01/06/93 - 146
Dobrinja (water line) -Sarajevo - 12/07/93 - 27
Sarajevo (residential street) - Sarajevo 28/11/93 - 11 Ciglane Market (fruit market) - Sarajev 06/12/93 – 20 Alipasino Polje (children playing) Sarajevo 22/01/94 - 10 Cetinjska St (children playing) Sarajevo 26/10/94 7
Sarajevo (Livanjska Street) Sarajevo - 08/11/94 - 7
Sarajevo (flea market) Sarajevo - 22/12/94 - 9
Tuzla (plaza) - Tuzla 24/05/95 - 195

APPROPRIATION AND PLUNDER OF PROPERTY

18. Shortly after launching an attack on the Republic of Bosnia and Herzegovina, Bosnian Serb forces quickly suppressed armed resistance in most villages and cities. In the course of consolidating their gains, Bosnian Serb military and police personnel, and other agents of the Bosnian Serb administration, under the direction and control of RADOVAN KARADZIC and RATKO MLADIC, systematically and wantonly appropriated and looted the real and personal property of Bosnian Muslim and Bosnian Croat civilians. The appropriation of property was extensive and not justified by military necessity. It occurred from April 1992 to January 1993 in the municipalities of Prijedor, Vlasenica, and Bosanski Samac, among others.

19. The appropriation and looting of said property was accomplished in the following manner and by the following means, among others:

A. Thousands of Bosnian Muslim and Bosnian Croat civilians were forced into detention facilities where they remained for protracted periods of time. Upon entering these internment facilities, the personnel who ran the internment facilities systematically stole the personal property of the detainees, including jewelry, watches, money and other valuables. The detainees were rarely provided receipts for the property taken from them or given their property back upon their release.

B. Civilians interned in these camps witnessed and/or were subjected to physical and psychological abuse. After witnessing or experiencing serious abuse, thousands of internees were forcibly transferred from these camps to locations inside and outside the Republic of Bosnia and Herzegovina. Before being forcibly transferred, many detainees were compelled to sign official Bosnian Serb documents wherein they "voluntarily" relinquished to the Bosnian Serb administration title to and possession of their real and personal property.

C. In many instances, Bosnian Muslim and Bosnian Croat civilian detainees were taken from internment camps to their homes and businesses and forced to turn over to their escorts (Armed Serbs) money and other valuables. In other instances, they were used as laborers to load property from Bosnian Muslim and Bosnian Croat homes and businesses onto trucks for transportation to parts unknown. This occurred with the consent and approval of those in control of the detention facilities.

D. Many Bosnian Muslim and Bosnian Croat civilians who were not interned in camps were forced to stay in their communities where they were subjected to physical and psychological abuse from Bosnian Serb military and police and their agents, paramilitary forces and lawless elements of the Bosnian Serb community. Conditions for many became intolerable and they left. Before leaving, many civilians were compelled to sign official Bosnian Serb documents wherein they "voluntarily" relinquished to the Bosnian Serb administration their rights to their real and personal property. In some cases, Bosnian Muslim and Bosnian Croat civilians who left their communities were permitted to take with them limited amounts of personal property and money, but even that property was stolen from them at Bosnian Serb checkpoints or at other locations.

E. In many instances during and after the Bosnian Serb military take-over of towns and villages, Bosnian Serb military, police and their agents, entered the homes of non-Serb civilians and plundered the personal property of non-Serb civilians.

DESTRUCTION OF PROPERTY

29. Persecution throughout the occupied territory by Bosnian Serb military, police and their agents, or third parties with their acquiescence, involved the systematic destruction of Bosnian Muslim and Bosnian Croat homes and businesses. These homes and businesses were singled out and systematically destroyed in areas where hostilities had ceased or had not taken place. The purpose of this unlawful destruction was to ensure that the inhabitants could not and would not return to their homes and communities. The cities, villages and towns, or Bosnian Muslim and Bosnian Croat portions thereof, where extensive destruction of property occurred include, but are not limited to the following:

Destruction of Towns/Villages - Municipalities

Grebnice -	Bosanski Samac	-	19-22 April 1992
Hrvatcka Tisina	Bosanski Samac		19-22 April 1992
Hasici -	Bosanski Samac	-	19-22 April 1992
Derventa -	Derventa	-	4 April 1992
Vijaka -	Derventa	-	4 April 1992
Bosanski Brod -	Bosanski Brod	-	3 March 1992
Odzak -	Odzak	-	July 1992
Modrica -	Modrica	-	Late April 1992
Vidovice -	Orasje		29 April and 4 May 1992
Gradacac	-Gradacac	-	mid-1992
Piskavice	- Vlasenica	-	22 April 1992
Gobelje -	Vlasenica		23 April 1992
Turalici	Vlasenica	-	29 Apri 1992
Djile	- Vlasenica	-	1-3 May 1992
Pomol –	Vlasenica		1 May 1992
Gaj -	Vlasenica -		1 May 1992
Besici -	Vlasenica		- 1 May 1992
Nurici -	Vlasenica	-	1 May 1992
Vrsinje -	Vlasenica	-	1 May 1992
Dzamdzici -	Vlasenica	-	8 May 1992
Pivici -	Vlasenica	-	11 May 1992
Hambarine -	Prijedor	-	23 May 1992
Ljubija -	Prijedor	-	23 May 1992
Kozarac -	Prijedor	-	24 May 1992
Biscani -	Prijedor	-	20 July 1992
Carakovo -	Prijedor	-	20 July 1992
Rizvanovici -	Prijedor	-	20 July 1992
Sredice -	Prijedor	-	20 July 1992
Zikovi -	Prijedor	-	20 July 1992

Milosevic, Slobodan (also Slobovan), Born August 20,

1941, in Serbia, was a minor Serb politician until he began extremist talk about revoking Kosovo's autonomous status because the majority of the populations was Muslim. His Serb Nationalism won him Serb support, and was a reversion to pre- WW II Serb dominance that Tito abolished when he created a republic that gave the different republics a right to secede from the federation.

The formation of a federation conflicted with the way the French, British, and Russians set Serbia to control this new nation with the *1914 Secret Treaty of London*. Tito's wanted a federation to curb Serb aggressiveness. It is hard to explain to people that Serbs have a different concept of right and wrong than the rest of the world.

Milosevic's wife, Markevic, whose parents were Communist Party members of Jewish ethnicity, fled to Russia after Slobodan's extradition to The War Crimes Tribunal The Hague. Even though the War Crimes Tribunal states every accused War Criminal will have a speedy trial, Milosevic is still awaiting trial after two years while incarcerated in The Hague. Chances are he will be set free with the reason given that he did not receive a speedy trial.

William, Perry, Born in October 11, 1927 Vandergrift, Pennsylvania. He was the 19th U.S. Secretary of Defense, from February 1994 to January 1997 and co-director of the Center for International Security and Arms Control, 1988-1993. He has received decorations from Germany, England, Korea, France, Albania, Poland, Ukraine, Japan, and Belarus. He also worked in technical research, taught math at Santa Clara University, received B.S. and M.S. at Stanford University and a Ph.D. from Pennsylvania State University all in mathematics.

Rose, Lt. General Sir Michael: In January 1994, British Lieutenant General, Michael Rose, assumed military commands of the UN forces in Bosnia and Herzegovina. Within weeks he won praise for his ability to combine diplomatic skills with military judgment. But all of this disappeared after he was called to Britain and made a Lord and given a title. Because of his caustic comments against the Bosnian Muslims and strong support for the Serbs, he lost his worldwide support.

Haris Siladjic, Prime Minister of Bosnia until 1996, was outspoken in his criticism of a UN that shirked its responsibilities. He called Sir Michel Rose a liar to his face and before television cameras. Sir Michael's face flushed but he did not respond.

Siladjic favored a secular democracy representing all minorities. He was ousted as Prime Minister of Bosnia in 1996 when the war was ending.

Talbott, Strobe, Under Secretary of State in the Clinton Administration, and Mr. Clinton's roommate at Oxford University in England where both were Rhodes Scholars. He is presently President of the Brookings Institution. He was Deputy Secretary of State in the Clinton Administration and worked previously as the Washington bureau chief of *Time* magazine, and author of *The Russia Hand: A Memoir of Presidential Diplomacy* as well as *The Russia Hand,* which he called a memoir of the Clinton Presidency. Mr. Talbot viewed the American support for Russia's first president, Boris Yeltsin, as the most important issue during the Clinton years in the White house. While Yeltsin threatened to intervene in Bosnia and used atrocities and terror tactics in Chechnya (giving the Chechen capital, Grozny one of the worst bombardments ever witnessed in history with the city receiving some four thousand bombs, rockets, and artillery shells per hour). The inhumane attacks he approved on civilian target are enough to charge him with war crimes. But Mr. Talbot, saw in Yeltsin a man who represented democracy in Russia and supported a war criminal.

Tito (Josef Broz) born in Croatia, was a Communist Partisan fighter in WW II, fighting the German occupation of Yugoslavia and executed his Rival. Mihailovic, the leader of the pro-British Chetniks in 1946.

The pro-Tito cell of Communist British intelligence operating out Brinidisi, Italy, funneled all the British weapons and supplies to Tito and he began a ruthless campaign of killing off any potential opposition to his Rule. 200,000 Croats and Bosnians who fought alongside the German Army against Stalin surrendered to the British and turned over to Tito who marched them into the mountains of Bosnia in winter and left them to freeze to death.

Tudjman, Franjo, President of Croatia and communist leader of Croatia before and during the Bosnian War. Tudjman, a hard line Communist, was clever enough to get support from the very strong pro-German element, the Domo Branci, which served as a Croatian home guard for the Germans in WW II. The Domo Banci has been labeled as fascist by Croatian Communists, did not bother Tudjman.

At the beginning of Yugoslavia's breakup, Croatia refused to allow the Yugoslav Army to cross from Serbia into Slovenia after Slovenia declared its independence from the *Yugoslav Federation.* The when Croatia declared its independence, the Yugoslav Army began a campaign of terror through atrocities and massacres, as Croatia was relatively defenseless.

Belgrade Serbs were in full control of the Yugoslav Army, which is more proof that Yugoslavia was really Greater *Serbia*. Serbs never allowed any of the other nations to be an equal partner the Creation of the *Kingdom of Slovenes, Croats, and Serbs* that was set up by the *1914 Secret Treaty of London*1914 Secret Treaty of London. In 1929, the name was changed to Yugoslavia but was always meant to be *Greater Serbia*.

The United Nations managed to halt hostilities in Croatia in 1992, which gave hope to Muslims in Bosnia that they could also break away from Serb dominated Yugoslavia and become independent. Although there had been peace in the Balkans under Tito, who was a Croat and understood the Serb aggressiveness, this disappeared with Milosevic.

Tudjman at an early stage in the war began cooperating with Bosnians in defending themselves against Serb aggression, which was being directed out of Belgrade.

In Herzegovina, a small group of men dressed as Muslim Army soldiers committed atrocities in a Herzegovina village. A journalist at the scene said he overheard the "Muslim" leader of the group speaking English with "a Yorkshire accent." From this comment by the journalist was the insinuation that this was a *Black Operation,* meant to create friction between Muslims and Croats, and likely done by Brits.

Tudjman was always the pragmatic Communist. As the war proceeded, he could see that the Serbs were much better equipped militarily and stronger than both Bosnia and Croatia (see August 31, 1995, news from the *Wall Street Journal* Where Milosevic gave 512 tanks, 506 armored personnel carriers, 18 transport helicopters and 8,700 tons of fuel to the Bosnian Serbs, but the UN Security Council prevented Bosnia from getting any arms. Tudjman later joined with the Serbs to divide Bosnia between them.

As the war progressed, Tudjman realized that the Serbs meant to keep Croatian Serb territory carved out of Croatia and that Croatia would receive from the division of Bosnia., territory that was to make up for the loss of Croatian territory to the Serbs. It was about this time, that he received an offer from Iran whereby Iran would fly in weapons to Zagreb, and Croats and Bosnians would share fifty-fifty the weapons that Iran had sent by the planes...

The first two planes from Iran were seized and all the weapons were kept by Croatia. However, Iranians sent a third plane and the Croatians allowed the Iran to keep their plane and shared the weapons with Bosnia this third time. After several other shipments of weapons, the two first planes were returned to Iran.

Tudjman also began getting arms from Catholic countries of Eastern Europe they saw that the Russian military was supporting Serbia. This fear of Russia coming back into their countries helped fuel their sympathies for fellow Catholic Croats. Tudjman's most important support came from the secret and very powerful Herzegovina Mafia (see February 7, 1996, Radio Netherlands news report on this Mafia) that was spread worldwide and gave him support. With all this help, Tudjman had the power to recover all of Croatian territory from the Serbs and sure that Serbia could never threaten Croatia again.

There is speculation that the Freemasons influenced Tudjman's support of Serbia's aggression in Bosnia at the beginning of the war. Why mention the Freemasons? At the very core of this secret society of Freemasons are the *Knights Templar,* founded in 1119 in Jerusalem by Catholic monks dedicated to fighting Islam and destroying it. By 1306 they had moved from Palestine to Paris, France, but had become so secret that even the Catholic Church and the French King did not know of them.

Lord David Owen's rabid hatred of Muslims was matched by Eduard Balladur of France. Lord Owen was fired from his position as the EU representative but refused to be fired and yet remained in that post. His bigotry might be explained by the House of Lords support for the 1914 Secret Treaty of London that promised Serbs a Greater Serbia if they would murder Archduke Ferdinand. Were the Lords what British Prime Minister, John Majors, meant when he said, "If I allow the arms embargo to be lifted on Bosnia, my government will fall."

Yeltsin, Boris, first elected President of Russia. A controversial figure most Russians know as the *drunk*, his ordering the Russian military to commit atrocities in Chechnya brought international condemnation as well as a vote of no confidence from the Russian parliament.

In one instance, when someone mentioned the name of Bosnia Yeltin became so enraged he was almost incoherent. He appeared to be little more than a puppet who received his instructions from the old Soviet military which controlled the new Russian Army. Yeltsin's conduct in conducting the Chechen War should have led to his indictment for War Crimes by The Hague.

The United Nations failed to condemn the invasion of Iraq in 2003 by the United States and Britain. Mr. George W. Bush obtained three years of exemption from the War Crimes Tribunal in The Hague for all Americans, on the basis that frivolous accusations against Americans would arise from U.S. military operations in Iraq and Afghanistan. However the failure by the United States to adhere to the International Conventions on the treatment of prisoners was based on the advice of White House legal Counsel, Gonsales, who said the terrorist threat to the United States rendered "obsolete Geneva's strict limitation on questioning of enemy prisoners."

The Bosnian war was four years of deprivation when electricity, gas, and water were cut off and trees from around Sarajevo were cut to warm homes. There was the constant breaking of ceasefires and truces by the Serbs and sniping at unarmed men, women, and children. Serbs also used bullets that could penetrate seven walls of concrete and brick of an apartment building that created fear and murdered innocents.

There was the shelling of markets where people gathered to buy food. After one such vicious shelling, Serbs claimed the bodies were mannequins smeared with red paint, and not real bodies.

Were the *Oklahoma City Bombing* and the *October 2001 Anthrax Scare* in the United States a **Black Ops** by the CIA or Pentagon to demonize *Muslims as terrorists*. Muslims are a peaceful people and murder rates in Muslim countries are much lower than murder rates in western nations. The suicide attack by Muslims on Mumbai is confusing when viewing this low rate of murder in Muslim countries.

News reports in this documentary show that the UN Security Council, Secretary Boutros Boutros Ghali, EU observer, Lord Owen, Lt. General Sir Michael Rose and leaders of Western Governments and International Organizations were callous to the destruction of Bosnia and efforts by Serbs to push Bosnians into terrorism was in vain.

The UN Peacekeepers failed to protect Bosnia's civilian population. It seems remarkable that the UN leadership and the UN Security Council ruled against Bosnia's right as to defend itself which was its right as a member of the United Nations. While UN left the Bosnians to be massacred the EU worked to save Chechens from Russian abuses. While the Bosnian conflict was going the massacres in Rwanda saw one million people die which was more duplicity by UN agencies.

The reader can read a summary of War Crimes indictments against The author is critical of the United Nations and its lack of handling the situation in Bosnia and elsewhere. The hope of the world was that the United Nations would be the place where peace could be secured but it has not. The declaration of war on Iraq by the United States was done despite a UN committee that was investigating charges by President Bush of the United States that Iraq posed an imminent danger to the world with weapons of mass destruction.

When Germany and France refused to contribute to the *coalition forces* invading Iraq, the Bush Administration accused them of disloyalty and threatened to boycott French and German goods. The Bush-Blair led invasion resulted in an estimated 30,000 non-combatant Iraqi civilians killed, the antiquities museum ransacked, the economic collapse of a country already impoverished by eleven years of economic sanctions which resulted in the deaths of an estimated 500,000 Iraqi children from malnutrition and disease. The invasion was like putting out the welcome mat terrorists to come into the power vacuum of Iraq and establish their base for future terrorist operations.

The Iran-Iraq War, instigated by the CIA to maintain high oil prices by creating scarcity is another crime to investigate. The derivatives market has ruined the economies of many poor nations by those abusing the rules and regulations. An overhaul of the United Nations, the World Court, the world's derivatives (commodities) markets, and International War Crimes Tribunal is needed if we expect to see freedom, equality, and progress in the future.

"Our cause was so just, so sacred, that had I known all that has come to pass, had I known what was to be inflicted upon me, all that my country was to suffer, all that our posterity was to endure, I would do it all over again." - Confederate States President, Jefferson Davis

Bibliography: Best source on the Bosnian Conflict and world news in general was Radio Netherlands. The next best news sources were Die Deutsche and *Wall Street Journal*. It might be noted that *The Wall Street Journal* started out pro-Serb but changed with more information that showed the war was aggression by Serbia on Bosnia.

ABC- TV, United States
BBC, Whitehouse, London
Bloomberg TV, New York City, USA
Asian News Program, channel 33, Houston, Texas
Beijing Radio, Beijing, P.R. China
Channel 17, Houston, Texas.
Christian Science Monitor Radio, United States
CNN (Cable News Network)
Die Deutsche Welle, Cologne, Germany
ECO, Spanish language news on Channel 33, Houston, Texas
Eye on Asia, Television program aired over Houston, Texas television.
French Television, international program presented in Houston, Texas.
Houston Post, Houston, Texas
Iranian News on Los Angeles television. Los Angeles, California, U.S.A.
Radio, Moscow, Russia
PBS (Public Broadcast Service) radio in America.

PBS-TV, *MacNeil-Lehrer Report* United States
Radio France, Paris, France
Radio Netherlands, Hilversum, Netherlands
Spanish Radio. Madrid, Spain
Swiss Radio International, Switzerland
The New York Times, daily newspaper published in New York City, U.S.A.
The Wall Street Journal, daily financial newspaper noted for journalistic accuracy, United States.
The Washington Post, published daily in Washington, D.C. and influential in Washington U.S.A.
The Washington Report on the Middle East, bimonthly magazine published in Washington, D.C.
VH-1 Television, Houston Texas, U.S.A.
VOA. Voice of

www.ingramcontent.com/pod-product-compliance
Lightning Source LLC
Chambersburg PA
CBHW062120280526
45788CB00001B/5